FOURTH EDITION

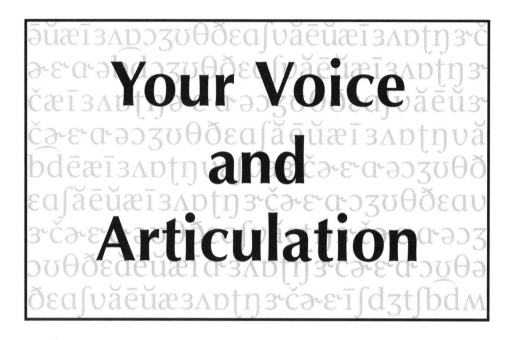

Your Voice and Articulation

ETHEL C. GLENN

University of North Carolina, Greensboro, Emeritus

PHILLIP J. GLENN

Southern Illinois University at Carbondale

SANDRA FORMAN

Northern Kentucky University

An International Publisher

8700 Shoal Creek Boulevard
Austin, Texas 78757-6897
800/897-3202   Fax 800/397-7633
www.proedinc.com

© 1998 by PRO-ED, Inc.
8700 Shoal Creek Boulevard
Austin, Texas 78757-6897
800/897-3202   Fax 800/397-7633
www.proedinc.com

Printed in the United States of America

1 2 3 4 5 6 7 8 9 10   08 07 06 05 04

Contents

Chapter 12   **Affricative and Nasal Consonants
and Central Vowels**   **188**

Chapter 13   **Glides (Semivowels)
and Diphthongs**   **208**

Appendix A   **Enunciation, Pronunciation,
and Sound Games and Exercises**   **235**

Preface

If you have had courses in public speaking or interpersonal communication, you may wonder just what lies ahead from a book entitled *Your Voice and Articulation.* How will this study differ from earlier lessons you may have had in acting or oral interpretation of literature?

Think of voice and diction (articulation) as one component of many different communication performances—giving a speech, engaging in a conversation, participating in a group meeting, acting in a play, reading aloud, or talking on the radio or on TV. Developing a pleasant and impressive voice enhances your opportunities for success in any communication performance. Pronouncing sounds and words in a way that is understandable and does not attract attention makes you a more effective communicator.

If you are from a part of the country where regional dialects are the norm, perhaps you have been teased when you travelled to other parts of the country. Southerners are often laughed at when they go north or west, for example, since the Southern dialect is so distinct. If you have a regional or ethnic dialect, part of your goal may be to change your pronunciation pattern. If you already speak Standard American English, you may view the time spent in this course as strengthening your speech skills rather than remediating them. Both goals—correction and enhancement—can be met by careful study of the contents of this book.

Like it or not, people make judgments about us by the way we talk. Ideally judgments should be based on *what* we say, not *how* we say it, but it just doesn't work that way. The kind of improvement that the study of voice and diction offers can be an asset to you in both the business and social worlds. If your primary goal is such self-improvement, that's great! You will find much in this book to help you reach that end.

If, on the other hand, your long range plans include a career in one of the performing professions—acting, public speaking, or the media—your goal is to take an important first step in preparing yourself for that profession. You can move toward both personal and professional goals by mastering better voice and speech usage. Along with this enhancement comes added self-confidence. In much the same way that you feel more poised when you know you *look* your best, your self assurance increases when you are secure in the knowledge that you *sound* your best.

This book offers you clear explanations of the processes by which we produce our voices and speech sounds. Four chapters are devoted to the characteristics of voice—volume, pitch, rate, and quality. Exercises for improvement accompany the explanation of each characteristic. We also include step-by-step guidelines to each sound in American English. With each sound we have provided lists of words and sentences which contain that sound for your practice. Some are nonsense sentences—we hope they will be fun for you. For many students, just acquiring this knowledge about the complex process of voice production and sound formation is sufficiently interesting and valuable in and of itself—as an area of study rather than a self-improvement tool.

Finally, we invite you to celebrate the English language with us by sharing some of its great literature from a variety of sources—novels, short stories, plays, poetry, and speeches. Starting with Chapter 3, the end of the introductory section, each chapter ends with short passages that have been purposely selected because they can stand alone. The readings bear no relationship to the chapters they follow. Some teachers skip around from chapter to chapter. Speech majors may prefer to focus on the classic and contemporary speeches, while Broadcasting majors may prefer the media copy. Theatre majors usually enjoy the monologues or the passages from plays. Few classes will have time to do all the readings. Some readings may be assigned and can be rehearsed, others may be done "cold" or spontaneously.

As you practice reading aloud, as well as in your everyday conversations, try to incorporate newly acquired pronunciations and vocal techniques. Remember, voice and diction is a component of all oral performance, not an end in itself. It is an essential ingredient in effective communication. Use this text as a work and practice book to develop voice and speech skills that will be instrumental in your achieving that effectiveness.

Ethel C. Glenn
Phillip J. Glenn
Sandra Forman

Key Terms

Abdominal breathing: respiration that results when the diaphragm flattens, the visceral organs move forward, and air moves lower in the lung area

Accent (dialect): sounds from a speaker's first language extended to a second language; speech habits typical of a group of natives or residents of a geographic region

Accent (stress): syllable within a word, or a word within a phrase, emphasized or made predominant by changes in pitch, volume, and duration

Adam's apple: projection in the front of the throat formed by the thyroid cartilage, the largest cartilage in the larynx

Affricative consonant: the phonemes [tʃ] and [dʒ]; consonants formed by a stop followed immediately by a fricative-type release

Allophone: variant of a phoneme; sound that exists between two closely related phonemes

Alveolar ridge: hard ridge immediately behind the teeth

Amplification: enlargement, enrichment, and expansion of sound

Articulation: obstruction, molding, or reshaping of outgoing airstream to form language sounds; act or manner of articulating sounds

Arytenoid cartilages: ladle-shaped structures attached directly to vocal folds in the back of the larynx

Aspirated: pronounced or produced so that breath is heard; characteristic of the [h] sound in particular

Assimilation: modification of adjacent sounds in connected speech

Back vowels: the phonemes [ɑ], [ɔ], [o], [ʊ], and [u]

Beat: a rhythmic stress or accent; a particular tempo

Bernoulli effect: rush of air pulling vocal folds back together after voice vibration

Bilabial consonant: phoneme produced when place of articulation is the two lips

Bronchi: tubular passages from the trachea to the lungs

Central vowels: the phonemes [ʌ], [ə], [ɝ] and [ɚ]

Chest resonance: amplification and reinforcement of the voice from vibrations in the ribs and thorax

Clavicular breathing: respiration accompanied by movement of the upper chest and shoulders

Cognate pair: two sounds identically articulated except that one is voiced and the other is voiceless

Consonant: group of speech sounds characterized by a relatively significant degree of obstruction of the outgoing airstream

Cricoid cartilage: ring-shaped structure, larger in back than in front, forming the base of the larynx

Decibels: units of sound intensity; degree of loudness

Denasality: vocal quality that results from insufficient nasal resonance during speech

Dentalized: produced near the upper front teeth

Diacritical mark: print symbols used in most dictionaries to indicate pronunciation of the orthographic alphabet

Dialect: variation pattern in speech characteristics of a language, usually geographically or socioeconomically defined

Diaphragm: dome-shaped muscle separating the abdomen from the chest cavity; used in respiration

Digraph: a union of two separate symbols that represent a single sound

Diction: practice and study of pronunciation, articulation, and enunciation

Diphthong: the phonemes [eɪ], [aɪ], [ɔɪ], [aʊ], and [oʊ]; two vowels blended to produce a single phoneme

Duration: length of individual sounds within overall words

Emphasis: prominence or importance given to certain words or phrases

Enunciation: production of well-articulated sounds; clear pronunciation

Epiglottis: tongue-shaped cartilage that lowers over the vocal folds during swallowing

ESL: English as a Second Language

Esophagus: food passage from the mouth and pharynx into the stomach

Exhalation: act of expelling air from the lungs

External intercostals: muscles between the ribs that pull the thorax upward and outward

Extrinsic muscles (larynx):   tissues that attach the larynx to the hyoid bone and control "bobbing" of the larynx

Falsetto: unnaturally high pitched voice, especially in a man

False vocal folds: tissues above the glottis that pull together in swallowing; aid the epiglottis in preventing food from entering the lungs; no role in sound production

Fricative consonant: the phonemes [f], [v], [θ], [ð], [s], [z], [ʃ], [ʒ], and [h]; consonants produced by tensing certain articulators to narrow the passageway so that outgoing air is emitted with friction

Front vowels: the phonemes [i], [ɪ], [e], [ɛ], and [æ]

Fundamental frequency: vibration rate of vocal folds measured without overtones

Glide (semivowel) consonant: the phonemes [ʍ], [w], [l], [r], and [j]; consonants produced with movement of the articulators during formation

Glottal fry: grinding sound (much like bacon frying) produced in the glottis by overly slow vocal-fold vibration

Glottal shock (stop):   clicking sound sometimes substituted for stopplosives; caused by overrapid closure or opening of vocal folds

Glottis: opening between the vocal folds

Habitual pitch: customary pitch range (highness or lowness) within which a person speaks

Hard palate: front part of the roof of the mouth, just behind the gum ridge; separates oral and nasal cavities

High vowels: the phonemes [i], [ɪ], [u], and [ʊ]

Hyoid bone: U-shaped structure at the base of the tongue; the larynx is attached to the bottom of it

Inflection: pitch change that occurs within individual syllables or words

Inhalation: act of expanding the chest cavity so that air rushes in to equalize the resultant air pressure change

Internal intercostals: muscles between the ribs that pull the thorax downward and inward during exhalation

Intonation: overall pattern of pitch changes through phrases and sentences; spoken melody

Intrinsic muscles (larynx):   tissues attached to the inside of the larynx; aid both in the motion of the larynx and in sound production

IPA: International Phonetic Alphabet; specific marking system that assigns each sound a single pronunciation symbol

Jaw: set of two bones that form the framework of the mouth

Key (pitch):   general pitch level, ranging from high to low, used as a vocal adjunct to carry mood and meaning

Labio: of the lips; of sounds made by closing or rounding the lips

Larynx (voice box):   cavity containing the vocal folds and acting as an organ of the voice

Lingua: of the tongue; sounds formed with the aid of the tongue

Lips: either of the two fleshy, movable edges of the mouth

Lisp (lateral):   [s] or [z] with breath stream emitted over the side of the tongue because the tongue tip is pressed too hard against the teeth or gum ridge. Lisp: [θ] substituted for [s]

Loudness: intensity of sound interpreted comparatively by the ear; measured in decibels

Low vowels: the phonemes [æ], [ʌ], [ɔ], and [ɑ]

Lungs: two spongy, porous, cone-shaped organs filling the chest cavity and serving as air reservoirs

Meter: repetition of a single rhythmic pattern; cadence; a musical measure

Mid vowels: the phonemes [e], [ɛ], [ɝ], [ɚ], [ə], and [o]

Monotone (monopitch):   unvaried key or pitch in speaking or reading; lack of vocal modulation

Nasal cavity: air passage within the nose and directly above the roof of the mouth

Nasal consonants: the phonemes [m], [n], and [ŋ]; made by lowering the soft palate so air emits through the nose

Nasality: voice quality that results from excessive nasal resonance during speaking

Nasal resonance: amplification and reinforcement of the voice though secondary vibration in the nasal cavity

Omission: mispronunciation that results from leaving out a sound or sounds from a word

Optimal pitch: highness–lowness level at which the voice is most efficiently produced with the least effort

Oral cavity: cavity bounded by the lips and jaw at the front, the tongue at the base, the palate at the top, and the cheeks on the sides

Oral resonance: amplification and reinforcement of the voice through secondary vibrations in the oral cavity

Orthography: the standard alphabetic representation of the sounds of a language; orthographic English is our present-day printed alphabet, as compared with a phonetic or other alphabet

Overlaid function: function superimposed on organs and structures designed to serve a separate, basic biological function

Pause: absence of sound between speech units

Pharynx: upper part of the throat; the passage connecting the mouth to the esophagus or trachea

Phonation: vibration of the vocal folds to produce sound

Phoneme: smallest isolatable unit of sound in a language

Phonetic: of or having to do with speech sounds

Phrasing: the use of pauses or other vocal features to separate groups of words or thoughts into meaningful relationships

Pitch: highness or lowness of sound to the ear; frequency of vibration

Projection: energy, concentration, and desire to communicate coupled with forward placement; carrying power

Pronunciation: production of sounds within words, especially as compared with an arbitrary standard of correctness; utterance of words

Quality (voice):   combination of fundamental frequencies and overtones that characterizes and distinguishes individual voices

Rate: overall slowness or rapidity of speech, especially as determined by the time allotted to pauses

Relaxation: freedom from abnormal or undue tension—especially muscular—on the one hand, and laxness or inertia on the other; tonal responsiveness

Resonation: amplification and enrichment through secondary vibration; harmonics, overtones

Respiration: inhalation and exhalation of air; exchange of oxygen and carbon dioxide; motivating force for sound production

Rhythm: patterned repetition of stressed and unstressed vocal elements

Rib cage: structure formed by twelve pairs of bones attached to the spinal column in back, of which ten pairs are joined to the sternum in front

Semivowel: *see* glide

SLL: second language learner

Soft palate: back part of the roof of the mouth, between the hard palate and the pharynx

Sound waves: vibrations of a physical entity that cause pressure changes that in turn disturb and move through the surrounding air

Step: moving from one pitch to another between words or syllables

Sternum: breastbone; bone to which the seven upper pairs of ribs are attached

Stop-plosive consonant: the phonemes [p], [b], [t], [d], [k], and [g]; consonants produced by articulator closure followed by sudden release of air

Stress: *see* accent (stress)

Substitution: mispronunciation that results when one phoneme replaces another in a word

Suprasegmental: elements of spoken language such as stress, pitch, or juncture that take place at the same time as the utterance of vowels and consonants

Syntax: arrangement of words in phrases and clauses; structure of sentences

Teeth: upper- and lower-mouth bony appendages; one of several articulators of sound

Tempo: rate and rhythm of a given vocal passage

Thorax: bony structure constituting the chest cavity

Thyroid cartilage: two shield-shaped joined plates forming the front of the larynx

Timing: use of rate, rhythm, and tempo to convey meaning and mood in a speech or oral reading

Tone: vocal sound; voice quality; overall mood or emotional value of a speech or reading

Tongue: movable fleshy organ in the mouth—one of the articulators; the language of a people; a way or manner of speaking

Trachea: tube that connects the larynx to the top of the bronchial tubes; windpipe

Transposition: mispronunciation that results from reversing the order of sounds in a word

Unstressed: syllable within a word or word within a phrase that is not emphasized or accented

Uvula: fleshy structure hanging from the back of the soft palate

Velum: soft palate

Viscera: organs such as heart, liver, and intestines located in the trunk of the body

Vocabulary: a speaker's sum collection of words to which meaning can be attached; words and their meanings

Vocal folds: pair of ligaments within the larynx whose vibration produces sound

Voice box: *see* larynx

Voiced sounds: consonants produced with vibration of the vocal folds

Voiceless sounds: consonants produced without vibration of the vocal folds; whispered sounds

Volume: intensity of sound; degree of loudness or softness

Vowels: group of speech sounds characterized by freedom from articulatory obstruction and differentiated primarily by oral resonance

Windpipe: *see* trachea

SECTION I
Overview and Groundwork

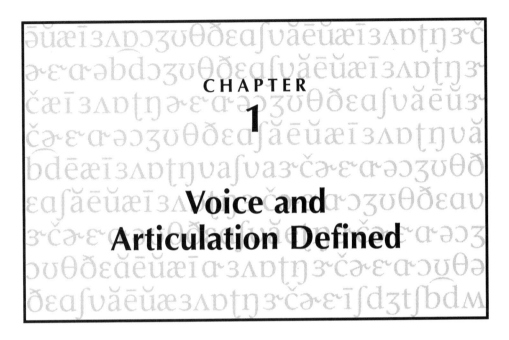

CHAPTER

1

Voice and Articulation Defined

Language most shows a man:
Speak, that I may see thee.

—BEN JONSON

THE NEED FOR SPEECH SKILLS

You are probably enrolled in a course called "Voice and Diction," or "Voice and Articulation," or something else that indicates a focus on one narrow aspect of oral communication—the human voice and the formation of specific language sounds. Or perhaps this text is the basis of only one section of a speech communication course that also has units in interpersonal communication, public speaking, or oral interpretation. Whatever the orientation of the course or your reason for studying voice and articulation, some general knowledge of the impact of your voice and your pronunciation patterns on the overall impression you make when you talk is necessary to help you establish your goals for the course and for your personal progress.

*There are moments when speech
is but a mouth pressed
Lightly and humbly against the
angels' hand.*

—JAMES MERRILL,
"A Dedication"

This course may be required in your degree program, as it is for a number of different curricula. Or you may have elected to take it because you sense that your own speech skills could improve or perhaps because someone has teased you about your dialect. Whatever your reason for enrolling in this course, you stand to benefit, because many professions in today's competitive job world demand at least some degree of clear and standardized speech.

If you are a communications major, you are probably preparing for a career in which the ability to speak well is obviously essential. It may be broadcasting, speech making, interviewing, leading small or large groups—whatever the situation, your job description will require you to speak to and in front of people. Or perhaps you plan to become a lawyer, a teacher, a minister, a politician, or an actor. These career choices all demand skill in speech for success.

The need for speech skill is not restricted to those careers where the requirement for it is obvious. Most businesses want their executives, managers, sales agents, secretaries, receptionists, and other employees who interact with the public to be able to speak clearly, distinctly, and with unobtrusive pronunciation patterns. Government employees, clerks in shops and stores, supervisors on assembly lines, people who work primarily on the telephone making reservations and appointments, pilots, bus drivers, and other people in transportation—these and many more occupations depend in part upon oral communication with others. The present time has been called the "information age" because the gathering and disseminating of information has become not only a large part of many occupations, but an expanding occupation in and of itself. In all probability, you will be called on to pass along information verbally, and you need to be able to do that as effectively as possible. The ability to speak well will be an advantage in most jobs and professions.

Eloquence is the power to translate a truth into language perfectly intelligible to the person to whom you speak.

—RALPH WALDO EMERSON

Not only in the job world, but also in social and interpersonal settings, effective use of the voice and clear pronunciation of words is an asset. This is a time of self-improvement, as shown by best-selling books on such goals as body shaping, dressing for success, handling difficult people, and improving your self-image. Many of these books deal with communication, ranging from the formal communicative act of public speaking to informal communication in a variety of interpersonal settings, such as parents talking with children or counselors working with the elderly.

This book will address not so much *what* you say as *how* you say it. Many of you will also take courses in public speaking or group communication to work on content, or the *what,* of your oral communication. This text focuses on the *how*—the skill of voice and speech production. And the emphasis is on self-improvement.

As a college student, you have moved steadily up the educational ladder, finishing elementary and then high school. You are rapidly becoming "an educated person." One of the primary characteristics by which people judge each other's intellectual achievements is by the way they talk. Your speech should reveal your academic progress, suggesting to listeners that you are all that you have worked so hard to become.

AS OTHERS HEAR YOU

Oh wad some power the giftie gie us
To see oursels as others see us!
It wad frae monie a blunder free us,
An' foolish notion.

—ROBERT BURNS,
To a Louse

If the tongue had not been framed for articulation, man would still be a beast in the forest.

—RALPH WALDO EMERSON

When Robert Burns wrote of the gift of being able to see ourselves as others see us, he could well have added several verses on *hearing* ourselves as others hear us. We use mirrors many times each day to check our appearance. But when was the last time you ran a quick check before class, work, or a social engagement to make sure that your speech sounds and voice were pleasing to the ear? Such a self-test would require a tape recorder, for your voice does not sound the same to you as to others. Even today, when tape recorders are readily available at nominal prices, a surprising number of people have never heard themselves speak. Others have never made use of top-quality recording equipment that produces a high-fidelity reproduction of their voices. The initial response to the play-back for most self-listening newcomers is a ghastly grimace and a groan: "Do I sound like *that?*"

The voice is characterized from the viewpoint of the listener, not the speaker. Loudness, pitch, rate, and quality are all measured by the impact of the voice on the receiver. You may think you are talking loudly or slowly enough, but others may find your volume so low as to be almost inaudible or your rate so fast that they cannot keep up with you. Dialects, accents, or any differences in pronunciation are identifiable by the way words sound to a listener. For example, even the most expert speech teacher probably would be unable to differentiate between *sit* and *set* merely by observing the position of the speaker's lips, teeth, and tongue, but would know instantly upon hearing the two words that the vowel sound had changed. And you may not realize that you have a dialect of any sort. Most people do not perceive the differences in their own pronunciation or inflectional patterns.

Your voice and articulation, then, must be evaluated by others. Working in a classroom with a critical teacher and discriminating but supportive fellow students, coupled with intensive tape recorder practice, you will gradually learn to hear yourself more as others hear you. The speech process, which has long been automatic for you, must be taken apart and examined, studied, and practiced step by step, then ultimately restored to the automatic level it now occupies. When people talk, most of the time they think about *what* they are saying, not *how* they are saying it. That is as it should be. Suppose you had to stop and think of the rules of English grammar before you could generate a sentence—rules for word order, verb tenses, or plurals. Speaking would be next to impossible. In the same way, you could not talk if you had to remember to inhale and exhale, to vibrate the vocal folds, and to place your lips, teeth, and tongue in certain positions.

Your willingness to interfere with this customarily unconscious process for a temporary period is important. After a few weeks in a course on voice and articulation, students often say, "I'm so conscious of my voice and pronunciation that I can hardly talk!" This sentiment describes a necessary growth period. Don't be discouraged and don't give up. The automatic aspects of the speech act will return, and newly learned vocal and articulatory control can become a habit. Your persistence and diligence can help you acquire pronunciation patterns and a clear, colorful voice that will be of lifelong benefit to you professionally and in the social world.

Fear is static that prevents me from hearing my intuition.

—HUGH PRATHER,
Notes to Myself

A HUMAN COMMUNICATION MODEL

The study of voice and articulation needs to be placed within a model of human communication that guides the bulk of current research and teaching. Among the several theoretical models that have been generated, all contain at a minimum the four elements of sender, message, channel, and receiver, with some provision for feedback. At their most basic, these models might look something like this:

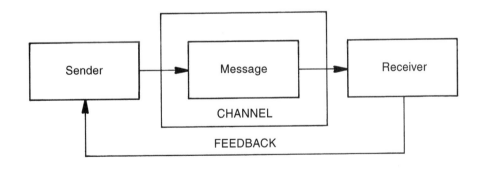

Voice and diction are primarily sender variables. They identify a particular aspect of the speech act that is limited only to oral communication. Written communication has comparable features—notably spelling, punctuation, and certain elements of style—but the comparison slights the immense impact of vocal quality on meaning. Comparing a pause with a period or comma, like comparing rising inflection with a question mark, is virtually useless, for in actuality the periods, commas, and question marks are merely visual attempts to symbolize the oral act.

Voice and diction are only two of the many components of the sender and the sender's message. Messages are usually thought of as *what* is said—the ideas and the choice and arrangement of words through which those ideas are expressed. Voice and articulation are thought of as *how* the speaker pronounces those words, at what level of loudness and pitch, and with what vocal variety. Yet while labeling voice and articulation as sender variables, we recognize that changes in *how* a message is uttered may directly affect the meaning of the message. Only context clues prevent wide misunderstanding when a language contains a number of different dialects and pronunciation patterns.

They spell it Vinci and pronounce it Vinchy; foreigners always spell better than they pronounce.

—Mark Twain,
The Innocents Abroad

Just as the *message* may be influenced by the sender's voice and pronunciation, so the *receiver* may decode and interpret a message in various ways in response to specific vocal and articulatory behaviors of the speaker. In some communication models, grating voice qualities and gross mispronunciations could be labeled *noise in the channel,* for they might truly interfere with message transmission and reception. More often than not, though, meaning is not lost to the receiver. Rather, the receiver makes judgments in addition to decoding meaning—judgments that involve perceptions of the intelligence and competence of the speaker.

Those of you who have studied communication models in your other courses will have discussed the circularity or interactive quality of these models. No model is designed to suggest that any aspect of the total communication process exists in isolation. Like a ripple effect, any change in any one part of the model will produce changes in all other parts of the model as they interact or circle back upon themselves. This premise can be applied to voice and articulation. One specific aspect of the total process—how words are said—may produce changes in other parts of the model—the message or the receiver, for instance.

In summary, voice and articulation are primarily sender variables, since they deal with specific skills and techniques a speaker uses in uttering messages. Yet the impact of the manner of utterance can alter not only the way in which a receiver interprets a message, but in some instances the message itself. If this were not the case, the study of ways to improve your voice and speech production would be pointless, since such study is designed to increase your rhetorical effectiveness—a receiver-based judgment.

READING ALOUD

Much of the time in this course you will be reading aloud—individual words, drill sentences and paragraphs, or the end-of-chapter passages from books, speeches, and plays that are provided for you as opportunities to incorporate pronunciation and voice principles as you learn them. A few suggestions on oral reading may help you as you prepare to read in class.

Reading aloud is different from spontaneous speech. The ideas are not yours, the word choice is not yours, the sentence structure is not yours, and the clues to the subtle shadings that are possible through vocal variation are nebulous and open to error. Yet the needs, even the demands, of the listeners do not change. They need to hear assimilated, connected speech with clear-cut vocal cues in order to process the psychological and emotional levels of the text, not just the information conveyed in dry and barren words alone.

The best oral reading is akin to the best of natural, conversational speech. Not only is it animated and interesting, but it falls on the listener's ear in phrases and thought groups—not as so many individual words strung together. Pauses, inflections, slight changes in volume, and minor alterations in rate separate the thought groups so that each is a unit a listener can decode and process *as* a unit. At the same time, assimilation, tempo, and inflectional patterns clearly tie the thought groups together so that the entire passage is received as a unified message.

As with good conversational speech, good reading clearly conveys the many shades of meaning that can be brought to words and thought groups by emphasizing them through subtle changes in pitch, volume, and duration. Indeed, different emphasis patterns are a significant aspect of the actor's or reader's unique interpretation of a manuscript. The lack of precise clues to the author's specific meanings underlies the challenge and fascination of translating the written word into an oral medium.

Set goals for your oral reading that bring it up to the best of your conversational speech. In platform speaking use the best of your conversational techniques in an amplified fashion. Do not let the focus on pronouncing words, projecting your voice, maintaining good posture, or in general "performing" cause you to lose touch with the basic nature of all oral communication, be it your own creation or your recreation of the words of another communicator. That basic nature is rhetorical—the securing of a response from a listener. The more natural, spontaneous, and artless you seem to be, regardless of how hard you may be working, the more the listener can focus on the *meaning* of your message. The sharing of meaning between a speaker and a listener *is* communication. And that's what it's all about!

COURSE GOALS

What, then, can you hope to accomplish during this course of study? To begin with, you may gain a new awareness of the importance of speech habits in daily life and how dialects contribute to the impressions people create. If you have international students in your class, you will become sensitized to the difficulties faced by second language speakers.

It is not sufficient to know what one ought to say, but one must also know how to say it.

—ARISTOTLE

On a theoretical level, you will first learn how human sound is produced, how your vocal mechanism is structured and how that structure works, and then how to gain more control over the final product—your own voice and speech sounds. With daily practice, your voice will gain more strength and flexibility.

According to your teacher's preference, you may or may not learn the International Phonetic Alphabet (**IPA**), a set of symbols to use in improving your articulation. You will learn how all the sounds of the English language are formed and some problems that occur in various formations. With your instructor's help, you will evaluate your own pronunciation habits. As a beginning step in your self-evaluation, complete the Personal Speech Background Inventory on the next page. It enables you to examine regional and family influences on your speech. Finally, use the drill and exercise material in this book to approach proficiency in Standard American English and thereby acquire further communication competence.

PERSONAL SPEECH BACKGROUND INVENTORY

_____   _____   _____
name   course   date

Classification: F S J S G Unclassified

Reason for taking this course: ( ) required for degree
                               ( ) advised for degree
                               ( ) elected
                               ( ) other (specify)

I was born in _____ , _____ , and lived there for
                     city   state

_____ years. Other cities I have lived in, and my age when I moved there, are:

_____ , _____ , _____

_____ , _____ , _____

_____ , _____ , _____

In general, people in these cities speak with regional dialects: _____ _____
                                                                   yes   no

What dialects? (mountain, Brooklyn, southern, etc.) _____

My parents speak or spoke in a dialect: _____ _____
                                         yes   no

My parents coached me, by direct teaching or corrective feedback, in word pronunciation:

_____ _____ If yes, occasionally _____ frequently _____
yes   no

I feel I speak in the following way:

_____ _____ _____ _____
no dialect   light dialect   moderate dialect   heavy dialect

Friends and acquaintances have _____ _____ _____
                               never   occasionally   often
commented upon my pronunciation pattern.

I would like to be able to speak Standard English if and when I want to:

_____ _____
yes   no

I would like to make the following changes in my voice: _____

_____

_____

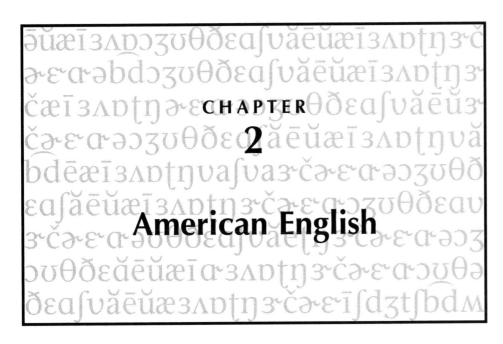

CHAPTER 2

American English

"England and America are two nations separated by a common language."

—ATTRIBUTED TO
GEORGE BERNARD SHAW

ORIGINS OF PRONUNCIATION STANDARDS

Although voice and diction are usually taught in the same course, and training in one of these areas bears directly on performance in the other, goals for voice improvement have not created the kind of controversy that surrounds standards for pronunciation. Few would argue against the goals of voice training—sufficient volume to be heard, pitch flexibility for interest and variety, and freedom from excessive quality problems such as nasality or hoarseness.

Diction or pronunciation training, however, depends upon the use of an arbitrary set of **phonemes**—the smallest isolatable units of speech sound. The implication of pronunciation instruction is that while a number of specific speech sounds may be available to convey the same orthographic (written-alphabet) letter, in actuality one pronunciation is preferable to another for some reason.

The history of the relationship between the spoken (phonetic) alphabet and the written (orthographic) alphabet is interesting. All languages developed first in the spoken form. Eventually a method was needed for transmitting talk to remote listeners or preserving it for a future time. A system for writing the spoken word was established and grew. In some languages, the written medium was *ideographic*—based on concepts or meanings of words or phrases. The Latin and Germanic languages, however, were *orthographic*, where written symbols were attempts to reproduce the sounds of the words. Yet whichever the writing system, the oral medium remained dominant; writing was merely a symbolic representation of the spoken word.

Read It Aloud _____

**They tell us Demosthenes
practiced with stones
To enunciate better, and
strengthen his tones.**

But over time, as specific languages such as English, French, German, and Spanish grew constantly more complex, the written mode gradually became the source of answers to questions about the "correctness" of the language. Today, if we want to know what a word means—the semantic or vocabulary feature—we look it up in the dictionary. The definition printed in the dictionary is the one we assume to be correct. If we want rules for grammatical relationships between words or how sentences may be constructed, we find them in books on language usage.

The same principle holds true in the language feature that you will be studying in this course—the pronunciation of words in American English. Imagine that before there was a written language, some scholars met to decide on a set of pictures or symbols that could be used for putting speech on paper. Suppose they agreed that the sound [b] should be drawn *b*, the sound [æ] should be *a*, and [θ] should be printed *th*—so that [bæθ] could be written *bath*.[1] Of course, no one knows exactly how the first dictionary was created, and the process surely was not this simple. The marking system probably evolved over many years, but the point remains—the standard for correct pronunciation was originally the pronunciation used by educated people of the day. Dictionaries of American English today present visual (orthographic) representations of the sounds (phonetics) spoken by the people, primarily by language scholars and community leaders.

Over the years, educators came to depend more heavily on printed guidelines to determine acceptable usage. While lexicographers (dictionary makers) continually strive in revised editions to change pronunciation guides and definitions to reflect changes in language usage, some teachers continue to insist that students conform to the dictionary as if it were law. But such conformity ignores the history of the development of language. English did not suddenly emerge as it is spoken today in America—or in England, for that matter. Indeed, the English language evolved with influences from the languages of the early Celts, the Angles and Saxons from Germany, the Romans, the Norse, the French, and other nationalities.

Over time, characters in the alphabet and the sounds those characters represent have changed considerably. Language is always changing, always evolving. Think of the number of new words that science and technology have added to the language in just the past decade. While there are "preferred" pronunciations in present-day speech, these standards likely will not govern American pronunciation 100 years from now. This text will examine standards and encourage you to use them, but it is important that you do not adopt a rigid attitude toward an arbitrary level of correctness. After all, English is spoken "correctly" in England, Scotland, South Africa, Australia, and many other places—and it sounds very different from the way it is spoken in the United States!

Read It Aloud _____

**If preachers preach and
teachers teach,
Why don't we say that
speechers speech?**

THE STANDARD AMERICAN DIALECT

FYI . . . _____

**A bird's larynx is called a
syrinx, and bird songs are
referred to as *dialects*.**

But what is the basis for speech standards represented in print? All speakers of English make choices—how to pronounce individual sounds, what syllables to emphasize, what words to use, and so on. What makes one choice "correct" and another not?

A **dialect** is a variation pattern of speech features within a given language that is characteristic of certain native speakers. (By contrast, **accent** usually refers to patterns from a speaker's native language spilling over into production of a second language; thus a person from Paris might speak English with a French accent.) Dialects can vary on a number of features, including vocabulary, rhythm, and pronunciation. These variations may mark certain geographic areas (New Orleans, Boston, Brooklyn), ethnic and national groups (Black, Hispanic, Eastern European), and socioeconomic distinctions (upper class, working class).

In the United States, one particular dialect—Standard American English—has gained widespread acceptance, and its pronunciational choices are reflected in most

_____

[1]Bracketed symbols are from the International Phonetic Alphabet. Until you learn it, refer to the chart on page 128 to understand the pronunciation. Brackets are used to distinguish IPA symbols from orthographic print.

print sources. Standard American English is associated most often with educated Americans, with Caucasian descendants of settlers from England, and with people living in parts of the North, Midwest, and West. There is a common misconception that speakers of Standard American have *no* dialect, that only people from places such as Alabama or New Jersey talk in a marked way. This is wrong—every person speaks with a dialect, choosing ways to pronounce sounds. Standard American is one dialect, and in this country it is the dialect most commonly accepted and employed in the entertainment, education, business, and political worlds.

SOCIAL IMPACT OF DIALECTS

Because Standard American is a preferred dialect in this country, many people evaluate others on how closely they adhere to it. This leads to a kind of linguistic snobbery that associates Standard American with "good" speech and labels other dialects as substandard or inferior. As this implies, people judge each other based on ways of speaking. Your dialect or accent choices will affect how people perceive you and react to you, and you will likewise react to others' speech. In this section, we will consider how dialects work in everyday life, how people react to certain dialects, and why you might wish to speak Standard American English in some situations.

Dialect does not mark a single category, such as region or ethnicity, in a straightforward way; rather it marks clusters of attributes. Your dialect may reflect your identity as "Southern," but it may also reflect that you are middle class, Black, or female. This raises an interesting question. Given that your speaking marks your membership in various, overlapping categories, how does one come to stand out? Why might people take your ways of speaking as indicating your gender in one situation, your education level in another, or your ethnic group in a third? This is a complex process, closely connected with how people stereotype others. (One could explain racism and sexism, for example, as errors in applying these categories—as explaining people's behavior too simply, and usually negatively, based on one factor such as race or sex without regard for the more complex *clusters* of attributes that we all represent.)

A second factor complicating the picture is that people do not employ dialects consistently. Much dialect variation is partial, meaning that speakers make a particular pronunciation or word choice in some opportunities but not all. For example, a midwesterner from Indiana may say *warsh* for *wash* but would not say *gorsh* for *gosh*. When we speak, we always are speaking in a particular situation, for a particular purpose, in interaction with particular others who also speak. Because these circumstances change, we adapt our ways of speaking accordingly. Under some circumstances, people may adjust their speech to be more like that of the people with whom they are speaking. Usage also affects pronunciation choice. In one study, linguist William Labov sent students out to ask clerks in particular New York City department stores questions in order to get them to answer, *fourth floor*. The students then would ask the clerks to repeat. He discovered that the clerks often would shift their pronunciation of *r* from nonstandard *fouhth flooh* to Standard American *fourth floor* between the first and second uses of the phrase.[2] The issue here is not that the clerks thought they were wrong the first time and corrected, but that the act of giving directions is different from the act of repeating oneself when the other has not heard you clearly—and different actions sometimes call for differences in speech. In short, for a number of reasons, speakers do not speak consistently in dialects.

Furthermore, language is dynamic and always changing. The spoken English of 100 years ago would sound strange to us, that of Shakespeare's time 400 years ago would be difficult to understand, and that of 1,000 years ago virtually unrecognizable. Dialects, too, evolve over time. The features that comprise Standard American as well as nonstandard forms do not remain constant. In the United States, geographical relocation,

---

[2]William Labov, *The Social Stratification of English in New York City* (Washington, DC: Center for Applied Linguistics, 1966).

God, all-powerful Creator of nature and Architect of the world, has impressed man with no character so proper to distinguish him from other animals, as by the faculty of speech.

—QUINTILIAN

FYI . . . —————

In 1850, fewer than half of all the people in the United States could read or write any language.

—ANDY ROONEY,
Communication is the Name of the Game

economic mobility, education, and mass media have all worked to lessen the impact of some nonstandard dialects. However, this does not mean that all nonstandard forms will die out. There is some suggestion, for example, that the gap between Standard American and the English of urban, lower-income African Americans is widening. Through dialects we identify ourselves and others as members of various groups, and we preserve and share culture. These remain important social processes, and people will continue to find ways to mark group membership through nonstandard language use.

Speaking is intimately linked to social interaction. How you speak influences how others perceive, judge, and respond to you, and how others speak influences how you perceive, judge, and react to them. Dialect and accent play prominent roles in these processes. Recall a time when you noticed someone's accent or dialect, whether in an interpersonal encounter or on television, radio, or in film. What brought it to your attention? Did you have trouble understanding that person? Did you find that way of speaking pleasing or attractive? Did that person sound uneducated? Did you find yourself wanting to hear more of that speech? Did you wish that person spoke more like you?

Research in the past four decades has explored how people perceive and judge each other based on dialects and accents. For the reasons discussed above—dialects continually change, they mark multiple rather than single group identities, and their usage is not constant—researchers face interesting challenges trying to determine the social impact of different dialects. A consistent finding across many of these studies is that people judge Standard American English speakers more positively on such dimensions as credibility, intelligence, ambition, and success when compared to speakers of nonstandard dialects.[3] This holds true whether the judges themselves speak primarily with a nonstandard or with Standard American dialect. Not only dialects but accented versions of English fare poorly when people compare them to Standard American, whether those rating the differences are native, English-speaking Americans, or nonnative speakers.[4] In some studies, nonstandard speakers have judged a nonstandard dialect as being more socially attractive. However, these same judges will still tend to rate Standard American English as superior in the attributes listed above.[5]

Consistent with the findings of these laboratory studies, field research, anecdotal evidence, and expert opinion confirm the widespread prejudice in the United States in favor of Standard American English and against nonstandard dialects. A hundred years ago, people might scarcely have questioned the assumption that the only proper and correct pronunciations are the standard forms. Early in this century, a few linguists and anthropologists began to challenge the premise that one version of a language was inherently better than another. Yet is was not until the Civil Rights movement of the early 1960s that the issue of nonstandard dialects made an impact on the thinking of American educators. African American activists demanded recognition of Black dialect as a highly functional communication system that provides an alternative to academic white English, an alternative that was different—nonstandard—but not *sub*standard. Similarly, students, black and white, wanted a place in the classroom for the jargon and speech patterns that filled their lives outside of school. In 1972, the Committee on College Composition and Communication adopted a position paper entitled "The Students' Right to Their Own Language." They argued that regional and ethnic dialects are *different,* not *deficient.*[6]

The educated Southerner has no use for an r *except at the beginning of a word.*

—MARK TWAIN,
Life on the Mississippi

"Mrs. Durbeyfield habitually spoke the dialect; her daughter . . . spoke two languages, the dialect at home, more or less; ordinary English abroad and to persons of quality."

—THOMAS HARDY,
Tess of the d'Urbervilles

. . . if in a tongue you utter speech that is not intelligible, how will anyone know what is being said? For you will be speaking into the air.

—THE BIBLE,
I Corinthians, 14:9

---

[3]Reid Luhman, "Appalachian English Stereotypes: Language Attitudes in Kentucky," *Language in Society,* 19 (1990), 331–348.

[4]Ruth Johnson, *The Relationship between Native Listener's Perceptions of Personality Traits of Nonnative Speakers and the Grammatical Errors and Phonetic Errors in Nonnative Speakers' Speech.* Unpublished doctoral dissertation, Tallahassee: The Florida State University, 1993. Also Tase-Rong Want, *Reactions of Native Speakers of English, Chinese, and Spanish to English Spoken by Native Speakers of English, Chinese, and Spanish.* Unpublished Master's Thesis, Carbondale: Southern Illinois University at Carbondale, 1995.

[5]Howard Giles, Angie Williams, Diane M. Mackie, and Francine Rosselli, "Reactions to Anglo- and Hispanic-American-Accented Speakers: Affect, Identity, Persuasion, and the English-Only Controversy," *Language and Communication,* 15: 2 (1995), 107–120.

[6]Committee on College Composition and Communication, "The Students' Right to Their Own Language," *College English,* 36:6 (1975), 711.

Yet prejudices in favor of Standard American remain. In the mass media, nonstandard dialect speakers often are portrayed as stupid, uneducated, or criminal, reinforcing various stereotypes. Unfair as it may seem, nonstandard dialects can work against you in education, professional, and social environments. Some educators argue that children who grow up speaking Black English and who are unfamiliar with the sounds, rhythms, and grammar of Standard American will have much greater difficulties in school. Because of this, some school districts have attempted programs to teach these children Standard American, virtually as a second language. Recent efforts in Oakland, California, have brought the new word "Ebonics" as a synonym for Black English into the vocabulary. Columnist Don Williamson writes about his ability to speak both Black English and Standard American English: "It meant better communication, which translated into better grades, better jobs and better overall opportunities. The ones who never learned both languages, never reached their potentials. Some didn't survive."[7]

A 1982 study found that speakers of Black English were clearly at a disadvantage in the job market compared to Standard American speakers.[8] Many speakers of a Southern dialect try to rid themselves of it, convinced that others in professional contexts will view them as quaint or laughable. Yet even the attempt to change may prove problematic. In a curious kind of reverse snobbery, nonstandard speakers who develop Standard American sometimes find themselves criticized or ostracized when they return to their nonstandard-speaking community of origin. Dialect choices display solidarity with certain groups, and a change in dialect may translate into a change, partial or complete, in group affiliation.

There is nothing inherently better about Standard American English. There is nothing inherently superior in saying *get* rather than *git*—each, in fact, represents a rather arbitrary association between a particular sound and a particular meaning. Judgments concerning preferred pronunciation standards are based in social and political considerations, not in any features of the dialects themselves. Any attempt to label a particular dialect good or bad, superior or inferior, misses this important point. Dialects, like languages, are not right or wrong; they all provide ways for people to communicate, to display solidarity with each other, and to create, share, and preserve culture.

Communication that seeks a response—and most communication falls into this category—is called **rhetorical.**[9] One can think of the broad range of dialects in American English as a range of possible choices in developing effective rhetorical strategies. All dialects are viable forms of communication; all function well in certain times and places. The effective communicator is one who has a sufficiently broad repertoire to choose the most rhetorically effective style for the particular situation. The idea of using different speech for different situations is not a new one. You probably already do this instinctively, talking casually around friends and more formally during a job interview. *Caynt* (can't), *boids* (birds), or *dese'n dose* (these and those) would go unnoticed in certain geographic areas and in some situations. But in other areas or situations, such pronunciational choices would tend to direct the listener's attention to the speaker's speech patterns and away from the message, hence reducing the rhetorical effectiveness. Furthermore, there is a chance that the attention focused on speech containing these dialect features would result in negative judgments about the speaker's intelligence, competence, or attractiveness. People do judge each other according to how they speak. In the United States, most people tend to perceive Standard America English more favorably than nonstandard dialects or accents. Given these trends, and

Read It Aloud _____

Rhetoric teaches the art of persuasion For speakers and speeches for any occasion.

[7]Don Williamson, " 'Talking Proper'; Black English Doesn't Help in Real Life." *Southern Illinoisan* (December 3, 1992.) A–1.

[8]Sandra L. Terrell and Francis Terrell, "Black English is a Liability in the Job Market," (paper presented at the American Speech-Language-Hearing Association Convention, Rockville, MD, Nov. 17, 1982).

[9]Speech communication experts continue to use the word *rhetoric* in its classic definition—any communication that seeks a response or in some way persuades the listeners. Two additional definitions are often heard: one equates rhetoric with the *style* of writing and speaking; the other suggests an oral or written message that is devoid of substance or potential action, as when a journalist labels a speech "mere rhetoric."

given the difficulty of changing these sorts of perceptions, you may wish to develop the ability to speak Standard American English.

This is not to suggest that if everyone were to speak Standard American, all prejudice would disappear. People will continue to stereotype others based on group attributes such as class, region, and ethnicity. You may develop superior Standard American English and still experience discrimination or peoples' unfair negative judgments of you. Nevertheless, the ability to speak Standard American remains an important communicative skill, and plenty of evidence suggests that possessing this skill will help you in many ways.

You are not being asked to give up the way you have always spoken. Your speech is a part of you and helps define who you are. We do ask, however, that you develop proficiency in Standard American English in addition to whatever dialect you presently speak. Just as learning a foreign language does not mean that you give up what you now have, so learning Standard American does not mean you will never talk again as yourself, whether "yourself" means urban Chicago or rural Mississippi. Develop the ability to use Standard American dialect if it will help you in any particular situation.

When should you use Standard American? You may wish to use it when people might judge your use of a nonstandard dialect negatively. When you are around Standard American speakers, you may want to use it. If you are considering a career in performance—theatre, film, television, or radio—you may be severely hampered if you cannot use Standard American. More generally, many people prefer to use it in their business, professional, and even social lives.

Think of your study in this course as an effort to increase your number of options among various dialects so that you broaden your repertoire of pronunciation behaviors. If you think of different dialects as different codes, than you can become a proficient "code switcher," adapting your speech to given listeners and situations. Such skill does not come easily, for speech patterns are deeply ingrained. You will need to work very hard if the speech patterns you acquired naturally in childhood were not relatively standard.

THE SOUNDS OF STANDARD AMERICAN ENGLISH

I myself have heard a common blacksmith eloquent, when welding of iron has been the theme.

—C. C. COLTON

Why is *oil* [ɔɪl] instead of *all* [ɔl] the preferable pronunciation for liquid grease or petroleum? Why should one more than five be called *six* instead of *sex*? Who said so? While we certainly admit some validity to the argument that "there is no such thing as Standard English," because no two persons speak with identical pronunciation patterns, we do believe that an inclusive range exists for each phoneme. Sounds within this range are called **allophones,** or variants of a phoneme. These are fine differences that can be thought of as speech sounds existing between two phonemes. Just as some people can hear minor differences in pitch between two notes on a musical instrument, some people can hear allophones while others cannot. The goal for you as a voice and speech student is to pronounce within that allophone range rather than substitute an entirely different phoneme. The symbol [ɔɪ] stands for a phoneme different from the symbol [ɔ], and [ɪ] is not the same sound as [ɛ].

We prefer *oil* and *six* because virtually every dictionary of American English uses the phonetic or diacritic symbol for [ɔɪ] and [ɪ] in these two words. Most educated people say *oil* and *six,* and educated people set standards for pronunciation. Given the wide range of possible variation within that dictionary standard, our goal of this text is to give you the tools to adjust your speech pattern accordingly. In many instances, the dictionary offers two or more pronunciations, admitting acceptable variation and leaving you some choice.

Standard American English, then, defines a range of pronunciation patterns as specified by dictionaries, not a precise right or wrong. Your goal is to work within that range, but to avoid moving out of the allophone range and substituting a different phoneme.

As you move through this book, it is inevitable that some of your teachers will question our choice of preferred pronunciation. This is the nature of the field and is reflected by the fact that many words in the dictionary have more than one *acceptable* pronunciation. In justifying our preferences, we agree with Abraham and Betty Lass, who say:

- This is the way our elementary school teachers first taught us to say the word. They taught us pronunciation with the same kind of zeal and thoroughness they taught us everything else.

- This is how we first heard the words pronounced. This is how we have always pronounced them. So they sound right and feel right to us.

- This is how we have heard educated people in our part and other parts of our country pronounce these words.

- We prefer our pronunciations because we have lived with them all our lives.[10]

FYI . . . —————

Eric LaSalle, who plays the role of Peter Benton in the popular TV series *ER*, was once dropped from Julliard because the faculty did not believe he could eliminate his inner-city dialect! He later mastered highly polished diction at New York University.

---

[10]Abraham and Betty Lass, *Dictionary of Pronunciation* (New York: Quadrangle/The N.Y. Times, 1976), p. 8.

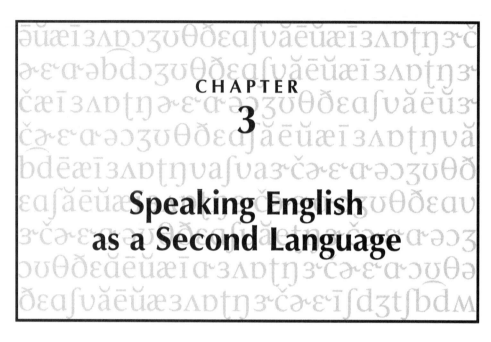

CHAPTER

3

Speaking English as a Second Language

There are doubtless many different kinds of sounds in the world, and nothing is without sound. If then I do not know the meaning of a sound, I will be a foreigner to the speaker and the speaker a foreigner to me.

—THE BIBLE,
I Corinthians 14: 10 & 11

INTERNATIONAL STUDENTS

FYI . . . _____

According to the 1995 *World Book Almanac,* Mandarin Chinese is the language with the largest number of speakers—975 million. English follows with 478 million, Hindi with 437 million, then Spanish with 392 million.

This chapter is directed toward those of you who have learned English as a second language (ESL). Born in a country that does not have English as its primary language, you came here to go to college, or perhaps moved here with your family while you were in high school. You probably studied English in your native land, but may not have mastered the language sufficiently to feel confident in your oral English communication skills. Many international students who come to the United States for higher education have enough knowledge of English to pass the written TOEFL exam (Test of English as a Foreign Language) required by many universities for admission. But they may be less able to converse freely and to make themselves understood, especially if they speak with a heavy accent.

Many Departments of English on college campuses offer ESL courses. These courses concentrate mostly on vocabulary and syntax, both formal and conversational. A growing number of voice and diction teachers, usually in Departments of Speech Communication, are reporting that international students are being advised or are electing to take also a basic speech production class. This enables them to focus their attention on pitch, inflection, and rhythmic patterns that are so important in speaking and listening in any language.

This course is ideal if you want to make your accent more understandable. You will be introduced to the individual sounds, called *phonemes,* of spoken American English. In some classes, you will learn the International Phonetic Alphabet, a marking system that assigns one symbol to each sound. Other teachers prefer using diacritical marks, those symbols that indicate length, assimilation, or position of vowel sounds. Learning one of these systems is essential, since English spelling often fails to predict pronunciation. Some spoken vowel sounds have many different spellings—look at the high back vowel [u], for example; that one pronunciation may be spelled twelve different ways! (See page 178.) You need to be able to look up pronunciations in either a standard or a phonetic alphabet dictionary. Understanding the marking system enables you to figure out how the word should be said.

HOW LANGUAGE IS ACQUIRED

Babies who are born free from hearing or speech organ difficulties and who are placed in an environment where they hear adults and sometimes older children talk will learn to talk with little direct *teaching* taking place. This is the way most people learn their first language. The ease with which children learn to talk and the relatively regular timetable by which they master sounds and words have led researchers to hypothesize an innate language acquisition capacity in the brain. The development of language goes hand-in-hand with the child's physical and mental development. The process is markedly similar all over the world, regardless of the particular language involved. The process also allows for the natural acquisition of more than one language, provided the linguistic environment offers the stimulus of two or more languages during the child's early years. In many homes where the father speaks one language and the mother speaks another, the children grow up speaking both languages with ease.

There is some indication, however, that the capacity to acquire language decreases with age. This suggests that the sooner children can be exposed to a second language, the more naturally they will learn it. The adult second-language-learner (SLL) may be more adept at rules of conversation, such as questions and answers or turn-taking behaviors. And the adult SLL has a wider frame of experience from which to process word meanings, contexts, and general frames of reference.

But a major drawback for the adult SLL is acquiring the phonemic and the *suprasegmental* features of the second language—the elements of spoken language such as stress, pitch, or juncture that take place at the same time as the utterance of vowels and consonants. This difficulty is one of the reasons that many adults can read and write in other languages in which they cannot carry on a conversation.

All of the spoken languages in the world are articulated from a single cluster of sounds that can be produced by the human vocal mechanism, (see pages 34–35). Each language draws from this larger cluster, using only some of the available sounds. No one language uses all of the sounds, and some languages use fewer sounds than others. Excluding diphthongs, Hawaiian has only five distinctly different vowels and seven consonants, while Spanish has five vowels and nineteen consonants. English, in comparison, has eleven vowels (represented in spelling by only five symbols) and twenty-four consonants. During the infant babbling and prespeech stage, from about three months to a year old, most babies produce a far greater number of sounds than will later be identified as meaningful phonemes of their own language. Their organs of articulation are flexible, not as yet set to accommodate only what is required of them for their native language. As we grow older, we lose some of this flexibility. Some of you may have genuine difficulty trying to "roll" your r's or do "Bronx cheers" by vibrating your lips or tongue. Most babies do these with ease.

Knowing this will help you to understand why it may be difficult to master an American English accent, or to speak English with a minimal carry-over of pronunciations from your first language. Many adults learn to pronounce a second language almost accent free, but the task may not be an easy one, for adults have passed the time when pronunciation comes naturally. This, however, is an excellent reason why you should be taking this course. This is an "academic" approach to language learning, necessary when your capacity for natural acquisition has lessened due to age. You will "be

Just for Fun . . .

"Doctor," a woman asked a renowned physician, "can you tell me why it is that some people are born unable to speak?"

"Why," replied the doctor, "it is due either to some congenital inhibition of the faculty of articulation, or to some anatomical deficiency in the organs of vocalization."

"There now," she said triumphantly to her husband, "see what it is to have an education? I've asked Henry why it was, and all he could say was " 'because they're naturally born that way.' "

"Speak in French when you can't think of the English for a thing."

—LEWIS CARROLL,
Alice in Wonderland

FYI . . .

Ralph Waldo Emerson called the English language "the sea which receives tributaries from every region under heaven." Why? Because English has evolved for over 2,000 years, and has "borrowed" from many languages including Celtic, Latin, Greek, Anglo-Saxon, German, Danish, Dutch, French, Spanish, Italian, Hindi, and other languages from Africa, North America, and Asia.

taught" to recognize fine differences between sounds, to learn to pronounce sounds that do not occur in your own language, and to speak with the rate, rhythm, and inflectional pattern that approach those of native American English speakers.

THE ACADEMIC APPROACH TO ESL

The academic approach to pronouncing American English has *theory* or knowledge value that extends beyond learning just enough everyday talk to get by. For example, you will learn about your anatomy, about the organs of speech and about how they work. You will learn the production differences between voiced and voiceless consonants, so that if you do not hear them easily, you can put your fingers on your throat in the "Adam's apple" area and feel the vibration. You will learn what it means to produce a sound high in the mouth, or to articulate it toward the front or toward the back. All this technical information can help you improve your pronunciation, if you will study it carefully, experiment with your mouth and the sounds, and learn just what it is you are doing when you substitute one sound for another. This means you are not solely dependent on your ear alone for changing your accent.

As you work with your classmates through these sounds, you will have the opportunity to hear native speakers as they produce the sounds in isolation, in clusters, in minimal pairs, in phrases, and in sentences and paragraphs. Imitation is the beginning point in learning pronunciation, and as you hear the other students and the teacher make these sounds, you can practice by imitating their pronunciation.

A word of caution, however, seems necessary here. All Americans do not talk alike. In fact, pronunciation and *paralinguistics* (those vocal effects that go along with, and in many cases modify, the pronunciation) may vary so much that you almost think you are hearing another language. Those of you who have traveled in other English-speaking parts of the world—England, Scotland, Ireland, Australia, South Africa—will recognize that the English language comes in many varieties. The origins and social impact of dialects were discussed in Chapter 2.

You may be somewhat confused about the correct pronunciation of a few sounds, especially if you are in the southern part of the United States, where many natives have regional dialects. Some of those natives are taking this course for a reason similar to your own—to modify their dialects. A *dialect* is a variation pattern in speech characteristics of a language, usually geographically or socioeconomically defined, while *accent* means sounds from a speaker's first language carried over into a second language. All people are not as precise in differentiating between these two terms as we are. You may hear someone speak of a "Southern accent" of a "French dialect." More correctly, ESL speakers have an *accent* when they speak English, while native United States speakers have *dialects*.

The differences between student pronunciations may be used as a basis for discussion. For example, the three front vowels [ɪ], [ɛ], and [æ] are closely related in their position in the mouth, as you will learn in Chapter 11. Southerners often substitute [ɪ] for [ɛ], as in saying *tin* when they want to refer to the number *ten*. Students whose native language is Spanish are not accustomed to hearing or saying [ɪ], for that sound does not occur in their language. They will often produce [i] when [ɪ] is called for, so that the word *city* may come out *ceetee*. Discuss these substitutions. Why do they occur? How can students master the preferred pronunciation? Do not be bothered by a variety of American speech patterns, but use that variety as a tool toward a better understanding of English sound structure.

Within any language, small differences may be heard in the way various speakers produce sounds and words. We talked about this in Chapter 1, describing the *allophone,* the slight variation in the way that the articulation organs are placed so that a minimal change occurs in the resultant sound. You can hear an example of that difference if you will say [l] at the beginning of the word *like,* then say it at the end of the word *tile.* Do you feel that your tongue is a bit further forward in your mouth on the first word than on the second and that the second [l] is somewhat darker? Sounds are influenced by the other sounds that come before or after them. We are not interested in having you identify and produce these fine differences. They are not necessary in making your speech intelligible. Most native speakers are not even aware that the differences exist. Concentrate on trying to produce each sound as it is described and illustrated in Section III.

YOUR LANGUAGE ENVIRONMENT

Much of your success in mastering English as a second language will depend upon how conducive your living environment is to daily practice. If your family has moved to the United States and you are living at home with them, and if your family continues to speak its native language around the house and at meals, your progress will be slower. Learning a new language is a gradual process, and we usually think in terms of four to five years to reach proficiency. That time can be shortened with daily immersion in the new language; it will probably be lengthened if the student does not have daily conversational practice. Conversation improves all aspects of your speech—vocabulary, syntax, pronunciation—and offers you good practice in understanding topic contexts and appropriate social interaction rules.

If your family plans to stay here for any length of time, then all members need to become better English speakers. Encourage them to use English around the house, invite people from church or school to come for "English evenings," and broaden your circle of friends so that you do not spend all your time with others from your own country. We all find comfort and ease in being around those who are like us, who know us, and with whom we can relax and talk freely. Talking freely is much simpler in your native language, since the native language is the one in which you think until you become skilled in the new language. As long as you must continue to search your mind to translate words and to structure word order, you will not feel comfortable. But in the case of learning a second language, nothing is more true than the old adage, "Practice makes perfect." Use every opportunity to talk with and listen to native English speakers.

If you are living in a dormitory, seek out English speakers. Perhaps you are sharing an apartment with other students from your own country. Follow the same suggestions we gave to students living with their families. Taking courses in Linguistics, English, and Speech Communication Departments is a great way to aid your mastery of American English, but it will not ensure that you become a fluent and understandable speaker unless you reinforce the classroom in your outside interactions. Those of you holding down a part-time job while you are in school probably have a higher motivation to improve quickly, for you know that your job security may depend on the clarity with which you speak.

YOUR COMMUNICATION STYLE

Another important factor in learning a second language is your communication style in your first language. Some people are naturally more outgoing, talkative, and enthusiastic than others, using more vocal and tonal expressiveness when they speak. They may be more willing to experiment, unafraid to make mistakes if they try new words or thoughts. Other people are quiet, shy, reticent, and may hold back on participating fully in speaking situations. Often the more reserved speakers use a softer volume, less pitch variation, and shorter turns at talk. Reticent speakers may have more difficulty in acquiring pronunciation skills in a second language. They may be more fearful of being laughed at or sounding silly in their way of speaking. When people are hesitant and unsure about the accuracy of their answers or whether what they are doing is correct, they often use a softer voice. Even young children will mumble an uncertain reply, seeming to believe that if the listener cannot hear them clearly, perhaps

nice—they all stood up together and asked me if I could see okay. They all sang 'José, can you see . . . !' "

OUR FAVORITE 2ND LANGUAGE JOKE: JoJo, the little dog, was walking down the street when he passed an office with a sign in the window: "Secretary wanted. Must be able to type 80 wpm, use the computer, and speak a second language." JoJo walked in, took the sign from the window, and stood on his hind legs in front of the receptionist. "What do you want," she asked. "You don't think you could handle that job?" JoJo nodded. "Well," said the receptionist, "let's see you type." JoJo sat down and promptly typed a perfect page, averaging 100 words per minute. "What about the computer?" asked the receptionist. JoJo booted it up and ran a copy of the company's latest financial report. "All right," replied the receptionist, "but what about a second language?" JoJo looked up earnestly. "Meow," he replied.

The English have no respect for their language, and will not teach their children to speak it. . . . It is impossible for an Englishman to open his mouth, without making some other Englishman despise him.

—GEORGE BERNARD SHAW, *Pgymalion*

that listener will not realize the answer is wrong! Adding a low level of volume to an accent makes the speaker more difficult to understand since the listener must strain to hear as well as to understand.

Many ESL speakers, especially those newly arrived in the United States and lacking confidence in their speech skills, may be slow to initiate conversations. They fear they will not be understood. When they do converse, they may treat topics more simply, with less elaboration, than they would in their own language. This is natural, since these speakers are not only struggling with the language, but are also working to become acculturated, to find their way around new cities, to learn the intricacies of day-to-day survival, to acquire appropriate behaviors in business and social situations, and to take in the host of new knowledge required to go to college in a foreign country. Just learning where the campus buildings are and what processes are required to register for classes can be a daunting experience, even for a native.

Situation and personality factors may make second language learning an even more difficult task. You need to work against any tendency to hold back, to avoid asking necessary questions, to sit silently even when you know the answers, or to escape from conversations. Rather than avoiding speech situations, plunge ahead and take advantage of every chance you get to talk and to listen to different speakers. Use all your opportunities to practice, for you will progress more rapidly if you participate whenever possible.

YOUR PERSONAL GOAL

What should you hope to gain from this course and from additional English studies that you may undertake? Some international students have approached us saying, "I want to get rid of my accent." This is not only an unrealistic goal, but it denies the positive aspects of using speech as a means of identification. A noticeable accent that is clear and understandable gives the listener immediate cues as to your country of origin. It makes you unique and interesting. Many listeners find accents pleasing to the ear and will pursue a conversation just to hear the speech patterns. Other listeners are fascinated by the accent's suggestion of travelers from distant lands that those listeners have not been able to visit. They may want to hear all about your homeland.

Elimination of an accent is not the goal. Rather, you should aim toward modification of your pronunciation so that you become completely *intelligible* to the listener. *Intelligibility* means that you are capable of being understood, that the listener not only hears, but can interpret each articulated sound distinctly and unmistakably so that full *comprehension* of all your words and ideas can take place. This is far more than merely the way you pronounce sounds, for it includes ample loudness, sufficient slowness, full and flexible use of the articulators, especially the lips (no mumbling!), eye contact, and other vocal and nonverbal features of oral communication. With these features operating at their best, you can substitute some of your sounds without any ill effect. Your goal should be a moderated accent that is clear and distinct, so that people do not have to ask you to repeat yourself frequently.

At the same time that you are gaining skill in oral English, each day you are also learning more about the United States, the customs, habits, and behaviors. You are also learning how to listen in English. This knowledge, combined with added skill in the language, will lead you toward *cultural competence*. You will be amazed at how much you learn during your years of American college or university study. All this learning comes to you more easily if you have a good command of the language.

You may wish to buy or check out from the library some additional books that would help you. We highly recommend Avery and Ehrlich's *Teaching American English Pronunciation*. These authors analyze 14 major languages according to the problems their speakers will have in learning English. Morley's two practice manuals, *Rapid Review of Vowel & Prosodic Contexts* and *Intensive Consonant Pronunciation Practice* provide

---

FYI . . . ———————

Incomprehensible is an anagram of problem in Chinese. An anagram is another word or phrase made by rearranging the letters of a first word or phrase. English allows for hundreds of anagrams. What about your native language? Can you form anagrams in it? What might be an English anagram for *one hug*? or *a sentence of death*? See answer in the Appendix.

"I speak Spanish to God, Italian to women, French to men, and German to my horse."

—Charles V
(Charles the Wise)
1337–1380

additional practice material to supplement this textbook. Some other references are suggested below.

REFERENCES

AVERY, PETER, AND SUSAN EHRLICH. *Teaching American English Pronunciation.* Oxford, New York, Toronto: Oxford University Press, 1992.

CHENG, LI-RONG LILLY. *Assessing Asian Language Performance.* Rockville, Maryland: Aspen Publishers, 1987.

COOK, VIVIAN. *Second Language Learning and Language Teaching.* London, New York: Edward Arnold, 1991.

LARSEN-FREEMAN, DIANE, AND MICHAEL H. LONG. *An Introduction to Second Language Acquisition Research.* London, New York: Longman, 1991.

MORLEY, JOAN. *Extempore Speaking Practice.* Ann Arbor: Univ. of Michigan Press, 1992.

——. *Intensive Consonant Pronunciation Practice.* Ann Arbor: Univ. of Michigan Press, 1992.

——. *Rapid Review of Vowel and Prosodic Contexts.* Ann Arbor: Univ. of Michigan Press, 1992.

WODE, HENNING. *Learning a Second Language: An Integrated View of Language Acquisition.* Philadelphia: John Benjamins, 1981.

PASSAGES TO READ ALOUD

In the Preface we told you that beginning with Chapter 3 we would offer paragraphs and passages at the end of each chapter for reading aloud, either in class or for you own practice at home. Remember that these reading passages have no direct relationship with the chapter they follow. They come from a number of different types of literature. Oral reading gives you a chance to practice the pronunciation and voice skills that you are working to acquire. We hope you find these selections interesting and challenging.

MEDIA COPY FOR PRACTICE

Many of you may be planning careers in radio and television. The following fictional passages represent some of the different kinds of copy that broadcasters encounter. Practice reading them aloud. More media copy may be found at the end of Chapter 6.

Network Newscasts

DATELINE: CHICAGO

The American Medical Association has released the results of a study on the relationship between the smoking habits of parents and the number of colds and sore throats contracted by their children. Doctors in the Jackson City Pediatric Clinic kept records for a four-year period on over 500 patients between the ages of two and eleven, noting both the number and severity of upper respiratory infections.

Parents were interviewed to determine whether one or both of them smoked cigarettes in the home. Results indicated that children from homes where both parents smoked had over three times the number of colds and sore throats with more severe symptoms, than children from nonsmoking homes. "The evidence is clear," said Dr. Michael Turner, director of the research. "Smoking parents are making their small children sicker than they need to be." The clinic plans to continue gathering data for further study.

DATELINE: WASHINGTON D.C.

The nation's public colleges and universities reeled today under a congressional budget decision to do away with all federal direct grants and loans to students in state-supported institutions. The move, labeled by its opponents as the "private school supremacy" measure, will make federal funding available only to students who attend privately owned colleges and universities. The measure assumes that large sums of state tax money used to support public colleges should be balanced by a federal tax infusion into the private schools.

The National Council of Institutions of Higher Learning has fought the measure bitterly, arguing that it directly opposes the basic concept of public education. The full impact will be felt in the fall of next year when the measure goes into effect.

DATELINE: NEW YORK

Anti-nuclear arms protesters today caused a major snarl in mid-Manhattan traffic as they marched by the thousands into the Times Square area at noon. Protesting the recent withdrawal of the United States from the nuclear disarmament talks in Stockholm, the demonstrators refused to follow police injunctions to move out of the streets. Several hundred were arrested and taken to jail, but the majority remained in the streets until National Guardsmen arrived in the late afternoon, and the crowd began to disperse. Surprisingly, no accidents or injuries were reported.

DATELINE: PANAMA CITY, PANAMA

A large outbreak of yellow fever—a form of malaria—among the Cuna Indians in the San Blas area of eastern Panama has health authorities working round the clock to fight the disease through treatment of those already infected, immunization for all others, and a massive spraying effort designed to kill off the yellow fever mosquito, the culprit in this deadly infection.

Authorities say this is the worst outbreak since the Cuban epidemic at the turn of the century, at which time the theory of transmission by mosquito bites was verified. While the disease, caused by a virus, is infectious and most often fatal, it fortunately is not contagious. The most effective means of control is eliminating the mosquito by spraying insecticides and draining grounds. Panamanian officials say they hope to have the outbreak under control in the next twenty-four hours.

DATELINE: HAWAII

Seismologists at the East–West Center in Honolulu today recorded significant tremors believed to be a submarine earthquake on the island of Krakatau in Indonesia. The volcanic island suffered one of the worst eruptions in the history of the world in 1882, when thousands of people were killed in a series of explosions that were heard 3,000 miles away.

Krakatau has been dormant since a minor upheaval in 1927, at which time the island was evacuated of all inhabitants. It has remained abandoned since then. Scientists note that another major eruption of the volcano could have far-reaching consequences in the form of massive tidal waves that could sweep hundreds of miles across the ocean, flooding islands and seaports in their wake. Weather stations across the Pacific Ocean will continue to monitor the volcano carefully.

Local Newscasts

State health officials today urged immediate passage of legislation to make rabies immunization mandatory for cats. Rabies vaccination has been required for dogs since 1937, but cats have been exempt since it was generally believed they did not carry the dread disease. In recent years, however, a number of cases of rabies in cats have been reported by veterinarians in several locations across the state.

Although several counties and a few cities presently have local laws requiring vaccination of cats, officials feel statewide control is necessary. Supporters believe the measure will pass both the House and the Senate without serious opposition. Cat owners will pay two to ten dollars to have their pets immunized, a process that must be repeated every two to three years.

Chemy-Con Industries continued its battle against Environmental Protection Agency officials today as its appeal hearing opened in the Tenth District Court. The EPA has blocked the Winfield County toxic-waste disposal site established by Chemy-Con on the charge that underground seepage presents a hazard to nearby Lake Wallace, a well-developed resort and fishing area. Environmental scientist Carmen Sanchez began the hearing with an elaborate presentation of charts and diagrams designed to explain the precise nature of the chemical waste produced by Chemy-Con and its absorption by the soil. The hearing is expected to continue for several days.

The local housing industry continued to show signs of a healthy recovery during the past month, when 105 permits were issued for new single-family dwellings. Beleaguered by over two years of recession, with high interest rates having brought construction to a virtual standstill, builders seem optimistic that the worst is over. Mortgage money, which reached an all-time high of 19 percent in January of last year, is now available at rates of 12 to 13 percent, making home purchase more attractive and more feasible to buyers who have been waiting out the recession. Housing experts believe the city needs six to eight hundred new single-family dwellings as well as a comparable number of apartment units in the next two years to meet the demand.

On the sports scene, fourth-ranked Carson College handed the first-ranked Tabor Tigers a stunning 21-to-7 defeat last night in the first of the two-game championship series. Wide receiver Wayne Jackson scored all three touchdowns on long passes from quarterback Reggie Dunbar. This dynamic duo had brought the Carson Cougars from the bottom of the league into the fourth place slot during the season with an average of three completions per game for over forty yards per throw.

Despite a week of special drills designed by Tabor defensive coach Earl Stanley to contain the Dunbar–Jackson combo, they were not to be stopped. Carson meets the Ponca City Panthers next Saturday, while Tabor will tangle with Oak Falls in a battle for third place. Tickets are still available for both games.

Mack Mahoney, longtime manager of the world championship Darby Deacons, and Sam Simon, hard-slugging shortstop for the Raytown Raiders, were elected to baseball's Hall of Fame on Friday. They will be inducted at the Hall of Fame Museum in Cooperstown, New York, in a special ceremony on June 25.

Chosen by the Committee on Veterans from a number of nominees, Mahoney, who retired in 1969, seemed surprised by the news when Committee spokesman Arthur Adams reached him at his ranch in Arizona. Simon, who now owns and manages a large chain of car wash establishments in Illinois and Indiana, said he was delighted with what he called "the greatest honor of my career." He still recalls the seventh game of the 1965 World Series, when the Raiders shut out the Brevard Bulldogs—his most exciting moment in baseball.

Public Service Announcements

Do you want to stop smoking, but feel you lack the willpower to quit on your own? Then attend the Smok-No-Mor Clinic at the Carter Street Methodist Church this Friday and Saturday.

The Smok-No-Mor program was designed by nationally famous Dr. Edgar Morris, who has personally trained the workshop leaders. The technique is built on the group-sharing concept of Alcoholics Anonymous.

A ten-dollar fee covers your participation from 7 to 10 P.M. both Friday and Saturday evenings. You must attend both sessions to benefit from the program. Interested persons should call the church office to make reservations. Call soon, for enrollment is limited.

Friends of the Palace will assemble this Saturday to begin the massive cleanup job following the fire in the theater five weeks ago. Insurance investigators had delayed cleanup while they sifted through the charred remnants of stage properties, scenery, and costumes hoping to find clues to the origin of the fire. Arson had at first been suspected, but it was finally determined that the fire began in a dimmer board used to control the stage spotlights.

Anyone interested in joining the Friends of the Palace should show up on Saturday morning at eight o'clock, wearing old clothes and face masks, since soot and fumes are still strong in the old building. Palace board members plan to have renovation complete and the theater back in operation in about three months.

Enter your cat in the annual Bryant Park cat show by calling Park Director Ernie Lane at 378-2153. The show, a highlight of the park's spring activities, has categories for everything from common house cats or even alley cats to pedigreed pusses with papers to prove prestigious parentage.

Judges will be marking entrants for appearance and personality all day on Saturday, March 21. However, your cat need stay only two hours to qualify. "Cats are so temperamental," said director Lane, "that we prefer keeping them only short periods of time. Besides, last year over a thousand cats were entered, so there are plenty on hand at any one time for visitors to enjoy seeing."

Don't forget—call 378-2153 to enter your feline friend. Prizes range from $25 to $100 for the several categories of winners.

The Department of Agriculture will hold another cheese giveaway this Sunday afternoon at the Ebenezer Baptist Church. Church officials agreed to administer the giveaway, the third in the city during the past six months. The last time, people lined up for several blocks to receive the five-pound boxes of processed cheese, surplus purchased by the Department of Agriculture as part of its price-support program for the nation's dairy farmers.

Any family eligible to receive food stamps is eligible for the cheese. Pastor Jeremy Walker has announced that the line will form in the church parking lot, but asks that recipients not begin to gather until after one o'clock, so that churchgoers will have left the parking area.

Members of MADD, Mothers Against Drunk Drivers, will meet this Friday night at the Central YMCA to plan their strategy for handling the upcoming New Year's Eve celebration. Last year MADD volunteers stayed on duty all night to pick up and take home people who called in asking for a ride because they had had too much to drink. The effort was highly successful, with rides furnished to 127 callers, most of whom had heard the phone number repeated every half hour all New Year's Eve afternoon and night by local radio and television stations. Drunk driving arrests were significantly lower than in previous years.

MADD members will repeat the offer this year. Anyone wishing to join the organization or to volunteer to stay on duty New Year's Eve should attend the meeting at the Y at 7:30 P.M. Friday.

Commercials

Wise investors need an up-to-the-minute report on the latest stock market conditions. Do you depend only on the skimpy reporting in your local newspaper? Well, let *Darien's Daily Digest* furnish you in-depth information on what to buy, what to sell, and trends in the market as they are happening. *Darien's* is a computerized, televised service available through your local cable TV company. For a small monthly fee, you can have a full thirty-minute analysis at the touch of your dial from 6:00 A.M. to midnight, five days a week. Have *Darien's Digest* in your home or office. Never again have to wait and worry about market conditions. Call your local cable TV company or *Darien's* toll-free number, 800-623-7184. That's *Darien's Daily Digest*—800-623-7184.

Are you in the market for a new television set? Is the picture on your old set fuzzy? Is the color weak? Does it take three or four minutes to warm up?

Price Appliances has the CSA zq100 on sale this week only. Dan Price took advantage of a special factory overstock offer to order 500 of the twenty-one-inch models just for this special promotion. All solid-state, the zq100 is designed to give you years of reliable, maintenance-free performance. And for this week only, the set is available for just $399.99—a full $100 below the usual cost.

Come to Price Appliances on High Meadows Road today and take home a brand-new CSA that will give you and your family countless hours of top-quality TV viewing at a price you can afford.

Is it time to paint your house again? You only painted it two years ago, yet you see cracking and peeling in several spots, and the color seems to have faded into drabness? Next time buy O'Rourke's quality paint and see it last for years and years. Whether you are a do-it-yourselfer or hire a professional to do the painting, insist on O'Rourke's Sunproof Super Latex House Paint for long life and long-lasting color. O'Rourke offers a wide range of color choices, and our experts in the paint department will help you estimate quantity and answer any of your questions on painting techniques. A complete line of paint accessories is also available. So, visit your nearby O'Rourke store before you paint again. You and your house will be glad you did.

Jacques Continental Restaurant in the Forest Park Shopping Center offers the finest in French cuisine for a dinner that goes beyond food alone and into an environmental eating experience. Cordon Bleu chef Henri Dubois creates his culinary masterpieces surrounded by a staff of professionals dedicated to making each patron's meal a sensual delight. In the elegant rococo decor, French-speaking waiters will lead you from a tempting aperitif through to the delicate after-dinner chocolate and demitasse, followed by a fine brandy. And all to the accompaniment of a chamber music quartet. Call Jacques today for reservations for a dinner you will long remember.

Monthly bills about to get you down? Are you over your head with charge accounts and time payments? Well, let Cameron's Consumer Credit Consolidation Corporation lump all those charges into a single loan, where you make only one payment a month, and that payment adjusted to your income so that you have some money left over for yourself after payday. Many of our customers—through no fault of their own—have overextended themselves and now face past-due payments and bill collectors who harass and embarrass them. If you have a steady job, Cameron's can help free you from the daily pressure and worry about cash in hand by helping you rearrange your bills in a more manageable plan. Call Cameron's today—consolidate those "easy payments" that are making your life so hard.

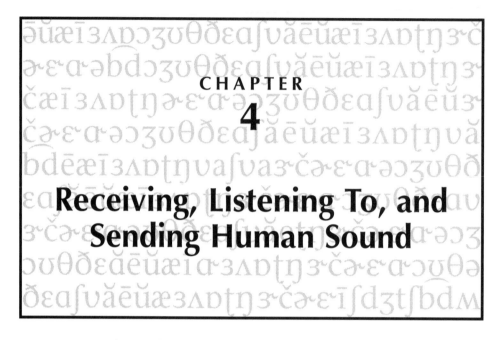

CHAPTER
4

Receiving, Listening To, and Sending Human Sound

The angel ended, and in Adam's ear
So charming left his voice, that he awhile
Thought him still speaking, still stood fixed to hear.

— JOHN MILTON,
Paradise Lost

WHAT IS SOUND?

Sound can be discussed from two different viewpoints. Physicists and speech scientists describe sound as the activity and resulting effect of a vibratory body or mass—the initiation of **sound waves.** Psychologists and speech teachers focus on the impact the vibrations make on the human ear—the reception of sound waves. When you hear a sound, you judge its highness or lowness by assigning pitch according to your own aural perception, governed by your memory. The physicist or speech scientist judges pitch by determining the rapidity or frequency at which the physical body vibrates, with each complete vibration called a *cycle* or *Hertz (Hz).* (See Figure 4–1.) Whereas speech scientists chart human-voice sound waves onto *oscillograms,* speech teachers help students find that combination of frequencies and resonating patterns most pleasing to the human ear.

In simplest terms, sound is produced when some physical entity with the capacity to vibrate is set in motion. These vibrations create pressure waves that move out from the vibrating body through the surrounding medium, most often air or water. The ripples resulting from a pebble tossed into a pond demonstrate this principle. The water itself does not move from the center of the pond to the shore, but the ripples do. In the same manner, the air does not move when we speak, but the sound waves or vibrations move through it. They are detected by the ear, then perceived by the brain.

Familiar examples of vibrating bodies that initiate sound waves that the human ear can process are violin strings, clarinet reeds, metal tuning forks or rods, and the

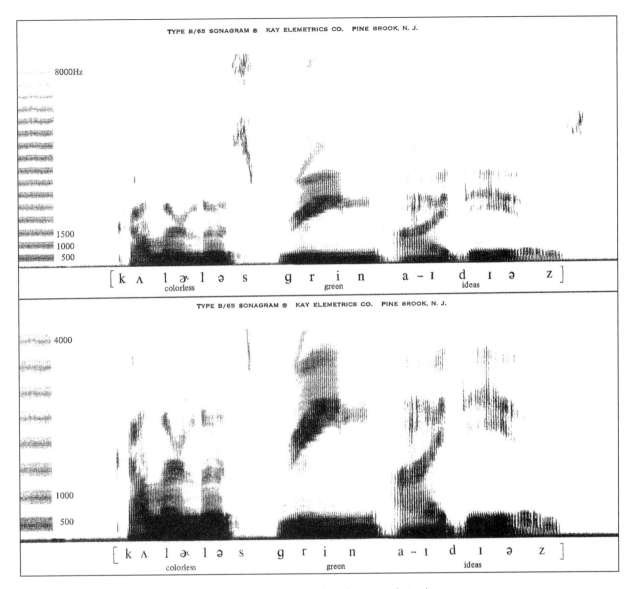

Figure 4–1 A sound spectrograph, or "voiceprint," of the first three words in the sentence "Colorless green ideas sleep furiously," coined by linguist Noam Chomsky to illustrate his theory that a group of words does not have to make sense in order to be a sentence. The upper graph extends to 8000 Hz, so the peaks of the consonants may be seen. The lower graph is at 4000 Hz and more clearly demonstrates the lower frequency of the vowel sounds.

human vocal folds. Many sounds lie outside the frequency range of human hearing. For example, a high-pitched whistle that humans cannot receive can be heard at some distance by a dog and is often used by owners to call their dogs.

Sound is characterized by three features: pitch, loudness, and quality. (Human speech adds a fourth feature—rate or timing, to be considered later.) These features correlate with the three physical properties of sound: frequency, amplitude or intensity, and harmonic construction. The frequency at which a physical body vibrates in part determines the pitch (highness or lowness on a musical scale) of the sound. Amplitude (the strength with which the airwaves strike the eardrum) determines loudness. And the combination of pure tones that blend as the vibration passes through various resonating chambers becomes the quality of the sound. (Each of these processes will be discussed in subsequent chapters.) When the movement of the vibration or wave through the air is relatively pure and even, a simple tone or sound results. As additional frequencies are blended, the result becomes more complex and may be disharmonic.

The human voice is a fascinating generator of sound. Think of the many different people you know—yet no two voices are identical. Given the limited scope of the vibrating body (vocal folds), the potential range of pitches from very low to very high and the possible changes in volume from whispers to shouts are remarkable.

STOP AND TRY THIS

Explore the potential flexibility of your own voice by playing the "Listen to My Voice" game—by yourself, with a friend, or into a tape recorder.
Think of a quality, then try to imitate that quality with your voice:

"Listen to my voice—shouting!"

"Listen to my voice—whispering!"

"Listen to my voice—growling!"

In each case, repeat the whole phrase while trying to use the particular voice quality described. Other interesting qualities are squeaking, drawling, racing, slowing, croaking, whining, twanging, snapping, and rolling. In fact, your voice qualities can go as far as your imagination takes you.

RECEIVING SOUND

Hearing

All speech, written or spoken, is a dead language, until it finds a willing and prepared hearer.

—Robert Louis Stevenson

To the human ear (see Figure 4–2), sound is vibration within the range of frequencies that the inner ear can receive and the brain can process. Vibrations are carried or transmitted through the air by the motion of air particles. The waves move through the outer ear to the tympanum (eardrum), which in turn vibrates and sets the ossicles in motion. The ossicles consist of the malleus (hammer), the incus (anvil), and the stapes (stirrup)—terms that generally describe the shape of these three smallest bones in the body. The stirrup causes vibration of the oval window, the thin membrane that connects the middle and inner ear. Next the cochlea, a pea-sized, "snail-like" canal containing thousands of tiny hairs, processes the sound impulses, which then travel to the brain along the auditory nerve. The brain processes the impulses so that the hearer can respond by assigning meaning to the sound.

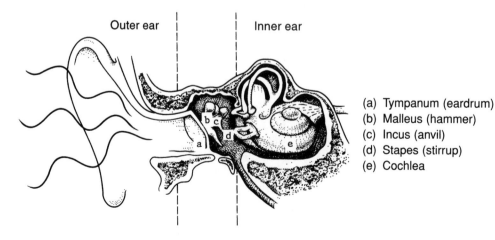

(a) Tympanum (eardrum)
(b) Malleus (hammer)
(c) Incus (anvil)
(d) Stapes (stirrup)
(e) Cochlea

Figure 4–2 The ear.

Good hearing is essential to the development of a clear voice and accurate pronunciation of speech sounds. Children learn to talk by hearing speech and by imitating what they hear. By contrast, teaching hearing-impaired children to speak is difficult, and the chances are negligible that they will ever speak as distinctly and with the same balanced resonance as hearing persons.

Listening

Unfortunately, many individuals whose hearing is perfectly normal do not become good listeners. Listening requires that we pay special attention to incoming sounds, filtering (selecting from) a variety of internal and external competing messages. Listening also requires concentration, for the listener must try to assign an accurate meaning to the incoming signal. Good listening is an active process, although it can appear to be passive since the listener may simply sit still. During active listening, the pulse speeds up and brain wave activity increases.

Self-motivation is a key factor in improving listening ability. Many students attend classes expecting them to be uninteresting or boring. Anticipating boredom, they may tune out from the active listening process, often openly engaging in competing tasks such as writing letters, reading the newspaper, or drafting an essay for another course. Years of watching television have conditioned many young people to expect constant entertainment, frequent breaks in the program, and a kind of listening that can usually be done with far less than full attention. Students must work hard to offset these influences as they listen in the classroom.

For the voice and diction student, good listening is the crucial component of progress. Listening must be fine-tuned, much as a complex stereo system is. The ability to discriminate minimal phonemic differences and to hear these differences in yourself, your classmates, and your instructor is central to your ability to produce those sounds when you speak. You need to be able to recognize the most subtle changes in pitch and volume, as well as to distinguish shifts in various vocal qualities. These abilities all depend on your effectiveness as a listener. Your determination to suspend thoughts of life outside the classroom, to concentrate fully for the fifty to eighty minutes you are in class, and to give complete attention to what you hear will give you a genuine advantage over those poor listeners whose warm bodies may occupy other classroom seats.

One may really indeed say that that is the essence of genius, of being most intensely alive, that is being one who is at the same time talking and listening.

—GERTRUDE STEIN,
Portraits and Repetitions

Your ears will always lead you right, but you must know why.

—ANTON VON WEBERN

Speed Bump

SPEED BUMP reprinted by permission of Creators Syndicate.

THE HUMAN VOCAL MECHANISM

The vocal mechanism is comprised of four systems: respiration, phonation, resonation, and articulation. Although these systems can be discussed separately and sequentially, in reality they operate almost in unison when a person speaks. As a speaker or listener, you are unaware of going through a series of steps to produce or receive the vibrations that become sounds and words. Only when you study voice and speech is it necessary to isolate and examine each of the four systems to understand and improve your use of them.

Respiration

Respiration is the term for the overall process of **inhaling** and **exhaling** air. Voice coaches more often use the word *breathing* for the controlled inhalation and exhalation needed to produce sound. If vocal sound is produced by vibrating airwaves, obviously the quality with which the airwaves are initiated will affect the product—the voice.

The parts of the body involved in respiration are the lungs, diaphragm, rib cage and intercostal muscles, bronchi and trachea (see Figure 4–3). The **thorax** (chest cavity) is shaped by the **rib cage.** Twelve pairs of ribs are attached to the vertebrae. The topmost ten pairs are attached to the **sternum** (breastbone); the two lowest pairs have no frontal attachment and are called *floating ribs*.

The **lungs** lie within the rib cage and are filled with microscopic air sacs called *alveoli*. Within these air sacs, a crucial exchange of gases—the absorption of oxygen from the fresh air and the removal of carbon dioxide from the blood—takes place. Air moves out of the alveoli through tiny air tubes (*bronchioles*), through the **bronchi** (bronchial tubes) and the **trachea** (windpipe), and then out the mouth or nose.

Although some muscle fiber is present in the lungs, the lungs themselves are not muscles and hence cannot move independently. Instead, they depend for movement on the muscles between the ribs and at the base of the lung cavity. Between the ribs and mostly toward the sides of the body are a number of connecting muscles called the **external intercostals.** These muscles can cause the rib cage to move upward and outward. At the base of the lung cavity is a large, dome-shaped muscle called the **diaphragm,** which controls the size and shape of the lower portion of the cavity.

When the external intercostal muscles expand the ribs outward and upward and the diaphragm contracts downward, the lungs, which are attached to the sides of the chest cavity, expand with the expansion of the cavity itself. A vacuum is then created, and air rushes in to equalize the pressure. When the **internal intercostal muscles**

The devil hath not,
  in all his quiver's choice,
An arrow for the heart like a
  sweet voice.

  —LORD BYRON

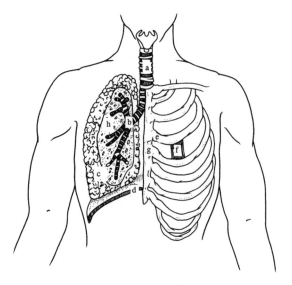

(a) Trachea (windpipe)
(b) Bronchi (bronchial tubes)
(c) Lungs
(d) Diaphragm
(e) Rib cage
(f) Intercostal muscles between ribs
(g) Sternum (breastbone)
(h) Alveoli

Figure 4–3   The breathing mechanism.

begin to contract the ribs inward and the diaphragm relaxes upward to the base of the lungs, air is forced out of the lungs, or exhaled.

This process of inhaling and exhaling happens thousands of times each day. For most people respiration is accomplished without thought and without sound. Noisy respiration, such as heavy sighing or snoring, or the snuffled nasal sounds of the breather with a head cold, may signal a problem. When a person is ready to speak, the outgoing air is channeled to vibrate with and through the vocal folds, initiating vocal sound.

Exhaled air is the power source of voice and speech production. Controlled abdominal breathing is important for the speaker. Because the abdominal area, controlled by the action of the diaphragm, is a greater distance from the air passages (nose, mouth, and throat) than the upper chest area controlled by the intercostal muscles, we call abdominal breathing "deep breathing." Speakers and singers need to breathe deeply, not in a shallow, upper-chest manner. Practice in deep breathing should become a daily routine, from which you can expect a number of benefits.

Deep breathing is healthful.   As air moves in and out of the body, a critical exchange of gases takes place within the lungs. Oxygen, basic to all functions of the circulatory system, is taken into the bloodstream, while carbon dioxide, a waste product of metabolism, is removed and then exhaled.

STOP AND TRY THIS

Lean back in your chair, relax, and take a good deep breath.

1. Lay your hands gently across the area just above your waistline. Do you feel a gentle rise and fall as you inhale and exhale?

2. Now place your hands around your rib cage, thumbs to the back, fingers toward the front. Try to push your hands in and out as you inhale and exhale.

3. Now try to move both the abdominal area and the rib cage area by breathing even more deeply and fully. Can you sense the motion and feel the vibration in your fingertips?

4. When you are filled with air, gently begin to blow out, with your lips rounded. No sound is necessary. Just feel the slow, steady blow as the air is exhaled.

You can help assure yourself of adequate oxygen intake if, several times each day, you spend a few minutes outdoors breathing deeply, where you are more likely to encounter fresh air. People who live or work in large metropolitan areas where pollution from cars and factories deprives them of clean air face potentially serious lung problems. Brown lung and black lung are diseases brought on by pollutants breathed into the lungs. And the message is clear for those who will hear it: cigarette smoke is harmful to the lungs, throat, and mouth. You can do your voice and body a great favor by not smoking.

Deep breathing is natural.   Deep breathing (remember that it is also called abdominal or diaphragmatic breathing) is natural. Watch a person sleeping on his or her back. You will see a gentle rise and fall of the area just above the navel and waistline and below the triangle formed by the lower ribs as they round downward from the sternum and toward the sides and back of the body. As the diaphragm contracts downward the visceral organs move outward, thus creating the rising motion that accompanies inhalation. The falling motion of exhalation occurs as the sleeper's diaphragm moves back up into its relaxed position. (See Figure 4–4.)

Is there a difference between this relaxed, natural breathing in sleep and the type of breathing recommended for voice and speech work? The answer is both *no* and *yes*.

"By climbing up into his head and shutting out every voice but his own, 'Civilized Man' has gone deaf. He can't hear the wolf calling him brother—not Master, but brother. He can't hear the earth calling him child—not Father, but son. He hears only his own words making up the world."

—URSULA K. LEGUIN,
*Buffalo Gals and
Other Animal
Presences*

EXHALATION
Relaxed diaphragm

INHALATION
Contracted diaphragm

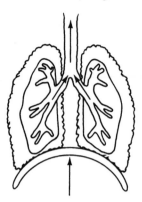
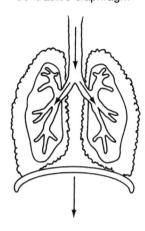

Figure 4–4 Diaphragm movement during breathing.

No, the two processes do not differ in the working of the respiratory system. Downward contraction of the diaphragm and the concurrent outward and upward lift of the rib cage by the external intercostal muscles cause an enlargement of the lung cavity, resulting in air pressure changes and the creation of a vacuum. Air rushes in to equalize the pressure, and inhalation has occurred. Exhalation results when the diaphragm relaxes upward and the rib cage is moved down and in, forcing air back out of the lungs. This process is the same in either type of breathing.

However, the answer is "yes" when we compare the two types of breathing on other bases. Nonspeech breathing occurs almost totally *involuntarily:* we do not have to think about it. But at least in the practice and exercise stages, and often in performance situations, speakers consciously control inhalation and exhalation, bringing a *voluntary* aspect to the process. Another major difference is *timing.* In regular daily breathing, the time allotted to inhalation and exhalation is relatively the same. But when you begin to speak, you must inhale very rapidly, then exhale slowly, sustaining the outgoing air so that you can speak several words or sentences without pausing to inhale again.

A third difference is *size* or *power.* You do not need as much strength, muscular control, or quantity of air for quiet breathing. Just as it takes a great deal more muscular energy to throw a ball than to keep your arm quietly at your side, so speaking requires more power and energy than life-sustaining breathing. Do not forget that while you are using rapidly inhaled air to produce voice and speech sounds, your body still must supply its oxygen needs and remove its carbon dioxide. Speech breathing is *added* to life breathing, not substituted for it. Therefore, speech breathing needs to be "bigger" in every way—deeper into the lungs and abdominal cavity, wider in the chest, and with more tension in the muscles.

Deep breathing improves the voice. Like any other muscle, the diaphragm can be strengthened and made more responsive to command. Lung capacity increases as the rib cage and diaphragm extend the size of the chest cavity. The result is more breath coming from a greater distance with increased strength or power.

The effect of improved breath control on the voice is found primarily in three vocal elements. The first is the ability to *project* the voice so the speaker can be heard and understood even in large auditoriums or at a considerable distance from the listener. Later we will talk in some detail about projection—how it differs from loudness and why it is important even when speakers use microphones. For now, understanding that adequate projection is to a large degree a matter of good breathing techniques will help you understand the value of respiratory control.

The second vocal element that profits directly from controlled breathing is the power to *sustain* the voice, both in individual speech units and over time. Sustaining individual units is a simple matter of taking in enough air to complete long phrases or sen-

FYI . . .

Being born with a silver spoon in your mouth may be more advantageous than you realize. Recent experiments by a Washington, DC, internist have indicated that the uvula may hold the key to curing hiccups. The next time an "attack" occurs, try this: Exhale completely. Breathe in short, shallow breaths. Open your mouth, keep your tongue flat, and—using a mirror—place the handle tip of a spoon into your mouth and touch the uvula until the hiccuping stops. Be careful not to touch your throat lest you gag.

Believe it or not, this works!

tences without having to pause for an additional intake of air. Although most modern prose is written in a style that seldom demands long phrases or groups of words, classical prose, drama, and much poetry may require a long segment of uninterrupted speech.

Sustaining power also consists of the ability to talk for long periods without losing one's voice or having it grow excessively weak and hoarse. People whose voices tire easily usually do not put sufficient air behind the sound, and hence force the vocal folds and intrinsic muscles of the larynx to work harder to compensate. This in turn may contribute to excessive tension in the upper torso and throat. Either excessive tension or inadequate breath supply can cause the voice to tire prematurely, and often we find both problems present in the same speaker, since weakened exhalation may contribute to tracheal and laryngeal tension.

The third and final vocal element that can improve with controlled respiration is vocal *quality*. This important vocal characteristic will be more fully explained in Chapter 8. Quality is the result of melding phonation and resonation so that several frequencies—tones and overtones—are combined such that the ear receives them as a single sound. Quality is the element that causes two voices to sound different, even if they produce the same words with the same pitch, rate, and loudness. Good breathing helps prevent such voice quality problems as harshness, hoarseness, or gutturalness, as well as problems of breathiness, weakness, or lightness.

FYI . . .

Dizziness, lightheadedness, blackouts, numbness in the extremities, tension, chest pains, and shortness of breath can often be attributed to an imbalance of carbon dioxide (CO_2) and oxygen in the bloodstream. Breathing too rapidly and too deeply—hyperventilating—causes excessive amounts of CO_2 to be expelled from the body. When the normal level of CO_2 in the blood and brain falls, alarming symptoms may result. The treatment: regular practice in slow, diaphragmatic breathing.

STOP AND TRY THIS

See if you can read this in one breath:

> You're a regular wreck, with a crick in your neck, and no wonder you snore, for your head's on the floor, and you've needles and pins from your soles to your shins, and your flesh is a-creep, for your left leg's asleep, and you've cramp in your toes, and a fly on your nose, and some fluff in your lung, and a feverish tongue, and a thirst that's intense, and a general sense that you haven't been sleeping in clover;
>
> But the darkness has passed, and it's daylight at last, and the night has been long—ditto ditto my song—and thank goodness they're both of them over!

> —GILBERT AND SULLIVAN,
> "Lord Chancellor's
> Nightmare," *Iolanthe*

Phonation

Phonation is the production of sound through vibrations of the **vocal folds.** The vocal folds are located in the **larynx,** above the trachea but below the **pharynx** (the upper part of the throat) (see Figure 4–5).

STOP AND TRY THIS

Recite a nursery rhyme—"'Mary Had a Little Lamb," "Little Jack Horner," "Baa Baa Black Sheep"—or any other rhyme or short poem in a strong, clear voice.

Before you begin speaking, place your fingers lightly on your throat and swallow several times. The area that moves upward and downward is your larynx and adjacent muscles. Keep your fingers on the larynx while you recite the nursery rhyme. Do you feel the strong vibration that comes from the vocal folds and surrounding muscles?

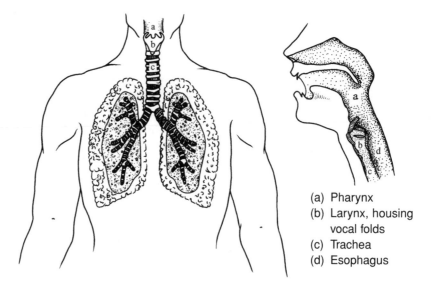

(a) Pharynx
(b) Larynx, housing vocal folds
(c) Trachea
(d) Esophagus

Figure 4–5   Location of the larynx.

Read It Aloud _____

Glossolalia **means talking in tongues;**
It must be hard on the mouth and the lungs.

The larynx is formed by three sets of cartilage and suspended from the **hyoid bone** (see Figure 4–6). The largest of the cartilages, the **thyroid,** consists of two shield-shaped joined plates at the front of the larynx. The **cricoid cartilage,** much like a signet ring, larger in the back than the front, is at the base of the larynx. Below the cricoid cartilage are the rings of the trachea, which shape the top of the windpipe. The third major cartilage forming the larynx is the **arytenoid,** shaped somewhat like a ladle and flexibly joined to the cricoid cartilage at the back. The vocal folds are attached directly to the arytenoid cartilages, which move in conjunction with movement of the folds.

These cartilages form a protective shield or shell covered by muscle tissue. The vocal folds are attached to the inside of the cartilage shield, just above the trachea. The outgoing airstream passes through the **glottis,** the opening between the folds (see Figure 4–7). The **epiglottis** is a tongue-shaped structure attached to the inside of the thyroid cartilage and just above the vocal folds. It rests upright during normal phonation but lowers over the glottis during swallowing, thereby preventing food particles from entering the lungs.

The vocal folds are often called the "vocal cords" (never chords!), but this is a misnomer. They are not like rubber bands or cords, but are folds or lips of muscle attached behind the thyroid cartilage in the front and to the flexible arytenoid cartilages

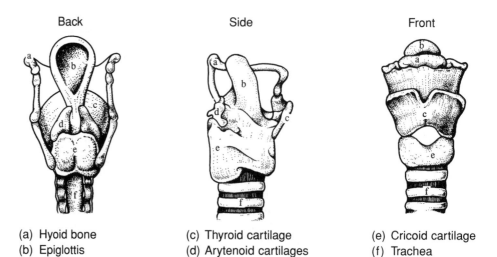

(a) Hyoid bone   (c) Thyroid cartilage   (e) Cricoid cartilage
(b) Epiglottis   (d) Arytenoid cartilages   (f) Trachea

Figure 4–6   Structure of the larynx.

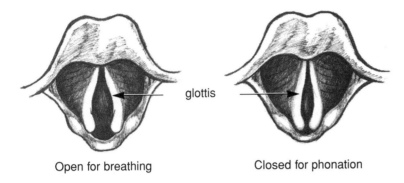

Open for breathing   Closed for phonation

Figure 4–7   The vocal folds.

in the back. The folds open for routine breathing and close for phonation. Closure of the glottis causes air pressure to build in the trachea, and its release sets the vocal folds to vibrating and thereby producing sound. Changes in the pressure of the exhaled air and in the tension of the vocal folds produce varying frequencies of vibration. We hear these as changes of pitch and loudness. Your heredity and nutrition have predetermined the length and thickness of your vocal folds, placing certain limits on the pitch range and vocal flexibility that you can acquire.

Resonation

Resonation is the process whereby vibrations from the vocal folds move through chambers or cavities, causing secondary vibrations (overtones) that blend with the original to create a harmonic construction. Resonance is the acoustical result of combining an original, or fundamental, tone with a series of overtones. A single vibrating body emitting a single vibratory frequency would produce a pure tone. However, because the ear itself has resonance properties in its vibrating membranes, a human being probably cannot hear a pure tone, even one produced by a vibrating body as simple as a tuning fork, without resonance added during the transmittal and reception process.

The human vocal mechanism contains a number of resonating chambers, primarily the **pharynx,** the **oral cavity,** and the **nasal cavity** (see Figure 4–8). Some

FYI... _____

Cats have two sets of vocal folds, somewhat similar to the true and false vocal folds in humans, except that in cats, the upper set of membranes (false vocal folds) function fully. Growling and purring are thought to initiate primarily in the false vocal folds, while the lower set of membranes, the true vocal folds, are used to produce meowing. And cats have a "vocabulary" more than twice the size of dogs. They can call, purr, murmur, growl, and make distinct and recognizable vowel and consonant sounds.

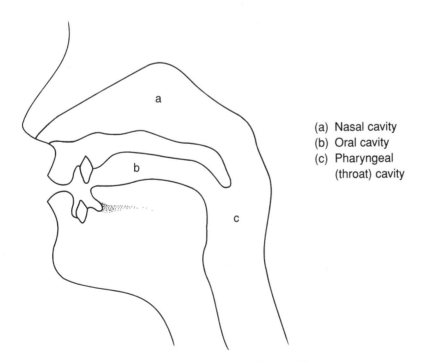

(a) Nasal cavity
(b) Oral cavity
(c) Pharyngeal
     (throat) cavity

Figure 4–8   Primary resonating cavities.

additional resonance is added by vibrations in the chest cavity. As we speak, these cavities vibrate and the frequencies emitted blend with and modify the vibration from the vocal folds, so that the resulting sound is a blend of several tones or frequencies. Speakers do not produce pure tones, for all voice sounds are modified in these various resonating chambers.

Resonance not only amplifies and enlarges vocal tone but adds richness and brilliance to it. Much of the emotional quality that the voice can convey results from resonance. Without resonance, the voice would be flat and colorless, and intensity and amplitude (distance and loudness) would be significantly reduced. Compare the human resonating mechanism to a stringed instrument, such as a guitar or violin. If just the strings could be stretched tightly in midair, then plucked or bowed, only a small, twangy note would be emitted. Without the hollow wooden box to act as a sounding board, resonating the initial vibration, very little sound would be produced. The wooden box is the principal resonating chamber, and many elements, such as the size, shape, type, and age of the wood and the craftsmanship of the box, affect the tonal quality of the music produced by the instrument.

Similarly, your voice quality is affected by the size, shape, and general condition of your resonators. Nasal cavities blocked by swollen mucous membranes resulting from colds or allergy attacks cannot vibrate in the same manner as unobstructed, healthy nasal passages. Chest congestion, throat infections, or misshapen or missing teeth can also reduce or alter resonation.

The timbre of the music from a guitar or violin is also highly subject to the skill of the performer. Good tonal quality does not just happen, but is the result of training, practice, and native ability. Extensive training and practice will not guarantee an Itzak Perlman or Andrés Segovia—innate talent is also required—but the performer can produce vastly better music than would have been possible had he or she never studied or rehearsed.

The same is true of your voice. Certain inborn elements, combined with years of usage habits, place some limits on the alterations you can make in the tonal quality of your voice. However, with proper, extensive practice your voice can become richer, more resonant, and free from problems of imbalanced resonance.

> *Speech is the mother, not the handmaid, of thought.*
>
> —KARL KRAUS

STOP AND TRY THIS

Take a moment and feel the vibratory action of resonance.

1. Lay your fingers gently on your cheeks. Say [eɪ] as in *ate* or [i] as in *eat* and sustain the sound. Can you feel the slight vibration in your cheeks? It will be more subtle than nasal or vocal fold vibration, but you can feel it in your fingertips.
2. Lay the index finger of each hand gently along the sides of the nose. Hum and sustain an [m] and then an [n] sound. You should feel a significant level of vibration.

This is resonance in action!

Articulation

Read It Aloud ————

**From the tip of the tongue
  To the jut of the jowl,
Articulators move
  To shape consonant
  and vowel.**

The last system in the human vocal mechanism, **articulation,** is the obstructing, molding, and reshaping of outgoing airwaves by one or more of the articulators. These articulators are the **lips, tongue, teeth, palate, gum ridge,** and **jaw** (see Figure 4–9). By moving and shaping the articulators into different positions, we reshape the airstream. The resulting changes in the vibrating air become the varied sounds that are utilized as the phonemes of languages. Articulation as an area of study in courses in

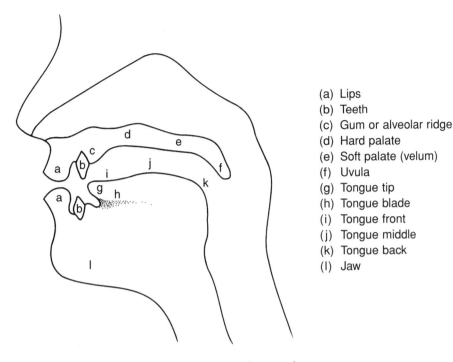

(a) Lips
(b) Teeth
(c) Gum or alveolar ridge
(d) Hard palate
(e) Soft palate (velum)
(f) Uvula
(g) Tongue tip
(h) Tongue blade
(i) Tongue front
(j) Tongue middle
(k) Tongue back
(l) Jaw

Figure 4–9   The articulators.

voice and speech production assumes a major role, for it involves an examination of the formation of each of the over forty distinct phonemes of English. Moreover, dialects are defined primarily as differences in articulation. Much of the remainder of this book will be devoted to a detailed study of articulation.

SPEECH AS AN OVERLAID FUNCTION

Speech functions are secondary to more basic biological needs in all four systems of the vocal mechanism. For example, the discussion of breathing mentioned the role of ingoing and outgoing air in the oxygenation and purification of blood. The larynx and vocal folds serve as a pressure valve that closes during heavy straining or lifting to give additional strength to other parts of the body. The bearing down that accompanies labor during childbirth makes heavy use of the closure of the glottis. A closed glottis also helps prevent food from going into the lungs.

All parts of the mouth serve in ingesting food; chewing, salivating, and swallowing are all necessary to the digestive process. The mouth and the nasal passages keep harmful bodies out of the trachea or esophagus. Breath is taken in and out through the mouth and nose, where it is warmed and filtered.

Understanding the primary, or underlying, functions of the parts of the vocal mechanism is helpful in learning to protect and control the various muscles and organs used in speaking. Good breathing habits promote good health as well as clear, strong voices. Nasal passages free from colds and infection contribute to balanced resonance and better vocal quality. Careful chewing and swallowing of food aid digestion and in the process utilize the muscles around the lips and tongue that contribute to clear enunciation.

Speech is clearly an **overlaid,** or secondary, **function,** for all parts of the vocal mechanism are used for other purposes, even by those who cannot speak. The study of voice and articulation stresses healthy functioning at the primary level as an aid toward improved use of the mechanism at the secondary, or speech, level.

Writing is an abuse of language; reading silently to oneself is a pitiful substitute for speech.

—GOETHE

PUTTING IT TOGETHER

Now that you understand the anatomy and physiology of the human vocal mechanism and the characteristics of voice, the next four chapters will further explain and provide a variety of exercises for you to improve the use of your own voice. You will begin by concentrating on respiration—the breathing that is the foundation of the voice. The production elements of phonation and resonation will be incorporated as you move through the characteristics of volume, pitch, rate, and voice quality. Clear articulation is always needed as you do in-class sentence and paragraph drill work.

Putting all the elements and characteristics together is not unlike the dancer who must think of arms, head, posture, legs and feet—all while remembering a series of planned steps, fitting them to the music, and giving interpretation and meaning to the performance. Each element can be isolated and practiced separately, then pulled together in a unified whole. You must think about what you are going to say as well as work to include ample volume, clear pitch, controlled rate, accurate pronunciation, and all the other aspects of speech performance. This is a cumulative process, growing as we add each new chapter.

CLASSIC PROSE FICTION FOR PRACTICE

The gamblers . . . were still more easily recognizable. They wore every variety of dress, from that of the desperate thimble-rig bully, with velvet waistcoat, fancy neckerchief, gilt chains, and filigreed buttons, to that of the scrupulously inornate clergyman than which nothing could be less liable to suspicion. Still all were distinguished by a certain sodden swarthiness of complexion, a filmy dimness of eye, and pallor and compression of lip. There were two other traits, moreover, by which I could always detect them;—a guarded lowness of tone in conversation, and a more than ordinary extension of the thumb in a direction at right angles with the fingers.

—EDGAR ALLAN POE,
"The Man of the Crowd"

The cloud, which had scattered so deep a murkiness over the day, had now settled into a solid and impenetrable mass. It resembled less even the thickest gloom of a night in the open air than the close and blind darkness of some narrow room. But in proportion as the blackness gathered, did the lightnings around Vesuvius increase in their vivid and scorching glare. Nor was their horrible beauty confined to the usual hues of fire; no rainbow ever rivalled their varying and prodigal dyes. Now brightly blue as the most azure depth of a southern sky—now of a livid and snakelike green, darting restlessly to and fro as the folds of an enormous serpent—now of a lurid and intolerable crimson, gushing forth through the columns of smoke, far and wide, and lighting up the whole city from arch to arch—then suddenly dying into a sickly paleness, like the ghost of their own life!

—EDWARD G. E. BULWER-LYTTON,
"The Last Days of Pompeii"

"But," I went on, "when I first saw Mr. Martin, I must admit I too gave vent to an exclamation of surprise. I was standing next to an old soldier whose right leg had been amputated. We had walked in together, and his face had struck me. It was one of those heroic faces marked by the seal of war and on which are written the battles of Napoleon. This old soldier had a particular air of frankness and good-humor which always impresses me favorably. He was no doubt one of those troopers who are surprised at nothing, who find something to laugh at in the last grimace of a dying friend, who bury or plunder him lightheartedly, who challenge bullets with authority, whose deliberations finally are brief, and who would fraternize with the Devil himself."

—Honoré de Balzac,
"A Passion in the Desert"

What chiefly characterized the colonists of Merry Mount was their veneration for the Maypole. It had made their true history a poet's tale. Spring decked the hallowed emblem with young blossoms and fresh green boughs; Summer brought roses of the deepest blush, and the perfected foliage of the forest; Autumn enriched it with that red and yellow gorgeousness which converts each wildwood leaf into a painted flower; and Winter silvered it with sleet, and hung it round with icicles, till it flashed in the cold sunshine, itself a frozen sunbeam. Thus each alternate season did homage to the Maypole, and paid it a tribute of its own richest splendor.

—Nathaniel Hawthorne,
"The Maypole
of Merry Mount"

Mr. Bingley was good-looking and gentlemanlike; he had a pleasant countenance and easy, unaffected manners. His sisters were fine women, with an air of decided fashion. His brother-in-law, Mr. Hurst, merely looked the gentleman; but his friend Mr. Darcy soon drew the attention of the room by his fine, tall person, handsome features, noble mien, and the report which was in general circulation within five minutes after his entrance, of his having ten thousand a year. The gentlemen pronounced him to be a fine figure of a man, the ladies declared he was much handsomer than Mr. Bingley, and he was looked at with great admiration for about half the evening, till his manners gave a disgust which turned the tide of his popularity; for he was discovered to be proud; to be above his company, and above being pleased; and not all his large estate in Derbyshire could then save him from having a most forbidding, disagreeable countenance, and being unworthy to be compared with his friend.

— Jane Austen,
Pride and Prejudice

Fearful indeed the suspicion—but more fearful the doom! It may be asserted, without hesitation, that no event is so terribly well adapted to inspire the supremeness of bodily and of mental distress, as is burial before death. The unendurable oppression of the lungs—the stifling fumes of the damp earth—the clinging to the death garments—the rigid embrace of the narrow house—the blackness of the absolute Night—the silence like a sea that overwhelms—the unseen but palpable presence of the Conqueror Worm—these things, with thoughts of the air and grass above, with memory of dear friends who would fly to save us if but informed of our fate, and with consciousness that of this fate they can *never* be informed—that our hopeless portion is that of the really dead—these considerations, I say, carry into the heart, which still palpitates, a degree of appalling and intolerable horror from which the most daring imagination must recoil. We know of nothing so agonizing upon Earth—we can dream of nothing half so hideous in the realms of the nethermost Hell.

—Edgar Allan Poe,
"The Premature Burial"

I still remember that vigil very distinctly: the black and silent observatory, the shadowed lantern throwing a feeble glow upon the floor in the corner, the steady ticking of the clockwork of the telescope, the little slit in the roof. Looking through the telescope, one saw a circle of deep blue and the little round planet swimming in the field. It seemed such a little thing, so bright and small and still, faintly marked with transverse stripes, and slightly flattened from the perfect round. But so little it was, so silvery warm—a pinhead of light! . . . And invisible to me because it was so remote and small, flying swiftly and steadily towards me across that incredible distance, drawing nearer every minute by so many thousands of miles, came the Thing they were sending us, the Thing that was to bring so much struggle and calamity and death to the earth. I never dreamed of it then as I watched; no one on earth dreamed of that unerring missile.

—H. G. Wells,
"The War of the Worlds"

It is not often that hope is rewarded by fruition, as completely as the wishes of the young men of the garrison were met by the state of the weather, on the succeeding day. It may be no more than the ordinary waywardness of man, but the Americans are a little accustomed to taking pride in things, that the means of intelligent comparisons would probably show, were in reality of a very inferior quality, while they overlook, or undervalue advantages that place them certainly on a level with, if not above most of their fellow creatures. Among the latter is the climate, which as a whole, though far from perfect, is infinitely more agreeable, and quite as healthy, as those of most of the countries which are loudest in their denunciation of it.

—James Fenimore Cooper,
The Pathfinder

The room was full of old women, shop assistants, and house porters—all with bits of paper in their hands. In one a coachman of sober habits was advertised as being let out on hire; in another an almost new, second-hand carriage, brought from Paris in 1814, was offered for sale; in still others were offered for sale: a serf girl of nineteen, experienced in laundry work and suitable for other work, a well-built open carriage with only one spring broken, a young, dappled-grey, mettlesome horse of seventeen years of age, a new consignment of turnip and radish seed from London, a summer residence with all the conveniences, including two boxes for horses and a piece of land on which an excellent birchwood or pinewood could he planted; there was also an advertisement containing a challenge to those who wished to purchase old boot soles with an invitation to come to the auction rooms every day from eight o'clock in the morning to three o'clock in the afternoon.

—Nikolai Gogol,
"The Nose"

It was already one in the morning; the rain pattered dismally against the panes, and my candle was nearly burnt out, when, by the glimmer of the half-extinguished light, I saw the dull yellow eyes of the creature open; it breathed hard, and a convulsive motion agitated its limbs.

How can I describe my emotions at this catastrophe, or delineate the wretch whom, with such infinite pains and care, I had endeavored to form? His limbs were in proportion, and I had selected his features as beautiful. Beautiful! Great God! His yellow skin scarcely covered the work of muscles and arteries beneath; his hair was of a lustrous black, and flowing; his teeth of a pearly whiteness; but these luxuriances only formed a more horrid contrast with his watery eyes, that seemed almost of the same color as the dun white sockets in which they were set, his shriveled complexion, and straight black lips.

—Mary Wollstonecraft
Shelley,
Frankenstein

We now worked in earnest, and never did I pass ten minutes of more intense excitement. During this interval we had fairly unearthed an oblong chest of wood . . . three feet and a half long, three feet broad, and two and a half feet deep. It was firmly secured by bands of wrought iron, riveted, and forming a kind of trellis-work over the whole. On each side of the chest, near the top, were three rings of iron—six in all—by means of which a firm hold could be obtained by six persons. Our utmost united endeavors served only to disturb the coffer very slightly in its bed. We at once saw the impossibility of removing so great a weight. Luckily, the sole fastenings of the lid consisted of two sliding bolts. These we drew back—trembling and panting with anxiety. In an instant, a treasure of incalculable value lay gleaming before us. As the rays of the lanterns fell within the pit, there flashed upward from a confused heap of gold and of jewels, a glow and a glare that absolutely dazzled our eyes.

—EDGAR ALLAN POE,
"The Gold-Bug"

While they were talking, the rain began to beat down upon the roof like running horses. As soon as the rain stopped, they climbed out of the house and moved about cautiously. They learned that many other houses had been struck by the lightning or twisted by the cyclone. Chimneys were shattered, barns and sheds were rolled out into the middle of roads. One neighbor's house roof was lifted completely off and borne out into the field. Many fences were blown down, and the cattle looked strange, roaming in new parts.

The minister and the doctor and two of the townsmen made the rounds of all the houses, asking if any people had been killed or injured, but there were none. Little groups of people gathered in streets and roads and lanes. They spoke in awe of the suddenness of the thing, and of the miracle that no lives were lost. All at once they realized the shadows had grown long and slanting. Just before the moment of setting, the sun flared out with a quick, strange brightness, as if to assure them of a safe and fair tomorrow.

—PEARL WALLACE CHAPPELL,
Stella

The panther was a female. The fur on her belly and thighs glistened white. Several little spots, like velvet, formed pretty bracelets around her legs. The muscular tail was also white, but ending with black rings. The upper part of her dress, yellow like burnished gold, smooth and soft, had these characteristic spots, in the form of roses, which distinguishes panthers from all other feline species. This tranquil and formidable hostess snored in a pose as graceful as that of a cat sleeping on the cushion of an Ottoman. Her blood-stained paws, nervous and well armed, were stretched in front of her head which rested upon them, and from which darted her sparse and straight whiskers, like silver threads.

—HONORÉ DE BALZAC,
"A Passion in the Desert"

The cause of so much amazement may appear sufficiently slight. Mr. Hooper, a gentlemanly person, of about thirty, though still a bachelor, was dressed with due clerical neatness, as if a careful wife had starched his band, and brushed the weekly dust from his Sunday's garb. There was but one thing remarkable in his appearance. Swathed about his forehead, and hanging down over his face, so low as to be shaken by his breath, Mr. Hooper had on a black veil. On a nearer view it seemed to consist of two folds of crepe, which entirely concealed his features, except the mouth and chin, but probably did not intercept his sight, further than to give a darkened aspect to all living and inanimate things. With this gloomy shade before him, good Mr. Hooper walked onward, at a slow and quiet pace, stooping somewhat, and looking on the ground, as is customary with abstracted men, yet nodding kindly to those of his parishioners who still waited on the meeting-house steps. But so wonder-struck were they that his greeting hardly met with a return.

—NATHANIEL HAWTHORNE,
"The Minister's Black Veil"

. . . I gazed round for a means of diverting her thoughts. On one side of the road rose a high, rough bank, where hazels and stunted oaks, with their roots half exposed, held uncertain tenure; the soil was too loose for the latter; and strong winds had blown some nearly horizontal. In summer, Miss Catherine delighted to climb along these trunks, and sit in the branches, swinging twenty feet above the ground; and I, pleased with her agility and her light, childish heart, still considered it proper to scold every time I caught her at such an elevation, but so that she knew there was no necessity for descending. From dinner to tea she would lie in her breeze-rocked cradle, doing nothing but singing old songs—my nursery lore—to herself, or watching the birds, joint tenants, feed and entice their young ones to fly; or nestling with closed lids, half thinking, half dreaming, happier than words can express.

—EMILY BRONTË,
Wuthering Heights

I gazed at this queenly apparition for at least half an hour, as if I had been suddenly converted to stone; and during this period, I felt the full force and truth of all that has been said or sung concerning "love at first sight." My feelings were totally different from any which I had hitherto experienced, in the presence of even the most celebrated specimens of female loveliness. An unaccountable, and what I am compelled to consider a *magnetic* sympathy of soul for soul, seemed to rivet, not only my vision, but my whole powers of thought and feeling upon the admirable object before me. I saw—I felt—I knew that I was deeply, madly, irrevocably in love—and this even before seeing the face of the person beloved. So intense, indeed, was the passion that consumed me, that I really believe it would have received little if any abatement had the features, yet unseen, proved of merely ordinary character; so anomalous is the nature of the only true love—of the love at first sight—and so little really dependent is it upon the external conditions which only seem to create and control it.

—EDGAR ALLAN POE,
"The Spectacles"

On an early morning in April, just about the time the sun was due above the housetop, little Jim turned over in his bed. He looked for Rita, but her corner was empty. She had left his milk, though, so he began to drink it. He could not see very clearly and a funny smell was in the air. Then he heard the firemen's bell ding, ding, ding, ding. It was much more fun to see them coming back when they were not hurrying so. He would not bother to see them leave. He finished his milk, caught hold of his nightshirt in front and climbed the little ladder to the attic. The attic was very, very hot and all full of smoke, but little Jim knew the way. He moved to the window and crawled out on his balcony to look for the fire trucks returning.

—PEARL WALLACE CHAPPELL,
"Buttons"

Poor little warbler, how unlucky you were to fall out of your nest last evening before your wings were grown. Forlorn little bird, you are no heavier than a feather and no bigger than a fly. You have made yourself at home here, perching on my finger, nestling in my hair, pecking at my hand and answering the sound of my voice. Who gives you this confidence in my strength, and why do you rely on me to sustain and comfort your weakness? This fold of my sleeve in which you take refuge is not your nest. This hand that feeds you is not your mother's beak. You cannot be so easily deceived, nor have you forgotten your family. You hear the cry of your frantic mother as she hunts for you in the branches of neighboring trees. She would fly through this window if she dared, and you would go to her if you were able. I see that you recognize her cries. Your bright black eyes seem ready to swim with tears. Your head turns restlessly from side to side. Your tiny throat utters feeble notes of protest.

—GEORGE SAND (PEN NAME
OF AMANDINE DUPIN),
*The Intimate Journal of George
Sand,* June 25, 1837

The war did not interfere with the traffic of the peddler, who seized on the golden opportunity which the interruption of the regular trade afforded, and appeared absorbed in the one grand object of amassing money. For a year or two his employment was uninterrupted, and his success proportionate; but, at length, dark and threatening hints began to throw suspicion around his movements, and the civil authority thought it incumbent on them to examine narrowly into his mode of life. His imprisonments, though frequent, were not long; and his escapes from the guardians of the law easy, compared to what he endured from the persecution of the military.

—JAMES FENIMORE COOPER,
The Spy

The afternoon sun was warm on the five workmen there, busy upon doors and window-frames and wainscoting. A scent of pine-wood from a tent-like pile of planks outside the open door mingled itself with the scent of elder-bushes which were spreading their summer snow close to the open window opposite; the slanting sunbeams shone through the transparent shavings that flew before the steady plane, and lit up the fine grain of the oak panelling which stood propped against the wall. On a heap of soft shavings a rough grey shepherd-dog had made himself a pleasant bed, and was lying with his nose between his forepaws, occasionally wrinkling his brows to cast a glance at the tallest of the five workmen, who was carving a shield in the center of a wooden mantelpiece.

—GEORGE ELIOT (PEN NAME
OF MARY ANN EVANS),
Adam Bede

5
Relaxation and Breathing

Man is so made that he can only find relaxation from one kind of labor by taking up another.

—ANATOLE FRANCE

RELAXATION

Before you begin any session on voice exercises, you need to be sure you are working at the proper level of **relaxation.** Central to all vocal exercising is the need for a balance between excessive muscular tension on the one extreme and laxness on the other. As few students in today's stressful society come to class *overly* relaxed, most of your attention must be directed toward relieving the stiffness and rigidity of the entire body, especially the upper torso. In some people this tension is so great that you can see shoulders held rigidly and tight neck muscles standing out, or arms held stiffly away from the body rather than hanging freely beside the hips.

Relaxing and removing tension does not mean moving to the opposite extreme of limp, flaccid muscles, but rather a middle ground that finds muscles pliant and resilient—a state of *muscle tone responsiveness*. With tautness gone, muscles are alert and energetic, ready to work for you instead of against you.

Could you serve a tennis ball with your arm limp? Of course not, for you would need to bring the muscles into this state of muscle tone responsiveness, in which they are ready to help you grip, control, and move the racket through the air. The muscles of the chest cavity, spine, neck, and shoulders—indeed, the entire upper torso—need to be in a state of tonal responsiveness for you to profit from vocal practice.

Read It Aloud _____

For your voice to sound pleasant, remember these facts: "Eliminate tension" and "learn to relax."

> STOP AND TRY THIS
>
> Make a tight fist, tense all your arm muscles up to your shoulder, hold your arm rigidly to your side, and squeeze all your muscles until they almost tremble. Your arm is completely overtensed. Now, pantomime holding a tennis racket and serving. You simply could not do it without relaxing some of those tight muscles.
>
> Then go to the opposite extreme: let your arm go limp, loosening every muscle. Let it flop by your side. Could you hold a tennis racket with your arm so totally relaxed?

Control of Mind and Body

Achieving relaxation and tonal responsiveness requires total coordination of the mind and body. The signals that send messages to the muscles come from the brain. The mind must exert control and direction. To relax mechanically or purely physically when your mind is racing in different directions or absorbed with an uncomfortable self-consciousness is almost impossible. You need to work in a supportive classroom environment, as well as practice privately, to overcome any embarrassment about your body. If you are worried about looking silly to your classmates, you will not be able to achieve unity of mind and body during the exercises. Self-conscious giggling or unwillingness to try exercises that may seem foolish to you will seriously interfere with your progress.

Total integration of mind and body is a subject worth pursuing on its own. Specialists whose techniques are used as the basis for training in this area include F. Matthias Alexander, Moshe Feldenkrais, and Jose Silva.[1] Their training systems employ *functional integration,* in which the mind exerts control over the body. A circular response pattern follows: a more relaxed, healthy body in turn promotes a controlled and effectively functioning mind.

Much of the time we think very little about the way our bodies are feeling. But then an illness or accident causes pain or discomfort, making us all too aware of our physical selves. Mind–body control, with its focus on using thought processes to create an efficient and responsive physical self, is basic to a healthy and competent use of the speaking voice.

Performance Anxiety

Another benefit of mastering relaxation techniques is the potential for control of performance anxiety. Few emotions are more common yet more individually devastating than stage fright. Anyone who has given a speech, performed in a play, sung a solo, or participated in any form of public performance has likely had butterflies in the stomach, breathing irregularities, sweaty palms, shaky knees, or a quavering voice—all physical manifestations of a fear of appearing in front of a group of people.

Students ask more questions about stage fright than about any other aspect of public speaking. Many have difficulty believing that stage fright is normal. Unfortunately, some speech training programs have advertised a goal of "eliminating" stage fright, as if it were a disease to be cured. While a few people suffer from *trait anxiety—*

---

[1]See F. Matthias Alexander, *The Resurrection of the Body* (New York: Dell, 1978); Sarah Barker, *The Alexander Technique: The Revolutionary Way to Use Your Body for Total Energy* (New York: Bantam, 1981); Moshe Feldenkrais, *Awareness Through Movement: Easy-to-do Exercises to Improve Your Posture, Imagination, and Personal Awareness* (San Francisco: Harper SF, Reprint ed., 1991); and Jose Silva and Philip Miele, *The Silva Mind Control Method* (New York: Pocket Books, 1991).

a fear of communicating in almost all situations—the vast majority of us are subject to *state anxiety*. State anxiety is brought on by pressure or stressful situations, such as job interviews or public speeches. Total elimination of state anxiety is not only almost impossible but is also undesirable. A certain amount of nervous tension causes a flow of adrenaline into the blood that is stimulating and energizing to the performer. The secret is to learn to use this nervous energy, to harness it for a vigorous and enthusiastic performance, and to control the extreme physical symptoms of excessive nervousness. Central to that control is relaxation.

Stretching exercises, regulated deep breathing, or shaking the hands and feet to stimulate the flow of blood to the extremities can help you relax backstage before a performance. Using mind–body techniques as you prepare to move to the platform or podium will help you control the physical symptoms of nervousness. Audio tapes that induce light states of self-hypnosis are available commercially and are useful in conditioning your attitude over a longer period. A tonally responsive body, ready to do the bidding of the mind, can relax and handle the normal pressure of a performance situation much better than a tense, stiff, untrained body. If stage fright worries you, increased mental concentration and frequent practice of relaxation exercises like the ones that follow can help you control your fear and feel more comfortable about public performances.

The following exercises are designed to help you achieve a state of muscle tone responsiveness. Remember that a body attuned to the mind and a mind unified with the body are of the utmost importance as you learn to recognize and relieve harmful muscle tension.

EXERCISES FOR RELAXATION

1. Sit on a sofa or easy chair. Lean back, extending your feet comfortably in front of you on the floor. Rest your hands comfortably in your lap or at your sides. Close your eyes. Concentrate on quiet, deep breathing. Be aware of the gentle rise and fall of the area around your diaphragm. Think of nothing at all but the gentle inward and outward flow of air. Feel as if you could easily drift off to sleep.

2. Lie on your back on a mat or carpet. Flex your toes as tightly as possible. Release. Try to isolate each muscle as best you can as you proceed up the body, flexing and releasing—one leg at a time for calf, knee, thigh; then buttocks, abdomen, chest, and back; and finally the neck and face. Try to distinguish between the feeling of tension and the feeling of relaxation.

3. Repeat exercise 2, but this time concentrate solely on the extremities—toes, feet, ankles, legs; fingers, hands, arms, shoulders. Concentrate all your thoughts on one part of your body at a time. Try to feel a conscious flow of energy from your brain to the isolated part. Tell that part to relax, to let go, to drain off all tension, and to lie limp and totally inactive. Keep each part fully relaxed as you move up the arms and legs to other parts. This is also an excellent way to fall asleep if you are having insomnia.

4. Engage in a restful fantasy. Close your eyes as you settle into a comfortable chair or stretch out on your bed or the floor. Imagine you are walking along a quiet beach, with the warm sun on your back and the sand between your toes. Or imagine that you are walking in a lovely garden with no one else around. See and smell the flowers; enjoy the symmetry of the trimmed and shaped hedges and shrubs. Or imagine a peaceful forest, with a canopy formed by the leaves on the tree branches. Dried leaves crunch beneath your feet as you walk. Crickets chirp and birds sing softly.

   Project yourself as fully as you can into one or more of these fantasies, or into any peaceful fantasy scene you find personally relaxing. Close out the outside world. Drift with your drifting thoughts.

5. Give yourself a massage. Start by gently rubbing your forehead and temples with a circular motion. Move on to your eye sockets; rub gently around them and over

your eyelids. Massage your cheeks, then your ears and ear lobes. End by rubbing the back of your neck and shoulders with a kneading action that helps relieve tension.

6. With the entire class in a circle, give a neck and shoulder massage to the person in front of you so that each person gives and receives a relaxing rub. Turn the circle the other direction, so you give and receive from a different person. This is an excellent way to begin a practice workout or rehearsal.

7. Slowly and easily move your head toward one shoulder, then the other. Repeat several times. Keep the action slow and controlled. Do not force your neck into extreme positions that are uncomfortable. Sudden, jerking movement may damage muscles and tendons.

8. Stretch toward the ceiling as completely as you can. Go up on your toes. Reach with your arms and fingers. Try to lengthen and stretch every muscle. After several seconds in a full stretch, let your body flop over into a rag doll position—upper body bent at the waist, hanging as loosely as possible with the arms swinging freely toward the floor. After a few seconds, slowly rise, lifting from the upper spine, inhale deeply, assume a comfortable, erect posture, and exhale fully. Repeat the entire exercise several times.

9. With a partner, test your ability to completely relax your arms. "Give" your partner your arm with all its weight: let your partner lift it up and down, but do nothing yourself to help out. The degree of relaxation can easily be checked if your partner suddenly releases your arm when holding it up high: if you are not holding your own muscles taut, your arm should fall freely and easily to your side. Many people have trouble giving control of their bodies, even just their arms, to another person. Group exercises in building physical trust can be helpful, provided they are led by skilled trainers. Such exercises include failing backward into the arms of a comrade, letting people toss you from one group to another, or simply taking "blind" walks, letting another lead you through mazes of people or furniture while your eyes are shut.

"But wait a bit," the Oysters cried
"Before we have our chat;
For some of us are out of breath,
And all of us are fat!"

—Lewis Carroll,
Alice Through the Looking Glass

BREATHING

As you learned in Chapter 4, the human voice depends on exhalation, or outgoing air, as its power source. Although some sounds can be produced without phonation, or whispered, they will not carry far enough to reach the average listener's ear. A voice that is clear, strong, and well supported requires control and skillful use of the respiration system. Deep breathing practice is the best way to achieve that proficiency. The following series of exercises will help you, provided you establish a daily practice routine. Two to three minutes, at least three times a day, is required to achieve and maintain the desired level of control. Voice exercises should be done frequently, but only for short periods. Combining deep breathing with daily routines can be helpful: deep-breathe in the shower, while you blow-dry your hair or shave or put on makeup, while you walk across campus or drive to school, while you wait in line in the cafeteria, or during a large, less-than-exciting lecture in order to stay awake. You must keep up these breathing exercises throughout the semester in order to improve other aspects of your voice.

When you feel reasonably sure that your body—especially the upper torso, including the shoulders and throat—is in a state of muscle tone responsiveness, begin to practice abdominal breathing, using some of the following exercises.

BREATHING EXERCISES

1. Place your fingertips lightly halfway between your navel and your breastbone, in the triangle formed by the lower, floating ribs and the waistline. Gently but

firmly inhale so that the air seems to travel all the way down to the area where your fingers are resting. The area should move outward as you inhale, then gently flatten back inward as you exhale.

Caution: When put on the spot and asked to take a deep breath, many people will gasp heavily, raise their shoulders high, and suck in their diaphragm area. By now you should realize that the respiratory mechanism does not work that way—the diaphragm and visceral organ area should move outward, not inward. If you suck in, you are in fact doing only shallow, clavicle or upper-chest breathing—the opposite of deep, abdominal breathing. None of the benefits to your voice discussed earlier can occur from shallow, clavicle breathing.

If you have difficulty feeling the outward thrust of the abdominal wall, lie flat on your back on the floor or the bed. Because this position restricts the upward motion of your shoulders, it can help you isolate the diaphragm action more easily.

Continue to practice inhaling and exhaling with a strong motion of the diaphragm until you know that you are in control of the muscle. All other breathing exercises depend on this initial mastery. Doing the following exercises with a sucked-in abdomen and shoulder breathing will do you no good at all in improving your voice.

2. This exercise can be done either on your back or sitting up straight. If you choose to sit, watch your posture.

Place your right hand on your abdomen below your rib cage. With the other hand, block your left nostril with your thumb. Count to six and inhale slowly through your right nostril, keeping your mouth closed. (You should feel the abdominal area *push out*.) After a full inhalation, block both nostrils and count to twelve. Remove your thumb and exhale slowly through your left nostril, again counting to six. (You should feel the abdominal area *pull in*.) Repeat the exercise several times.

Be careful to keep your shoulder and upper chest as relaxed as possible. The only movements should occur in the area of the diaphragm.

3. Inhale deeply, then see how far you can count on one breath. Speak in a clear, projected tone as rapidly as you can yet enunciating each word distinctly. Make sure you do not unconsciously take an additional breath by gasping in air while you continue to count. It is possible to produce a distorted speech sound on inhaled air, but this is not a desirable method of phonation.

In counting, women should work toward an ultimate goal of forty-five to fifty. Men, who generally have larger chest cavities than women, should aim for fifty-five to sixty.

4. Inhale deeply, then produce a steady [s] sound, sustaining it as long as possible. Try to make the sound smooth, without any jerkiness or noticeable changes in loudness.

5. With a series of short breaths, repeat the word "ha" several times, breathing between each repetition. Keep your fingers on your abdominal area, feeling the steady series of short contractions. Try to make the sound free from breathiness, so that the "ha" is clearly "on top" of the airstream, not forced out so that exhalation is audible.

6. Light a candle and let it burn until the flame is strong and steady. Then, placing it six to eight inches from your mouth, blow out a steady airstream so that the flame actually bends over, almost to a 90-degree angle. Practice until you can keep the flame bent over for several seconds but without ever blowing out the candle. This exercise is helpful in learning to control exhaled air.

7. When you have mastered basic control of abdominal breathing, try this more advanced exercise which isolates muscle action and makes possible more specialized development. Count to four in the following manner. On one, inhale quickly and deeply, trying to expand only the abdominal area, keeping the intercostal mus-

cles and the rib cage still and the upper lung area relatively free of air. Hold this diaphragm contraction. On the count of two, pull out the rib cage with a strong action of the intercostal muscles, allowing the upper portion of the lungs to fill with air. You should now be very full. On three, maintain the contracted muscles so that the rib cage remains outward and the upper chest retains air while you relax the diaphragm and exhale air from the lower lungs. Finally, on a count of four, release the rib cage and the rest of the air.

If you have problems with step 3, as most people do at first, put your hands on your sides at the upper part of your rib cage, where the greatest expansion is possible. Breathe so that you push your hands firmly out. Do this two or three times until you feel in complete control of the action, then repeat the muscle action, but do not inhale any air. This will be very difficult, for in order to keep the vacuum to a minimum, you will need to pull upward on the diaphragm, supported by a strong push from the abdominal muscles, reducing the size of the lung cavity.

Although difficult to master, this exercise does much to strengthen control of the intercostal muscles and the diaphragm.

8. *The Fifty States:* Try to name as many of the fifty United States as you can in one breath. We have grouped them by number of syllables to facilitate rhythmic reading.

Maine	Iowa	Wisconsin	Pennsylvania
	Kentucky	Wyoming	West Virginia
Georgia	Maryland		
Kansas	Michigan	Alabama	Louisiana
New York	Missouri	Arizona	North Carolina
Texas	Montana	California	South Carolina
Utah	Nebraska	Colorado	
Vermont	Nevada	Connecticut	
	New Hampshire	Indiana	
Alaska	New Jersey	Massachusetts	
Arkansas	Ohio	Minnesota	
Delaware	Oregon	Mississippi	
Florida	Rhode Island	New Mexico	
Hawaii	Tennessee	North Dakota	
Idaho	Virginia	South Dakota	
Illinois	Washington	Oklahoma	

9. *The Picnic:* Fill in the blank in the sentence with the words in the list, beginning with sandwiches and adding one each time. How big a picnic can you describe with one breath?

On Saturday we went to the park. We brought a basketful of _____ for a picnic.

sandwiches	hors d'oeuvres
chips and dip	watermelon
cheddar cheese	salt and pepper
green grapes	mustard and relish
shiny red apples	hot dogs
chocolate bars	soda pop
a jug of wine	deviled eggs
dill pickles	potato salad
baked beans	Alka-Seltzer

10. (Inhale after each sentence.)

Don and Mary furnished a house. They bought a bed.

They bought a dresser to go with the bed.

They bought a mirror to go over the dresser that's by the bed.

They bought some carpet to go under the mirror that's over the dresser that's by the bed.

They bought a chair to sit on the carpet that's under the mirror that's over the dresser that's by the bed.

They bought a picture to put on the wall that's above the chair that sits on the carpet that's under the mirror that's over the dresser that's by the bed.

They bought some curtains to hang on the windows beside the picture that's put on the wall that's above the chair that sits on the carpet that's under the mirror that's over the dresser that's by the bed.

They bought a chest to go below the curtains that hang on the windows beside the picture that's put on the wall that's above the chair that sits on the carpet that's under the mirror that's over the dresser that's by the bed.

They bought a cat to sit on the chest that's below the curtains that hang on the windows beside the picture that's put on the wall that's above the chair that sits on the carpet that's under the mirror that's over the dresser that's by the bed.

Don and Mary took out a loan to pay for the cat that sits on the chest that's below the curtains that hang on the windows beside the picture that's put on the wall that's above the chair that sits on the carpet that's under the mirror that's over the dresser that's by the bed.

And now—Don and Mary have a cat, a chest, some curtains, a picture, a chair, a carpet, a mirror, a dresser, a bed, and a big debt!

FYI . . . _____

Did you ever think of the original meaning of a number of words that stem from the Latin *spirare,* **meaning "to breathe"? For example:**

aspire—to breathe upon
conspire—to breathe together
expire—to breathe one's last breath
inspire—to breathe into
perspire—to breathe through
transpire—to breathe across

Or even the word *spirit,* **which literally means "breathing"!**

PUTTING IT TOGETHER

Now that you understand the theory and process of correct abdominal breathing and know several exercises that you can do to improve your own breath control, we hope you will understand the importance of doing these exercises on a daily basis. As with any set of muscles in the human body, the muscles involved in respiration must be put through workouts if you want them to function for you at maximum efficiency. The improvement needs to be incorporated into your everyday speech so that it becomes a part of you.

Next we will examine two other vocal characteristics—volume and pitch. Volume means the loudness and softness of the voice and includes the concept of *projection,* which is important if you speak in public settings. Pitch is the highness and lowness of the voice and is the principal source of vocal variation and vocal color.

We hope you are finding time to read aloud the paragraphs at the end of each chapter. You may be reading some of them in class, but few voice and diction classes have enough time to cover all the practice material. You can do it on your own. Ideally, sit with your tape recorder at home and read several of the passages, then stop and listen. Reread them, making corrections and improvements in your voice and pronunciation.

MODERN PROSE FICTION FOR PRACTICE

Luis Horseman had chosen this camp with care. Here the plateau was cut by one of the hundred nameless canyons which drained into the depth of Many Ruins Canyon. Along the rim, the plateau's granite cap, its sandstone support eroded away, had fractured under its own weight. Some of these great blocks of stone had crashed into the canyon bottom, leaving behind room-sized gaps in the rimrock. Others had merely tilted and slid. Behind one of these, Horseman knelt over the fire. It was a small fire, built in the extreme corner of the natural enclosure. With nothing overhead to reflect its light, it would have been visible only to one standing on the parapet, looking down. Now its flickering light gave the face of Luis Horseman a reddish cast. It was a young face, thin and sensitive, with large black eyes and a sullen mouth. The forehead was high, partly hidden by a red cloth band knotted at the back, and the nose was curved and thin. Hawklike.

—Tony Hillerman,
The Dark Wind

Until the time is ripe, the monolith will permit no contact. When that time comes—when, perhaps, the Europans have invented radio and discovered the messages continually bombarding them from so close at hand—the monolith may change its strategy. It may—or may not—choose to release the entities who slumber within it, so that they can bridge the gulf between the Europans, and the race to which they once held allegiance.

And it may be that no such bridge is possible, and that two such alien forms of consciousness can never coexist. If this is so, then only one of them can inherit the Solar System.

Which it will be, not even the Gods know—yet.

—Arthur C. Clarke,
2010: Odyssey Two

Meandering back down the rocky hillside, I come upon a strand of green glass beads shining in the weeds. I pick the beads up, turning them this way and that in my hands, letting the sun play over them, before letting them drop again to earth. They are cheap, half broken. Suddenly they seem to me symbolic of this whole enterprise which strikes me as silly, a fool's errand, even though my grandfather told me in such detail on the telephone about the rocking chair, the terrible banging noises and rushing winds and ghostly laughter that began every day at sundown, driving them at last from their home. One feels that the true benefits of this trip may derive not from what is recorded or not recorded by the tape now spinning in that empty room above me, but from my new knowledge of my heritage and a new appreciation of these colorful, interesting folk. My roots.

—Lee Smith,
Oral History

Once a stone rattled down from the cliffs with a small metallic clatter that was uncomfortably reminiscent of the chatter of teeth, and then a twig cracked, and Victoria turned quickly; but there was no one there. Only the trees and the shadows and the rank grass—and a flicker of movement that might have been imagination or a bird flitting between the leaves. . . . A minute or two later the undergrowth rustled as though something or someone was moving stealthily away. The soft sound grew fainter until it was submerged at last by the silence, and though there were no more sounds, Victoria did not move. She sat quite still, listening intently, while the sun moved slowly down the sky and the deep blue shadow of the cliff crept forward across the cup of the crater.

—M. M. Kaye,
Death in Kenya

As Booth made his way up the stairs to the dress circle, he saw that there was an empty chair next to the presidential box. The policeman was not at his post. This was an unexpected bit of good luck. In the half-light from the proscenium arch, Booth opened the door and stepped inside the vestibule to the box. The President was only a few feet in front of him, silhouetted by calcium light. To the President's right sat Mrs. Lincoln and to their right a young couple occupied a sofa.

As the audience laughed, Booth removed from his right-hand pocket a brass derringer; and from his left-hand pocket a long, highly sharpened dagger. . . . Booth fired a single shot into the back of the President's head. Without a sound, Lincoln leaned back in the chair; and his head slumped to the left until it was stopped by the wooden partition. Mary turned not to Booth but to her husband, while in the wings, an actor stared, wide-eyed, at the box. He had seen everything.

—GORE VIDAL,
Lincoln

I've noticed, anyway, that unless a man is a bona fide genius, a Harvard education is a permanent liability. Not so much what they learn there, but what they presume about themselves ever after—the albatross of being a Harvard man: the aura, the atmosphere, the pronunciation problems, the tender memories of the River Charles. It tends to infantilize them and cause them to go dashing about the corridors of advertising agencies with their ties flapping behind them. It causes them to endure the dreadful food and ratty upholstery of the Harvard Club for the sake of impressing some sweet young thing with the glorious source of their B.A.

—ERICA JONG,
Fear of Flying

The lift was attached to one of the structural arches. It didn't go straight up; it followed a curved course. Except in one low corner of the interior, there was no light. And now the vast dome rumbled. Something parted, began to slide above them. Segments of the curved surface opened quickly and let in the sky—first a clear piercing slice. All at once there was only the lift, moving along the arch. The interior was abolished altogether—no interior—nothing but the open, freezing heavens. If this present motion were to go on, you would travel straight out. You would go up into the stars. . . . He came inevitably back to the crematorium, *that* rounded top and its huge circular floor, the feet of stiffs sticking through the curtains, the blasting heat underneath where they were disposed of, the killing cold when you returned and thought your head was being split by an ax. But that dome never opened. You could pass through only as smoke.

—SAUL BELLOW,
The Dean's December

The two pigs had quietly disregarded Augustus's orders to go to the creek, and were under one of the wagons, eating the snake. That made good sense, for the creek was just as dry as the wagon yard, and farther off. Fifty weeks out of the year Hat Creek was nothing but a sandy ditch, and the fact that the two pigs didn't regard it as a fit wallow was a credit to their intelligence. Augustus often praised the pigs' intelligence in a running argument he had been having with Call for the last few years. Augustus maintained that pigs were smarter than all horses and most people, a claim that galled Call severely.

"No slop-eating pig is as smart as a horse," Call said, before going on to say worse things.

—LARRY MCMURTRY,
Lonesome Dove

We buried Corrine in the Olinka way, wrapped in barkcloth under a large tree. All of her sweet ways went with her. All of her education and a heart intent on doing good. She taught me so much! I know I will miss her always. The children were stunned by their mother's death. They knew she was very sick, but death is not something they think about in relation to their parents or themselves. It was a strange little procession. All of us in our white robes and with our faces painted white. Samuel is like someone lost. I don't believe they've spent a night apart since their marriage.

—ALICE WALKER,
The Color Purple

Some warm nights during lightning storms, I heard my folks pacing the hallway carpet outside my room. I felt honored. I believed they guarded me from lightning. I pictured a blazing stick figure—white-hot zigzags, light for its blood—come to fry or kidnap me. I imagined them fighting him off using the brass umbrella stand or a huge pink wedding-present vase kept out there. But, listening I found: Momma was secretly petrified of electric storms. Sure, she joked about it, acted real ashamed, but (at first flash) she always hurried to my hall, the only one without a window. Pop rose with her, in his nightshirt, never sounding cross. They had their good talks then. I could see the candle come and go under my door's seam. I used to feel spooked of big gales till I found that Momma feared them. Then it seemed she was being scared for the both of us.

—ALAN GURGANUS,
*The Oldest Living Confederate
Widow Tells All*

The terrain lost all resemblance to the cold prairie that had surrounded their old cave. Iza found herself depending more and more on knowledge of memories more ancient than her own as the clan passed through shaded glens and over grassy knolls of a full temperate forest. The heavy brown barks of oak, beech, walnut, apple, and maple were intermixed with supple, straight, thin-barked willow, birch, hornbeam, aspen, and the high brush of alder and hazelnut. There was a tang to the air Iza couldn't readily identify that seemed to ride on the warm soft breeze from the south. Catkins still clung to fully leafed birches. Delicate petals of pink and white drifted down, blown blossoms of fruit and nut trees, giving early promise of autumn's bounty.

—JEAN M. AUEL,
The Clan of the Cave Bear

After forty minutes, her sneakers were muddy and soaked, her legs were aching and she had accomplished nothing. She stopped to rest at a clearing where the riding classes from the stable would pause and regroup. There were no other hikers around and she could not hear any sounds of riders on the trails. The sun was almost completely gone. I must be crazy, she thought. This is no place to be alone. I'll come back tomorrow. . . . Halfway down she came to a large rock and paused to rest on it. . . . When her breathing became even, she wiped her hands on her light-green jogging suit. She grasped the side of the rock with her right hand as she prepared to hoist herself up. And felt something. Kitty looked down. She tried to scream, but no sound came, only a low, disbelieving moan. Her fingers were touching other fingers, manicured, with deep-red polish, held upward by the rocks that had slid around them, framed by the blue cuff that had intruded upon her subconscious, a scrap of black plastic, like a mourning band, embracing the slender inert wrist.

—MARY HIGGINS CLARK,
While My Pretty One Sleeps

Well, it was done. Morgaine had had her will. So she would see Lancelet and welcome him as her husband's kinsmen, no more. The other madness was past and gone, but she would see him and that was better than nothing. She tried to banish all this with thoughts of the feast. Two oxen were being roasted, would it be enough? And there was a huge wild boar taken in hunting a few days ago, and two pigs from the farms nearby, being baked in a pit yonder; already it smelled so good that a group of hungry children were hanging around sniffing the good smell. And there were hundreds of loaves of barley bread, many of which would be given away to the country-folk who came to crowd around the edges of the field and watch the doings of the nobles, the kings and knights and Companions; and there were apples baked in cream, and nuts by the bushel, and confectionery for the ladies, honey cakes, and rabbits and small birds stewed in wine. . . . if this feast was not a success, certainly it would not be for the want of good and abundant food!

—Marion Zimmer Bradley,
The Mists of Avalon

La Mouette was returning for her master, and as he climbed into the waiting fishing boat, and hoisted the little sail on the single mast, it seemed to Dona that this moment was part of another moment, long ago, when she had stood upon a headland and looked out across the sea. The ship drifted on the horizon like a symbol of escape, and there was something strange about her in the morning light, as though she had no part in the breaking of the day, but belonged to another age and to another world.

She seemed a painted ship upon the still white sea, and Dona shivered suddenly, for the shingle felt cold and chill on her bare feet, while a little wave splashed upon them, and sighed, and was no more. Then out of the sea, like a ball of fire, the sun came hard and red.

—Daphne du Maurier,
Frenchman's Creek

Sheila Webb opened the front gate, walked up to the front door and rang the bell. There was no response, and after waiting a minute or two, she did as she had been directed, and turned the handle. The door opened and she walked in. The door on the right of the small hall was ajar. She tapped on it, waited, and then walked in. It was an ordinary quite pleasant sitting room, a little overfurnished for modern tastes. The only thing at all remarkable about it was the profusion of clocks—a grandfather clock ticking in the corner, a Dresden china clock on the mantelpiece, a silver carriage clock on the desk, a small fancy gilt clock on a whatnot near the fireplace and on a table by the window, a faded leather travelling clock, with ROSEMARY in worn gilt letters across the corner. . . .

Sheila started violently as there was a whir and a click above her head, and from a wooden carved clock on the wall a cuckoo sprang out through his little door and announced loudly and definitely: *Cuckoo, Cuckoo, Cuckoo!* The harsh notes seemed almost menacing. The cuckoo disappeared again with a snap of his door.

—Agatha Christie,
The Clocks

She thought she was ugly, for she was so much taller than her small and ungenerous schoolmates. Sometimes she envied them their ordinary prettiness, their mincing ways, their sweet little simpers, their tiny little voices, and she would gaze at them wistfully. They laughed at her hair, her height, her great blue eyes, and she did not know it was envy, though subconscious. She felt herself gawky and graceless and odd. When she looked at herself in the little smeared mirror above the kitchen sink in her aunt's house she did not see miraculous beauty, or color, or perfect contour. She saw distortion and did not know it was the distortion of others.

—TAYLOR CALDWELL,
Ceremony of the Innocent

In horror she watched as a woman in a dark green gown and cap was led past the Tower gates through a jeering mob. The woman looked to be in her late forties. Her chestnut-brown hair was streaked with gray. She walked directly, ignoring the guards who clustered around her. Her beautifully sculpted features were frozen in a mask of fury and hatred. Her hands were bound before her with thin wirelike strands that bit into her wrists. An angry red crescent-shaped scar at the base of her thumb glistened in the early morning light. As Judith watched, the crowd separated to make way for dozens of soldiers, marching in orderly fashion toward a draped enclosure near the execution block. The ranks parted to allow a slender young man in a plumed hat, dark breeches, and embroidered jacket to step forth. The crowd cheered wildly as Charles II raised his hand in greeting.

—MARY HIGGINS CLARK,
The Anastasia Syndrome

Barry the Blade entered the warehouse alone. Gone was the swaggering strut of the quickest gun in town. Gone was the smirking scowl of the cocky street hood. Gone were the flashy suit and Italian loafers. The earrings were in a pocket. The ponytail was tucked under his collar. He'd shaved just an hour ago. He climbed the rusted steps to the second level, and thought about playing on these same stairs as a child. His father was alive then, and after school he'd hang around here until dark, watching containers come and go, listening to the stevedores, learning their language, smoking their cigarettes, looking at their magazines. It was a wonderful place to grow up, especially for a boy who wanted to be nothing but a gangster.

—JOHN GRISHAM,
The Client

Literature was then delivering a heavy broadside against marriage, which was regarded as so unsatisfactory an institution that a divorce was no longer assumed to be a tragedy. If one knew the people who were getting divorced it usually turned out that there was some sadness attached; either there was some condition that had made for prolonged unhappiness, drunkenness or insane jealousy, or one partner had ceased to love a still loving partner; but the picture that was provoked by the news of a divorce was simply of the sensible cancellation of an arrangement that had appeared irksome. Yet everybody whom I met when I was still so newly married that they took note of my state showed a faith in marriage, gave signs that they thought it not an unreasonable hope that Oliver and I would be happy together for ever.

—REBECCA WEST,
Cousin Rosamund

Volume and Pitch

His voice no touch of harmony admits,
Irregularly deep, and shrill by fits,
The two extremes appear like man and wife,
Coupled together for the sake of strife.

—CHARLES CHURCHILL,
The Roschiad

VOLUME

Loudness

The human speaking voice is characterized by three features: volume (loudness and projection), pitch, and quality (vocal color). A fourth feature, timing or rate, characterizes speech rather than voice, but is equally important in effective voice and speech production.

Volume means the loudness or softness of sound to the human ear. To the scientist, vocal volume is the effect of the energy or intensity with which the outgoing air strikes the vocal folds and moves through the resonating chambers. Intensity is measured in **decibels** (db), the unit of assessment of the relative loudness of sound, which ranges from barely audible (1 db) to a level that is potentially painful to the ear (160 db).

A more general concern is not the measurement of the physical properties of sound waves at their source, but their perceptual effect on the human receivers. Therefore, think of vocal **loudness** in terms not of decibel levels but of the strength with which the vibration from the vocal folds and resonators strikes the eardrum and subsequently stimulates the nerve endings in the inner ear. Simply put, people judge loudness by how it sounds, not by how it is produced. Evaluations of loudness levels are more apt to be made by message receivers or listeners than by message senders or speakers.

Yet speakers hear their own voices and to some degree monitor loudness by aural perception. You can certainly tell when you say a word or phrase *louder* or *softer* than the immediately preceding word or phrase. But remember that you hear yourself by the conduction of vibrations through the bony structures of your head as well as by sound waves that enter your ear. This dual input causes you to hear your voice quite differently from the way other people may hear you. Bone conduction usually emphasizes the lower frequencies, making your voice sound stronger to you than it actually is.

Many beginning voice and articulation students think they are talking with ample volume when in reality others in the same room can barely hear them. So as you work to improve your volume level and learn to adjust it to various speech settings, you will need guidance and feedback from your instructor and classmates. Their perception of your loudness level is far more accurate than yours can be.

Read It Aloud _____

**If you want your voice
    to be heard in a crowd,
Be sure to project—
    or at least to talk loud.**

STOP AND TRY THIS

Say these words in order, following the directions:

1. peep [pip]
2. bib [bɪb]
3. dead [dɛd]
4. tat [tæt]
5. cook [kʊk]
6. gog [gɑg]

First Time Through:

1. softly
2. twice as loud
3. as loud as you can
4. half that loud
5. just a little bit softer
6. whisper

Second Time Through:

1. Your listener is next to you in the front seat of a car, and you don't want the person in back to hear.
2. The person you're talking to is slightly deaf.
3. You're in a large auditorium.
4. You're in your living room, alone with your mate or fiancée.
5. You answer the telephone in a room where the vacuum cleaner, blender, and TV are all running.
6. Your listener is across the street.

Think about what you just did. First, you concentrated on the physical and perceptual aspects—loudness and softness. The second time through, your focus was on the psychological motivation for altering volume. Environments, situations, relationships, and emotional states all influence the loudness of your voice. These psychological considerations provide the most effective approach for the improvement of your vocal volume. The term "projection" conveys a more useful concept than the word "volume," for projection connotes the psychological as well as the physical and perceptual aspects of loudness and softness.

Projection

Quiet, priestlike voice,
Too used to syllable damnations round
To make a natural emphasis worth while.

—Elizabeth Barrett Browning,
"Aurora Leigh"

A dictionary defines projection as "the act of throwing or shooting forward" by some external yet adjacent force, such as a bullet from a gun, an image from a motion picture projector, or your voice from your body, especially your vocal mechanism. That bullet, image, or voice is able to continue forward because of the property of inertia. The stronger the initiating force, the greater the resulting motion will be. Just as a bigger gun may shoot farther and with more power and a larger movie projector with a higher-wattage lamp can send a stronger, bigger image, the stronger the vibration from your vocal mechanism, the greater the audibility of your voice.

In Chapter 5, you learned that adequate projection is to a large degree a matter of good breathing techniques. Without the force behind the initiating airstream, the vibration will be too weak to carry.

As important as controlled breathing is the focus or placing of the tone. To gain full forward momentum, the voice needs to be focused toward the very front of the mouth or even outside it. This is called *forward placement.*

FYI . . . _____

Consider two terms from psychology, *introvert* and *extrovert*. The introvert is shy and withdrawn. The extrovert is outgoing, confident, and interested in other people. What kind of voices would you guess these two extreme personality types might have? We probably think of the introvert as having a soft, quiet, weak voice, while the extrovert would likely have a louder, stronger, more resonant voice. What does this suggest to you about the relationship between projection and attitude?

STOP AND TRY THIS

1. Lay your fingers on your pharynx or upper throat, just under your chin. Pull your voice downward to this area. Think of it as being down and far back. Say:

   "In learning voice placement I surely must note
   How cloudy and weak is this sound from my throat."

2. Puff your cheeks out with air. Lay your fingers gently on the puffs. Using a somewhat higher pitch, read the following, pushing the tones into your fattened cheeks.

   "Voice tones and words that are trapped in the cheek
   Will sound dimpy and wimpy and puny and weak."

3. Concentrate on completely relaxing and lowering your soft palate, so that you let all the air go through your nose. *Whine* as you say:

   "One of the worst of a listener's woes
   Is a voice that exudes from the speaker's nose."

In this exercise, you have focused your tone incorrectly—in your throat, your cheeks, and your nasal passages. As you likely have noticed, this incorrect placement will seriously interfere with your ability to project and may also lead to unpleasant vocal qualities.

Think of placing your tone right at the front of your mouth, on your lips, teeth, and the tip of your tongue. Think of sending the sound outside of your mouth, outside of your body, with the same sort of follow-through that a pitcher uses when throwing a ball, or a golfer when hitting a golf ball. Neither the pitcher nor the golfer stops the thrust or motion once the ball has left the hand or golf tee. Careful follow-through is essential if the ball is to continue its motion. Your voice needs the same follow-through for good projection to take place.

Some mechanical practice, such as breath control and relaxation exercises, can aid projection. Drills for clear enunciation of sounds can also help, for they focus your attention on the articulators, particularly the lips, thereby bringing the focal point of the tone forward. Clearly enunciated tones travel farther and with more audibility.

Of equal importance to drills and exercises is your attitude: you need to "think forward." You need to want your message to reach the receiver and to be *communication*, not just *speech*. This sense of outreach is helpful when working to improve projection.

Projection is not synonymous with loudness, although you may hear coaches and directors use the words *louder, more volume,* or *project* to get at the same behavior—increased audibility, clarity, and distinctness of the speaker's voice and speech. A very soft tone, well projected, can be heard at the back of a large auditorium. Yelling, on the other hand, may be loud, but because it depends upon tightened throat muscles and a forced tone, it may be diffused so that it is not understandable. Clear projection, not mere loudness, is your goal.

Perhaps you were blessed with a "voice that carries"—though not always a blessing when you are overheard telling secrets or gossiping from across a large area or even a nearby room! If so, your voice tones are focused and directed naturally, and you will have little trouble making yourself heard in a large lecture hall or theater. But do not despair if you were not so gifted naturally, for good projection can be acquired with diligence and practice. The following exercises will help you.

EXERCISES FOR PROJECTION

Note: Before every exercise, check your abdominal support for ample inhalation and controlled exhalation.

1. Read the following paragraph slowly and deliberately. Start low, but gradually build as you focus solely on a single spot on the back wall, directing your tone only to that one spot. Once you have finished reading, improvise your own conversation with the wall rather than reading word for word. The importance of this exercise lies not in the exact wording of the paragraph but in the idea that you are speaking directly to an inanimate object.

    I am looking at a spot on the back wall. I am talking to that spot, and only to that spot. But that spot does not hear very well, and I must focus carefully or the spot will miss my message. Listen, spot—hear and know what I say. My voice is clear, the room is quiet—hear me, if you will.

2. Say the words *green, blue, yellow, orange,* and *red,* beginning very softly with *green,* then increasing your projection with each word until you are very strong on *red.* Have five distinctly different levels of volume. After four or five repetitions, change and come downward, starting with a strong *red,* ending with a soft *green.* Repeat four or five times. Do not alter your pitch during this exercise, only your volume.

3. Stand in the center of the room (or the middle of the stage if you are working in a theater). Position your voice at various locations on the walls and ceiling, in accordance with the ideas expressed in the following words. Say these words slowly:

here	there
up	down
high	low
right	left

I would rather be kicked with a foot than be overcome by a loud voice speaking cruel words.

—Elizabeth Barrett Browning

top	bottom
above	below

side by side

Add other "place" words and change the order randomly.

4. Certain ideas, concepts, or emotions call for various loudness levels. Maintain clear projection, but alter your volume according to the content of the following sentences:

Soft or Low Volume

1. The baby's just started his nap.
2. Father died peacefully in his sleep last night.
3. Please lower your voice—I have a terrible headache.
4. Would you mind taking off your hat? I can't see the speaker.
5. If we tiptoe, maybe she won't find out how late we came in.
6. Oh, look—it must have snowed all night—the world is solid white.
7. She's had three kittens already—there'll be another one any second now.
8. If you leave me, I don't think I want to go on living.
9. Where would I find the books by Erle Stanley Gardner?
10. Please hand me a hymn book from beside you.
11. Honey, wake up—I hear a noise downstairs—someone's in the house.
12. Pass this note over to Shirley—don't let the teacher see you.
13. Did you hear that Mr. Edwards was fired?
14. Shhh, don't let on that you know he's been watching you.
15. Let's sneak out of the tent and go catch a bullfrog and put it in Mr. Farley's sleeping bag.
16. What did you get for the answer to the third question?
17. I wanted to ask you if you would—would you—would you go steady with me?
18. Let's leave at intermission—I can't take any more of this awful play.
19. Slowly she opened the huge, creaking door and crept into the haunted castle.
20. See that man over there at the next table? He looks just like Dad.

Moderate or Medium Volume

1. Can you cash a check for more than the amount of the groceries?
2. Harry, you'll have to stay after school today to finish your assignment.
3. Pat, please bring me the file on the Ipswich transaction.
4. Pass the gravy after you've served yourself.
5. Truthfully, your honor, I was only going thirty-five miles an hour—I had just looked at my speedometer.
6. Could you have the alterations finished by tomorrow night?
7. Your transmission needs a complete overhaul.
8. Would you like to have lunch tomorrow or the next day?
9. Please wait your turn at the end of the line.
10. Hand me the screwdriver from that peg on the back porch.
11. Would you like to go to a movie or maybe go dancing next Friday night?

12. Grind a chuck roast for me—medium-sized chunks for chili.

13. Please take a letter to Consolidated Industries. I need it to go out in the afternoon mail.

14. I'm sorry—I'm just not interested in subscribing to any more magazines right now.

15. Hold still while I make sure the light is absolutely right.

16. I'm sorry your car broke down, but I made it clear that there would be no make-up exams in this class.

17. Take two of these tablets after each meal for one full week.

18. What time do you think you'll get home today?

19. That is undoubtedly the silliest thing you've ever said.

20. I'd like to order a large pepperoni pizza to be delivered.

Strong or Full Volume

1. No, you cannot go outside and play—I've told you three times already.

2. Let's get this straight—I did not borrow your new sweater—I don't know where it is.

3. Turn down the TV—the phone's ringing.

4. Good evening, ladies and gentlemen. I want to thank you for inviting me to speak to you this evening.

5. No, no, bad dog—bad dog. On the paper—go on the paper!

6. I've told you for the last time—I am not interested in jogging or running.

7. If you don't quiet down right now, class, we won't go outside at recess.

8. Take a ten-minute break, chorus; then we'll pick up with Act Two.

9. I'm not hungry! Why do you keep trying to force me to eat all the time?

10. The first item on the agenda today is Dave's report on his recent sales campaign.

11. Officer, a man just ran out of that store as if he might have stolen something.

12. When I grab the ledge, swing the ladder about two feet toward the window.

13. All clerks in the back, please come to the checkout counter—all clerks report to the counter.

14. The meeting will please come to order. The secretary will read the minutes of the last meeting.

15. The congregation will please rise as we sing hymn number 489, "Faith of Our Fathers."

16. Joe, bring me another sack of pine bark from the truck when you come back.

17. And now, I bring you the woman of the year—the next president of the United States.

18. If you think you're going to blame this whole thing on me, think again.

19. The phone call is for you—do you want me to take a message?

20. I love this spot—it's windy, but you can see for miles.

Very Loud (But Don't Yell or Tense Your Throat Muscles)

1. Heads up—the sandbag's falling!

2. Tim—ber!

3. "Friends, Romans, Countrymen, lend me your ears!"

4. Get out of the street!

5. Touchdown! Touchdown! We want a touchdown!

6. Stop that man—he stole my purse!

7. Bravo! Bravo! Encore!

8. Give me your attention, please—quiet! Quiet!

9. Get out of the building—it's on fire!

10. Swing the crane over this way!

11. Stop! You're about to back over my bicycle!

12. Come back here, do you hear me? Come back!

13. Oh, no—they're going to crash—look out!

14. Watch out behind you—he's got a knife!

15. You bring back that shoe, you dumb dog!

16. Here—over here—throw me the ball—throw it to me!

17. You take your hands off me right this minute!

18. Mother—mother—over here—here we are—over here!

19. This situation is intolerable! We demand action now!

20. Hey! Wait for me! I'll walk over with you!

5. With the instructor or one student serving as a Marine drill instructor (DI), the group all together repeats a simple response four or five times, significantly increasing the loudness each time. For example, the DI asks, "How do you like speech class?" The group answers, "We like it just fine, sir! (ma'am!)" "I can't hear you," intones the DI, and the group repeats its response as long as the DI wishes to continue. (You've seen this in a dozen movies about the Marine Corps.)

Check repeatedly that your throat does not tense up, your tongue does not retract, and your jaw does not lock. Stronger responses come from increased pressure from the diaphragm and added forward focus on the articulators.

6. If your class is held in a regular classroom, make arrangements as individuals or as a group to hold some sessions in a large auditorium, a lecture hall, or even a cafeteria to practice projection. We subconsciously adjust our volume level to the amount of space around us. You will find it easier to work at full volume in these larger spaces. If no large area is available, go outside for a practice session.

7. Practice on a microphone with some of the media copy found in this chapter and elsewhere in the book. Beginning speech students often mistakenly believe that projection is not necessary if they are speaking into a microphone. Yet the same clarity of enunciation and forward placement are required for a good radio or television voice as on a platform or behind a podium. In fact, microphones may amplify and highlight poorly placed tones and lazy and careless lip and jaw movements.

PITCH

Begin low, speak slow;
Take fire, rise higher;
When most impressed
Be self-possessed;
At the end wax warm,
And sit down in a storm.

—THE REV. JOHN LEIFCHILD,
"Lines on Public Speaking"

The second feature of the human voice is **pitch.** Like volume, pitch can be studied from both a physical and perceptual viewpoint—by examining the physical properties of sound and the effect the vibrations have on the human ear.

To the scientist, pitch is determined by the frequency with which the vocal folds vibrate. Remember, volume is the intensity of the vibration; pitch is the speed of the vibration.

The length and thickness or mass of the vocal folds place certain limitations on an individual's pitch range. Just as some people inherit long fingers, big noses, or thick eyebrows, certain persons have longer, thicker vocal folds. Generally, the longer and thicker the vocal folds, the lower the pitch will be. To a large degree, this explains why men's voices are usually pitched lower than women's; resonance explains the rest of the difference.

Within the predetermined structural limitations of the vocal folds, much pitch variation is possible. This variation is a combination of two factors: changes in the pressure with which air is released through and across the glottis and the tension created by the vocal folds themselves. The stronger the air pressure and the more tension in the vocal folds, the greater the frequency of the vibration. Higher pitches result from greater frequencies.

Note: In thinking about pitch as a result of the frequency or rate of vibration, make sure that you do not confuse this measure of rate with speech rate, to be discussed in Chapter 7. When someone talks too fast or too slowly, the issue is not vocal fold vibration and pitch but speech rate, which varies with the length of individual sounds and pauses.

Read It Aloud ───────

**The pitch of your voice moves from high down to low,
While the rate gives a choice to talk fast or go slow.**

STOP AND TRY THIS

Gently place your fingers on your larynx and begin counting from one to at least eight or nine—higher if you can. *One* should be said at the lowest pitch you can produce comfortably. Then step up one note on the scale with each number you speak. Using a piano or pitch pipe is helpful in maintaining clear, whole-tone steps.

If you are producing a well-supported, sufficiently projected tone, you will feel noticeable changes in your larynx as you go up the scale. Later we will discuss the significant difference between this natural tension and tension in the muscles surrounding the larynx.

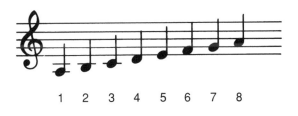

1   2   3   4   5   6   7   8

As noted in Chapter 4, frequencies of vibration are measured in *cycles* (single completed motions of the vibrating body). Cycles in turn are expressed as *hertz* (abbreviated *Hz*), with one hertz equaling one cycle per second. Most humans with fairly normal hearing can perceive a range of from 20 to 20,000 cycles. In speaking, the fundamental vibration is usually around 125 to 140 Hz for men and between 200 and 250 Hz for women. In singing voices, this range extends from around 80 Hz (produced by the E that is an octave and a half below middle C) for the lowest bass voice to 1365 Hz (the F a little over two octaves above middle C) for a coloratura soprano (Figure 6–1).

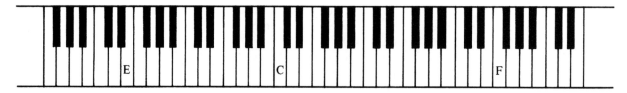

Figure 6–1 Singing-voice range, represented on keyboard.

Speakers and listeners think in terms not of frequencies, cycles, and hertz but rather of the highness and lowness of the sound to our ear. People often make personality judgments about others based on their voice pitch level. The authors were disappointed to learn that Abraham Lincoln had a weak, high-pitched, somewhat squeaky voice. It seems like such a tall, masterful man whose powerful ideas and commanding language led him to construct many fine speeches should sound like Raymond Massey, Gregory Peck, or other actors who have depicted Lincoln with a rich, resonant voice!

Optimal and Habitual Pitch

Despite the capacity to produce a wide variety of pitches, people talk mostly within a relatively small pitch range. For most of us, that range reflects the pitch most appropriately produced by the physical structures we have inherited. This appropriate pitch—which reflects the most comfortable and functional use of the vocal folds to produce the fundamental vibration, amplified by balanced resonance—is called **optimal pitch.** Your optimal pitch might be described as the pitch at which nature and heredity designed you to speak.

Habitual pitch is the pitch that is used most frequently by a speaker in conversational settings. Ideally, and for most people, habitual and optimal pitches are the same. Some people, however, habitually speak either higher or lower than the pitch that comes naturally from their inherited physical structure. A habitual pitch that does not accurately reflect the age, sex, or personality of the speaker is usually not the optimal pitch for that speaker. Such a pitch may result from poor physical or mental health, but is more often a matter of acquiring and perpetuating poor speech habits. If you wish to change your habitual pitch, you will need to devote considerable time to voice and breathing practice, for you will be altering a deep-seated habit. Substantial changes are possible, however, if you feel that your habitual pitch is too high or too low.

To find your habitual pitch, tape-record a segment of one of your conversations. Listen to it several times. You will discover that despite pitch steps and inflections (discussed later in this chapter) upward and downward several tones, you say a number of key words, especially nouns and verbs, at about the same pitch. This is your habitual pitch. Then try to make the same determination by listening to yourself without recording your voice—through your own ears and head bones. Try making your general pitch higher, then lower, and then return to your natural level so that you clearly recognize your habitual pitch.

To find your optimal pitch, start from the central tone that you identified as your habitual pitch. Using a "speak-sing" quality, where the tone is sustained slightly longer than in a usual spoken word but not held like a sustained vibrato in singing, count downward several whole steps. You should reach a point at which you can go no lower without seriously altering your voice quality. Now sing while counting upward, until you slide into a very comfortable, natural-sounding tone. That is your optimal pitch. If you cannot go down at least four or five steps, your habitual pitch is probably lower than your optimal pitch. If, however, you can step down as much as seven or eight whole tones, you are probably speaking habitually at something higher than your optimal pitch.

Changing Your Habitual Pitch

Don't look at me, sir, with—ah—in that tone of voice.

—Punch, XCVII, 38

As with most other dimensions of voice evaluation, you must depend more heavily on those who listen to you—teachers and other students—than upon your own ear to determine the appropriateness of your pitch. Because of bone conduction and resonance, your pitch may sound somewhat lower to you than it does to other listeners. However, very few students complain that their pitch is too low; far more seem to feel it is too high. In general, lower pitches are perceived to be more desirable than higher pitches. Low pitches in men usually suggest strength and masculinity; listeners may think of a higher-pitched male speaker as weak or effeminate. Many people believe that low-pitched voices in women are sexy, while the higher pitches may suggest a less intelligent, flighty woman. These stereotypes have been perpetuated by actors and actresses, who often use pitch changes to help establish different characters.

If with the guidance of your instructor you determine that your habitual pitch is significantly different from your optimal level or does not seem to suit your age, sex, or personality, you may need special help from a voice and speech therapist to make a major change. If, however, the variance is only slight, daily exercise can help you raise or lower your pitch. Try the following:

1. This exercise requires a pitch pipe, piano, or other instrument that can help you hear pitches accurately. Many people, especially those with no musical background, have a problem distinguishing the pitches they are making. Trouble hearing a pitch accurately will make it more difficult to alter your habitual pitch, for your self-monitoring ability may be impaired. Practice making tones that coincide with those on the musical instrument, especially your optimal pitch and the two or three notes above and below it. Practice with the musical instrument until you can stay on or near pitch without it. We advise a few singing lessons for those with serious problems discriminating pitches.

2. Identify your optimal pitch level, as you did earlier. Using a sustained singing tone sing the following phrases at your optimal pitch. (Don't worry if you don't have a good singing voice; this is only for practice.)

   a. How are you?

   b. Long-lost soul.

   c. Free clean air.

   d. Calm old town.

   e. Nine coal trains.

   f. They labor late.

   g. Miles of smiles.

   h. Pure, beautiful truths.

   i. Round, brown mountains.

   j. Far away from home.

3. "Speak-sing" the ten phrases in the previous exercise in your optimal pitch, sustaining only slightly. Speak-singing is much like intoning.

4. Speak the same ten phrases without sustaining, yet note that all contain long vowel sounds that should be held. Sounds of longer duration are easier to produce at a natural pitch level. Can you retain your optimal pitch, or do you find yourself slipping back into your habitual pitch?

5. Beginning with your identified optimal pitch, sustain the vowel combination [ɑ]–[u] on a single note. Then repeat it one note higher. Then move one note lower than the original. End on your optimal tone. Repeat, stretching to two tones on either side of the optimum tone. Does it still sound and feel comfortable?

6. Return to your old habitual pitch and read the following:

> Voice pitch is often a determinant in a listener's evaluation of a speaker's credibility. Excessively high- or low-pitched voices can arouse suspicion or mistrust, for they may suggest lack of maturity, lack of clear sexual identity, or insincerity on the part of the speaker.

Has the old pitch begun to sound somewhat off to you? The more you practice in your newly discovered optimal pitch—provided it is produced with full vocal relaxation and good forward placement—the more strange the old habitual pitch will sound to you.

Now, again establish your optimal pitch. Intone [ɑ], [i], [u], [oʊ], and [eɪ], sustaining each. With your larynx, articulators, and ears tuned to this intoned sound, repeat the paragraph, trying to keep the overall focus of the pitch on the optimum.

7. As you work to habituate the optimal pitch, make sure you do not drift into a **monotone,** or **monopitch.** You must continue to use variation, although you will vary from your newly established optimal pitch rather than your old habitual pitch. The exercises in the rest of the chapter will help you develop pitch variation.

Keeping your pitch at the optimal level and using natural expression and variation, read the following verses from the New Testament:

a. The voice of one crying in the wilderness, prepare ye the way of the Lord, make his paths straight.

b. O generation of vipers, who hath warned you to flee from the wrath to come?

c. This is my beloved Son, in whom I am well pleased.

d. Follow me, and I will make you fishers of men.

e. Ye are the salt of the earth; but if the salt has lost its savor, wherewith shall it be salted?

f. Whosoever shall smite thee on thy right cheek, turn to him the other also.

g. Lay up for yourselves treasures in heaven; for where your treasure is, there will your heart be also.

h. Consider the lilies of the field, how they grow; they toil not, neither do they spin.

i. Ask, and it shall be given you; seek, and ye shall find; knock, and it shall be opened unto you.

j. What is a man profited if he shall gain the whole world, and lose his own soul?

k. Where two or three are gathered together in my name, there am I in the midst of them.

l. It is easier for a camel to go through the eye of a needle, than for a rich man to enter into the kingdom of God.

m. Whosoever shall exalt himself shall be abased; and he that shall humble himself shall be exalted.

STOP AND TRY THIS

Find and produce your **falsetto** voice. Say "one" at a comfortable, average pitch level, "two" one tone higher, and so on up the scale with "three, four, five . . ." etc. You will come to a tone, probably at "ten," "eleven," or "twelve," where you can no longer maintain the same voice quality. You should feel the tension shifting up from your pharynx to the back of your nasal passages as you slide into a high, tight falsetto tone. Men might use this voice to portray women, and women might try it to suggest a little girl. Voices of animals, such as mice, and "Munchkin" characters are often done in a falsetto.

Produce a **glottal fry.** Open your mouth wide and concentrate on the lower part of your pharynx and the larynx. Try to imitate the sound of bacon frying in a skillet by using your glottis to articulate a low-pitched, grinding sound. Actually, your vocal folds are moving too slowly to produce a full tone, and you are using the glottis as the place of articulation. Many speakers who don't use enough breath support will drop into a glottal fry on the last word or two of a sentence. This grinding sound in the glottis or at the back of the palate is used to portray gruff, gravelly-throated characters, such as Lurch in the old TV show "The Addams Family," or quacky animals, such as Donald Duck.

Vocal Color

My words are little jars
For you to take and put upon a shelf.
Their shapes are quaint and beautiful,
And they have many pleasant colours and lustres
To recommend them.

—Amy Lowell,
"A Gift"

For the majority of you who already use your optimal pitch habitually, the primary pitch improvement could be to increase pitch variation. Most speakers can comfortably move through at least one octave in average speaking situations—about eight whole tones and the intermediate half steps. Greater extremes are possible if you consider the high tones of the falsetto voice or the low tones associated with glottal fry.

Yet many people use only a few notes when reading or speaking in public. The result is the **monotone** or **monopitch** voice, familiar to us all as a major cause of boredom in listeners. When monopitches are accompanied by lack of variation in rate, loudness, and overall voice quality, as they usually are, and a generally lethargic delivery, teachers, directors, and coaches will call for "more enthusiasm, more animation, more vigor, more pep, more dynamism, more eagerness, more forcefulness!" All these terms ask listless, monopitch speakers to liven up and use vocal variety, an essential ingredient of effective oral delivery.

Achieving enthusiasm, vocal color, and pitch variation depends upon a combination of a positive, vigorous attitude, an energetic, well-controlled body, and skillful use of the vocal mechanism. A positive attitude will enable you to *think* with vitality; an energetic, healthy body will help you *feel* vital and alive; and extensive practice can help you learn to use your vocal mechanism to its fullest potential. The following exercises are a start toward achieving this last goal.

EXERCISES FOR VOCAL COLOR

1. Starting with the lowest tone you can produce with a clear, controlled voice, say "one, two, three, four," and so on up the scale. How many notes can you include? Ten? Twelve? Fourteen? Then begin on the highest note and count down. If you are not making at least nine or ten distinct tones, try pushing a half step more at each end of the scale until you can stretch your range.

2. Repeat exercise 1, this time using the word *ho* instead of numbers. Keep the [h] well supported so that outgoing air cannot be heard as it moves across the vocal folds. Again push a half step lower, then return to a half step lower than your

optimal tone. Continue pushing downward as long as natural-sounding tones can be produced without strain in the throat.

3. Make a siren with your voice. Start low in pitch and volume and say "zow," gliding up until you are very loud and high in pitch. Without stopping, glide back down to your lowest pitch and volume. You will need to practice spacing your breath so that you have enough left to produce the final tone. The whole sound is one, long, sustained glide up and down and suggests a siren passing by. This will help you stretch your pitch range and improve your volume flexibility.

4. Increase your sensitivity to subtle variations in pitch by counting up and down the chromatic scale as well as the more familiar diatonic scale. The diatonic scale has eight tones—an octave—with fixed intervals of half and whole notes; the chromatic scale uses all the half steps. It would probably be helpful to use a piano when you begin this exercise, but eventually you should be able to do it without accompaniment.

DIATONIC SCALE

do   re   mi   fa   so   la   ti   do

CHROMATIC SCALE (ascending)

do   di   re   ri   mi   fa   fi   so   si   la   li   ti   do

CHROMATIC SCALE (descending)

do   it   te   la   le   so   se   fa   mi   me   re   rah   do

Steps and Inflection

As you counted up one note at a time in the diatonic scale in the last exercise, each number should have been a single pitch, like this:

one   two   three   four   five

Moving from one pitch to another between words or syllables is called **stepping.** In the siren exercise in the preceding section, you slid from one pitch to another. Sliding or changing pitch within a syllable is called **inflection.** Count upward, inflecting each number from one whole note to the whole note above it:

What is the difference in effect created by gliding from one tone to another instead of stepping?

EXERCISES FOR INFLECTION

1. Say the following in steps, using only one tone per word. The notes on the scale merely suggest high and low notes and need not be duplicated exactly. Rather, work within your own optimal pitch range.

Repeat, using the phrases "Don't do that" and "No, no, no." Alter the pitch pattern as many ways as you can, always stepping from one tone to another.

2. Now, instead of stepping, slide from one pitch to another. Create a short scenario that might be reflected in the words *where* and *there,* inflected as follows. In print, they would probably be written, "Where? There. There? Where."

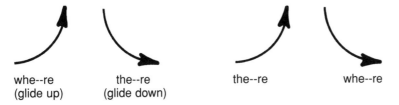

How does the meaning of the words change as you alter the inflection pattern?

3. In the following dialogue, reminiscent of an early television skit about John and Marsha, say only the two names as written. However, use pitch inflection to suggest the thoughts in parentheses.

She: Sam? (Is that you?)

He: Jennie. (*Sheepishly:* Yes, it's me.)

She: Sam? (How late is it?)

He: Jennie. (Pretty late.)

She: Sam! (How dare you stay out so late!!!)

He: Jennie. (I'm sorry, honey.)

She: Sam. (Sorry, my foot.)

He: Jennie. (Don't be mad—come on, now.)

She: Sam. (*Tearful:* You don't love me anymore.)

He: Jennie. (Sure I do, baby. Please don't cry.)

She: Sam? (Are you sure?)

He: Jennie, (Sure I'm sure.)

She: Sam. (Well, all right.)

4. Try to combine step and inflection in the following statements. You will probably find that you step more often in the first five sentences and glide more often in the last five. What's the difference?

a. I wish you wouldn't do that!

b. Don't give up yet! Hang on!

c. Stop the man in the yellow car!

d. Go, team, go! Kick that ball!

e. Hup, two, three, four. Right, left, right, left. Hup, two, three, four.

f. The river flows to the sea.

g. The young king dreams of fame and glory.

h. Flying kites is an ideal pastime for a spring day.

i. He sleeps beside the gently flowing stream.

j. The magic carpet floated through the clouds.

Do you find that you are using a wider pitch range with the first five sentences? Probably so. Heightened emotions, strong commands, and expressions of excitement call for more extremes in high and low pitches. Straightforward or factual statements and quieter moods and emotions make less demands for extremes and can be meaningfully conveyed within a limited range of four or five tones. Even the subtle variation of only two or three tones can prevent a monotone.

5. Repeat the following sentences with the different moods or emotions suggested. Note the changes in your pitch.

a. "Go away and leave me alone." (sad, angry, frustrated)

b. "It's all mine now." (elated, greedy, defensive)

c. "I can't stand this." (laughing hysterically, depressed, in pain)

d. "Let me go with you." (pleading, suggesting, demanding)

e. "He won the contest." (jealous, incredulous, excitedly happy)

6. Imagine that you are telling the story "Goldilocks and the Three Bears" to a group of small children. Say the line, "Somebody's been tasting my porridge" first as Papa Bear, then as Mama Bear, and finally as Baby Bear. Note your natural use of extreme pitch variation, coupled with changes in voice quality, to achieve these characters. Try repeating the line as it would be spoken by each of the three characters, but retain the same pitch throughout. Sounds ridiculous and empty, doesn't it?

Key

Although pitch is continuously varied within phrases and sentences, paragraphs or passages usually evoke an overall pitch level called **key**. Key is generally high, middle, or low. High keys are associated with material involving excitement or emotional intensity such as that of fear or rage. Middle keys are generally used for less emotional material, such as narrative or descriptive passages or unembellished information. Low keys are associated with more somber emotions, such as sadness and depression; funeral passages; or old age or sickness.

EXERCISES FOR KEY

Try reading aloud the following short paragraphs, maintaining an overall key but also keeping variety within it.

High Keys

1. "I won't go with you. I don't care if you are my own father. My mother told me to stay here and to wait till she got back. You let go of me. I won't go with you!"

2. "Look out! He's going to fall! The rope has slipped from one end of the scaffold—it's about to come loose. Somebody do something! Hang on, Joe!"

3. "If you come near me, I swear I'll kill you! I hate you and everything about you. You've cheated me for the last time—now get out of here!"

4. "Please let me go! I'll give you all my money, but please don't hurt me!"

5. "Eeeek—there's a mouse in my closet—I hate mice—somebody do something. Help me!"

6. "We are the little men who live in the glade, We frolic in the sunshine and slumber in the shade."

7. All the tiny chipmunks chattered and clattered as they scurried up and down the tree trunks carrying the smallest acorns to their secret hiding places.

8. The high-pitched whine of the whirring machine pierced his ears so intensely that he shrieked in pain and clapped his hands over the sides of his head.

9. One, two, button my shoe; three, four, open the door.

10. Whee! This is so exciting—I love it—spin it faster—make it go faster!

Middle Keys

1. Harry got up at 6:15, just as he had every morning for the past twenty-two years. He showered, shaved, and put on a white shirt and tie with his dark suit. In the kitchen, Mildred fixed eggs and toast, the same as always.

2. Please turn off the air conditioner when you leave the building. The automatic on–off control is not functioning properly, causing the motor to run continuously when it is not disengaged manually. The management will appreciate your cooperation.

3. In Washington today, the Senate Select Committee on Postinaugural Protocol voted to give a one-minute standing tribute to all outgoing members.

4. "I would like to order a medium cheese pizza with pepperoni and mushrooms. I want it delivered to 1906 Maple Street. The name is Chapman."

5. The chairman of the board called a meeting of the executive officers in order to report to them about the growing concern among stockholders that dividends might be sharply reduced in the coming fiscal year.

6. She stood in line almost an hour, hoping to get tickets to the concert. But when she reached the ticket window, she was greeted with a "Sold Out" sign. The couple in front of her had bought the last seats in the auditorium.

7. "Please come and see us when you have time. You and John used to visit more often—we haven't seen enough of you in the past year. I know how busy you've been, but we really do miss you."

8. "Your term papers will be due on April 27. Don't forget to include a bibliography as well as your foot- or endnotes. And unless you have an exceptionally good reason, your paper must be typewritten—no longhand."

9. They stayed in the store for over two hours, trying on one dress after another. But nothing seemed right—this one didn't fit, that one's color was wrong, another was too expensive. The shopping expedition was a failure.

10. They sat down after dinner to watch television—first the news, then a game show, followed by their favorite sitcom. By 8:30, they were ready for popcorn and cocoa.

Low Keys

1. Laura sat with her head in her hands, shoulders hunched pitifully into her neck and jaws. She could not cry. The depth of her loss outweighed the comfort of tears. It would be a long time before such relief would come.

2. The old man walked slowly down the brick pathway with its broken fragments letting random weeds and grass shoots find their way through the once neat pattern. He moved slowly, the pain of stiffened joints evident in each carefully negotiated step.

3. Death came quietly into the small bedroom, where it found the little girl with no resistance left. She was too tired to draw any more of the breaths the disease had made so difficult. Quietly, easily, she gave up, surrendering that small and fragile body to a world where breath was not important.

4. Students and teachers filed quietly out of the auditorium. They all loved the old building. The news that it was to be torn down was sad indeed, yet they knew the headmaster was right—the old must make way for the new.

5. "I promise that I'll love you forever. I'll never feel this way about anyone else, I'm sure of it. I want to spend the rest of my life with you, loving you and taking care of you."

6. The spotted fawn stood silently gazing down on his mother. She did not move as he gently nudged her, his small nose quivering with a sense of apprehension. His ears still throbbed with the crack of the rifle, but his small heart had not yet understood the finality of its meaning.

7. Release all thoughts from your mind. Today, tomorrow, yesterday—all are gone. Only the sound—OHM—OHM—PAHD-NAY—only the sound is real and here. Repeat the sound—OHM, OHM, PAHD-NAY, OHM.

8. "Sleep, my dear, sleep. You are tired—it is late. Relax—rest—just let go. The day is over—there is nothing more you can do before morning. Close your eyes, now, and go to sleep."

9. I don't know what's the matter with me, doctor. I'm tired all the time. I don't have any energy—it's almost impossible for me to get out of bed in the morning. What could be wrong with me?

10. I'm sorry I've been so neglectful of you lately. I know how unfair I've been to keep you dangling. But the truth is—I've met someone else. I've put off telling you—I really can't go on this way any longer.

Color Words

In addition to a flexible and responsive vocal mechanism and focus on the psychological or emotional values in the content or meaning of a selection, vocal color can be improved by utilizing the relationship between *sound* and *meaning* in certain words. *Onomatopoetic* words are words whose sense or meaning is in some way implied by their phonemic structure. Many of these words may have been coined in an attempt to reproduce vocally some natural sound or action. The use of *POW, ZAP,* and *BAM* in *Batman* comics to suggest fighting noises is an example.

Certain phonemic features, such as the abruptness and clean attack of the plosives, as opposed to the smoother, more gently articulated glides and nasals, create a psychological relationship between the sound of the phoneme and certain moods. Longer vowels, such as [i], [u], [ɔ], and [aʊ], seem to suggest greater distance and time spans than do short vowels, such as [ɪ], [æ], and [ʌ]. Many words clearly suggest the state or action they denote:

click	cackle	tranquil	giggle	pop
slap	mimic	lovely	burp	tinkle
droop	flit	whirl	crunch	crash

hop	bang	flick	creak	grind
ripple	stretch	blip	zigzag	wilt

Another place where vocal color can be found in words is in those pairs of words that are opposite not only in meaning but in the phonemic image they create. This image can be received aurally by a listener and can be felt orally as well as heard by the speaker. Feeling or sensing the mood values of sounds as they are formed by your articulators is helpful in achieving good vocal color. Try the word *far:* as you move from the quiet, voiceless [f] to the wide-mouth, elongated [a] and gently round back into the [r], let your mind picture great distance; then experience that sensation of distance in your articulators. Now form the following pairs, trying to be aware of the word meanings in your mind and sensing them as the sounds move across your articulators.

hot—cold	bitter—sweet
green—red	cruel—kind
sad—happy	smooth—rough
shut—open	tall—short
huge—tiny	mean—nice

Emphasis on colorful words, whether or not they are specifically onomatopoetic, is helpful in achieving vocal color. Be sensitive particularly to adjectives and adverbs, for they add depth, dimension, and detail to nouns and verbs. "The door opened" becomes much more interesting as "The *creaking* door opened *slowly.*" But you, the oral reader, must make *creaking* and *slowly* carry vivid images. Without vocal color from the reader or speaker, the words lose their mood-inducing potential.

Concentrate on the images conveyed in the specific color words in the following selections:

"Courtroom Colors"
SHARON THOMAS

The judge had visions of purple,
Although his robe was black.
The jury was in the pink.
They felt they had the knack.
The D.A. made his opening statement.
His color? Bold Gold!
The witness, a pale yellow,
Wasn't sure what should be told.
The defendant appeared to be
The deepest blue the court had seen,
For he knew that his attorney . . .
Was just plain green.

"White"
SHARON THOMAS

White! Everything's white. You'd think this earth had no color . . . just white.
　　For everything in sight is white.
White! All white. From ceiling to floor . . . it's white. Furniture, drapes, blankets, sheets. Is this my plight? To see only white?
White! Every uniform is white. They come and they go as if their heels were on fire. But if their heels did ignite . . . I bet the flame would be white.
White! Everything that enters is white. The white coats bring me an anemic diet of cauliflower and egg whites. Even my appetite is white.
White! Why must everyone have a passion for white? "Look what the florist just brought," said the nurse. "Your office staff sent them. How nice." Now I hate to be trite . . . but did they have to send me carnations of white?

FYI . . . _____

The 10 most beautiful words in the English language, according to Wilfred Funk, the dictionary-writer, are: *dawn, hush, mist, murmuring, lullaby, tranquil, luminous, chimes, golden,* **and** *melody.*
　The 10 ugliest words in the English language, listed by the National Association of Teachers of Speech, are: *gripe, plump, plutocrat, crunch, phlegmatic, flatulent, cacophony, treachery, sap,* **and** *jazz.*

—ANDY ROONEY
Communication is the Name of the Game

I would lay emphasis above all things, on the speaking voice. People rely far too much on that deceptive gadget, the microphone.

—CORNELIA OTIS SKINNER

White! Is everything beyond this room white? If I could fully see out the window there, would all be void of color? While lying here I can only view the heights . . . the clouds of white.

White! If I ever leave this world of white . . . I'll seek the world of brighter hues. With all my might, I can't imagine how anyone could delight in white.

White! Someone here thought that white was right. But why? What could their motive be? Maybe out of spite, they made everything white.

White! Not only the external, but the internal is white. They've diagnosed my illness. I have a parasite. And yes . . . it's white!

PUTTING IT TOGETHER

You should now have a clear understanding of the impact that volume and pitch have on your voice. Volume not only determines whether or not you will be heard, but it enables your voice to add many shades of meaning to the words you read or speak. Pitch is the element that contributes the most to vocal color and variety, as well as providing flexibility to interpret the words we say, adding additional layers of meaning through changes in key, step, and inflection.

The next chapter will present the characteristic of speech called *rate*—the fastness or slowness of speech, and the ways in which pauses and sound duration can change the meaning and add variety and interest to your voice. *Emphasis* is also covered in Chapter 7, although it is not just an element of rate. Emphasis occurs through changes in pitch and volume as well as rate.

You should be including voice practice in your daily life and study time. Go over all the exercises in this chapter and the previous one, working on a few each day. Is your ear for your own voice getting sharper? Do you hear flat and monotonous pitches? Has anyone asked you to speak louder? Do you run out of breath when you have to read aloud? Regular practice and honest self-monitoring will enable you to use your voice more effectively.

MEDIA COPY FOR PRACTICE

Network Newscasts

DATELINE: TOKYO

On Saturday, Japan's newly formed government urged the United States in unusually strong terms to get its economic house in order and do its part to support the dollar. Prime Minister Koto Nakura said he and his cabinet expect the United States to abide by an international agreement on stable currency exchange rates. The White House recently has indicated it will allow the dollar to slide rather than jeopardize the U.S. economy. The Japanese, still unwilling to discuss a voluntary trade balance policy, have been harsh in blaming Washington's budget deficit for recent heavy drops in stock markets around the world. Washington officials have not yet responded to this latest attack.

DATELINE: AMMAN, JORDAN

Arab leaders gathered Saturday for their largest summit in five years, and Jordan's foreign minister pledged they "will not fail" to reach agreement on a position towards Israel in the long-running Israeli-Palestinian conflict. But both Arab and Western officials expressed doubts that the meeting would produce the strong anti-Israeli stance that the Jordanian government seeks from other summit participants. A full color guard met leaders of the active members of the Arab League at Amman's military airport. The summit opens officially today with a speech by League leader Ali Nassan, a moderate whose peace plan has been given a tentative nod of approval by both sides. Washington officials, while hopeful of a settlement, have taken a "wait and see" position.

DATELINE: MEXICO

An Air Hispaniola DC-10 airliner with 141 people aboard crash-landed at Monterrey Airport when part of its main landing gear broke off, but there were no serious injuries, officials said yesterday. The exact circumstances of the Monday night crash remained unclear, but there were accounts of an engine fire and a hydraulic problem on the plane's left side. An Air Hispaniola employee at the airport referred inquiries to airline offices in Mexico City, but repeated calls to the number went unanswered. Air reservation offices in Dallas and Chicago had no information about the crash or about continued service into Monterrey.

DATELINE: SEOUL, SOUTH KOREA

Hundreds of students shouting "Fair elections" battled police at three universities Friday, and a dozen people shaved their heads to protest the opposition's failure to agree on one presidential candidate. Police fired tear gas at Seoul National University to disperse 1000 students hurling fire bombs and rocks. The violence broke out after a rally to demand formation of a neutral interim government to ensure the honesty of presidential elections, expected in mid-December. The government has rejected the demand. Seoul streets are quiet tonight, but officials fear another outbreak when classes resume on Monday.

DATELINE: WASHINGTON, D.C.

House Republicans Friday proposed a $30 billion deficit-reducing plan with the general backing of the White House, the first sign of significant progress in the bipartisan budget negotiations between Congress and the administration. Democrats did not embrace the proposal but said that it showed the first important movement by the administration toward accepting larger tax increases and less money for the military. Until Friday, the White House negotiators had shown no willingness to compromise on these issues. The proposal also calls for $14 billion in spending cuts, the sale of federal assets, and some fees for use of government services.

Local Newscasts

Railroad and utility crews spent another day at the scene of the fiery crash between a freight train and a gasoline tanker at the intersection of South Elm and Parker Streets. Long identified by both railroad workers and truckers as a dangerous crossing, the intersection has been closed since yesterday afternoon while crews work to restore telephone and electric wires melted when the 8,000 gallons of gasoline in the truck exploded and burned. Officials expect the work to be completed sometime late this evening. Meanwhile, all traffic to and from the airport has been rerouted over Walker Road. An investigation into the exact cause of the accident is under way.

There's a new man in the front office of the city's underground Metro system. Robert Martin is the new chief operations officer. He's no stranger to Metro—he's been director of administration and finance for five years. Martin says his first step will be to develop a new image for Metro, one that will offset the negative publicity from the series of holdups on the trains last year. No further incidents have occurred since a staff of security guards were hired to ride the lines. Martin wants to promote the image of a safe and clean environment in the subway. He replaces Thad Wallace, who retired earlier this year.

The Austin County health director, who had threatened to boycott next week's AIDS conference in Crestwood Park, has agreed to participate in the event after being pressured by county commissioners. Dr. David DeVito had stated earlier that he felt it was inappropriate for the Health Department to sponsor the conference because it had been planned without his knowledge and without the knowledge of the county commissioners, who make up the Board of Health. He added, however, that his office was deeply committed to the concept behind the conference—the further dissemination of information about AIDS. For this reason, he has agreed to attend the meeting, which begins on Monday morning.

An unusually high number of dead dolphins have been washing up on the beaches in Marino County recently, but it is not clear whether they died from the same bacteria that killed scores of the mammals on the East Coast this summer, officials say. Marine biologist Jack Concannon said dolphins have been migrating through the area, which could account for the number of dead ones washing ashore. But Professor Jim McDonald of the state university's Marine Institute disagreed. "They've been migrating for years and years, and if that was the case, we should have been seeing this high percentage of dead dolphins every year, but we have not. This is most unusual, and is probably the result of the red tide that swept the coast last week." Marine biologists continue to look for causes.

The number of brush fires across the state was reduced from 121 to 78 on Saturday, but officials said one fire in Pleasant Valley threatened several homes, and weather and wind conditions were providing no reason for optimism. Personnel from the Division of Emergency Management, as well as the Forestry Division, manned a command center in Anderson to keep watch over the fires. They were keeping a close eye on weather conditions, warning that although the number of fires and the acreage destroyed had decreased drastically from Friday to Saturday, the danger was still high. An Air Force National Guard team dropped over twenty tons of flame retardant onto key targets on Friday, thus containing several of the most dangerous areas. Fire fighters will remain on alert through the next several days, fearful that without rain, conditions could become critical.

Public Service Announcements

For just turning eighteen, I think I'm doing great. I've got a good job, I bought a car, and I'm going to college at night with the help of a federal loan. But right now, there's something special I've got to do—for myself and for my country. I've got to go to the post office and register with Selective Service. It's easy to do, it takes only a few minutes, and it's the law. Are you an eighteen-year-old male? Have you registered yet? You can complete this simple requirement at any downtown or branch post office. You owe it to yourself and to your country.

The fifteenth Art on Paper show, the largest art event at the Underwood Art Gallery on the A & M campus, opens October 23. More than 100 artworks by national and area artists will be displayed through November 29. Most of the drawings are contemporary, but a few date to the 1930s and 1940s and represent the work of established artists. The work of sixteen area artists, twelve from the A & M faculty and four city residents, will be displayed in the show. The gallery is open from 10 to 5 daily, and there is no admission charge. Through the past fifteen years, almost 2000 works have been shown in this annual display, sponsored by the Parker Paper Company. Most of the works in the show are for sale and can be purchased now, although the show will be left intact until it closes in late November.

The Greenhill Oratorio Society will begin rehearsals of its twenty-seventh presentation of Handel's *Messiah*, to be performed Sunday, December 7, in the Memorial Auditorium at the Greenville Avenue Civic Center. Joseph McGee, music director of the society, again will conduct the chorus and orchestra. Interested area singers may sing in the performance if they attend next Monday night's rehearsal, to be held at 7:30 in the sanctuary of St. Paul's United Methodist Church on Friendly Avenue. Rehearsals will be each Monday and Thursday during the month of November. Singers do not have to be members of the society in order to participate. Newcomers are welcome.

For a gastronomically glorious experience, be sure to attend the Food Festival at the Greenville Avenue Civic Center Friday through Sunday. The finest and freshest gourmet foods have been gathered from Italy, France, Spain, Mexico, and other countries participating in this unusual event. Booths will be well stocked with meats, cheeses, breads, oils, pastas, chilies, and ethnic foods of every variety. An array of luscious desserts from pastries to distinctive chocolates will round out this culinary extravaganza. Sponsored by the Restaurant Association of Greater Dallas, the Food Festival offers an outstanding opportunity to stock your pantry with hard-to-find specialties from around the world. Don't miss it!

An antique medical exhibit will be held at Eastern Medical College June 1 through 14. Featured will be exact replicas of a wide assortment of medical supplies, including complete surgical rooms and doctors' examining rooms, from turn-of-the-century offices and hospitals.

      The exhibit hours are 2 to 7 P.M. weekdays and Sunday, with doors open from 10 A.M. till 8 P.M. on Saturday. Mock surgical reenactments will be staged each day at 3 and 5 P.M. The public is encouraged to attend, free of charge. After the exhibit closes at Eastern, it will return to its home at the Smithsonian Institution, in Washington, D.C.

Commercials

Are you sitting on a fence? A fence that separates the future from the past? A fence between progress and stagnation? A fence that divides inexperienced, unseasoned leadership from experience and knowledge of state government? We can stay on the fence, or we can move ahead with Roger Thornton's strong leadership to set our feet on a forward course. So, let's get off the fence and get on with the business of effective state government by electing Roger Thornton as the next governor of North Dakota.

It's the season for keeping warm. Carter Furriers brings you a beautiful Norwegian blue fox jacket that will warm your soul as well as your body. This is the elegance you've dreamed of, just in time for the holiday season. The jacket comes in blue or black, sizes ten through sixteen, and can be bought at either our downtown or our Southpark store. Give yourself an early Christmas present, or hint to that special Santa Claus of yours that a jacket from Carter's would be the perfect addition to your holiday wardrobe. Carter Furriers is open until 10 P.M. Monday through Saturday for your shopping convenience.

The new Mercantile Bank Gold Account offers you a unique way to combine a credit card with an all-purpose line of credit. When you open a Gold Account, you automatically establish a $10,000 line of credit, and you may qualify for larger amounts based on your past savings record. Your special Gold Account Card will entitle you to make cash withdrawals of up to $500 a day until you reach your line-of-credit maximum. It also entitles you to free checking and free custom-designed, personally imprinted checks. Free traveler's checks and a no-fee credit card, as well as quarterly statements especially prepared to aid you in income tax preparation, are among the other exciting features available to qualified customers. Come in today and talk with your Mercantile banker about the Gold Account, an all-purpose approach to all your banking needs.

Carpetworld offers a special on Saxony Plush stain-resistant carpet, on sale this weekend only for the low price of $9.95 a yard, including padding and installation. A revolutionary breakthrough in carpet manufacture makes this the most stain-resistant carpet on the market—most household food and drinks wipe up easily, even after sitting overnight or for several days. We guarantee this is a first-quality carpet, free from manufacturing defects, which, with proper care and maintenance, will provide you years of pleasure and beauty. Our installation workmanship is of the highest professional standards demanded by the carpet industry. Call Carpetworld today, and one of our experienced sales agents will measure your home and give you an estimate free of charge.

Mothers-to-be will find exactly what they've been looking for at Expectantly Yours, the maternity shop located in the Broadmore Shopping Center. Expectantly Yours carries a complete line of dresses, pants, shirts, and underthings designed to flatter the figure of the expectant mother. Sundresses, swimsuits, and even designer jeans carry special labels from top designers—Argosy, Poile, Ravensly, to mention just a few. No need for the expectant mother to feel dowdy or to be depressed about her appearance. She can be a fashionplate in clothes from Expectantly Yours—Broadmore Shopping Center, West St., and Arden Road. Come in and see for yourself.

Rate and Emphasis

First among the evidences of an education I name correctness and precision in the use of the mother tongue.

—Nicholas Murray Butler

RATE

In addition to volume, pitch, and quality—the three major characteristics of voice—there is a fourth way to describe the production of human speech and its impact on the listener. In the preceding chapters, these characteristics were identified in terms of both production and listener impact. In production, volume is a matter of the intensity of vocal fold vibration, pitch is frequency, and quality is the combination of overtones and resonance. From the point of view of the listener, volume becomes a matter of loudness or softness, pitch of highness or lowness, and quality of richness and tone.

The fourth feature, **rate,** characterizes speech more than voice as such, yet with its components of rhythm, duration, and pause it is so integral to human oral communication that it must be viewed as a basic voice characteristic. Because rate, especially pausing, is a primary way of creating oral thought segments, **phrasing** is considered a part of rate. And since pausing and alterations in sound duration are key elements in stressing certain words or phrases in the overall utterance, *emphasis* is discussed in this chapter.

Unlike volume, pitch, and quality, *rate* means the same in terms of both production and listener impact: it is simply a matter of the fastness or slowness of the speech utterance. The words **tempo** and **timing** more accurately denote this phenomenon, for they refer specifically to the rate or velocity of any given passage of speech or music. *Rate* is commonly accepted among speech teachers to mean the overall slowness or rapidity of speech, and especially the time allotted to pauses.

Rate is often measured in the number of words spoken per minute. This measure can be somewhat misleading, since it does not account for the average number of syllables of the words in a passage. A highly complex, scientific essay might contain many words of five or six syllables. A simple children's story would probably have mostly two- and three-syllable words. This difference will obviously affect the number of words read per minute. Despite this limitation, there are some guidelines for determining whether your overall rate is too fast or too slow.

The rapidity of any segment of speech is determined by three factors: the duration of the individual sounds, the speed of assimilating and blending one word into the next, and the presence or absence of pauses. Use the following exercise to assess your overall rate in terms of words per minute (WPM) before moving on to duration, word blending, and pauses.

YOUR WPM RATE

Read the following paragraph through twice to yourself to make sure you understand it and can read it aloud without stumbling. Then, using a clock or watch with an accurate second hand, read the passage aloud. Note the number of seconds that have elapsed at the three checkpoints indicated in the text. Do this quickly out of the corner of your eye, but don't stop reading. Better, have someone else time the reading for you.

> The word *rate,* like many words in our language, has a number of different meanings. It may mean a placed value, such as the rate charged for goods or services, or the ratio of value used to assess taxes. *Rate* may describe a relative quality or condition, as when we say "at any rate" to mean "anyway." To *rate* can mean to regard or consider, as in "The judges rated his performance the highest of any contestant." *Rate* can mean rank, as in "We rated in the top 10 percent of the class." Special rank or privilege is implied in the phrase "She really rated," although that particular usage may be considered slang by some purists.

(time check 1)

> Currency from one country is transferred into currency from another country at a given rate of exchange for that particular day. The number of miles a vehicle can travel in a given period is its speed, another form of rate.

(time check 2)

> In the navy, a ship is rated by its force or magnitude. *Rate* also has the totally different meaning of scold or chide, perhaps more familiar to you in the kindred word *berate. Rate* is certainly a word of many meanings.

(time check 3)

If you reached one minute at checkpoint 1, you are reading too slowly. If, however, you made it almost to checkpoint 3 before one minute elapsed, your rate may be overly rapid. Reaching checkpoint 2 in sixty seconds is about the average rate.

The average rate for material of average complexity that is read aloud or delivered partially prepared, as in the case of an extemporaneous speech delivered from an outline, is between 145 and 175 WPM. Conversational speech tends to be a bit faster, although individual segments of conversation are usually shorter than one minute, so an even rate is more difficult to measure. Listeners can process short speech segments that are overly fast more easily than they can handle long passages that are too rapid.

If your average rate is from 115 to 130 WPM, you are probably speaking too slowly and will lose the attention of your listeners. From 130 to 145 is somewhat slower than average, but might be suitable for passages of highly complex or difficult material, especially if the listeners are expected to retain details, as with the more important parts of lectures. Somber emotional passages or eulogies are often read at slower rates.

A rate between 175 and 190 WPM is on the fast side, but would be appropriate for light or humorous material, or prose of intensified emotions, such as exciting descriptions or narrations of fear or chase scenes. Past 200, you will be perceived as speaking very rapidly. Although most listeners can process rapid rates, they cannot continue to give attention over time, for such processing is much more difficult and straining than listening at more conventional rates.

Compare your rate with the suggested times for the following passages. You don't have to duplicate these times, but extreme variation should cause you to question your rate. These passages are designed especially to show how language choice and mood can affect WPM rate.

Arthritis
(127 words—one minute)

Arthritis terminologically defines a complex classification of rheumatic diseases affecting the joints and connective tissue. Nonarticular rheumatic conditions include fibrositis and bursitis, inflammatory processes that best respond to a combined physiotherapy and use of anti-inflammatory agents to reduce swelling and pain. Osteoarthritis causes a degenerative change in the cartilage within the joints and may lead to crippling if deterioration is severe. The great crippler, however, is rheumatoid arthritis. While its manifestations are primarily in the joints, systemic involvement is commonplace. The inflammatory process affects the actual lining of the joints, and the synovial membrane secretes excessive viscid lubricating fluid, causing swelling. Treatment for rheumatoid arthritis includes rest, mild exercise, and drugs ranging from simple acetylsalicylic acid (aspirin) to the complex Adrenocorticosteroids, or synthetic steroids.

Charlie's Pride
(155 words—one minute)

The solemn little procession moved slowly up the narrow street. The six pallbearers handled the plain wooden casket with seeming ease, yet not one of them looked strong enough to make the trek from the State Street Funeral Parlor to the small cemetery where Charlie's pennies, paid weekly for so many years, had reserved a space especially for him. Only a few other souls straggled along beside the shabby cortege. Charlie had lived longer than most of his associates, those who shared warmth from trash-can fires, drafts from cheap bottles of wine, and bunks at the Salvation Army when winter made street sleeping too miserable and too dangerous. His monthly pension check had furnished him better food and warmer clothing than those without income—and the ultimate luxury of his own cemetery lot. "I don't know where I'll sleep tonight," he used to say, "but I know where I'll go for my final sleep."

Decided by a Hare
(200 words—one minute)

Billy Boy Bunny hopped and jumped with joy as he saw his mother coming back toward their home in a hollow hole near the root of an old oak tree. She was carrying the better half of a fresh carrot in her mouth, and he knew the tasty treat was for him. But about that time, his brother, Barnabus Bunny, woke from a nice long nap, stretched, scratched his ears, and said, "My, I'm hungry!" As he looked out the door of the hole, he, too, saw Mother Rabbit nearing their home. "Oh, good," he said, "Mama is bringing me a carrot. Just what I wanted!"

Billy Boy began to fret and worry, for he knew that even if Mama gave him the carrot, Barnabus would take it away from him, just as he always did. "I hate him," Billy Boy thought to himself. "I hate him because he is bigger and stronger than I am, and he is mean."

Mama Bunny arrived, and in no time sensed the conflict between her two sons, just as wise mothers usually know when their children are troubled. So she promptly ate the carrot herself, with Billy Boy and Barnabus looking on forlornly.

Duration

When you learned the orthographic alphabet and its accompanying diacritical marks, you learned that orthographic vowels have both long and short versions, usually marked *ā* for the long *a*, or *ă*, for the short *a*, for example, each with its own pronunciation. The phonetic alphabet has a different symbol for each sound and separates vowels from diphthongs. The concept of long and short is not retained in the symbols assigned to the sounds in the IPA, but the idea of length in individual phonemes is an important and useful way of getting at some major pronunciation problems.

Individual sound length is called **duration.** As you have seen, duration is one of the elements of speech rate. Certain phonemes are inherently longer than others. While some differences exist among the consonants, the widest variation is in the vowels and diphthongs. Consider the length difference between [ɪ], [ɛ], [æ], or [ʊ], all short sounds, and [i], [eɪ], [aɪ], or [u], all longer phonemes. Under certain circumstances any of these sounds may be altered in duration, but in general the vowels divide as follows:

Short	Medium	Long
ɪ	e	i
ɛ		eɪ
æ		ɑ
a		ɔ
	o	oʊ
ʊ		u
ɚ		ɝ
ə	ʌ	
		aɪ
		ɔɪ
		aʊ

The primary difference between the sounds in each of the following pairs is one of duration, with the diphthongs including the slight slide into another pure vowel:

e — eɪ

o — oʊ

ə — ɝ

ə — ʌ

The variant [ɒ] is a short sound that occurs between the two longer back vowels [ɑ] and [ɔ]. The primary difference between the vowels in *far* and *hot* is duration. [ɔ] can also be produced in varying lengths—long in *saw* or fairly short in *awkward*.

When short sounds are held longer than they should be held, a pure vowel may be turned into a diphthong. If you call your pet a [kæ ət], you've turned [æ] into a diphthong [æə]. The same would be true for [hɪ ət] for *hit*, or [bʊ ək] for *book*. Sometimes elongation is so extreme that the result is a triphthong—[kæɪət] for *cat*—or even the addition of the consonant [j], as in [kæjət].

Deliberately elongate the following short vowels in order to hear the difference:

1. fill [fɪ əl]
2. set [sɛ ət]
3. bag [bæ əg]
4. pick [pɪ ək]
5. kiss [kɪj əs]
6. bed [bɛ jəd]
7. cab [kæ jəb]
8. with [wɪ jəθ]
9. egg [eɪjəg]
10. Dallas [Dæɪjələs]

Now repeat the words, keeping the vowel short and crisp. Concentrate on moving quickly to the consonant that follows the vowel.

The other primary problem of duration is just the opposite—failing to give enough time to the longer vowels, particularly the diphthongs. If a diphthong is shortened, we usually omit the second of the two pure vowel sounds. For instance:

Word	Problem
fail [feɪl]	[eɪ] is shortened and shifted downward in the front of the mouth to [ɛ], resulting in [fɛl].
my [maɪ]	Becomes [ma] or is shifted slightly backward to the bottom of the mouth to [mɑ].
oil [ɔɪl]	Becomes [ɔl].
down [daʊn]	[ʊ] is omitted, changed to [ə], or shifted slightly upward in the front of the mouth to produce [dæən].

In a few dialects such as that of the Atlantic tidewater region, speakers alter the diphthong [aʊ] by dropping the first rather than the second pure phoneme, while shifting slightly from the [ʊ] to the [u] position. This gives [ə but ðə hus] for *about the house*, for example.

The diphthong [oʊ] suffers from shortening mostly at the ends of words where the stress is divided between the two syllables rather than being strongly on one or the other or where [o] is probably more appropriate. The central vowel [ə] is substituted for the [o], so that *yellow* becomes [jɛ lə]. In a more extreme substitution, [ɚ] is used, resulting in [jɛ lɚ].

When the front vowel [i] is not given sufficient time to develop fully, [ɪ] usually results, particularly in words followed by the consonant [l]. *Feel* may be said as [fɪl], or *heel* as [hɪl].

Experiment with the length of the vowel sounds in the following words:

Long	Short	Long	Short
heap	hip	spite	spit
bait	bet	foil	fall
seal	sill	loin	lawn
eye	eh	sound	sand
age	edge	fellow	Feller

Although the durational differences among consonants are not as wide or subject to as much diversity among various speakers as are those among the vowels and diphthongs, some subtle differences exist. These subtleties are most noticeable in comparisons of the voiced and voiceless fricatives; the voiced version of each cognate pair tends to be longer. Compare the consonants in the following pairs, noticing the slight elongation of the voiced sound:

Initial		Final	
feel	veal	leaf	leave
face	vase	half	have
thigh	thy	sooth	soothe
thin	then	sheath	sheathe
sue	zoo	base	bays
seal	zeal	niece	knees
shah	Zsa Zsa	ruche	rouge
Shawn	genre	ash	azure

Duration is an excellent way of adding vocal color to your speech. Many words with short vowels connote fast motion or quickness. Examples would be *quick, fast, flick, flit, twitter, rapid, snap, lickety-split, zip, whiz, sprint, clap, dash,* and *scamper.* If in saying these words you give only a short duration to the vowel, you will enhance their meaning. Many words that contain long vowels or diphthongs connote distance or longer time; these can be enhanced by giving longer duration to the vowel. Such words might include *slow, long, far, wide, high, bawl, mope, drawn out, louder, dawdle, creep, crawl, poke along,* and *lazy*.

Not only individual words but sentences, paragraphs, or whole selections may have greater impact if you work on the duration of sounds. Flexibility in articulating phonemes allows you to make your sounds more crisp or staccato if you wish. Reading material that is brisk, fast-moving, lighthearted, or highly tense might call for a throbbing, clattering, rat-a-tat liveliness suggested by shortened duration. On the other hand, you can slow down your overall production of vowels and, by use of more legato, suggest a slower, calmer, easier-going mood and setting. Try for variation of duration in the following sentences.

Words do not change their meanings so drastically in the course of centuries as, in our minds, names do in the course of a year or two.

—MARCEL PROUST

Crisp, Short Words—Cut the Sounds Short:

1. "Quick," said Will. "Billy fell in the well and is yelling."
2. He let the cat out of the bag when he whispered the facts about Annie.
3. "Sit on it," Ed irreverently instructed Elmer when he was fed up with him.
4. Flip the flapjacks and stack them in the pan on the back burner.
5. Jack's utter stupidity left him without a thought in his head.
6. Above the dusty cabbage patch the blackbirds flocked looking for tidbits.
7. As fast as you can, run after that brat who kicked me in the shin!
8. The man grabbed an apple off the shelf and began to nibble it without even thinking that it wasn't his.
9. We played kick-the-can in the alley in back of the tenement building.
10. The squirrels chittered and chattered as they ran up and down the trunks of the elm tree.
11. *Wham! Bam! Zip!* and *Zap!* are words used when Batman and Robin catch criminals.
12. It is silly to tickle little kids in the ribs until they giggle and snicker.
13. The hummingbird flitted quickly from the wisteria to the redbud, searching for nectar.
14. I zipped my zipper, flipped on my slippers, and slipped into the back of the class at fifteen after.
15. "The Trouble with Tribbles" was an episode in which Captain Kirk encountered an unusual dilemma.
16. We clapped the erasers against the blackboard to get rid of the chalk dust.
17. We went to bed just after we had let the cat out and cut off the heat.
18. The trucker carried a cot and a pad to make a bed in the back of his van.
19. Fred read to his kids from a big yellow book with pictures.
20. Let's plan a quick trip to Mississippi.

Long, Slower Words—Hold the Duration:

1. The old coal-mine shaft was damp and drafty.
2. Long, lazy days in July and August spoil me for fall's heavy work load.
3. The wounded boy dragged his lame knee painfully behind as he tried to walk.
4. The roll of the ocean is a sound that pounds on the coastline night and day.
5. Slowly and ploddingly we worked our way along the icy highway during the storm.

6. Uphold the oath you have taken to be a loyal patriot of the United States of America.

7. "Smile while your heart breaks" is the theme of at least a thousand songs, stories, and poems.

8. Great and famous leaders do not come along during every decade.

9. Boy wore a loincloth just like Tarzan's, while Jane was more modestly clothed.

10. How long have you owned your house in the mountains?

11. Row, row, row the boat, but don't go into the ocean in an open rowboat.

12. Skylarks fly high into the sky, then swoop downward toward the ground.

13. Romeo, Othello, Bassanio, Petruchio, Iago, Orlando, Antonio, and Horatio are but a few of the names that show Shakespeare's fondness for final *o*'s.

14. The coils in an automobile must be oiled often or they will foul up and fail to operate, causing an awful, annoying noise.

15. 1 like a night-light to show me the way when I sleep in a strange house.

16. *Three Coins in the Fountain* was a movie set in Rome, a beautiful European city.

17. Open oodles of oblong noodles so you can create a tasty treat for our evening meal.

18. Her downtown penthouse was high in a tall tower overlooking the surrounding panorama.

19. Hamoud found an old towel useful for wiping oil from his new boots.

20. I don't know why Clarice employs only a few students.

Read the following poem on colors and think about its images. Note that the word meaning is enhanced through long and short vowel sounds.

> White is a slow color, for it is snow,
>   clouds, diapers, and old age.
> Black is faster—a big badness, magic,
>   ebony, a pit of embers.
> Green is very long—trees, fields, new
>   and unripe, doubts, and green-eyed
>   monsters.
> Red is quick—blood bleeding, anger flashing,
>   young things blushing.
> Gold is leisurely, with its coins, curls, chrome
>   on my Chrysler, the canary's cage.
> Pink leaps up with pinafores, petunias, healthy
>   infants, cherubs' skin.
> Gray and brown move slowly by—drizzles,
>   ashes, earth, grass in winter.
> Colors move, and in their motion lies a
>   world of images and secret thoughts.

The following passages from Shakespeare also demonstrate the effectiveness of using short and long sounds.

SHORT SOUNDS

> Eye of newt, and toe of frog,
> Wool of bat, and tongue of dog,
> Adder's fork, and blindworm's sting,
> Lizard's leg, and howlet's wing
>
> —*Macbeth*

Scale of dragon, tooth of wolf,
Witch's mummy, maw and gulf
Of the ravined salt-sea shark,
Root of hemlock digged i' th' dark,

—*Macbeth*

This is the excellent foppery of the world, that when we are sick in fortune, often the surfeits of our own behavior, we make guilty of our disasters the sun, the moon, the stars; as if we were villains of necessity; fools by heavenly compulsion; knaves, thieves, and treachers by spherical predominance; drunkards, liars, and adulterers by an enforced obedience of planetary influence; and all that we are evil in, by a divine thrusting on. An admirable evasion of whoremaster man, to lay his goatish disposition on the charge of a star.

—*King Lear*

I have of late—but wherefore I know not—lost all my mirth, forgone all custom of exercises; and indeed, it goes so heavily with my disposition that this goodly frame the earth seems to me a sterile promontory;

—*Hamlet*

What a piece of work is a man, how noble in reason, how infinite in faculties; in form and moving how express and admirable, in action how like an angel, in apprehension how like a god: the beauty of the world, the paragon of animals!

—*Hamlet*

And who doth lead them but a paltry fellow,
Long kept in Britain at our mother's cost,
A milksop, one that never in his life
Felt so much cold as over shoes in snow?

—*King Richard the Third*

If we be conquered, let men conquer us,
And not these bastard Britaines, whom our fathers
Have in their own land beaten, bobb'd, and thump'd,
And, in record, left them the heirs of shame.

—*King Richard the Third*

LONG SOUNDS

Now entertain conjecture of a time
When creeping murmur and the poring dark
Fills the wide vessel of the universe.
From camp to camp, through the foul womb of night,
The hum of either army stilly sounds,
That the fixed sentinels almost receive
The secret whispers of each other's watch.

—*King Henry the Fifth*

The poor condemned English,
Like sacrifices, by their watchful fires
Sit patiently and inly ruminate
The morning's danger; and their gesture sad,

Investing lank-lean cheeks and war-worn coats,
Presenteth them unto the gazing moon
So many horrid ghosts.

—King Henry the Fifth

When sorrows come, they come not single spies,
But in battalions: first, her father slain;
Next, your son gone, and he most violent author
Of his own just remove; the people muddied,
Thick and unwholesome in their thoughts and whispers
For good Polonius' death, and we have done but greenly
In hugger-mugger to inter him;

—Hamlet

Foul whis'prings are abroad. Unnatural deeds
Do breed unnatural troubles. Infected minds
To their deaf pillows will discharge their secrets.
More needs she the divine than the physician.

—Macbeth

To-morrow, and to-morrow, and to-morrow,
Creeps in this petty pace from day to day,
To the last syllable of recorded time;
And all our yesterdays have lighted fools
The way to dusty death.

—Macbeth

Out, out, brief candle!
Life's but a walking shadow, a poor player
That struts and frets his hour upon the stage
And then is heard no more. It is a tale
Told by an idiot, full of sound and fury,
Signifying nothing.

—Macbeth

. . . like the baseless fabric of this vision,
The cloud-capped tow'rs, the gorgeous palaces,
The solemn temples, the great globe itself,
Yea, all which it inherit, shall dissolve,
And, like this insubstantial pageant faded,
Leave not a rack behind.

—The Tempest

Assimilation

Ifyourunallyourwordstogetherlikethisitdoesn'tmatterhowcarefulyouareaboutduration foryourspeechratewillsoundawful. This problem is the opposite of "I / see / the / dog, / the / dog / sees / the / cat" style of reading, where words are presented almost in isolation. The latter approach characterizes the beginning-to-learn reader or a person who has poor skills in reading aloud. The first, run-together sentence suggests the overly rapid reader or speaker who lets each word tumble out of the mouth, bumping into the words before and after it.

Sounds in natural speech are assimilated, that is, a sound is blended into the sounds that go before and after it. Words are also assimilated into the words that precede and follow them as they are blended together to create thought groups and sen-

---

FYI . . . _____

Have you ever heard a drive-through attendant over the speaker as you try to place your order? "Can o'tacure border fleas?" Through the crackling static, did you make out "Can I take your order, please?" When you have ordered, you may hear "ankoo. Dry roun' peas," so you'll know you've been thanked and told to "Drive around, please." Clear articulation could help these transmissions significantly.

tences. Thought groups and their separation will be discussed in the next section on pausing. In preparation for that section, practice the following exercises to make sure you are assimilating sounds correctly. Overassimilation results when a speaker goes too fast and fails to pronounce all the sounds. The result is not only the slurring of sounds, but in many cases, the actual omission of required phonemes, particularly those at the ends of words. While a few people may speak so deliberately that they sound staccato and stiff, far more are guilty of rushing and slurring so that they seem to mumble and swallow their words.

Say the following phrases first overly deliberate, then slurred, then correctly.

Phrase	Overly Deliberate	Slurred
1. did you?	[dɪd/ju]	[dɪ dʒju or [dɪ dʒə]
2. right now	[raɪt/naʊ]	[rɑ naʊ]
3. it is a	[ɪt/ɪz/ə]	[ɪs ə]
4. give me	[gɪv/mi]	[gɪmɪ]
5. watch out	[watʃ/aʊt]	[ʃaʊt]
6. I wish you would	[aɪ/wɪʃ/ju/wʊd]	[ɑ ɪʃ jud]
7. Did you eat?	[dɪd/ju/it]	[dʒit]
8. go to the show	[goʊ/tu/ðə/ʃoʊ]	[gɔt ð foʊ]
9. how do you do?	[haʊ/du/ju/du]	[haʊ du]
10. cats and dogs*	[kæts/ænd/dɔgz]	[kæs n dɔgz]
11. big and little	[bɪg/ænd/lɪt əl]	[bɪg ɪt lɪl]
12. up and out	[ʌp/ænd/aʊt]	[ʌpn naʊt]

Omission of phonemes can occur in the middle of a word as well as at the ends of words in connected speech. This is a pronunciation problem, yet it often results from faulty timing and overassimilation. Do you tend to omit a sound or syllable in the following words?

Word	Do You Say?
probably	[prɑ blɪ]
secretary	[sɛ kə tɛrɪ]
interesting	[ɪn ɚ stɪŋ]
government	[gʌv ɚ mənt]
environment	[ɪn vaɪr mənt]
usually	[juz lɪ]
something	[sʌm (p) n]
strength	[strɛnθ]
virtually	[vɝtʃlɪ]
company	[kʌmp nɪ]
laboratory	[læb ə torɪ]
library	[laɪ bɛr ɪ]
history	[hɪs trɪ]
geography	[dʒɑg rə fɪ]
interpretation	[ɪn tɚ pə te ʃn]

Many words have certain sounds that change as the word moves from a stressed to an unstressed position in a phrase or sentence. Such variation is not only acceptable but desirable and is not an assimilation problem. It would, however, be a pro-

*In the [t] in *cat,* the *stop* position of the stop-plosive consonant is formed but the *plosive* is not. You can feel this in your mouth by putting your tongue in the position for [t], then moving to the next phoneme without completing the plosive.

nunciation problem if the unstressed sound were used in a word that is intentionally emphasized to create an unusual interpretation. A familiar illustration of this point is the word *of*. Most of the time we pronounce it [əv]. Yet if you are reading Lincoln's Gettysburg Address, you would need to say "[ɑv] the people," not "[əv] the people."

The following words change according to the degree of emphasis they are accorded in a sentence:

Word	Stressed	Unstressed	Should Not Be
of	[ɑv]	[əv]	[ʌv]
was	[wɑz]	[wəz]	[wʌz]
for	[fɔr]	[fər] or [fɚ]	[fɝ]
when	[ʍɛn]	[ʍən]	[ʍɪn]
from	[frɑm]	[frəm]	[frʌm]
you	[ju]	[jə]	[jʌ]
and	[ænd]	[nd] or [n]	[ənd] or [ən]
or	[ɔr]	[ər] or [ɚ]	[ɝ]
to	[tu]	[tə]	[tʌ]
be	[bi]	[bɪ]	[bə]

To sensitize yourself to assimilation, try timing word pickup with others. First, go around the class with a series of telescoped sentences. **Telescoping** is a process in which the second speaker says the first word of his phrase or sentence at exactly the same time that the first speaker says the last word of her phrase or sentence; the third person repeats with the second person; and so forth. If we were to transcribe the process, it would look like this:

1.   Apples are <u>red</u>.
2.   <u>Trees</u> are <u>green</u>.
3.   <u>Clouds</u> are <u>white</u>.
4.   <u>Buttercups</u> are <u>yellow</u>.
5.   <u>And</u> so on.

Continue practicing until group members are always timing the first and last words exactly together:

6. <u>Dirt</u> is <u>brown</u>.
7. <u>Cheeks</u> are <u>pink</u>.
8. <u>Royal</u> robes are <u>purple</u>.
9. <u>Fresh</u> carrots are <u>orange</u>.
10. <u>Dark</u> red is <u>magenta</u>.
11. <u>Pale</u> purple is <u>lavender</u>.
12. <u>Summer</u> skies are <u>blue</u>.
13. <u>Winter</u> skies are <u>gray</u>.
14. <u>Some</u> cars are <u>beige</u>.
15. <u>Spades</u> and clubs are <u>black</u>.
16. <u>Yellow</u> and green make <u>chartreuse</u>.
17. <u>Coins</u> and candlesticks are <u>silver</u>.
18. <u>Deep</u>, rolling seas are <u>azure</u>.
19. <u>Red</u> and purple make <u>fuchsia</u>.
20. <u>Crowns</u> and curls are <u>golden</u>.
21. <u>Nothing</u> I know is puce.

As you no doubt have discovered, telescoping is difficult because it prevents us from hearing the complete idea. It is even more difficult in the middle of a thought than at the beginning and end of sentences. Practice the following in a group until you can time the telescoping perfectly. Note that all speakers in the group must assimilate carefully to have the exercise work smoothly.

1. Once upon a time, a little girl <u>dreamed</u>
2. <u>she</u> visited a Christmas tree. <u>The</u>

3. <u>little</u> girl, whose name was Meg, had a <u>lively</u>
4. <u>imagination</u>. Often she would lie under the Christmas <u>tree</u>
5. <u>looking</u> up through its branches at the <u>bright</u>
6. <u>lights</u> and garlands of tinsel. What fun it would <u>be,</u>
7. <u>she</u> thought, if I were only two <u>inches</u>
8. <u>tall</u> and could climb all the way to the <u>top.</u>
9. <u>One</u> evening, a few days before <u>Christmas,</u>
10. <u>she</u> was in her favorite spot under the tree, looking <u>up,</u>
11. <u>when</u> she fell asleep. In her dream, she <u>met</u> a
12. <u>wonderful</u> clown named Snowy. Together <u>they</u>
13. <u>set</u> out to climb the tree. But being only two <u>inches</u>
14. <u>tall,</u> Meg found she could not make <u>it to</u>
15. <u>the first</u> branch off the floor. Snowy <u>used a</u>
16. <u>broomstraw</u> he found on the floor to pole-<u>vault</u>
17. <u>into</u> the tree, then lowered icicles for Meg to <u>climb.</u>
18. <u>Together</u> they visited colored glass balls, <u>birds,</u>
19. <u>cherubs,</u> soldiers, and many special <u>decorations,</u>
20. <u>finally</u> arriving at the star on the very top of the tree.

Now read the story again, but this time do not telescope. Rather, the second speaker should pick up immediately *after* the first, so that the result is a completely smooth phrase, just as if only one person had spoken it.

Read the following sentences, being careful not to overassimilate: do not slur the sounds together too much. Blend the sounds naturally, however, so that you are not stiff and choppy.

1. Did you eat your dinner before you came over here?
2. Would you like to go to the show with me tomorrow evening?
3. Where did you get your jeans and shirt—Penney's or Sears?
4. Get your big feet off that wooden chair, and don't you scratch it.
5. I'm going to give you just ten seconds more to let go of my book.
6. What did you do over the weekend? Did you go sailing?
7. It was raining cats and dogs, and I couldn't find my umbrella.
8. What do you call a bunch of guys who don't know what to do on Saturday night?
9. I'll bet you a dime that my team is better than your team.
10. Give me all those matches that you've been playing with.
11. I wish you wouldn't get your dander up every time I ask you a question.
12. It's a safe bet that she wouldn't touch okra with a ten-foot pole.
13. You'll find it right here when you come back from hunting and fishing.
14. Did you ever watch the way the young ones follow after their mothers?
15. Can't you keep your dirty fingers off your clean shirt?
16. Why can't you just enjoy your dinner without counting calories and enumerating nutritional elements?
17. Quit your bellyaching and complaining and get on with what you have to do.
18. Don't you think you ought to ask Professor Acton if you can see her after class?

Pauses

The third major determinant of rate is the time allotted between sentences, phrases, or words—that absence of sound called a **pause.** Pausing is the principal way of dividing thought groups. It is also a means for stressing certain words or groups of words.

A pause is much more than a blank space in a series of speech sounds. The expression *pregnant pause* is sometimes used to convey the sense of fullness and expectation that a well-delivered pause can create. Pauses require careful timing to be effective. Too short a pause fails to give listeners the needed time for absorption of the sounds and images. An overly long pause will result in the loss of listeners' attention—their thoughts may wander, or they may think the speaker has forgotten something.

Over the years we have found only a few students whose pauses were too long. But we have found many who failed to allow enough time between thought groups and sentences. Either the pauses were too short, or the speakers failed to pause often enough. Racing from one idea to the next without pausing makes the speaker sound thoughtless and hurried, as if he or she is merely rattling off a series of words without real meaning.

Meaningless pauses in the middle of a phrase or thought group are another potential problem. These can result from poor breathing techniques. As a general rule, we inhale during pauses. If the speaker runs out of breath before the end of a thought group, a broken phrase may occur. This is less of a problem in speaking than in reading, for speakers phrase more logically when generating their own sentences; people construct ideas in thought segments, which are inherently tied to inhalation. Material that is memorized or read from a manuscript, however, lacks the spontaneity of the speaker's creativity in syntax and word choice; it therefore presents more problems in making phrases and pauses natural and linked to meaning.

Attempts to alter rate and the time allotted to pauses by instructing the speaker to slow down are usually unsuccessful. The rattling speaker must learn to control tempo by thinking about the message and the meaning to be conveyed. "Think the thought" rather than "read the word" suggests the necessary approach. The result is an image of "ownership" of the message that the listener receives. The speaker conveys the impression that he or she is making up the words and that this is the first time they have been spoken. This desired spontaneity is the reason most public speaking instructors insist on the use of extemporaneous style—major ideas of the speech are outlined and rehearsed, but the precise words are chosen as the speaker delivers the speech, not written down and read or memorized.

Words, like eyeglasses, blur everything that they do not make more clear.

—Joseph Joubert

A **thought group** may be a phrase, a clause, or a sentence. One sentence may be a single thought group or may be made up of two or more thought groups. How many thought groups are in this sentence?

The little boy and his dog wandered slowly along the dusty path in the late afternoon.

Total agreement on the number of thought groups in any sentence would be impossible to reach, for we do not all interpret a text in precisely the same manner. However, most readers would agree that this particular sentence contains at least three thought groups:

1. The little boy and his dog
2. wandered slowly along the dusty path
3. in the late afternoon

Three aspects of the basic idea are identifiable: *who* did *what* and *when*. You could easily argue that the second aspect consists of two ideas—*what* and *where*. The sentence, then, contains either three or four thought groups.

However, this is such a short sentence and the three aspects of the idea are so interwoven that no significant pause is required to separate the thought groups. They hold together as a single unit and can be read through on one breath.

Suppose we added another phrase:

The little boy and his dog, having tired of fishing, wandered slowly along the dusty path in the late afternoon.

The new thought group has injected a different idea into the sentence, a contrast that does not flow freely in a single thought, as did the original sentence. To enable a listener to follow the shift in idea, the reader must pause before and after this new phrase. Try reading the sentence both without and with the pauses.

(no pause)   The little boy and his dog having tired of fishing wandered slowly along the dusty path in the late afternoon.

(pauses)   The little boy and his dog, having tired of fishing, wandered slowly along the dusty path in the late afternoon.

Do you hear the real difference when the pauses are included? Suddenly the sentence makes sense and seems logical. Thought groups are logical relationships among words that enable those words to create an idea. Pauses are the oral device for signifying the division between thought groups.

The following exercises will help you to control the timing of your pauses. But you must remember to think carefully about the groupings of words and their meanings as you read. Mechanical devices alone will not solve rate and pausing problems.

EXERCISES FOR PAUSING

1. *Punctuation.* Punctuation frequently gives a clue to phrasing. Most major sections of a paragraph are separated by periods, and commas or dashes separate units within sentences. Although readers often add oral punctuation—pauses where no punctuation mark is found in the printed sentence—they seldom totally ignore the author's punctuation, for it is a guide to conveying the intended meaning.

   Read the following phrases, noting the different groupings suggested by punctuation marks. A comma suggests a lesser pause than a semicolon or period.

   1. One, two, three; four, five, six.
   2. One two; three four five, six.
   3. One two, three four, five six.
   4. One, two three, four, five six.
   5. One two three four; five, six.
   6. A, B, C, D, E, F, G.
   7. A B C, D, E F G.
   8. A B, C D, E F, G.
   9. A B C D; E, F, G.
   10. A, B C; D, E F; G.
   11. Red, green, blue, brown, black, white.
   12. Red green, blue brown, black white.
   13. Red; green, blue, brown; black, white.
   14. Red, green, blue; brown, black, white.
   15. Red, green, blue brown black; white.
   16. John, Tom, Ralph, Bob, and Henry.
   17. John Tom, Ralph Bob, and Henry.
   18. John, Tom Ralph, Bob and Henry.

19. John Tom, Ralph, Bob and Henry.

20. John Tom, Ralph Bob and Henry.

2. How do the following sentences change in meaning with the addition of punctuation marks?

1. (a) They had ice cream cake and candy at the party.

    (b) They had ice cream, cake, and candy at the party.

2. (a) Dogs and cats as well as rats and mice are kept in cages.

    (b) Dogs and cats, as well as rats and mice, are kept in cages.

3. (a) And then my friends walk with me.

    (b) And then, my friends, walk with me.

4. (a) My daughter Jane won a scholarship to college.

    (b) My daughter, Jane, won a scholarship to college.

5. (a) Ralph Terry and I are going skiing next weekend.

    (b) Ralph, Terry, and I are going skiing next weekend.

6. (a) I'm sorry I don't know how to spell it.

    (b) I'm sorry, I don't know how to spell it.

7. (a) Charles, an unforeseen problem has arisen.

    (b) Charles, an unforeseen problem, has arisen.

8. (a) He knew it was a light switch left on.

    (b) He knew it—was a light switch left on?

9. (a) I will; be cool!

    (b) I will be cool!

10. (a) The children would like to play, teacher.

    (b) The children would like to play teacher.

11. (a) And now you are on your own, Mother.

    (b) And now you are on your own mother.

12. (a) Repeat "many" hundreds of times.

    (b) Repeat many hundreds of times.

13. (a) How can you be yourself all the time?

    (b) How can you—be yourself all the time.

14. (a) Timmy your brother is here.

    (b) Timmy, your brother, is here.

15. (a) All my friends I know are at the party.

    (b) All my friends, I know, are at the party.

16. (a) Butter your bread and roll while it's hot.

    (b) Butter your bread, and roll while it's hot.

17. (a) Nureyev said, "The dancer is talented."

    (b) "Nureyev," said the dancer, "is talented."

18. (a) Nobody cares why you were the winner.

    (b) Nobody cares why—you were the winner.

    (c) Nobody cares—why, you were the winner!

19. (a) Don't ask me why—I'm with you.

    (b) Don't ask me why I'm with you.

20. (a) I don't think I know.

    (b) I don't think—I know!

3. A major problem in reading poetry aloud is phrasing it according to the layout on the line, rather than where it makes sense—between thought groups. Simply because you come to the end of a line is no assurance that the thought is complete. In the following poems, we have used a continuation mark—⌒—at the ends of lines where you might be tempted to break a phrase.

"Home Thoughts from Abroad"
ROBERT BROWNING

Oh, to be in England
   Now that April's there,
And whoever wakes in England ⌒
   Sees, some morning, unaware,
That the lowest boughs and the brushwood sheaf ⌒
   Round the elm-tree bole are in tiny leaf,
While the chaffinch sings on the orchard bough
   In England—now!

"An Old Sweetheart of Mine"
JAMES WHITCOMB RILEY

I can see pink sunbonnet and the
   little checkered dress ⌒
She wore when first I kissed her and she
   answered the caress
With the written declaration that, "as ⌒
   surely as the vine ⌒
Grew 'round the stump," she loved me,
   —that old sweetheart of mine.

"The Walrus and the Carpenter"
LEWIS CARROLL

The sun was shining on the sea,
   Shining with all his might:
He did his very best to make ⌒
   The billows smooth and bright—
And this was odd, because it was ⌒
   The middle of the night.

"Delight in Disorder"
ROBERT HERRICK

A sweet disorder in the dress
Kindles in clothes a wantonness:
A lawn about the shoulders thrown ⌒
Into a fine distraction,
An erring lace, which here and there ⌒
Enthralls the crimson stomacher,
A cuff neglectful, and thereby ⌒
Ribbands to flow confusedly,
A winning wave (deserving note)
In the tempestuous petticoat,
A careless shoe-string, in whose tie ⌒
I see a wild civility,
Do more bewitch me, than when art ⌒
Is too precise in every part.

4. We have marked suggested pauses for you in the following paragraphs—one slash to indicate a very short pause, two for a slightly longer pause, and three for a pause of significant length. Pausing must ultimately be determined by the reader, for superimposing pauses on your interpretation of the text can lead to a number of other problems. As a practice device, however, try the following, checking your perception against ours—would you pause and phrase in the same manner?

1. There is nothing more difficult to take in hand, / more perilous to conduce, / or more uncertain in its success, / than to take the lead in the introduction of a new order of things. / / /

2. The chief foundations of all states, / new as well as old or composite, / / are good laws / and good arms; / / / and as there cannot be good laws where the state is not well armed, / / it follows that where they are well armed / they have good laws. / / /

3. There are three classes in intellects: / / one which comprehends by itself; / another which appreciates what others comprehend; / and a third which neither comprehends by itself nor by the showing of others; / / the first is the most excellent, / the second is good, / / the third is useless. / / /

—Nicolo Machiavelli,
The Prince

4. They wonder much to hear that gold, / which in itself is so useless a thing, / / should be everywhere so much esteemed, / that even men for whom it was made, / and by whom it has its value, / should yet be thought of less value than it is. / / /

5. Plato by a goodly similitude declareth, / why wise men refrain to meddle in the commonwealth. / / / For when they see the people swarm into the streets, / and daily wet to the skin with rain, / / and yet can not persuade them to go out of the rain, / / they do keep themselves within their houses, / seeing they cannot remedy the folly of the people. / / /

—Sir Thomas More,
Utopia

6. The use of sea and air is common to all; / / neither can a title to the ocean belong to any people or private persons, / forasmuch as neither nature nor public use and custom permit possession thereof. / / /

—Elizabeth, Queen of England
(1533–1603),
"To the Spanish Ambassador"

7. I know I have the body of a weak and feeble woman, / / but I have the heart and stomach of a king, / and of a king of England / too; / / and think foul scorn that Parma or Spain, / or any prince of Europe / should dare to invade the borders of my realm. / / /

—Elizabeth, Queen of England
(1533–1603),
"Speech to the Troops"

8. I am no lover of pompous title, / but only desire that my name may be recorded in a line or two, / which shall briefly express my name, / my virginity, / the years of my reign, / the reformation of religion under it, / / and my preservation of peace. / / /

—Elizabeth, Queen of England
(1533–1603),
"To Her Ladies"

5. In the following paragraphs, mark the pauses for yourself, using the system of one, two, or three slashes.

1. There is, nevertheless, a certain respect, and a general duty of humanity, that ties us, not only to beasts that have life and sense, but even to trees and plants.

2. Some impose upon the world that they believe that which they do not; others, more in number, make themselves believe that they believe, not being able to penetrate into what it is to believe.

3. Arts and sciences are not cast in a mold, but are formed and perfected by degrees, by often handling and polishing, as bears leisurely lick their cubs unto form.

4. Is it not a noble farce, wherein kings, republics, and emperors have for so many ages played their parts, and to which the whole vast universe serves for a theatre?

—MICHEL DE MONTAIGNE,
Essays

5. Now blessings light on him that first invented this same sleep! It covers a man all over, thoughts and all, like a cloak; 'tis meat for the hungry, drink for the thirsty, heat for the cold, and cold for the hot.

6. Demonstrations of love are never altogether displeasing to women, and the most disdainful, in spite of all their coyness, reserve a little complaisance in their hearts for their admirers.

7. I would have nobody to control me, I would be absolute; and who but I? Now, he that is absolute can do what he likes; he that can do what he likes, can take his pleasure; he that can take his pleasure, can be content; and he that can be content, has no more to desire. So the matter's over; and come what will come, I am satisfied.

8. He that publishes a book runs a very great hazard, since nothing can be more impossible than to compose one that may secure the approbation of every reader.

—MIGUEL DE CERVANTES,
Don Quixote

9. I shall stay him no longer than to wish him a rainy evening to read this following discourse; and that if he be an honest angler, the east wind may never blow when he goes a-fishing.

10. We may say of angling as Dr. Boteler said of strawberries: "Doubtless God could have made a better berry, but doubtless God never did"; and so, if I might be judge, God never did make a more calm, quiet, innocent recreation than angling.

11. Thus use your frog: put your hooks through his mouth and out at his gills, and then with a fine needle and silk sew the upper part of his leg with only one stitch to the arming wire of your hook or tie the frog's leg above the upper joint to the armed wire; and in so doing use him as though you loved him.

12. Look at your health; and if you have it, praise God, and value it next to a good conscience; for health is the second blessing that we mortals are capable of—a blessing that money cannot buy.

—IZAAK WALTON,
The Compleat Angler

6. *Pauses to emphasize.* A preceding pause is a useful way of making a word or phrase stand out as more significant than it otherwise would be. You can convey disgust if your voice connotes aversion while you turn up your nose and say, "You ate worms?" But the impact is much greater if you put a sizeable pause before the final word: "You ate—worms?" The disgust becomes total repugnance. Even more emphatic is a pause both before and after a word or phrase, "I can't imagine being—married to—a person like that!"

In the following exercise, read the sentence first as written. Then reread it, taking a sizeable pause at the slash mark. Note the added emphasis the word after the pause assumes.

1. (a) He used the word in its pejorative sense.
   (b) He used the word in its / pejorative sense.
2. (a) The story will make your flesh creep.
   (b) The story will make your flesh / creep.
3. (a) The old man was as dead as a dormouse.
   (b) The old man was / as dead as a dormouse.
4. (a) "God bless us every one!" said Tiny Tim.
   (b) "God bless us / every one!" said Tiny Tim.
5. (a) It is right that you do so.
   (b) It is / right that you do so.
6. (a) She was the most beautiful girl I had ever seen.
   (b) She was the most / beautiful girl I had ever seen.
7. (a) I cannot believe you never heard of Johnny Cash.
   (b) I cannot believe you / never heard of Johnny Cash.
8. (a) Every time you tell that story, it gets longer and longer.
   (b) Every time you tell that story, it gets / longer and longer.
9. (a) They bound him hand and foot to the stockade.
   (b) They bound him / hand and foot / to the stockade.
10. (a) I can sing and dance or I can cry.
    (b) I can / sing and dance / or I can cry.
11. (a) As I stood quietly God spoke to me.
    (b) As I stood quietly / God / spoke to me.
12. (a) Don't you realize it hurts when you do that?
    (b) Don't you realize it / hurts / when you do that?
13. (a) Do you believe in ghosts?
    (b) Do you / believe / in ghosts?
14. (a) Everywhere you looked there were slimy slugs crawling on the sidewalk.
    (b) Everywhere you looked there were / slimy slugs / crawling on the sidewalk.
15. (a) The room spun round and round as I grew dizzy.
    (b) The room spun / round and round / as I grew dizzy.

EMPHASIS

Not all words in a thought group are of equal importance. While many stir up specific ideas and images in speakers' and listeners' minds, many other words are merely **syntactic** devices that suggest relationships among the "meaning" words and allow us to construct sentences. **Emphasis** is vocalic stress that allows us to give more importance to key words or phrases. Categorizing words according to the parts of speech gives us a general guideline for identifying the most important words.

Nouns and verbs are usually the major words in a sentence, for they tell who or what the sentence is about and what that person or object is doing. For example, if "The little boy and his dog wandered slowly along the dusty path in the late afternoon" were reduced to nouns and verbs, the result would be "boy dog wandered path afternoon." That almost makes sense, doesn't it? It gives an impression of who did what. The other words in the sentence add specificity and make clearer the relationship between the key words, but the principal idea is already established.

Adjectives and adverbs modify nouns and verbs, respectively. They add specificity, description, or differentiation. They may be somewhat less important in establishing the basic meaning of a phrase or sentence, but they are certainly vital in bringing a multidimensional quality to the message. They add fullness, vividness, and contextual detail. Without them our language would be a most inadequate representation of the wealth of variety in human experience. Adjectives and adverbs offer the reader the best opportunity for using all the inherent flexibility in the human voice to color, animate, and vivify the images in the verbal picture.

Prepositions, conjunctions, and articles are primarily useful tools for establishing relationships between the other words in a sentence. The knowledge that food was *on* the table rather than *under* the table may well be an important piece of information if you are hungry, but it does not rank with the importance of the food itself. Stressing these parts of speech can alter meaning: "I was going *to* the store" instead of "I was going *from* the store" establishes a time sequence. "Bacon *and* eggs" would suggest that we don't normally have those two items together—something unusual or special is being added to the bacon. But these special situations occur less often than the use of unstressed prepositions, conjunctions, and articles. For the most part, the student reader has a tendency to overstress these "little" words. Articles are the most troublesome, so that the stressed forms [eɪ] and [ði] are often used when the unstressed [ə] and [ðə] are needed.

In spontaneous speech the relationship between pronunciation variables, especially the rate factors of duration and assimilation, and emphasis as a vocal tool for enhancing meaning becomes most obvious. Natural, spontaneous, connected speech is the outward manifestation, or performance aspect, of the linguistic competence that the human mind possesses. As we speak, we generate sentences that draw from our total vocabulary and our knowledge of the rules of sentence construction. This ability to group words into meaningful relationships carries with it the ability to alter certain features in the vocal production of those words so that subtle differences in meaning are added. As a mature, linguistically competent speaker, you have so mastered this ability to use vocal variation as an integral part of your daily speech that you think nothing about it. Only when you must enlarge upon these natural features—as in a public speaking situation, or in the much more difficult task of trying to convey someone else's words as if you had generated the sentences yourself, as in reading aloud—does a problem emerge.

You would not say to your friend or roommate, "I / just / saw / [ði] / best / movie /." We simply don't talk that way. Instead you probably would have said, "I just saw [ðə] *best* movie." Emphasis would fall on the word that most clearly conveyed the full range of your intended meaning. As you formed that sentence to express an idea, you did *not* think about vocabulary, syntax, pronunciation, duration of sounds, or any of the myriad other features inherent in your utterance. Your linguistic competence allowed you to handle the entire process without conscious thought. The result was natural, connected human speech.

We could go through all the possible meanings implied by this sentence, and the resultant shifts in emphasis:

"*I* just saw the best movie." (*You* didn't see it.)

"I *just* saw the best movie." (Only a few minutes ago.)

"I just saw the best *movie.*" (Not a play or TV program.)

As a speaker with an idea to express, you unconsciously use your vocal mechanism in a manner that allows the listener to perceive such subtle differences in the intent of your message. Because you *can* emphasize by altering rate, volume, and pitch, you can come much closer to creating a genuine understanding between you and your listener, much closer than merely the words themselves—without vocal coloring—could ever bring you.

PUTTING IT TOGETHER

You now know that rate is far more complicated than just talking fast or slow. Duration of sounds, assimilation of one sound into another, and pauses contribute to rate. Pauses are a major tool used to emphasize and make certain words and phrases stand out.

Chapter 8 will deal with the more elusive characteristic of voice *quality*—a combination of resonance and placement. Quality distinguishes one voice from another. Even when those two voices may be at about the same pitch and volume level, the quality may differ greatly. People are recognized by their voice quality rather than volume, pitch, or rate. Several exercises in Chapter 8 are designed to help eliminate unpleasant voice qualities, but can also be useful in the creation of characters such as roles in a play or different speakers in a story. Spend time practicing these qualities to see how much flexibility you can master.

CLASSIC SPEECHES FOR PRACTICE

Some of the finest prose in English or any other major language can be found in the speeches of great orators. Read aloud the stirring words in the following passages from classic speeches.

> What tenderness, what regard, respect, or consideration has Great Britain shown, in their late transactions, for the security of the persons or properties of the inhabitants of the Colonies? Or rather what have they omitted doing to destroy that security? They have declared that they have ever had, and of right ought ever to have, full power to make laws of sufficient validity to bind the Colonies in all cases whatever. They have exercised this pretended right by imposing a tax upon us without our consent; and lest we should show some reluctance at parting with our property, her fleets and armies are sent to enforce their mad pretensions. The town of Boston, ever faithful to the British Crown, has been invested by a British fleet; the troops of George III have crossed the wide Atlantic, not to engage an enemy, but to assist a band of traitors in trampling on the rights and liberties which, as a father, he ought ever to regard, and as a king, he is bound, in honor, to defend from violation, even at the risk of his own life.
>
> —JOHN HANCOCK,
> "The Boston Massacre,"
> March 5, 1774

> I hold that it is not only necessary to use the military power when the actual case of invasion shall occur, but to authorize the judicial department of the Government to suppress all conspiracies and combinations in the several States with intent to invade a State, or molest or disturb its government, its peace, its citizens, its property, or its institutions. You must punish the conspiracy, the combination with intent to do the act, and then you suppress it in advance. . . . This is a familiar principle in legislative and judicial proceedings. If the act of invasion is criminal, the conspiracy to invade should also be made criminal. If it is unlawful and illegal to invade a State and run off fugitive slaves, why not make it unlawful to form conspiracies and combinations in the several States with intent to do the act?
>
> —STEPHEN A. DOUGLASS,
> "The John Brown Raid,"
> January 1860

Wouldst thou know whether thy name be written in the Book of Life, why then read what thou hast written in the Book of Conscience, thou needest not Ask who shall Ascend up into heaven. For to search the record of Eternity, thou mayest but descend down into thine own heart and there read what thou art and what thou shalt be. Tho' God's Book of Election and Reprobation be closed and kept above with God, yet the Book of Conscience is open and kept below in thy very bosom, and what thou writest here, thou shalt be sure to read there. If you write nothing in this Book but the black lines of Sin, you will find nothing in God's Book but the red lines of Damnation; but if you write God's word in the Book of Conscience, you may be sure God hath written your name in the Book of Life at the great day of judgment when all Books shall be opened there.

—JEMIMA WILKINSON,
undated sermon,
around 1789

I begin, men of Athens, by praying to every god and goddess that the same good-will which I have ever cherished toward the commonwealth and all of you, may be requited to me on the present trial. I pray likewise—and this specially concerns yourselves, your religion, and your honor—that the gods may put it in your minds not to take counsel of my opponent touching the manner in which I am to be heard—that would indeed be cruel!—but of the laws and of your oath, wherein (besides the other obligations) it is prescribed that you shall hear both sides alike. This means not only that you must pass no precondemnation, not only that you must extend your good-will equally to both, but also that you must allow the parties to adopt such order and course of defense as they severally choose and prefer.

—DEMOSTHENES,
"The Oration on the Crown,"
30 B.C.

America, gentlemen say, is a noble object. It is an object well worth fighting for. Certainly it is, if fighting a people be the best way of gaining them. Gentlemen in this respect will be led to their choice of means by their complexions and their habits. Those who understand the military art will, of course, have some predilection for it. Those who wield the thunder of the State may have more confidence in the efficacy of arms. But I confess, possibly for want to this knowledge, my opinion is much more in favor of prudent management than of force, considering force not as an odious, but a feeble, instrument for preserving a people so numerous, so active, so growing, so spirited as this, in a profitable and subordinate connection with us.

—EDMUND BURKE,
"Against Coercing America,"
March 1775

That man over there says that women need to be helped into carriages, and lifted over ditches, and to have the best place everywhere. Nobody ever helps me into carriages, or over mud puddles, or gives me any best place, and aren't I a woman? Look at me! Look at my arm! I have plowed, and planted, and gathered into barns, and no man could head me—and aren't I a woman? I could work as much and eat as much as a man (when I could get it), and bear the lash as well—and aren't I a woman? I have borne five children and seen them most all sold off into slavery, and when I cried out with a mother's grief, none but Jesus heard—and aren't I a woman?

—SOJOURNER TRUTH,
NEW YORK CITY, 1853

The occasions of silence are obvious, and, one would think, should be easily distinguished by everybody: namely, when a man has nothing to say; or nothing but what is better unsaid: better, either in regard to the particular persons he is present with; or from its being an interruption to conversation itself; or to conversation of a more agreeable kind; or better, lastly, with regard to himself. . . .

When you say somewhat good of a man which he does not deserve, there is no wrong done him in particular; whereas, when you say evil of a man which he does not deserve, here is a direct formal injury, a real piece of injustice done him. This, therefore, makes a wide difference; and gives us, in point of virtue, much greater latitude in speaking well than ill of others.

—Joseph Butler,
"The Government
of the Tongue,"
undated sermon,
around 1740

The possession of knowledge does not imply the power of imparting it; profound thinkers and ripe scholars may be poor and ineffective speakers; if experience proves that men who are strong in the study may be weak on the platform or in the pulpit, and that even men whose books evince a masterly grasp of their subject may be distanced as teachers or preachers or public speakers by persons of greatly inferior gifts and attainments—then it is obvious that something more than the possession of ideas goes to the making of the orator. . . .

The palmy days of oratory, when it was regarded as an art on a level with painting, and sculpture, and poetry, when the severest canons of criticism were applied to it, when the great speaker cultivated his gift by laborious and varied discipline, speaking seldom, and only on occasions worthy of his powers, and grudging no pains to meet the claims of an exacting but appreciative audience—these days are long passed away.

—John Caird,
"The Art of Eloquence,"
November 9, 1889

The question now is: how shall we get possession of what rightfully belongs to us? . . . To have drunkards, idiots, horse-racing, rum-selling rowdies, ignorant foreigners, and silly boys fully recognized, while we ourselves are thrust out from all the rights that belong to citizens, it is too grossly insulting to the dignity of woman to be longer quietly submitted to. The right is ours. Have it, we must. Use it, we will. The pens, the tongues, the fortunes, the indomitable wills of many women are already pledged to secure this right. The great truth that no just government can be formed without the consent of the governed we shall echo and reecho in the ears of the unjust judge, until by continual coming we shall weary him.

—Elizabeth Cady Stanton,
July 19, 1848

If a good speaker—an eloquent speaker—is not speaking the truth, is there a more horrid kind of object in creation? Of such speech I hear all manner and kind of people say it is excellent; but I care very little about how he said it, provided I understand it, and it be true. Excellent speaker! but what if he is telling me things that are untrue, that are not the facts about it—if he has formed a wrong judgment about it—if he has no judgment in his mind to form a right conclusion in regard to the matter? An excellent speaker of that kind is, as it were, saying—"Everyone that wants to be persuaded of the thing that is not true, come hither." I would recommend you to be very chary of that kind of excellent speech.

—Thomas Carlyle,
"The Edinburgh Address,"
April 2, 1866

I do not mean to be disrespectful, but the attempt of the lords to stop the progress of reform reminds me very forcibly of the great storm of Sidmouth, and of the conduct of the excellent Mrs. Partington on that occasion. In the winter of 1824, there set in a great flood upon that town—the tide rose to an incredible height—the waves rushed in upon the houses, and everything was threatened with destruction. In the midst of this sublime and terrible storm, Dame Partington, who lived upon the beach, was seen at the door of her house with mop and pattens, trundling her mop, squeezing out the sea water, and vigorously pushing away the Atlantic Ocean. The Atlantic was roused. Mrs. Partington's spirit was up; but I need not tell you that the contest was unequal. The Atlantic Ocean beat Mrs. Partington. She was excellent at a slop or a puddle, but she should not have meddled with a tempest. Gentlemen, be at your ease—be quiet and steady. You will beat Mrs. Partington.

—SYDNEY SMITH,
"Mrs. Partington in Politics,"
October 12, 1831

. . . [T]he blessings of liberty are forever withheld from women and their female posterity. To them this government has no just powers derived from the consent of the governed. To them this government is not a democracy. It is not a republic. It is an odious aristocracy; a hateful oligarchy of sex; the most hateful aristocracy ever established on the face of the globe; an oligarchy of wealth, where the rich govern the poor. An oligarchy of learning, where the educated govern the ignorant . . . but this oligarchy of sex, which makes father, brothers, husband, sons the oligarchs over the mother and sisters, the wife and daughters of every household; which ordains all men sovereigns, all women subject; carries dissension, discord, and rebellion into every home of the nation.

—SUSAN B. ANTHONY, 1872

There is a vast, immortal want stirring on the world and forbidding it to rest. In the cursing and bitterness, in the deceit of tongues, in the poison of asps, in the swiftness of blood, in all the destruction and misery of the world's ruin, there is yet a vast insatiate hunger for the good, the true, the divine, and a great part of the misery of the ruin is that it is so great a ruin; a desolation of that which cannot utterly perish, and still lives, asserting its defrauded rights and reclaiming its lost glories.

—HORACE BUSHNELL,
"The Dignity of Human
Nature," undated sermon,
around 1845–1850

The ultimate reason for the greater effectiveness of spoken than of written matter is simply this, that the latter is dead and silent, the former quick with the glow and vitality of intelligence and emotion. In certain scientific observation you must eliminate what is called the personal equation; but in good speaking, the personality of the speaker, instead of needing to be discounted, is that which lends its special value to the result. What reaches the auditor is not thought frozen into abstract form, but thought welling warm and fluent from a living source.

—JOHN CAIRD,
"The Art of Eloquence,"
November 9, 1889

The policy of the public authorities of never taking an initiative, and always waiting to be urged to do their duty, is obviously fatal in a neighborhood where there is little initiative among the citizens. The idea underlying our self-government breaks down in such a ward. The streets are inexpressibly dirty, the number of schools inadequate, sanitary legislation unenforced, the street lighting bad, the paving miserable and altogether lacking in the alleys and smaller streets, and the stables foul beyond description. Hundreds of houses are unconnected with the street sewer. . . . The houses of the ward, for the most part wooden, were originally built for one family and are now occupied by several. They are after the type of the inconvenient frame cottages found in the poorer suburbs twenty years ago.

—JANE ADDAMS,
"Address in Support
of Hull House," 1887

One difference between the monarchy and the republic, which alone should suffice to make the people reject with horror all monarchial rule and make them prefer the republic regardless of the cost of its establishment, is that in a democracy, though the people may be deceived, yet, at least, they love virtue. It is merit that they believe they put in power in place of the rascals who are the very essence of monarchies. The vices, the concealments, and the crimes which are the diseases of republics are the very health and existence of monarchies. Cardinal Richelieu avowed openly in his political principles that "the King should always avoid using the talents of thoroughly honest men." . . . It is, therefore, only under a democracy that the good citizen can reasonably hope to see a cessation of the triumphs of intrigue and crime; and to this end the people need only to be enlightened.

—CAMILLE DESMOULINS,
"Live Free or Die,"
February 1788

Ought we to hesitate at such a moment? Shall we hesitate to take up arms against them because they were our countrymen? No! They are our countrymen no longer. They have by a solemn treaty united and identified themselves with Indians, and pledged their faith to carry on a war of murder and plunder against the principal inhabitants of Texas. They are worse than the natives of the forest with whom they are allied, and it is our duty as men, as Americans, and as adopted Mexicans to prove to those infatuated criminals and to the world that we have not forgotten the land of our birth, nor the principles of honor and patriotism we inherited from our fathers, and that we are not to be dictated to and drawn into crime and anarchy by a handful of desperate renegades.

—STEPHEN F. AUSTIN,
"Address against the
Fredonia
Insurgents,"
January 22, 1827

(In the following, Mrs. Nation alternately addresses a group of men and individual city officials.)

Men of Kiowa, I have destroyed three of your places of business. If I have broken a statute of Kansas, put me in jail. If I am not a law-breaker, your Mayor and Councilmen are. You must arrest one of us, for if I am not a criminal they are. . . . As Jail Evangelist of Medicine Lodge, I know that you have manufactured many criminals, and this county is burdened with taxes to prosecute the results of these dives. Two murders—one in the dive I've just destroyed. You are a butcher of hogs and cattle, but they are butchering men, women, and children, contrary to the laws of God and men. Your mayor and councilmen are more to blame than the jointists. . . . You are a partner of the dive-keeper, and the statutes hold you responsible. The man that rents the building is no better than the man who carries on the business, and you are a party to the crime. Now, if I have done wrong in any particular, arrest me.

—CARRIE NATION,
Kiowa, Kansas, 1900

It is our glory that while other nations have extended their dominions by the sword, we have never acquired any territory except by fair purchase or, in the case of Texas, by the voluntary determination of a brave, kindred, and independent people to blend their destinies with our own. . . . Our past history forbids that we shall in the future acquire territory unless this be sanctioned by the laws of justice and honor. Acting on this principle, no nation will have a right to interfere or to complain if, in the progress of events, we shall still further extend our possessions. Hitherto in all our acquisitions the people, under the protection of the American flag, have enjoyed civil and religious liberty as well as equal and just laws, and have been contented, prosperous, and happy. Their trade with the rest of the world has rapidly increased, and thus every commercial nation has shared largely in their successful progress.

—JAMES BUCHANAN,
Inaugural Address, 1857

I appeal to any white man to say if ever he entered Logan's cabin hungry, and he gave him not meat; if ever he came cold and naked, and he clothed him not. During the course of the last long and bloody war, Logan remained idle in his camp, an advocate of peace. Such was my love for the whites that my countrymen pointed as I passed and said: "Logan is the friend of the white man." I had even thought to have lived with you, but for the injuries of one man. Colonel Cresap, the last spring, in cold blood, and unprovoked, murdered all the relations of Logan, not even sparing my women and children. There runs not a drop of my blood in the veins of any living creature. This called on me for revenge. I have sought it. I have killed many. I have fully glutted my vengeance. For my country, I rejoice at the beams of peace; but do not harbor a thought that mine is the joy of fear. Logan never felt fear. He will not turn on his heel to save his life. Who is there to mourn for Logan? Not one.

—LOGAN (Indian Orator),
Speech on the Murder
of His Family, 1774

"Eloquence," replied the ancient orator, "is action, still action, and ever action."
Action! what does that signify? Did he mean gesture? voice? attitude? bearing?
delivery? movement of ideas? the vivacity of the image? . . . Yes, all this at once.

—JOSEPH ROUX,
Meditations of a Parish Priest

BALANCED RESONANCE

If you were to listen to two different speakers use exactly the same pitch, level of loudness, and rate of speed as both read the same passage, the two voices would nevertheless sound significantly different to your ear. This difference is the result of the vocal element called **quality.** Review the material on resonance in Chapter 4. You learned there that resonance, or secondary vibration, occurs in the pharynx, oral cavity, and nasal cavity.

Resonance is a major determinant of voice quality. When one of the three primary resonators is over- or underused or out of balance with the other two, problems with voice quality may result. The exercises that follow are designed to help you achieve balanced resonance and to add more nasal resonance to your voice. A good balance of nasal resonance is difficult to achieve, but does much to strengthen and enrich the voice. Before you begin the following exercises, identify the resonators and your control of the degree of vibration in each:

STOP AND TRY THIS

1. *Locate and isolate pharyngeal resonance.* Focus your voice toward the back of your mouth and say [ɑ] while laying your fingers gently

---

on the outside of your upper throat area and trying to produce a heavy vibration. Keeping this focus, say the nursery rhyme "Mary Had a Little Lamb," maintaining heavy vibration in the upper throat but using only minimal resonance in the oral and nasal cavities. Exaggerating the openness of the mouth and keeping the pitch low will help you overstress pharyngeal resonance.

2. *Locate and isolate oral resonance.* Close your lips and puff your cheeks out two or three times, shifting your concentration to the mouth and away from the throat. Lay your finger gently on your cheeks and prolong the sound [i], sensing the vibration with your fingertips. Keeping this focus on the oral cavity, say "Mary Had a Little Lamb," using as little pharyngeal and nasal resonance as possible. Exaggerating the movement of the lips in articulating will help you achieve overstressed oral resonance.

3. *Locate and isolate nasal resonance.* Hum an [ŋ] sound, sustain it, and lay your fingers gently on either side of the nose. Feel the heavy vibration. At the same time, sense the downward, relaxed position of the back of your soft palate. If you have trouble sensing the soft palate, try shifting back and forth between the sounds [ŋ] and [æ]; you should feel the palate moving up and down. In the downward position, most of the air is being emitted through the nose. With this focus, say "Mary Had a Little Lamb," trying to nasalize all the sounds. Keeping your pitch low will help you to achieve overstressed nasal resonance.

Certain frogs have additional vocal sacs that they can inflate, and the subsequent vibration adds rich, resonant tones to their croaking voices.

You have now isolated the three principal areas of postglottal resonance. Resonance also occurs in the chest; you can feel it if you lay your fingers gently on your rib cage at the side or on the upper chest at the front. Chest resonance seems to be stronger at certain lower pitch levels, and more noticeable in some voices than in others. The voices of actors Patrick Stewart and James Earl Jones have strong chest resonance. There are no specific exercises for improving chest resonance. Good posture that opens the lungs to the fullest and deep breathing in a relaxed upper torso will allow fullest chest resonance.

EXERCISES FOR IMPROVING PHARYNGEAL AND ORAL RESONANCE

I will aggravate my voice so that I will roar you as gently as any suckling dove; I will roar you as 'twere any nightingale.

—WILLIAM SHAKESPEARE, *A Midsummer Night's Dream*

1. To ensure that your throat is fully open and relaxed, yawn deeply, emitting a big sigh as you exhale. Your throat is now relaxed.

2. With your head tilted back, lay your fingers gently on the front of your throat in the pharynx area, on either side of the passageway. Now, ease your fingers down two to three inches so that you pass the larynx, then stop at the sides of the upper trachea. Move your fingers up and down several times until you are sure you have identified the passageway and the muscles on either side of it. Return your head to its natural position, keeping your fingers on your throat. Now, pantomime screaming—make no sound, but act it out. What do you observe about the muscles of the throat? You should have felt a great deal of tension. Such tension prevents the pharynx from resonating fully and should be avoided.

3. Standing up or sitting straight in a chair, let your head drop as far back as is comfortable. Sustain on one breath, in a singing tone, [ɑ-oʊ-u]. Check your throat with your fingers to make sure you are not tensing up. Now drop your head to the side. Repeat [ɑ-oʊ-u]. Then drop your chin on your chest, repeat the sounds, drop your head to the other side, and again repeat. The sounds will become al-

FYI... _____

The 17 year cicadas mate, leave eggs in trees, and soon the eggs hatch and the young fall and burrow into the ground. They spend 17 years in the ground before they claw their way out to live a brief 4 to 6 weeks. Male cicadas sing lustily, a high-pitched hum and buzzing sound, in order to attract females. If we could only communicate with the opposite sex once every 17 years, our voices would doubtless be lively and animated!

most a chant. Listen to the pharyngeal resonance change as you move from one position to another.

4. Pinch your nose and say [ɑ]. Let go of your nose and say [ɑ]. Alternate opening and closing your nostrils, repeatedly saying [ɑ]. Try to eliminate any stress on nasal resonance by keeping the two sounds as much alike as possible. Concentrate on vibration in your cheeks.

5. Try to keep your throat open and free and focus clearly on oral and pharyngeal vibration as you practice the following sentences, which contain no nasal sounds.

   a. Fight the good fight fearlessly.
   b. She freely spiced the rice with herbs or flavor additives.
   c. Whittle twigs of teak wood as well as oak, acacia, or poplar trees.
   d. Take daily walks beside the big skyscrapers at Wall Street.
   e. I hope you will be able to assist Betty Baker with her project for physics laboratory.
   f. Theodore thought that thistles were a cactus species, but they are just a prickly bush.
   g. The volatile oil evaporated because Eva Vail failed to close the vapor lock attached to the vat.
   h. Wet your whistle with the water in the yellow tub beside the wastebasket.
   i. Patty Parker petted the pretty white rabbit that her daddy gave her for Easter.
   j. Dare we eat dates, dewberries, cold duck, cold fish, and apple cider?

EXERCISES FOR IMPROVING NASAL RESONANCE

1. Hum [m], [n], and [ŋ], sustaining the tones. Feel the vibration in your nose.
2. Say [m]—[ɑ]—[n]—[ɑ]—[ŋ]—[ɑ]. Repeat several times, almost as a chant. Concentrate on the movement of your soft palate and the vibration in your nose.
3. Intone the syllables [ɑm] and [neɪ] several times, until you are chanting. Place the sound in the upper part of the nose, sensing the area between the eyes as the focal point.
4. Pinch your nostrils so that you block nasal resonance while saying the following word pairs:

   feet—beat
   sit—flit
   bet—wet
   hat—cat
   got—cot
   taught—fought
   cute—butte
   rut—shut
   fight—tight
   goat—boat

Now repeat, adding the following rhyming words that begin with [n]. Try to keep the first and third words as free from nasal stress as possible, but clearly feel the vibration in your nose on the [n].

   feet—neat—beat
   sit—knit—flit

bet—net—wet

hat—gnat—cat

got—not—cot

taught—naught—fought

cute—newt—butte

rut—nut—shut

fight—night—tight

goat—note—boat

5. Achieving balanced nasal resonance is to a large degree a matter of directing just enough but not too much air through the nasal passages—a small amount on all sounds, a significant amount on the three nasal consonants. Try to achieve that balance on the following pairs of words, which contrast nasal consonants with nonnasal consonants.

[n] *and* [t]	[m] *and* [t]	[n] *and* [g] *and* [ŋ]
bean—beat	scheme—skeet	bin—big—bing
twin—twit	skim—skit	din—dig—ding
men—met	gem—jet	pin—pig—ping
scan—scat	scam—scat	rin—rig—ring
con—cot	calm—cot	win—wig—wing
fawn—fought	warm—wart	ban—bag—bang
soon—suit	zoom—zoot	fan—fag—fang
shun—shut	hum—hut	ran—rag—rang
rain—rate	fame—fate	tan—tag—tang
Rhine—right	lime—light	han(d)—hag—hang
moan—moat	roam—wrote	

[n] *and* [l]	[m] *and* [l]
seen—seal	deem—deal
pin—pill	him—hill
ten—tell	gem—jell
can—Cal	am—Al
don—doll	dumb—dull
on—all	tomb—tool
coon—cool	firm—furl
bane—bale	time—tile
whine—while	tame—tale
bone—bowl	home—hole

6. Try for strong nasal resonance in the following sentences, which contain an excessive number of nasal sounds.

   a. Many men and women are under tension in modern America, and often end up in sanitariums.

   b. Modern Millie demanded remuneration commensurate with the male employees in similar management positions.

   c. Flinging the gauntlet once indicated wanting to engage in a duel with guns or other weapons.

   d. Hitting the ball, running to first base, stealing second base, sliding into third base, and heading home, the second baseman scored a run.

e. Mr. Magoo was once the spokesman for a company making lamps and other electrical equipment.

f. Nothing makes women notice a man faster than a nice smile and a firm handshake.

g. The thing to do is sing until your nostrils ring with tones and sound abounding in ample resonance.

h. Sam was running around with another woman, but Velma didn't mind, since the "other woman" was Sam's mother.

i. My mama makes me mad whenever she remembers and recounts the many mischievous misadventures of my immature adolescence.

j. Hopping, jumping, leaping, and running around and around the downtown fountain, the mad monsters finally, merrily mounted the monument.

FYI . . . _____

According to the Acoustical Society of America, a keyed-in mother can immediately identify at least a dozen kinds of cries in her newborn: discomfort, illness, wetness, frustration, rage, the play for attention, and so on. She knows the cry that needs to be attended to, the one that may be safely ignored, and even the one that is asking to be stopped before it gets out of control. (In the) discipline called "paralinguistics," we are learning how to listen better, not merely to the words, but to the tone, the timbre, the pauses, and the bodily movements that accompany verbal communication. Lacking this skill, speech is a treacherous tutor.

—Sidney Harris

PROBLEMS IN VOICE QUALITY

There is no index of character so sure as the voice.

—Benjamin Disraeli,
Tancred, Bk. II

Good voice quality is a product of balanced resonance, strong breath support, forward voice placement, and a vocal mechanism free from excessive tension. If one or more of these necessary elements is missing, the result will be a problem in voice quality. Problems in voice quality fall into six major categories:

1. nasality ⎫
2. denasality ⎭ *(problem of balanced resonance)*
3. harsh gutturalness *(problem of placement and tension)*
4. throatiness *(problem of placement)*
5. breathiness *(problem of breath support)*
6. hoarseness or huskiness *(problem of breath support, tension, or ill health)*

Actors or impersonators use these distorted voice qualities to help create certain distinct or unusual characters. For the speaker, radio or TV announcer, or actor playing straight roles, the distortions should be eliminated.

As with all aspects of voice evaluation, you are dependent upon your instructor and classmates to give you accurate feedback. We have previously explained the difficulty of trying to monitor your own voice as it sounds to you through your ear. Frequent tape recordings of your voice can help you pinpoint your problems and make progress.

If any of the following are problem areas for you, use the accompanying exercises to help eliminate the fault.

I'll speak in a monstrous little voice.

—William Shakespeare,
A Midsummer Night's Dream

Nasality

Three phonemes, [m], [n], and [ŋ], are directed primarily through the nasal passages and are articulated by a lowering of the soft palate. Some speakers direct *all* sounds through the nasal passages, resulting in excessive **nasality,** or *hypernasality*. This problem may result from an insufficiently tense soft palate that does not rise high enough in the back of the mouth to close off the airstream. Or it may result from tensing and tightening in the upper pharynx and nasal cavity so that normal resonance is exaggerated and disproportionate. Finally, a *cleft palate*, a congenital opening in the roof of the mouth, will make it impossible for the speaker to prevent air from escaping through the nasal cavity, resulting in a heavily nasal voice quality. Most infants born with cleft palate undergo corrective surgery early in life, so we hear only a few adult cleft palate speakers.

People usually associate nasality with a whining or groveling personality. The whine and pout of the petulant child is usually accompanied by a nasal voice. In addition some regional dialects, notably the east Texas twang, are nasal in character,

If you voice is excessively nasal, you probably lack sufficient tension in your soft palate and may be failing to use forward voice placement that focuses on the lips, teeth, and tip of the tongue.

EXERCISES FOR REDUCING NASALITY

1. Use a sustained singing tone on the word *la.* Alternately pinch and release your nostrils. Keep the focus of the tone in the lower part of your mouth so that you hear little or no difference between the pinched- and open-nostril sounds.

2. Alternately pinch and release your nostrils as you repeat each of the following words several times. Place far forward in your mouth. The open-nostril sound should be as near to the closed-nostril sound in resonance as possible.

a.	baby	f.	pauper
h.	bye-bye	g.	bow-wow
c.	barber	h.	wahoo
d.	papa	i.	whopper
e.	paper	j.	whipped

3. Feel your palate shift up and down as you move from the nasal sound to the vowel:

    a.   [m]—[i]—[m]—[i]—[m]

    b.   [n]—[æ]—[n]—[æ]—[n]

    c.   [ŋ]—[ɑ]—[ŋ]—[ɑ]—[ŋ]

    Repeat several times to exercise the soft palate muscles.

4. *Assimilation nasality,* probably the most common type of nasality, occurs when a nasal consonant carries over into the vowel that immediately precedes or follows it. Say the following pairs of words, listening carefully to the vowel sound to determine whether you are nasalizing it in the second word of the pair.

Vowel Precedes Nasal	*Vowel Follows Nasal*
back—ban	cat—mat
dip—dim	tall—mall
seep—seem	sake—make
kit—king	cue—new
tab—tan	fob—nob
rag—rang	wee—knee
sight—sign	sitter—singer
head—hem	hacking—hanging
tug—tongue	log eyelet—Long Island
cab—cam	blight—might

5. Separate the sounds in the following words that contain three phonemes normally said as one syllable. Blend two of the phonemes together, pause, start to produce the sound in parentheses, then switch suddenly to the bracketed sound. Keep the vowel completely free of nasality.

Word	*Say*	*Start to say*	*Switch to*
cape to *came*	[keɪ]	[p]	[m]
reap to *ream*	[ri]	[p]	[m]

work to *worm*	[wɝ]	[k]	[m]
fad to *fan*	[fæ]	[d]	[n]
shoat to *shown*	[ʃoʊ]	[t]	[n]
sit to *sing*	[sɪ]	[t]	[ŋ]
bash to *bang*	[bæ]	[ʃ]	[ŋ]
gauze to *gong*	[gɔ]	[z]	[ŋ]
rope to *roam*	[roʊ]	[p]	[m]
turf to *turn*	[tɝ]	[f]	[n]

6. Assimilation nasality is especially easy to fall into when two or more nasal consonants occur in the same word. Make sure you are not nasalizing the vowels in the following words:

maim	moon	norm
mama	noon	morn
name	Ming	mourn
main	among	mean
Nome	mime	men
moan	nine	many
numb	money	mine
mound	noun	known

7. The following sets of sentences are designed to help you check nasality. The first sentence in each set has no nasal consonants. One or two nasals are added to each revision of the sentence. As you move through, add only the nasal consonants—do *not* add nasality to any of the other words or sounds.

a. (1) Keep the back lot free of trash.
   (2) Keep the back lawn free of trash.
   (3) Keep the back lawn clean of trash.
   (4) Keep the back lawn clean and neat.
   (5) Make the green lawn clean and neat.

b. (1) Park the car over there across the street.
   (2) Park the van over there down the street.
   (3) Park the van over there down the lane.
   (4) Park the van on the corner down the lane.
   (5) Get inside the van on the corner down the lane.

c. (1) He relaxed after the stress of the whole day.
   (2) He relaxed after the strain of the whole day.
   (3) He reclined after the strain of the long day.
   (4) Sam reclined following the strain of the long day.
   (5) Sam reclined following the strain of the long afternoon.

d. (1) Throw the old papers out of the attic.
   (2) Throw the old newspapers out of the attic.
   (3) Throw down the old newspapers from the attic.
   (4) Bring down the old newspapers from the bedroom.
   (5) Bring down the morning newspapers from the bedroom.

e. (1) Babies creep with legs or feet before they walk.
   (2) Babies creep on hands or feet before they walk.
   (3) Babies creep on hands and knees before they walk.
   (4) Infants move on hands and knees before they walk.
   (5) Infants move on hands and knees before standing and walking.

f. (1) Dogs or cats are favorite pets for kids.
   (2) Dogs and cats make favorite pets for kids.

(3) Dogs and cats make nice pets for kids.

(4) Dogs and cats make nice friends for children.

(5) Canines and felines make nice friends for children.

g. (1) The weather forecaster predicted ice or sleet Tuesday or Thursday.

(2) The weather forecaster predicted rain or snow Tuesday or Thursday.

(3) The weather forecaster announced that there would be rain and snow Tuesday or Thursday.

(4) The meteorologist announced that there would be rain and snow Tuesday and Thursday.

(5) The meteorologist announced that there would be rain and snow on Sunday and Monday.

h. (1) The fire showed through the roof as the fire fighters arrived at the house.

(2) The flames showed through the roof as the firemen arrived at the house.

(3) The flames showed through the roof as the firemen rounded the corner by the house.

(4) The flames burned through the roof as the firemen rounded the corner by my house.

(5) The flames burned through the ceiling as the firemen rounded the corner by my home.

i. (1) She served coffee, tea, cakes, cheese dip, chips—lots of good party food.

(2) She served punch, tea, nuts, cheese dip, chips—lots of good party food.

(3) She served punch, tea, nuts, sandwiches, chips—many good party foods.

(4) She served punch, tea, nuts, sandwiches, chips—many interesting snacks.

(5) She served punch, Seven-Up, nuts, sandwiches, nachos—many interesting snacks.

j. (1) The car required service—the oil refilled, the wiper blades replaced, the radiator flushed.

(2) My car required service—the oil changed, the wiper blades replaced, and the radiator flushed.

(3) My car needed servicing—the oil changed, new wiper blades put on, and the transmission overhauled.

(4) My car needed servicing—the oil changed, new windshield wiper blades put on, and the transmission overhauled.

(5) My Nissan needed servicing—the motor oil changed, new windshield wiper blades put on, and the transmission fluid drained.

8. Compare the nasal quality of the first sentence in each of the following pairs with the nonnasal quality of the second sentence. Again, keep nasality out of all but the nasal consonants, but make sure those nasal consonants have ample vibration so that they sound rich and strong.

a. (1) The twin mother shunned the dome.

(2) The twit brother shut the door.

b. (1) Jane has seen the pinker mug.

(2) Jay has sealed the pickle jug.

c. (1) The hen with one wing is in the chicken nest.

(2) The head with a wig is above the chicory chest.

d. (1) The nook had a nail for a hanger.

(2) The book told a tale of a hatter.

e. (1) Mickie was mad at Timmy, the trainer.

(2) Ricky was glad to see Tippy, the trader.

f. (1) Match the neck with the moss green panel.

(2) Patch the deck and toss grease on the paddle.

g. (1) A chime will tinkle, tingle, and clangor.
   (2) A child will tickle, titter, and chatter.

h. (1) Sam's shinbone was torn with a wrench and a crunch.
   (2) The sheer blow left the poor wretch on a crutch.

i. (1) We dined on noodles, mustard, French fries, bean casserole, greens, and meat loaf.
   (2) We ate strudel, custard, fresh pies, beef casserole, grits, and a beet loaf.

j. (1) Steam the mocha and bring it in warm in mugs.
   (2) Steep the cocoa and serve it hot in cups.

Denasality

A good voice can transform the most conventional of sermons into something like a divine revelation.

—ALDOUS HUXLEY

Denasality, or *hyponasality,* is less common than nasality. It results when insufficient air is directed through the nasal passages or when nasal resonance is dampened or deadened. Denasality is the familiar quality of someone with a bad head cold. When nasal passages are totally blocked by swelling and mucous, [m], [n], and [ŋ] cannot be articulated correctly, even with a sufficiently lowered soft palate. Unable to move air through the nostrils, the speaker will shift to a sound that is articulated in the same position in the mouth, so that the bilabial [m] will become the bilabial [b], the lingua-alveolar [n] will become the lingua-alveolar [d], and the lingua-velar [ŋ] will become the lingua-velar [g]. The place of articulation remains the same, but the manner of emitting air changes. The person might say, "Sigig is hard if by does is stopped up."

Actors sometimes use denasality to connote stupidity. The big dumb dog stereotyped in the cartoon character who repeatedly asked, "Which way did he go, George? Which way did he go?" is an example.

If your classroom evaluation suggests that your voice is denasal, you need first of all to check with your physician. Do you have chronic colds or allergies that cause nasal congestion? Swollen tonsils and adenoids? A structural problem in your nose? If so, the condition requires medical treatment.

If your problem is faulty production, you may be tensing your soft palate all the time, preventing it from lowering to allow air to move through your nasal passages. Repeat exercise 3 from the previous section, sensing the motion in the palate. Or you may be failing to support and direct the tone with an ample airstream and good forward placement. Review the breathing and projection exercises in Chapters 5 and 6. In addition, practice the following exercises.

EXERCISES FOR REDUCING DENASALITY

1. Hum with a sustained tone. Move from [m] to [n] to [ŋ]. Lay your fingers gently on the sides of your nostrils. Continue humming until you can feel a strong vibration.

2. Sustain [wɑ], [lɑ], and [rɑ] several times. With your fingers on your nose, note that you now feel no vibration. Then move from these nonnasal sounds to nasal sounds, noting that you can now feel vibration in your nose:

   [wɑ] — [m]
   [lɑ] — [n]
   [rɑ] — [ŋ]

3. Continue to sense the change from nasal vibration to its absence as you repeat the following pairs of words:

Mack — tack	tone — taupe	fling — flit
mate — pate	shun — shut	glimmer — glitter

meal—deal	boon—boot	money—muddy
make—cake	whine—white	Danny—Daddy
night—white	hung—hub	dimmer—dipper
came—cape	Nome—pope	thinner—thicker
time—type	rink—Rick	finger—fitter

4. Be aware of nasal vibration as you read the following sentences.

a. Move along—don't lag behind.

b. Kings and queens have golden thrones.

c. Movies are magnificent entertainment.

d. Nights are meant for dreaming.

e. Mama's maiden name was Mary Mahoney.

f. Walking, jogging, and running are methods of removing unwanted pounds.

g. Ingrid Swenson is a young immigrant from the town of Bergen, Norway.

h. Single men and women often meet at church events, civic meetings, and friends' homes.

i. It must take millions of miles of macaroni to meet the annual requirements of American and Italian diners.

j. Incense, scented candles, and air fresheners all make a room smell fragrant and aromatic.

Harshness

Harshness, a gutteral, rasping, throaty sound, is focused in the larynx and pharynx. A prime factor in harshness is overly heavy vocal fold vibration caused by too much pressure from the outgoing airstream. This excessive pressure occurs when the internal and external laryngeal muscles, as well as the muscles in the pharynx and neck, are overly tense. The breath is blocked in the larynx, resulting in the heavy vibration. Focusing sound to the front of the mouth by carefully directing the vibration to the lips, teeth, and tip of the tongue can help eliminate harshness. Relaxation in the upper torso, especially the entire neck area, will help free the tone from the throat.

Gangsters and tough guys are sometimes portrayed with a harsh, rasping voice. Mean or ferocious cartoon characters such as giants and monsters often have this quality.

If you have problems with harshness, we suggest—as we do with all voice-quality faults—that you begin with a checkup from your physician. Consulting a specialist is advisable. Otolaryngologists (sometimes called otorhinolaryngologists)—formerly ear, nose, and throat doctors—have specialized equipment that helps them accurately diagnose any physiological problem. In particular, the laryngoscope permits them to see into the larynx.

If your problem is not physically based, then you need to practice relaxation and placement exercises that will help you produce a normal tone, free from harshness.

EXERCISES FOR REDUCING HARSHNESS

1. Repeat the relaxation exercises in Chapter 5.

2. Repeat the forward placement exercises in Chapter 6.

3. Begin with as large a yawn as you can make. Don't just fake it—try to really yawn. As you complete the yawn, sense the relaxed muscles in your throat.

4. Whisper [hɑ] very lightly, yet with good breath support. Repeat several times, keeping the laryngeal muscles relaxed. Then increase the volume until you have a soft

Read It Aloud _____

THE TONE OF VOICE
It is not so much the words you say
As the manner in which you say it;
It is not so much the language you use
As the tone in which you convey it.
"Come here!" I cried,
And the baby cowered and wept.
"Come here," I said,
And straight to my lap he crept.
Words may be soft as the summer air
But the tone may break the heart,
For words come from the mind
And grow by study and art;
But tone leaps from the inner self
And whether you know or care,
Goodness, kindness, and love,
Like hate and anger are there.
If quarrels you would avoid
And in peace and love rejoice,
Keep anger not only out of your words,
But keep it out of your voice.

—ANONYMOUS

You have all the characteristics of a popular politician: a horrible voice, bad breeding, and a vulgar manner.

—ARISTOPHANES,
Clouds

but well-supported [ɑ] following the voiceless [h]. Vary the timing of the [h]: First stretch it out so that you hear a great deal of escaping air. Then make it very short—a clean attack to the [h]—but prolong the [ɑ]. Finally, with full volume, say the [hɑ] quickly and clearly. Keep the larynx free from excessive tension by staying relaxed in the throat area and letting the diaphragm do the work for you.

5. The following sentences focus on voiceless consonants. Keeping your focus on your lips, teeth, and the tip of your tongue, whisper each sentence in a projected stage whisper.

   a.   Pitter-patter, pitter-patter fell the rain upon the roof.

   b.   Tiny Tina washed her socks in tepid water.

   c.   He cooked fish for thirty hungry street pavers.

   d.   She sells seashells to anxious tourists.

   e.   High school principals and teachers often forget how it feels to be a high school student.

   f.   Captain Pete, a ferocious pirate, was washed ashore on foreign soil.

   g.   Cease the constant prattle and talk about something significant.

   h.   Thirty-three fashionable friends shared a feast on the third of the month.

   i.   I wish I had washed my shirts in Dash instead of Finish, since Finish is for washing dishes.

   j.   Hotels, hostels, and hospices are all havens for the temporarily homeless.

6. Now repeat the sentences in exercise 5, this time voicing them fully. Keep the throat area as free from strain as when you only whispered. Do not confuse vocal fold vibration (which you can feel if you lay your fingers gently on the laryngeal area) with muscle tension. With sufficient practice, you can easily learn to tell the difference.

Throatiness

The throaty voice is one that seems to be trapped or entombed way back in the mouth and the upper pharynx. It can result from retracting the tongue too far back in the mouth, which prevents the sound from moving clearly forward. A muffled, throaty sound can occur because the speaker draws the chin down toward the chest, hampering the free opening of the pharynx. It may be caused by excessive tension in the upper pharynx and the back of the oral cavity. Or the speaker may simply focus the tone in the upper throat, failing to send the breath stream forward to the lips and teeth. The throaty voice is often accompanied by mild denasality. Some throaty voices contain a tension-based grating sound; others are merely muffled, not rasping.

The throaty voice, much like the denasal voice, often suggests someone big and dumb or stuffy and pompous. Picture yourself as delivering a self-important, bombastic message. Pull your chin way into your chest, lower your pitch, and see if you can produce a throaty, somewhat hollow voice. That's the quality you want to avoid in effective speaking.

Correcting the throaty voice is primarily a matter of producing vowels with adequate and well-placed tongue tension, but without the tongue bunched toward the back of the mouth. Hold the chin up and focus the sound on the lips, teeth, and tip of the tongue.

EXERCISES FOR REDUCING THROATINESS

1. Stand in front of a mirror with your head and eyes straight forward. With your palm out flat, place the back of your hand and fingers under your chin, patting upward, much as you might do to help remove a double chin. Keep the chin at a right angle to the larynx and trachea as you do the rest of these exercises—do not let it sag.

2. Say the four front vowels [i], [ɪ], [ɛ], and [æ], conscious of the forward placement of resonance in the tongue. Then say the four back vowels [ɑ], [ɔ], [ʊ], and [u]. Feel the resonance and slight upward bunching in the back of the tongue, but do not permit your tongue tip and blade to move backward. Repeat several times until the tone quality of these sets of vowels is very similar.

3. Push the tip of your tongue firmly against the back of your lower teeth and keep it there while you repeat the following pure vowels: [i], [ɪ], [ɛ], [æ], [ɑ], [ɔ], [ʊ], [u], [ɝ], and [ʌ]. You will find that to produce the back vowels you must round your lips and palate more than you normally would, since you are restricting the motion of the tongue. Then, repeat these ten vowel sounds, allowing the tongue to move as it will but avoiding throatiness.

4. Say the three diphthongs [eɪ], [ɑɪ], and [ɔɪ] (as in *bay, buy,* and *boy*), concentrating on the forward thrust of the [ɪ] that concludes each. Feel the heavy oral resonance. Then say the other two diphthongs, [ɑʊ] and [oʊ] (as in *bough* and *beau*). Keep the oral resonance just as strong, despite the back-of-the-mouth pull of the [ʊ] at the conclusion of each sound. Avoiding throatiness is easier with front vowels than with back vowels, for the tendency is to pull back with the tongue muscles when resonance is focused in the back of the tongue. The sounds should not be swallowed, but should be kept moving freely forward, even though production is in the back of the mouth.

5. The following pairs of words contrast front and back vowels. Keep the tongue down and the oral resonance equal as you move to the back vowel sound.

feet—foot	tab—tube	Beth—booth
fill—fool	keyed—could	lack—lock
set—sot	till—tool	mean—moon
dab—daub	left—loft	hid—hood
keep—cop	cam—calm	fair—far
bill—ball	see—saw	tack—talk
shed—should	lick—look	aim—alm

6. The following sentences contain many front vowels and bilabial consonants. The forward thrust of these sounds should help you avoid a throaty quality.

   a. Peter and Penelope picked pretty pink peonies for Pat and Priscilla.

   b. Barry built bigger and better beanbag chairs than Betty did.

   c. Melba Milton met Mildred Miller for a midmorning committee meeting.

   d. The wheel wheezed, whined, and whirred when not well oiled or spinning freely.

   e. Bill Bell named his dogs Jingle, Tinker, and Dinner.

   f. When the whistle blows, the ball is where the referee places it, not where the tackled player wishes it were.

   g. Packages of puppy biscuits were sent parcel post to all poodles, Pekingese, Pomeranians, pugs, and pointers.

   h. Brahms, Beethoven, and Bach—the three B's—produced many melodious masterpieces of classical music.

   i. Casper Milktoast was no meek, mealymouthed, mismatched malcontent. He was a mature, manly mass of mind and muscle.

   j. Welts, weals, and wens are all blemishes or lumps on the skin. A whelp is a newborn puppy. Why do some people say they have whelps on their bodies?

He spoke with a certain what-is-it in his voice, and I could see that, if not actually disgruntled, he was far from being gruntled.

—P. G. WODEHOUSE
The Code of the Woosters

Breathiness

If you've been running hard before you try to talk, if you're trying to whisper, or if you're trying for a Marilyn Monroe or Melanie Griffith sexiness, you might produce a breathy voice. Breathiness results from incomplete closure of the vocal folds when phonation lacks a well-supported column of air. What we hear from a breathy speaker is escaping air rather than the phonated or vocalized tone produced with fully closed vocal folds. Sometimes breathiness comes from inadequate tension in the larynx, but more often it is a matter of breath control. And in a very few cases, nodules (small growths) on the vocal folds prevent full closure, resulting in a breathy quality. This is a medical problem that can be detected by a specialist and surgically corrected.

Some voice teachers believe that the breathy voice comes from weakness or laziness. We believe, however, that the breathy voice demands strength, since the speaker must have considerably more air to produce speech when much air is escaping unused. So, although breathiness may suggest weakness, as in the stereotypes of the helpless female or the very ill, more effort is required to produce a projected breathy quality than is needed for a fully phonated tone.

Eliminating breathiness is primarily a matter of good breath control. The exhalation of the outgoing column of air should be strong and steady. We hope you are continuing daily practice of the breathing exercises introduced in Chapter 5. Mastery of breath control is the key to eliminating a number of voice quality faults, especially breathiness.

The other major cause of breathiness is lack of adequate tension in the vocal folds. This is difficult to correct, since we do not have direct, voluntary control of the muscles of the larynx. Try the following exercises to strengthen laryngeal tension and eliminate breathiness.

EXERCISES FOR REDUCING BREATHINESS

1. Tighten the laryngeal muscles by swallowing hard, then continue to push downward, prolonging the completion of the swallow.

2. Tighten the laryngeal muscles by pantomiming a scream. Your throat muscles will also tighten. Then, consciously relax the outer throat muscles, but retain the tension in the larynx.

3. Stiffen your entire upper torso, including your arms, hands, and fingers. Can you feel the laryngeal muscles tighten? Then relax completely. Then tense again. Then let all the muscles go as limp as possible. Can you feel the alternate tensing and release in the larynx?

4. Produce a series of **glottal stops** or **shocks,** clicking sounds made by overrapid opening and closing of the glottis. Standard American English does not contain any glottal stops, although we frequently hear them in contractions such as *couldn't* and *didn't* or in phrases in which *the* follows a voiceless stop-plosive, such as "kick the ball" or "up the river." The IPA symbol for a glottal stop is [ʔ]. You can produce the sound by saying *didn't* as if it were [dɪʔnt]—follow the [dɪ] with a rapid click in your glottis. This is a common and acceptable sound in cockney English, where, for instance, the word *statue* may be pronounced [stæʔ ju].

   Although you should generally avoid glottal stops, they can increase tension in the larynx to eliminate breathiness. Repeat the following words and phrases, first with a glottal stop, then without it.

couldn't	up the tree
didn't	keep the peace
wouldn't	hit the dog

hadn't	hurt the head
isn't	kick the can
wasn't	pack the trunk

5. As in controlling nasality, assimilation is a problem in controlling breathiness. There is a strong tendency to carry over the breath-escaping quality of the five voiceless fricatives—[f], [θ], [s], [ʃ], and [h]—into a neighboring vowel. Keep the vowel sound in the second of each of the following pairs of words as free from breathiness as the first:

Fricative Precedes Vowel		*Fricative Follows Vowel*	
I've	five	lea	leaf
old	fold	owe	oaf
rows	throws	bow	both
ought	thought	four	fourth
oil	soil	ray	race
ail	sail	eye	ice
eat	sheet	was	wash
our	shower	mutt	mush
owe	show	with old	withhold
otter	hotter	Ida owe	Idaho

6. Ample volume and good projection can help you overcome breathiness. Maintain above-average loudness as you read the following verses from the Old Testament. They contain relatively few voiceless fricatives to tempt the speaker into assimilation breathiness.

   a. And the Lord God planted a garden eastward in Eden.

   b. The woman who thou gavest to be with me, she gave me of the tree, and I did eat.

   c. The voice of thy brother's blood crieth unto me from the ground.

   d. And Cain went out from the presence of the Lord, and dwelt in the land of Nod.

   e. Mighty men which were of old, men of renown.

   f. Babel; because the Lord did there confound the language of all the earth.

   g. Remember this day, in which ye came out of Egypt, out of the house of bondage.

   h. And the Lord went before them by day in a pillar of fire.

   i. Thou shalt not take the name of the Lord thy God in vain.

   j. Honor thy father and thy mother; that thy days may be long upon the land which the Lord thy God giveth thee.

7. Continue strong projection as you read more Old Testament verses. These, however, contain more voiceless fricatives, making assimilation breathiness more likely. Monitor it carefully.

   a. Now the serpent was more subtle than any beast of the field.

   b. And they sewed fig leaves together, and made themselves aprons.

   c. And Noah begat Shem, Ham, and Japheth.

   d. In sorrow thou shalt bring forth children.

e.   And the rain was upon the earth forty days and forty nights.

f.   While the earth remaineth, seedtime and harvest, and cold and heat, and summer and winter, and day and night shall not cease.

g.   The voice is Jacob's voice, but the hands are the hands of Esau.

h.   Thy brother came with subtlety, and hath taken away the blessing.

i.   This is none other but the house of God, and this is the gate of heaven.

j.   Behold, the bush burned with fire, and the bush was not consumed.

FYI . . . ─────────────

How does a new word get into a revised edition of a dictionary? Random House requires that the word be used in at least five reputable sources during a one-year period. Some of the new words in recently revised Random House College and Complete Unabridged Dictionaries are *dis, cyberpunk,* and *cybersex.*

The editors at Webster's, the other major publisher of English Language Dictionaries, are considering whether to include *duh* in the next edition, along with *phat* and *dis.* As we've said, language is constantly changing.

Hoarseness or Huskiness

The hoarse voice sounds like a combination of breathiness and rasping that lacks full phonation. You are familiar with the total loss of voicing or phonation that accompanies laryngitis, an inflammation of the larynx. In severe cases of laryngitis, resulting from heavy vocal strain and misuse, or from infection accompanying a bad cold or a raw, sore throat, a person may not be able to speak above a whisper. The condition is usually temporary, and a few days of total voice rest, coupled with medication in the case of infection, will restore full voicing.

The hoarseness or huskiness we are concerned with is a chronic rather than an acute problem. Only partial loss of voicing occurs, and so the speaker produces a sound somewhere between a whisper and full phonation. The sound may range from mild huskiness, with minimal loss of voicing, to barely more than a whisper. The degree of huskiness may also vary with the situation, such as the time of day and the fatigue level of the speaker.

Hoarseness should always be evaluated by a doctor. A chronically husky voice may be caused by nodules on the vocal folds; these are usually nonmalignant and can be removed surgically. More serious growths, including malignancies, also may be first indicated by hoarseness. Persistent allergies can be at fault, particularly when a postnasal drip causes the speaker to repeatedly cough or clear the throat. Pollutants in the air—cigarette smoke, chemical or industrial fumes, dust, or soot—may irritate the membranes of the larynx and cause hoarseness.

When the possible physical causes for a chronically husky voice have been eliminated, we look to poor usage of the vocal mechanism as the reason. One of three sources, or a combination of them, can usually be identified: lack of breath support; tension and strain in the larynx; and placement in the throat instead of at the lips, teeth, and tip of the tongue.

Lack of breath support causes the speaker to have to work the vocal folds more heavily in order to produce a projected tone. Strain may result. Or the strain may come from the speaker's repeated efforts to lower or raise pitch merely by tightening the vocal folds and intrinsic laryngeal muscles rather than fully using the overall vocal mechanism.

Strain may come from trying to talk too loud without good projection or from yelling a great deal the way cheerleaders or parents of small children often do. In yelling, the focal point of the placement is kept in the throat and larynx, rather than being brought forward and upward into the front of the mouth and nasal passages. Persistent irritation of the membranes of the larynx results, and a hoarse or husky voice is the outcome.

Or the strain may be the result of simply having to talk too much. Actors, singers, teachers, public speakers—people who must use their voices constantly in their daily work—may experience periodic hoarseness, no matter how skillfully they use their vocal mechanism. This is a matter of overuse, not misuse. Review of breathing and placement exercises is important for them, but sometimes an overworked voice, like an overworked body, simply must rest awhile.

If you are evaluated as chronically hoarse or husky, you can profit from the laryngeal area relaxation exercises in this chapter, as well as all the relaxation exercises in Chapter 5. The deep breathing exercises in Chapter 5 and the forward placement exercises in Chapter 6 and earlier in this chapter will also help. Controlled abdominal breathing, upper torso relaxation, and frontal voice placement will help you eliminate huskiness.

Other Problems

A few other unusual voice qualities occur, although less frequently than the six major ones that we have identified. A *strident* voice is one that is high-pitched and strained, discordant, and usually overly loud. A *thin* voice is one that is weak, often high-pitched, and particularly lacking in nasal and oral resonance. Closely related to the thin voice is the *flat* voice, one that has little or no vibrato or distinguishable overtone quality.

Frequent *glottal attacks*—clicks or crackles from the throat—characterize the speaker who misuses the glottis as an articulator, particularly for stop-plosive consonants. The *choked* or *strangled* voice croaks and seems unable to get out of the throat. Extreme fear or physical trauma, such as a heart attack, usually accompanies this voice quality.

A *muted* or *muffled* voice is similar to the throaty or entombed one, but the restraint may be just inside the oral cavity instead of in the larynx. Poor articulation, including lazy lip and jaw movement, is usually the cause. A *blurred* or *muzzy* quality is similar, but the cause is more apt to be drunkenness or a partial paralysis of one or more of the articulators, as with the numb tongue or lips that may follow a dentist's Novocain injection.

Stage fright sometimes produces a *quavering* or *wavering* voice, even in those who normally have good breath support. This shake or tremble is one of many possible physical symptoms of performance anxiety. Others include excessive perspiration, knocking knees, butterflies in the stomach, tremulous hands, and a flushed face. A few people have this voice quality all the time, either by temperament or because of extremely poor breathing and phonating techniques.

Finally, certain problems of pitch or loudness may be labeled voice quality problems—overly high or overly low habitual pitches, monopitches, and voices that are too loud or too soft.

Developing a pleasing voice quality should be a goal for all speakers. Your effectiveness in reaching your listener will depend in part upon the agreeableness of your voice. A smooth and easy yet vibrant and enthusiastic voice that is clear, well placed, well modulated, and free from any of the problems we have been discussing will be an asset to an oral communicator.

PUTTING IT TOGETHER

Chapters 4–8 have covered the four aspects of the vocal mechanism—respiration, phonation, resonation, and articulation. We have discussed and provided exercises for the characteristics of voice—volume, pitch, rate, and quality. Some instructors prefer to intersperse this voice work with the accumulation of the sounds of the English language (Chapters 9–13). Some may have started with Chapters 9–13, then gone back to Chapters 4–8. No one way to offer the material is best. It is a matter of personal preference.

If you have followed the order of the chapters as they are laid out, you will now be ready to begin the study of sounds—how they are formed and how your own pronunciation can be improved. You will not leave behind the chapters on voice, for as you read sentences and drills designed to practice specific sounds, you will be continually reminded of the need to make the best use of all vocal elements.

Vocal Warm-Up

The following brief Vocal Warm-Up works well for performers to use in readying themselves to speak in public. The warm-up relaxes and stimulates the various muscles of the vocal mechanism, increases the flow of blood, and moves the speaker toward a state of tonal responsiveness (see Chapter 5.)

1. Relaxation:
   a. The rag doll—hang over with your upper torso and arms dangling limply.
   b. Gently roll the neck and shoulders, settling in a comfortable "back and down" position.
   c. Swing your arms freely from the shoulders.
2. Deep Breathing:
   d. Do the 1-2-3-4 exercise—number 7 on pages 46–47.
   e. Take a deep breath—sustain the sound of s–s–s–s (exercise 4 on page 46.)
   f. "Ha-ha-ha" riding out on the top of the airstream (exercise 5 on page 46.)
3. Volume and Pitch:
   g. Do the siren on the word "wow." (exercise 3 on page 66.)
   h Count to five, increasing volume. Again, decreasing volume. Again, going up in pitch. Again, going down in pitch.
4. Resonance:
   i. Hum—sustain m, n, and ng.
   j. Shift from ng to ah—back and forth several times
   k. Say "one-up, nine-up" several times, exaggerating the n sounds.
5. Articulation:
   l. Say rapidly but clearly "ba, be, bi, bo, bu" several times. Repeat with m and p.
   m. Widen your mouth as much as it will go—say "eee." Now round the lips forward into "ooo." Repeat several times.
   n. Do a Bronx cheer, blowing air across your lips like a horse neighing.

CONTEMPORARY SPEECHES FOR PRACTICE

It seems that we can't pick up a newspaper today without hearing about yet another corporate downsizing, a euphemism for laying people off. Monsanto has had its fair share as well. These are wrenching times for a company—often heartbreaking times.

Sometimes there appear to be substantial business reasons for reducing the size of the work force. Other times it seems to be just another fad, for who knows what the right size of an organization is, especially when all the issues and complexities of life on this planet are taken into consideration.

Corporations often tell themselves they must do this to increase profit for shareowners, to be competitive in a changing global economy, to adjust to radical changes in the marketplace, to respond to technological change. And all of these things may be true. But as Chesterton pointed out, change is about the narrowest and hardest groove a person can get into. "As an ideal," he says, "change itself becomes unchangeable."

—Virginia Weldon
Senior Vice Pres., Monsanto Co.
"Faith and Values In
A Corporate Environment"
January 24, 1996

CIBC has an open staffing policy. We feel that we need to attract the very best candidates for every position. To do this, we have a policy which treats each employee with the same respect that one would give an outside candidate. All jobs up to and including senior vice-president are posted.

So, what does real empowerment look like in practice?

Our customers will deal with employees who will own all aspects of providing the solutions to the customer's needs.

Our employees will have control over much more of their lives and will know the boundaries of what they can do and what they are responsible for.

They will be supported by managers who will be able to provide clear direction, remove obstacles and make management decisions within a well understood framework that is clearly communicated throughout the entire organization.

> —Michèle Darling
> Executive Vice President,
> Human Resources, CIBC
> "Empowerment: Myth or Reality"
> February 14, 1996

The Japanese have a term for the kind of attitude and action they want their employees to nurture; it is *kaizen*. Kaizen simply means to continuously find small ways to improve yourself and what you do. It is an attitude that manifests itself in action. How does one do that? It is a matter of improving one's character, one's personality, one's relationships, and by increasing one's skill level. In Japan it is training, training, training, with a capital T which stands for self-improvement. Beginning in 1974, when my daughter was an exchange student in Japan and has been there many times since, I have studied the great attention the Japanese give to training. During a more recent year's study in that country, she had no difficulty in finding classes in any subject. Her particular course work that I attended when visiting her were classes in Japanese gardening and in flower arranging. Also, I sat in on the classes that she was teaching. She instructed doctors, their wives, and teachers in English. How many of us are taking Japanese, Chinese, Russian, or some other foreign language for self-improvement?

> —William I. Gorden
> Professor Emeritus, Kent State University
> "Values—Joining Together
> and Merging Individual Goals"
> March 2, 1996

I, along with everyone else in this room, have had to make choices, compromises, tradeoffs. It's foolish to believe that any woman, or man, for that matter, can have it all. . . . We won't always make the right choice. It's only human to make mistakes. Life is never a charted, swift and upward progression. There will always be interruption and discontinuity. What counts is that you turn these experiences into growth. I have to agree with Bateson who suggests in her book that life is an improvisational art. One must continually refocus, reassess, and redefine. Also keep in mind that each day we face all kinds of choices which can affect the quality of our lives. . . . Recognize too that while there are limits to how much we can have in life, the possibilities for leading fuller and more satisfying lives are almost limitless. No one can have it all, but you can have more if you look beyond a narrow ambition to include other things that give life purpose and meaning.

> —Claudette Mackay-Lassonde
> Chairman and CEO, Enghouse Systems Limited
> "Let's Stop Fooling Ourselves:
> No Man or Woman Can Have It All"
> March 19, 1996

I believe in Music! Someday, many, many years from now, I'd like to have that on my tombstone. In just four little words, it sums up one of the most important lessons I've learned in my young life: that music is a powerful vehicle for transferring emotion. Its scope of influence can be seen in a broad, public sense and shared with many people simultaneously. Or, it can convey the most private, intimate thoughts that only two can share. It can mean the same thing to different people at the same time, or different things to the same person at different times. When I look around my life and my world, I find countless examples of how music is familiar, but new; timeless, but ever changing; public, but very private—all at the same time.

The most common and yet stirring example of the public marriage between music and emotion is patriotism. Picture, if you will, a stadium filled with 50,000 raucous fans. They are all decked out in their school colors, anxiously awaiting the kick-off. Suddenly, a hush of silence falls over the entire crowd, all 50,000 rise to their feet and ask the same question: "Oh, say, can you see by the dawn's early light what so proudly we hailed at the twilight's last gleaming?"

—SANDRA CALL WILDER
EMPLOYER SPECIALIST,
EMPLOYEE RESOURCE MANAGEMENT
"I Believe in Music: The Power of Song"
March 22, 1996

Young workers are going to have to accept the fact that we must save more for our own retirements, as well as bear a share of our parents' Social Security benefits. For individual pensions to accumulate and provide an adequate retirement income, they will have to be based on substantial contributions. This means that workers will have to continue to pay a portion of Social Security, contribute the rest to a personal, mandatory account, and contribute additional savings to their personal account. But it is my belief that young workers will accept this burden if they are given the opportunity and the incentive to save more money themselves, watch their money grow, and know that the money will be there for them when they retire. . . . It is crucial for all Americans that we begin to confront Social Security today. To avoid action now is a moral and economic assault on future generations. If we seize the opportunity, however, I believe we can embark on a course that will boost national savings, invest in the future, and secure our ailing retirement system.

—HEATHER LAMM
BOARD OF DIRECTORS, THIRD MILLENNIUM
"Retirement in the 21st Century:
A Young Worker's Perspective"
March 26, 1996

Highly effective communicators consciously select their response to events that occur around them. They are not passive and reactionary. They take responsibility and they take the initiative. They offer solutions to the pressing communication challenges confronting an organization. Many people are aware of problems, but they don't offer solutions. I suppose they have been beaten and knocked down too many times. Highly effective communicators get back up after getting knocked down. . . .

The effective communicator also needs to have the right attitude when faced with a crisis or even a routine assignment. Over the years, I have learned that given two people with the same set of skills, the person with the positive, can-do attitude will generally perform better in most situations. In the business you are in, attitude really makes the difference. Attitude is critical. A smiling, happy person is a joy to be around. They lift your spirits. They can have a tremendous positive effect on an organization.

—RAMON L. HUMKE
PRESIDENT AND COO,
INDIANAPOLIS POWER & LIGHT CO.
"Highly Effective Communicators"
March 28, 1996

First, we have to promote the understanding that quality makes good sense from a business perspective. To be understood—and to be persuasive—we must speak in the language of business, plainly and clearly.

Second, we must continue to emphasize the need for incremental improvements as well as breakthrough achievements. Total Quality is a journey, not a destination. Like many journeys, it is a journey that carries the hope of self-renewal without self-destruction.

And last, we must never forget that the real bottom line is people. At the end of the day, the success or failure of a business depends on management's ability to harness the willing participation and creativity of people.

Now perhaps more than ever the business of business is people. That is an awesome responsibility and for all of us in this room an inspiring challenge.

—Laurie A. Broedling
Senior Vice President,
Human Resources and Quality,
McDonnell Douglas Corp.
"The Business of Business is People:
Total Quality Management"
April 8, 1996

The future in America has almost always rather closely resembled the recent past. In truth, genuine revolutions have been rare in modern history. Although technology has progressed steadily and with wonderful results in comfort and productivity, there have been relatively few truly revolutionary technology shifts in human history.

Gutenberg's printing press was revolutionary. It took learning out of the hands of political and priestly elites and put it into the hands of the people. . . . Steam power and the internal combustion engine also deserve the term revolutionary, for they have created genuinely profound changes in how we produce goods, where we live, and how we conduct our lives. . . . Will the computer bring about a genuine revolution? Will its convergence with telecommunications and video technology create the much-heralded Information Revolution? Perhaps. Given the fact that the future usually resembles the recent past, however—the fact that genuine technological revolutions are tantalizingly rare—we must await the verdict of history.

—Ervin S. Duggan President and CEO,
Public Broadcasting Service
"The Information Superhighway"
April 10, 1996

Did you see the movie "Apollo 13?" Remember how all America was united in its concern about the three lost astronauts?

The spirit of that togetherness was so touching because we don't have much of that unity now, do we? In place of unity it's special interest. It's the information haves versus the information have-nots. It's the immigrants who arrived in America a generation ago versus immigrants who arrived yesterday. And yes, it's men and women.

Probably not since the Civil War have we experienced so much conflict and so much self-righteous thinking. Right now as a society too many of us are performing as solo acts. That's a very hard way to proceed. And it's pretty lonely. Let's go back to "Apollo 13." Remember that scene when a simulation of all the equipment that is on the space rocket is put on a table. A team is told to use that equipment—and only that equipment—to build a device that will take care of the carbon dioxide aboard the ship. They do it! It works.

—Marilyn Carlson Nelson
Vice Chair, The Carlson Co.
"Women As Players: The Time is Now"
April 11, 1996

But if you take the time to listen and be honest in your reactions—and if you create a setting that recognizes that ideas come in all shapes and sizes—and are willing to follow the creative mind wherever it goes—something you can never predict—people begin to understand a basic fact: If you have an idea you believe in and can express it, it will be considered. Let me assure you that this is more, much more, than just an exercise in employee relations. The fact is that several of our better animated features have come out of the Gong Show and some of our other major winners out of similar kinds of programs in other parts of the company. I love going to our gong shows. I can be the emcee, the judge and the jury. Being part of the creative process is the best part of my job.

> —MICHAEL EISNER
> CEO AND CHAIRMAN OF THE WALT DISNEY CO.
> "Managing a Creative Organization"
> April 19, 1996

The outlook for these poor children is grim. Because they had the misfortune to be born to disadvantaged parents they are denied, for the most part, adequate nutrition, decent medical and dental care, and a safe and secure environment. As a result, by age 5 or so, they are less alert, less curious, and less effective at interacting with their peers than more privileged children. Thus, they begin school already behind. They, most likely, attend the most poorly staffed, overcrowded, and ill-equipped schools. Poor children, in short, are more likely than more advantaged children to have health problems, to not do well in school, to be in trouble with the law, and, as adults to be unemployed and on welfare. Progressives argue that unless society intervenes with meaningful programs and adequate support, many of these poor children will fail. But the current plan sponsored by Republicans and supported for the most part by Democrats is to reduce programs aimed at helping the poor and their children. This reduction process has been underway since 1981 when President Reagan took office.

> —D. STANLEY EITZEN
> PROFESSOR EMERITUS, COLORADO STATE UNIV.
> "Dismantling The Welfare State"
> April 25, 1996

We have a tendency to deal with China as if our basic objective with respect to China should be social reform, to change its governmental institutions, to bring about a different perception of the role of plebes, women, and other worthwhile objectives. But, of course, the Chinese do not consider it self-evident that we should tell them how to run what they consider their domestic affairs. And the reason they want to talk to us is because of concerns with Japan, Russia, India and other neighbors. So the problem we have in relations with China is to go back to fundamentals, to separate the desirable from the important, and to recognize that if we want to take on China, as so many heroes of our domestic debate in both parties seem to be eager to do, this is not the same as taking on the Soviet Union. No other Asian country will support us. We'll be alone. And we will be right back to the situation that . . . President Nixon overcame, namely, that a foreign policy in which we lose contact with China will undermine the flexibility of our American foreign policy around the world.

> —HENRY KISSINGER
> FORMER U.S. SECRETARY OF STATE AND
> CHAIRMAN, KISSINGER ASSOCIATES, INC.
> "United States Foreign Policy"
> April 29, 1996

And now, the last story I want to tell you today—is that of Vivian Pinn. Vivian first announced to her family that she wanted to be a doctor—when she was just four years old. That was fifty years ago. And even though there were few women physicians—and even fewer black women physicians—back then, her family gave her nothing but encouragement. When she entered the University of Virginia School of Medicine in 1963, she sat in the back of the room and waited for another woman or person of color to enter the class. It wasn't until the roll was called that she realized she was the only one.

Last November, Dr. Pinn received the Elizabeth Blackwell Award from the American Medical Women's Association for her outstanding contributions to the cause of women in medicine. And last year, Ladies' Home Journal listed her as one of the 10 most important women in medicine. She's been president of the National Medical Association, the national organization of African-American physicians. And today, she is the first director of the Office of Research on Women's Health at the National Institutes of Health.

—Nancy W. Dickey, MD
Chair, American Medical Association
"Our Sisters' Sicknesses, Our Sisters' Satchels"
May 4, 1996

In our time, religion is almost always seen as something primarily political, but this is because the political has claimed more and more of our lives. Politics looks more like a religion than religion looks like politics. Religion, contrary to its own inclinations, has been forced to become political because the laws of the public order increasingly embody principles and practices that are directly opposed to the tenets of religion, and of Christianity in particular. There is nothing secret about this. Anyone who objectively, say, reads the morning newspaper followed by reading the Ten Commandments cannot help but be aware that some deep conflicts exist in the soul of the democracies. As the state has gained control over the educational and cultural process, it has excluded anything that it did not directly control.

—James V. Schall, S. J.
Professor, Georgetown Univ.
"The 'Good News' Reconsidered"
May 5, 1996

I was covering a story about an AIDS hospice that was struggling to survive. . . . One of the nurses quietly pointed out a woman whose son was going to die at any moment, in a room at the end of the hall. When I saw the woman walking toward her son's room, I approached her and touched her shoulder. As we walked together, I said, "I'm so sorry," and we talked for a moment. I said to her, "You could give a wonderful gift to this hospice, if you would allow me, in a very tasteful way, to photograph you with your son. People will see this picture and be moved by it, and hopefully they will support the hospice. . . .

She agreed. She sat by her son's bed, and I photographed her from the doorway of the room. She was crying, and she was holding her son's withered hand to her face. That one powerful image moved the story from the inside of the paper to the front page of the metro section. The photograph spanned five columns.

—Sharon J. Wohlmuth
Teacher, Photojournalist and Author
"Courage to Create"
May 13, 1996

When it comes to activity let me remind you that activity is cumulative. You don't have to go out and spend an hour getting a sweat up in order to have done something that's good for your heart and good for your well-being. Be a little more active in the things that you do. Get up to turn the television off by hand instead of by remote control. Shut one telephone extension off and walk to the next one. Stair climbing is one of the best exercises in the world you can do. You don't have to jog, just get out and walk. You don't have to go to a track, just go back and forth in front of your house. I'm on the road an awful lot and I spent a lot of my time in hotels. Rather than get dressed up to go out and try to walk on city streets or on the grounds around the hotel, I just walk up and down the hotel corridors. To be sure, the maids look at me and wonders why I'm coming by for the third time, but I get my exercise and I feel better.

—C. Everett Koop, M.D.
Former U.S. Surgeon General
"Prevention of Disease is Cheap and Effective"
June 18, 1996

For my money at least, somebody who knows how to use both sides of his or her brain—the right as well as the left—is the type of person I want working at Chrysler in today's highly uncertain, super-competitive global economy.

But frankly, that type of person is difficult to find, especially given today's academic climate at most mainstream colleges and universities—including, by the way, those schools and those programs that purport to specialize in what most people would think of as the "right brained" subjects!

In fact, it's my firm opinion that one of the biggest things wrong with many programs in the so-called "softer" subjects today is that many of the people teaching those subjects feel a profound sense of inadequacy when they compare themselves to their counterparts in the physical sciences. . . . In the company of a genuine scientist, most mainstream professors of the social sciences feel like "touch-football enthusiasts who have wandered by mistake into the locker room of the Pittsburgh Steelers."

—Robert A. Lutz
Chairman and COO, Chrysler Corporation
"The Higher Education System"
May 29, 1996

If we are not to become a nation accused by our children of "generational malpractice," we must act now to reform our government, our elections, and our personal lives. We must accept limits on what we can afford, personally and collectively. Otherwise, we may well be remembered in a few short years as the last comfortable Americans—a selfish, short-sighted generation willing and eager to consume more than it produced—and then only too ready to pass along the tab for its excesses to posterity. And in doing so, risk everything we have built up over 200 years.

When I graduated from high school, the national debt took 7 cents out of every tax dollar that I paid. It is now 19 cents; and almost certainly my children will have to spend 25 cents out of every tax dollar they pay just to service the debt that my generation imposed upon them. That is more than "generational malpractice"—that is "fiscal child abuse."

—Richard D. Lamm
Former Governor of Colorado,
Director for the Center for Public Policy and
Contemporary Issues, Univ. of Denver
"The New Agenda: The Entitlement Problem"
June 1, 1996

Several weeks ago a friend sent me a eulogy which he had written and delivered at his uncle's funeral service. In that eulogy, he described a story that really touched me. Two weeks before his uncle died, his family gathered around him and he requested that they take out the picture albums. He started at the beginning of the first album and pointed to pictures of him growing up, his family, and his home. Near the end of that first album he stopped and stared at a picture of himself at the age of 18. He was all dressed up in a suit and looking very serious. He pointed to the picture and said, "This is the day that my life began. This is when I finished school."

And with great pride and joy he continued, "After that, all of the rest of the pictures in all of these other albums are but chapters of a wonderful story, and I was the author."

—David W. Magill
Superintendent, Lower Meriod School District
"Give Your Dream A Life With Design"
June 5 and 6, 1996

SECTION III
The Sounds of American English

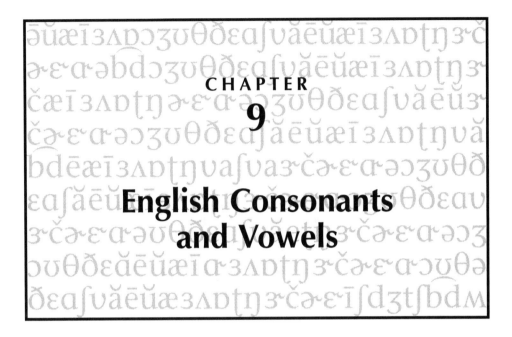

CHAPTER

9

English Consonants
and Vowels

Speak clearly, if you speak at all;
Carve every word before you let it fall.

—OLIVER WENDELL HOLMES

The sounds of the English language are divided into two broad categories—**consonants** and **vowels.** In elementary school you may have learned that "a, e, i, o, u, and sometimes y" are vowels and all the rest are consonants. A more formal distinction between the two categories can be drawn by examining the degree of obstruction of the outgoing airstream. In defining articulation, we said that it was a process of reshaping vibrating air. This is done by moving the tongue, lips, lower jaw, and soft palate and changing the positioning and relationship of these movable organs to the teeth and hard palate—the firmer, more stationary organs. Consonants are sounds that result from a relatively significant degree of obstruction; vowels are sounds that are basically free from obstruction and that depend more upon resonation of the oral cavity for their distinctiveness.

CONSONANTS

In studying consonant formation, we must examine three aspects of each sound. First, the method of obstructing and releasing the air determines whether the sound will be a **stop-plosive** (produced by exploded air), a **fricative** (air forced through a narrowed opening with friction), an **affricate** (air released by a combination of plosive and fricative phonemes), a **nasal** (air directed through the nose), or a **semivowel** or **glide,** where obstruction is minimal. The second feature is the position of the organs of articulation during the formation of the sound—how tongue, teeth, lips, and palate are juxtaposed and where tension is created. Finally, consonants are classified by whether or not phonation is required. Although most speech sounds result from vibration of the vocal folds, several sounds are produced by shaping outgoing air that is not vocalized, in much the same way that a whisper is produced. Several English consonants are paired phonemes—which are similar except that one is vocalized (*voiced*) whereas the other is produced without phonation (*voiceless*).

Subsequent sections of this book will examine each consonant in terms of these three aspects—method of air emission, place of articulation, and phonation. Table 9–1 classifies the consonants on these bases.

The first duty of a man is to speak; that is his chief business in this world.

—ROBERT LOUIS STEVENSON

VOWELS

Vowels are characterized by the position of the articulators. The airstream is not obstructed during vowel production, so the manner of air emission is the same for all vowels. Because all vowels are produced with vibrating vocal folds, all are voiced. Vowels are products of **oral resonance,** a resonating action of the oral cavity on the outgoing air. As the size and shape of the resonating chamber are altered, the ensuing sound changes.

Vowels fall into two categories, pure vowels and diphthongs. A **pure vowel** is a single sound or phoneme. A **diphthong** combines two pure vowels, but the result is classified as a single sound. Pure vowels are classified according to the positioning of the articulators, particularly the tongue, and the shaping of the lips. If the primary point of tension occurs in the front of the tongue as it moves up toward the front of the palate, the resulting sounds are called **front vowels. Central vowels** are formed with tension in the midportion of the tongue and palate. **Back vowels** engage primarily the back part of the tongue toward the soft palate. The highness or lowness of the tongue in the mouth further defines differences in vowel sounds. The rounding of the lips and the opening of the lower jaw complete the shape of the oral resonance chambers. Figure 9–1 illustrates vowel position.

Table 9–1   IPA Consonants

MANNER OF EMISSION	STOP-PLOSIVES		FRICATIVES		AFFRICATES		NASALS	SEMIVOWELS	
Place of Articulation	Unvoiced[a]	Voiced	Unvoiced	Voiced	Unvoiced	Voiced	Voiced	Unvoiced	Voiced
Bilabial (two lips)	p	b					m	ʍ[b]	w
Labio-dental (lip–teeth)			f	v					
Lingua-dental (tongue–teeth)			θ	ð					
Lingua-alveolar (tongue tip–gum ridge)	t	d	s	z			n		l[c]
Lingua-post alveolar (tongue blade–back gum ridge)			ʃ	ʒ	tʃ	dʒ			r
Lingua-velar (tongue–hard or soft palate)	k	g					ŋ		j
Glottal (glottis)			h						

[a]Also called *voiceless.*
[b]Also classified as a combined *fricative-glide* and may be written [hw].
[c]Also classified as *lateral.*

STOP AND TRY THIS

Watch your mouth in a mirror as your lips move inward and your jaw drops slightly from the widened, almost smiling lip position of [i], as in *seat*—the first vowel in the International Phonetic Alphabet (IPA)—through [ɛ] *set* and [æ] *sat.* Now watch your lips round out as tension shifts backward, and begin the upward thrust that marks the shift from [ɑ] *calm* to [u] *cool.* Try this again as you begin to learn the symbols of the IPA, for although tongue action and tension are the principal determinants of vowels, the lips certainly contribute.

Read It Aloud ————

**Tongue twisters always
get me tickled,
Like trying to get Peter's
peppers pickled.**

DIACRITICAL MARKS AND THE IPA

He mouths a sentence as curs mouth a bone.

—Winston Churchill

Chapter 2 pointed out that over a long time span the guidelines for the oral use of language were written in grammar and style books and in dictionaries. Dictionaries are a chief source of the denotative, or lexical, meaning of words people either do not know or are uncertain about. Dictionaries also indicate the preferred or standard pronunciation of those words.

Most dictionaries indicate the particular sound or sounds of a word by means of **diacritical marks.** The marks used most often in American English are the *macron* and the *breve,* placed over vowels to indicate long or short sounds (hāte, hăt); the *circumflex,* for showing broadness or length in a vowel (hâre); the double dot, or *umlaut* (härt); and the single dot (hu̇d—"hood").

Diacritical marks vary somewhat from one dictionary to another. Table 9–2 presents a comparison of the marks used by several major dictionaries as well as the IPA. A key to the marks appears at the beginning of each dictionary and often also at the bottoms of pages throughout. We suggest that whether your instructor chooses a particular

As sheer casual reading matter, I still find the English dictionary the most interesting book in our language.

—Albert Jay Nock,
Memoirs of a Superfluous Man

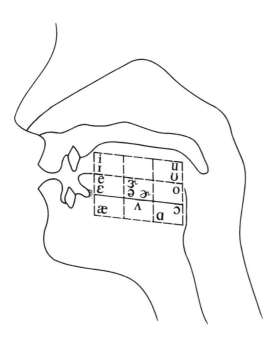

Figure 9–1   Vowel position.

Table 9–2   Phonetic and Diacritic Symbols for Standard American English Sounds

SOUND	IPA	AMERICAN HERITAGE	RANDOM HOUSE	WEBSTER'S THIRD INTERNATIONAL
Consonants				
put	[p]	p	p	p
but	[b]	b	b	b
tip	[t]	t	t	t
dip	[d]	d	d	d
cave	[k]	k	k	k
gave	[g]	g	g	g
foe	[f]	f	f	f
vote	[v]	v	v	v
thick	[θ]	th	t͟h	th
those	[ð]	*th*	th	t͟h
see	[s]	s	s	s
zone	[z]	z	z	z
shut	[ʃ]	sh	s͟h	sh
azure	[ʒ]	zh	z͟h	zh
hot	[h]	h	h	h
chuck	[tʃ]	ch	c͟h	ch
just	[dʒ]	j	j	j
me	[m]	m	m	m
not	[n]	n	n	n
sing	[ŋ]	ng	n͡g	ŋ
which	[ʍ]	hw	hw	hw
witch	[w]	w	w	w
you	[j]	y	y	y
rot	[r]	r	r	r
log	[l]	l	l	l
Vowels				
east	[i]	ē	ē	ē
it	[ɪ]	ĭ	i	i
ate	[e]	ā	ā	ā
set	[ɛ]	ĕ	e	e
sat	[æ]	ă	a	a
calm	[ɑ]	ä	ä	ä
saw	[ɔ]	ô	ô	ȯ
hotel	[o]	ō	ō	ō
foot	[ʊ]	o͞o	o͞o	u̇
food	[u]	o͞o	o͞o	ü
fun	[ʌ]	ŭ	u	ˈə
sofa	[ə]	ə	ə	ə
fir	[ɝ]	ûr	û(r)	ˈər
father	[ɚ]	ər	ər	ər
Diphthongs				
play	[eɪ]	ā	ā	ā
pipe	[aɪ]	ī	ī	ī
boy	[ɔɪ]	oi	oi	ȯi
out	[aʊ]	ou	ou	au̇
hope	[oʊ]	ō	ō	ō
Variants				
city	[ɨ]			
hot	[ɒ]	ŏ	o	ȧ
path	[a]	ȧ		

dictionary for the class or lets you select your own, you memorize the diacritical markings so that you can look up words quickly and easily.

If you do not own a good dictionary, you should purchase one. Any good current dictionary, such as the *American Heritage,* the *Random House,* or the *Webster's Third International,* will be useful. Desk dictionaries, such as the *Webster's New Collegiate* or *The American Heritage Third College Edition,* are probably more practical for the college student. You will need to familiarize yourself with the diacritical marking system used by your dictionary.

A few specialized dictionaries give only pronunciations, not word meanings. For many years, speech teachers depended upon Kenyon and Knott's *A Pronouncing Dictionary of American English* (Springfield, Mass.: Merriam), which uses the IPA. Although it was reprinted in 1995, it has not been significantly revised since 1956. Obviously, many words have been coined and the pronunciation of other words has changed since then. Abraham and Betty Lass's *Dictionary of Pronunciation* (New York: Quadrangle/The N.Y. Times, 1976) is more current, but it does not use the IPA. *A Concise Pronouncing Dictionary of British and American English* (London: Oxford University Press, 1972) uses the IPA, but is geared more to a comparison of British and American speech than to a comprehensive pronouncing dictionary.

Whatever your choice in dictionaries, or your instructor's particular requirement, we urge you to learn the marking system thoroughly so that you can use your dictionary with skill and ease.

THE IPA

As we mentioned earlier, many speech teachers will prefer that you learn the International Phonetic Alphabet, a system that provides a particular symbol for each sound, rather than simply using **orthographic** or print symbols to indicate pronunciation. Some dictionaries that use a standard diacritical system are beginning to introduce a few IPA symbols for added clarity, such as [j] and [ŋ].

We have found that using the IPA helps our students, for as we discuss the classification and the articulatory formation of each phoneme, they learn the phonetic symbol that represents it. They come to depend on their ears for the sounds, not for some mental predisposition to pronounce the word as it is spelled in print. Knowledge of phonemic construction, auditory training, and speech performance seems to us to advance as a whole more readily when we utilize the IPA. That is our personal bias; your instructor will choose the approach best suited to his or her teaching style.

Since the IPA is less well known, a brief history and explanation of it will help prepare you if your instructor decides to use it.

As early as the thirteenth century, a few sporadic attempts were made to adjust the English alphabet so that the written symbols more nearly represented the spoken sounds. But it was not until the late nineteenth century that concerted efforts produced the first workable phonetic alphabet, designed mainly to enable the deaf to "see" the various spoken sounds. Alexander Melville Bell, father of telephone inventor Alexander Graham Bell, included a sound classification system in his book *Visible Speech* (1867). This system became the basis for the alphabet perfected by Henry Sweet, published in his *History of English Sounds* (1874) and *A Primer of Phonetics* (1890). In 1888, the International Phonetic Association adopted the system as its official alphabet. Despite some minor modifications since then, the IPA remains the most widely accepted method for meeting the goal of most phoneticians—an alphabet with one and only one written letter for each speech sound. Incidentally, Sweet was a friend of George Bernard Shaw and the inspiration for the character of Henry Higgins in the play *Pygmalion* and the later musical version, *My Fair Lady.*

The IPA has not been used widely outside academic circles, but is generally accepted as a research and teaching tool. Students, faculty, and researchers often use the word *phonetics* to mean the alphabet itself. More precisely, phonetics is the study of the science of speech sounds. It comprises four major divisions—descriptive phonetics, historical phonetics, comparative phonetics, and experimental phonetics.

Dictionaries are like watches; the worst is better than none, and the best cannot be expected to go quite true.

—SIR JOHN HAWKINS, *Life of Johnson, Apothegms*

HIGGINS: *Remember that you are a human being with a soul and the divine gift of articulate speech: that your native language is the language of Shakespeare and Milton and the Bible; and don't sit there crooning like a bilious pigeon.*

—GEORGE BERNARD SHAW, *Pygmalion*

Just for Fun . . . —————

"A Plan for the Improvement of English Spelling" by Mark Twain

In Year 1 that useless letter *c* would be dropped to be replaced by *k* or *s*, and likewise *x* would no longer be part of the alphabet. The only kase in which *c* would be retained would be the *ch* formation. Year 2 might reform *w* spelling, so that *which* and *one* would take the same konsonant, wile Year 3 might well abolish *y*, replasing it with *i*, and iear 4 might fiks the *g/j* anomali wonse and for all.

Symbols such as [x] for the Scottish *loch* or the German *ich* and [ɫ] for the Welsh fricative *l* are available for studying other dialects of the English language or other languages, but our discussion will encompass only the sounds of American English. (See Table 9–2.)

Note that of the twenty-five consonant symbols, sixteen are identical to letters in our orthographic alphabet. This duplication can help you in learning the IPA, provided you do not go through a "translating" process. When you study a foreign language—French or Spanish, for instance—your instructor probably tells you to try to *think* in the language, not to translate every word. To learn the metric system, you must conceptualize the distances or other measures, not constantly relate them to inches, yards, or miles. In the same way, you should associate the sound, not the orthographic letter, with the phonetic symbol. If you do not, your phonetic transcription will probably contain such common errors as [cʌpd] for the word *cupped*—but there is no *c* in phonetics, only [k], and the final sound in the word is [t], not [d]. So, the visual relationship of the IPA to the orthographic alphabet can be both helpful and misleading.

Sound is best studied by listening to it, not by translating symbols or reading about it. The best way to understand [p]—a small "explosion" that results from closing the lips, building up air pressure, then suddenly releasing air by separating the lips—is to produce it, feel it, see it, watch your lips and other articulators in the mirror, and hear it by listening to the sound in your own voice and in others'. Although sounds are described and classified by the position of the articulators and the manner of sound emission, a surprising degree of variation in mouth placement and formation exists among speakers. This is well illustrated by those persons who through birth defect or accident lose some articulatory organ and still produce speech sounds clearly. Most of you will be striving only to improve everyday speech habits, not to overcome serious defects, and can therefore profit from seeing, hearing, and studying the significant differences and variations among the sounds of American English.

Ultimately your ear is your best guide. You may learn that [ɪ] is produced with the tongue slightly higher in the mouth and the jaw slightly more closed than in the sound [ɛ], but this tongue and jaw positioning will not help you distinguish [ɪ] from [ɛ] as much as your ear will. The ear, trained and sensitized by careful study of sound formation, including the study of IPA, is the speaker's most effective tool for monitoring his or her voice and speech production.

FYI . . . _____

A very obscure but interesting word exists that properly labels the subject you are studying: *orthoepy* [ɔr ˈθoʊ ə pɨ]. Coming from the root words *orth*, meaning "correct," and *epos*, the Greek word for "speech," orthoepy means the study of the customary pronunciation of a language. So, while you are in this course—and, we hope, throughout your career—you will be an orthoepist, believe it or not!

Balaam's ass spoke well once, but it never tried it again. Altogether it differed greatly from its brethren.

—C. H. Spurgeon

STOP AND TRY THIS

Begin a journal in which you write three to four sentences each day on some aspect of voice and diction. This can include observations about voices that you hear, problems you have expressing yourself, unusual dialects or pronunciations you hear, reactions to other persons' voices, comments about radio, film, or television personalities, or anything else about voice and speech that interests or impresses you.

Keeping such a journal helps you focus on habits that you are usually only aware of subconsciously. Raising your awareness to a conscious level is essential to changing your own voice and speech production.

DISTINCTIVE TERMINOLOGY

We will use several labels from time to time as we discuss articulation and speech production. As these terms often have overlapping connotations, we need to stress again the fine distinctions observed by most speech specialists.

- **Articulation** is the process of obstructing, molding, and reshaping outgoing air in order to form the distinct and different phonemes of any given language.

- **Enunciation** is clear, precise articulation. It implies freedom from mumbling or slovenly formation of sounds.
- **Pronunciation** is the choice of the phoneme considered "correct" for a given word, as determined by an accepted, arbitrary standard—usually, current editions of reputable dictionaries. Words are mispronounced in one of six ways:

1. *Omission* of a sound, such as saying [laɪ bɛrɪ] (liberry) for [laɪ brɛrɪ̩] (library), or [pɪtʃɚ] (pitcher) for [pɪktʃɚ] (picture).

2. *Substitution* of one sound for another, such as [lɛnθ] (lenth) for [lɛŋθ] (length), or [ɛk sɛt ɚ ə] (ex cetera) for [ɛt sɛt ɚ ə] (et cetera).

3. *Addition* of a sound that is not supposed to be in the word, such as [æθ ə lit] (athulete) for [æθ lit] (athlete), or [stə stɪs tɪks] (stastistics) for [stə tɪs tɪks] (statistics).

4. *Transposition* of two sounds, such as [hʌn dɚd] (hunderd) for [hʌn drɪd] (hundred), or [ækst] (axed) for [æskt] (asked).

5. *Misplacing the accent,* such as [ɪn kəm 'pɛr əbl] (in com *pare* able) for [ɪn 'kam pɚ əbl] (in *com* perable), or [æd 'maɪr əbl] (ad *mire* able) for ['æd mɚ əbl] (*ad* mirable). When the accent is misplaced, sound substitutions also occur.

6. *Unusual spellings* of words mislead the speaker. For example, *salmon* should be pronounced ['sæmən], not [sælmən]. The *l* is silent. And the word *extraordinary* is pronounced [ɛkstrɔdɪnɛrɪ] (ek straw di nary) not [ɛkstrə ɔrdɪnɛrɪ] (extra ordinary).

The following lists present some commonly mispronounced words.

Just for Fun . . . _____

How quickly can you find out what is so unusual about this paragraph? It looks so ordinary that you would think nothing is wrong with it at all, and in fact, nothing is. But it is unusual. Why? If you study it and think about it you may find out, but I'm not going to assist you in any way. You must do it without coaching. No doubt, if you work at it for long, it will dawn upon you. Who knows? Go to work and try your skill. Par is about half an hour.

—WILLIAM M. HILL

See answer in the Appendix.

Omissions	Substitutions	Additions
1. adjective	1. absurd	1. accompanist
2. company	2. chimney	2. brethren
3. cruelty	3. diptheria	3. burglar
4. environment	4. genuine	4. disastrous
5. February	5. heroism	5. escape
6. government	6. Italian	6. height
7. literature	7. partner	7. positively
8. poem	8. pronunciation	8. tremendous
9. recognize	9. sandwich	9. umbrella
10. understanding	10. welts	10. Washington

Transpositions	Misplace Accents	Unusual Spellings
1. aggravate	1. ascertain	1. almond
2. cavalry	2. deluge	2. bade
3. children	3. executor	3. chaos
4. introduction	4. formidable	4. chasm
5. larynx	5. guitar	5. epitome
6. modern	6. infamous	6. forehead
7. perspiration	7. maintenance	7. often
8. pretty	8. mischievous	8. poignant
9. professor	9. police	9. quay
10. secretary	10. theatre	10. toward

A final term, **diction,** is used as a general term for the study of voice and articulation. A course may be called "Voice and Diction," or students may talk of studying "diction." Used in these ways, "diction" includes the concepts of articulation, enunciation, and pronunciation. It thus has the broader scope of our phrase "speech production," encompassing the total act of creating sounds and words.

STOP AND TRY THIS

Many beginning speech students have difficulty identifying the stressed (accented) syllables in words. Three vocal alterations enable us to convey stress:

1. The syllable is higher in pitch:
   "di^sturb" rather than "di^sturb"
2. The syllable is longer:
   "pro t-e-c-t" rather than "p-r-o tect"
3. The syllable is slightly louder:
   "FOR ward" rather than "for WARD"

If you have trouble identifying stress, try emphasizing the *incorrect* syllable to see how strange it sounds. Always repeat with the correct stress:

Incorrect Stress	*Correct Stress*
beau TI fy	BEAU ti fy
BE lieve	be LIEVE
CON trol	con TROL
de PU ty	DEP u ty
dif FI cul ty	DIF fi cul ty
ex TRA	EX tra

Use your dictionary to identify and produce correct syllabic stress.

PUTTING IT TOGETHER

With this general understanding of how speech is structured, coupled with the theoretical principles outlined in Chapters 1 and 2, you are ready to begin a step by step examination of the spoken sounds of American English and to improve your own production of those sounds with as much vocal control and flexibility as you can master.

At the end of the last chapter, we said that you need to continue to think of all the elements of voice as you work on pronunciation—keeping your speech loud and clear, with ample pitch variation and good voice quality. In addition, you will now need to cumulate the sounds that are covered in each chapter. This process grows more difficult as you go along, for you are being introduced in each chapter to several sounds—clustered into vowels and consonants. Some will be no problem to you. Others will be harder to produce in a standard manner. Those that are difficult will require the most work.

As with any program that requires both mental and physical learning and skill, your rate of progress will depend on the amount of time you are willing to practice. Daily attention to this important element of your ability to communicate will be both beneficial and rewarding.

PLAYS FOR PRACTICE

Practice material in this chapter comes from plays, both classic and modern. Each reading is a long speech, with the character from the play identified. Ideally you would need to read the entire play to understand the passage. Since these selections are for classroom practice only, we have tried to choose speeches that make some sense without the total context.

Modern Plays

ELYOT (male): I should like to explain that if you hit me, I shall certainly hit you, probably equally hard, if not harder. I'm just as strong as you I should imagine. Then you'd hit me again, and I'd hit you again, and we'd go on until one or the other was knocked out. Now if you'll explain to me satisfactorily how all that can possibly improve the situation, I'll tear off my coat, and we'll go at one another hammer and tongs, immediately. . . . Do I love Amanda? Not very much this morning, to be perfectly frank. I'd like to wring her neck. Do you love her? That's the crux of the whole affair. If you do love her still, you can forgive her, and live with her in peace and harmony until you're ninety-eight.

—Noel Coward,
Private Lives

DIAN FOSSEY (female): . . . That's about the time I said to myself, You're all alone in this one. Like it was a monolog. It might as well have been. I could just as well have talked to the wall, without him sitting there, twiddling his pencil. There was a time when I believed everything a man would tell me. You know, the half-truths, whispered in semidarkness, the warm fuzzies that you hear from park officials, et cetera, et cetera. And don't leave the ladies out, either. I've got a pocket full of wine-and-cheese endorsements for my Save the Gorillas campaign, and I'm still wondering when I'm going to wake up and not be in a cold sweat, wondering whether my gorillas made it through the night or not. Forget about the long range stuff. Like, whether they'll make it through this century. I've already seen that handwriting on the wall. I'm just concerned about whether they make it through the night. I used to have dreams about all the people who said they were behind me. Dreams where everybody would be swaying back and forth, singing songs that you'd expect to hear in church, or in some commercial for Coca-Cola. But I woke up. And, when I woke up, everybody was gone.

—Lawrence M. Fogelberg,
*Nyiramachabelli, The Woman
Who Lives Alone in the Forest*

OSCAR (male): How can I help you when I can't help myself? You think you're impossible to live with? Blanche used to say, "What time do you want dinner?" And I'd say, "I don't know, I'm not hungry." Then at three o'clock in the morning I'd wake her up and say, "Now!" I've been one of the highest paid sportswriters in the East for the past fourteen years, and we saved eight and a half dollars—in pennies! I'm never home, I gamble, I burn cigar holes in the furniture, drink like a fish and lie to her every chance I get. And for our tenth wedding anniversary, I took her to see the New York Rangers–Detroit Red Wings hockey game where she got hit with a puck. And I *still* can't understand why she left me. That's how impossible *I* am!

—Neil Simon,
The Odd Couple

GERTRUDE (female): Hemingway was a mass of fears and prejudices. He said he has always carried a knife when he traveled in the company of men, because in those days when he was a boy, there were a lot of wolves about, and wolves was not a term for men who chased after women at that time. He said if a man sensed that you would kill, then you were let be and not interfered with in certain ways. Alice detested him forever after that. But I was patient with him. He was so young and his eyes were so passionately interested and he was sitting at my feet as though I was the goddess of intelligence. . . . He was a good fellow when he was young, I thought, and some of his really early stuff was not so bad. But he never got along with Alice and so our friendship did not last. It faded, but not the flowers of it—never the flowers.

—Marty Martin,
*Gertrude Stein, Gertrude Stein,
Gertrude Stein*

EARL OF GURNEY (male): My heart rises with the sun. I'm purged of doubts and negative innuendos. Today I want to bless everything! Bless the crawfish that has a scuttling walk, bless the trout, the pilchard and periwinkle. Bless Ted Smoothey of 22 East Hackney Road—with a name like that he needs blessing. Bless the mealy-redpole, the black-gloved wallaby and W. C. Fields, who's dead but lives on. Bless the skunk, bless the red-bellied lemur, bless "Judo" Al Hayes and Ski-Hi-Lee. Bless the snotty-nosed giraffe, bless the buffalo, bless the Society of Women Engineers, bless the wild yak, bless the Piccadilly Match King, bless the pygmy hippo, bless the weasel, bless the mighty cockroach, bless me. Today's my wedding day!

—PETER BARNES,
The Ruling Class

ASAGAI (male): In my village at home it is the exceptional man who can even read a newspaper—or who ever sees a book at all. I will go home and much of what I will have to say will seem strange to the people of my village. But I will teach and work and things will happen, slowly and swiftly. At times it will seem that nothing changes at all—and then again—the sudden dramatic events which make history leap into the future. And the quiet again. Retrogression, even. Guns, murder, revolution. And I even will have moments when I wonder if the quiet was not better than all the death and hatred. But I will look about my village at the illiteracy and disease and ignorance and I will not wonder long. And perhaps—perhaps I will be a great man—I mean perhaps I will hold onto the substance of truth and find my way always with the right course—and perhaps for it I will be butchered in my bed some night by the servants of the empire.

—LORRAINE HANSBERRY,
A Raisin in the Sun

CHERIE (female): I went to the Blue Dragon last night and just sang for the first show. Then I told 'em I was quittin'. I'd been wantin' to find another job anyway, and I picked up my share of the kitty. But darn it, I had to go and tell 'em I was takin' the midnight bus. They had to go and tell Bo, a course, when he come in a li'l after eleven. He paid 'em five dollars to find out. So I went down to the bus station and hadn't even got my ticket, when here comes Bo and Virge. He jest steps up to the ticket window and says, "Three tickets to Montana!" I didn't know what to say. Then he dragged me onto the bus and I been on it ever since. And somewhere deep down inside me, I gotta funny feelin' I'm gonna end in Montana.

—WILLIAM INGE,
Bus Stop

DRUMMOND (male): Are we now to halt the march of progress because Mr. Brady frightens us with a fable? Gentlemen, progress has never been a bargain. You've got to pay for it. Sometimes I think there's a man behind a counter who says, "All right, you can have a telephone, but you'll have to give up privacy, the charm of distance. Madam, you may vote; but at a price; you lose the right to retreat behind a powder-puff or a petticoat. Mister, you may conquer the air, but the birds will lose their wonder, and the clouds will smell of gasoline!" Darwin moved us forward to a hilltop, where we could look back and see the way from which we came. But for this view, this insight, this knowledge, we must abandon our faith in the pleasant poetry of Genesis.

—JEROME LAWRENCE AND ROBERT E. LEE,
Inherit the Wind

JAMES: (male): You see, music is—music has a—music starts with pitches. Sounds! High and low. A whole, huge range of sounds. And each one has its own emotional life. And then when you combine them and play them together—these two and these two—it has a whole new life. And then you can play them on different instruments—trombones, violins, flutes and drums—The combinations are infinite! And then when you put it all together, with a beginning, a middle, and an end, it grows into a—it transcends mere sound and speaks directly to your heart—because you hear it! I don't have the signs that can—I can't explain it, I'm sorry.

—Mark Medoff,
Children of a Lesser God

MOTHER (female): I was fast asleep, and—Remember the way he used to fly low past the house when he was in training? When we used to see his face in the cockpit going by? That's the way I saw him. Only high up. Way, way up, where the clouds are. He was so real I could reach out and touch him. And suddenly he started to fall. And crying, crying to me—Mom, Mom! I could hear him like he was in the room. Mom!—it was his voice! If I could touch him I knew I could stop him, if I could only—I woke up and it was so funny—the wind—it was like the roaring of his engine. I came out here—I must've still been half asleep. I could hear that roaring like he was going by. The tree snapped right in front of me—and I came awake. See? We should never have planted that tree. I said so in the first place; it was too soon to plant a tree for him.

—Arthur Miller,
All My Sons

Classic Plays

CATHERINE (female): My mother used to say: "Between husband and wife, there should be no secrets." And she was quite right. Married people have only too often brought down terrible catastrophes on themselves or their households just because they didn't tell each other everything. That is what happened to the Chief Justice of Beaupreau's wife. To give her husband a pleasant surprise, she shut up a little sucking pig in a chest in her room. Her husband heard it squealing, and thought it was a lover, so he out with his sword and ran his wife through the heart, without even waiting to hear the poor lady's explanation. You can imagine his surprise and despair when he opened the chest. And that shows you must never have secrets, even for good reasons.

—Anatole France,
The Man Who Married a Dumb Wife

LUKA (male): It was winter and I was all alone in the house. One day I hear noises at a window! . . . I picked up my rifle and went out. I look around and there I see—two men trying to open the window—and working so hard at it they didn't even notice me. I shout at them: Hey, you! Get out of here! And what do they do? They turn around and rush at me with an ax. I warn them, Keep away, I say, or I'll shoot, and at the same time I cover them with my rifle, now one, now the other. Down on their knees they went as if begging me to let them go. But by now I felt very cross with them—for the ax, you know. You devils wouldn't go away when I told you, says I, now break off some twigs from a tree, one of you. And now, I order one of you to lie down and let the other lash him with the twigs. So by my order they gave each other a fine lashing.

—Maxim Gorky,
The Lower Depths

MRS. HARDCASTLE (female): Fine spoken, madam; you are most miraculously polite and engaging, and quite the very pink of courtesy and circumspection, madam. And you, you great ill-fashioned oaf, with scarce sense enough to keep your mouth shut,—were you too joined against me? But I'll defeat all your plots in a moment. As for you madam, since you have got a pair of fresh horses ready, it would be cruel to disappoint them. So, if you please, instead of running away with your spark, prepare, this very moment, to run off with me. Your old Aunt Pedigree will keep you secure, I'll warrant me. You, too, Sir, may mount your horse, and guard us upon the way. I'll show you that I wish you better than you do yourselves.

—OLIVER GOLDSMITH,
She Stoops to Conquer

THE MAYOR (male): You, Luka, as Superintendent of Schools, must be particularly careful about the teachers. Of course they are learned men and have been educated at all sorts of colleges, but they have very strange peculiarities, naturally, inseparable from their vocation. One of them, for instance, the one with a fat face—I can't recollect his name—never seems able to go up to his desk without making a grimace and then begins smoothing his beard from under his cravat. Of course, if he makes a face like that at one of the boys it does not matter; it may be necessary. I can't judge; but just think if he does it to a visitor—that might be a dreadful thing; the Inspector or someone else might think it was meant for him. Goodness only knows what it might lead to.

—NIKOLAI GOGOL,
The Inspector General

RACHEL (female): But there is no forward in this! We have been thrown back into sheer barbarism! Once more all faith in happy future has been wiped out. Just ask a few questions around here! The worst feature of such a mad outburst of evil is not the death of some or the sorrow of others; it is that all courage is frightened out of the world. Mercy has fled, and all are crying for vengeance. Justice, kindness, forbearance, all our angels of light have fled away. The air is filled with fragments of mutilated corpses, and armed men are springing out of the ground. All others are in hiding—I can't dress a patient's wound without having to remember—I cannot hear a moan without getting sick at heart. And then the knowledge that no matter what I do, it won't help—it won't help!

—BJORNSTJERNE BJORNSON,
Beyond Human Might

MAX (male): My dear friend. You hold in your hands the solution to a puzzle over which the wisest men have racked their brains, you need only ask and you shall know all you wish to know. A single question—and you discover whether she loves only you. You could discover who your rival is, you could discover by what means he succeeded—but you refuse to say the word! Fate allows you a question, but you waste it! You torture yourself through days and nights, you'd willingly give half your life to discover the truth, but now that it's within your grasp, you don't even stretch out your hand! And why? Because the woman you love might turn out to correspond with your conception of women—and because your illusions are worth a thousand times more to you than the truth. Enough of this game, wake the girl, and be content with the proud knowledge that you might have accomplished a miracle.

—ARTHUR SCHNITZLER,
Anatol

GWENDOLEN (female): Jack? No, there is very little music in the name Jack, if any at all, indeed. It does not thrill. It produces absolutely no vibrations. I have known several Jacks, and they all, without exception, were more than usually plain. Besides, Jack is a notorious domesticity for John! And I pity any woman who is married to a man called John. She would probably never be allowed to know the entrancing pleasure of a single moment's solitude. The only really safe name is Ernest.

—OSCAR WILDE,
The Importance of Being Earnest

JEAN (male): One time I went into the Garden of Eden with my mother to weed the onion beds. Close to the kitchen garden there was a Turkish pavilion hung all over with jasmine and honeysuckle. I hadn't any idea what it was used for, but I'd never seen such a beautiful building. People used to go in and then come out again, and one day the door was left open. I crept up and saw the walls covered with pictures of kings and emperors, and the windows had red curtains with fringes. I had never been inside the manor, never seen anything but the church, and this was more beautiful. No matter where my thoughts went, they always came back—to that place. . . . I sneaked in, gazed and admired. Then I heard someone coming. There was only one way out for the gentry, but for me there was another and I had no choice but to take it. I took to my heels, plunged through the raspberry canes, dashed across the strawberry beds and found myself on the rose terrace. There I saw a pink dress and a pair of white stockings—it was you. I watched you walking among the roses and said to myself: "If it's true that a thief can get to heaven and be with the angels, it's pretty strange that a laborer's child here on God's earth mayn't come in the park and play with the Count's daughter."

—AUGUST STRINDBERG,
Miss Julie

NINA (female): Men and beasts, eagles and partridges, antlered deer, mute fishes dwelling in the water, starfish and small creatures invisible to the eye—these and all life have run their sad course and are no more. Thousands of creatures have come and gone since there was life on the earth. Vainly now the pallid moon doth light her lamp. In the meadows the cranes wake and cry no longer; and the beetles' hum is silent in the linden grove. . . . Living bodies have crumbled to dust, and Eternal Matter has changed them into stones and water and clouds and there is one soul of many souls. I am that soul of the world—in me the soul of Alexander the Great, of Caesar, of Shakespeare, of Napoleon and of the lowest worm. The mind of man and the brute's instinct mingle in me. I remember all, all, and in me lives each several life again.

—ANTON CHEKHOV,
The Sea Gull

SHOEMAKER (male) (counting the wrinkles in his face): One, two, three, four— and a thousand. But it serve me right, yes sir. Because, let's see: why did I marry? I should have known after reading so many novels that men like all women— but women don't like all men. And I was so well off! My sister, my sister is to blame. My sister who kept saying: "You're going to be left alone." You're going to be this and that. And that was my undoing. May lightning strike my sister, may she rest in peace!

—FEDERICO GARCIA LORCA,
The Shoemaker's Prodigious Wife

MODERN PLAYS ACKNOWLEDGMENTS

Private Lives by Noel Coward. Permission granted by Doubleday, a division of Bantam, Doubleday, Dell Publishing Group, Inc.

The Odd Couple by Neil Simon. Permission granted by Doubleday, a division of Bantam, Doubleday, Dell Publishing Group, Inc.

Gertrude Stein, Gertrude Stein, Gertrude Stein by Marty Martin. Random House–Vintage, 1980. Copyright © Sea-Ker, Inc. Harry W. Martin III. By special permission Pat Carroll, Lucy Kroll Agency.

The Ruling Class by Peter Barnes. Reprinted by permission of Margaret Ramsay Ltd. and Heinemann Publishers (Oxford) Ltd.

Nyiramachabelli by Lawrence M. Fogelberg. By special permission of the author.

A Raisin in the Sun by Lorraine Hansberry. Reprinted by permission of Random House, Inc. Copyright © 1959.

Bus Stop by William Inge. By permission of International Creative Management, Inc. Copyright © 1955, by William Inge. Copyright © 1956, by William Inge. Copyrights renewed 1983, 1984 by Helene Connell.

Inherit the Wind by Jerome Lawrence and Robert E. Lee. By permission of Random House, Inc. Copyright © 1955.

Children of a Lesser God by Mark Medoff. By permission of William Morris Agency, Inc. © 1980, 1987, by Mark Medoff.

All My Sons by Arthur Miller. In *Arthur Miller's Collected Plays*. Copyright 1947, renewed © 1975 by Arthur Miller. All rights reserved. Reprinted by permission of Viking Penguin, Inc.

CHAPTER 10

Stop-Plosive Consonants and Front Vowels

Speak the speech, I pray you, as I pronounced it to you, trippingly on the tongue; but if you mouth it, as many of your players do, I had as lief the town crier spoke my lines.

—WILLIAM SHAKESPEARE,
Hamlet

STOP-PLOSIVE CONSONANTS

Remember that consonants are produced by obstruction of the airstream, as compared with the relatively unobstructed vowel sounds. One of the methods of obstruction and subsequent emission of air is the creation of a blockage that stops the airstream for a moment, after which a sudden separation releases the air. As the release is somewhat like a small explosion, the term **stop-plosive,** sometimes merely *stop,* sometimes *plosive,* is used to characterize the six sounds produced in this way—p, b, t, d, k, and g. In the IPA, they are written [p], [b], [t], [d], [k], and [g].

A second means of distinguishing among consonants is the place of the articulators during production. For the six plosives, three configurations of the articulators are responsible. For [p] and [b], the two lips are brought together to form the stop, air pressure is built up, and the air is suddenly released. For [t] and [d], the tip of the tongue presses against the upper gum ridge to create the obstruction. For [k] and [g], the back of the tongue and the soft palate move together to obstruct the outgoing air.

The third basis for distinguishing among the consonants is whether they require phonation (vocal-fold vibration) or are made without vibration of the vocal folds. Paired, or cognate, consonants are produced with the same manner of obstruction and the same positioning of the articulators, yet differ in phonation. If the vocal folds vibrate, the sound is *voiced.* A *voiceless* sound is produced without vocal-fold vibration. The six plosives are three such **cognate pairs,** with [p], [t], and [k] voiceless and [b], [d], and [g] their vocalized cognates.

[p] *AND* [b]

[p] **Is a Voiceless, Bilabial Stop-Plosive**

Production: To form the consonant [p], pull the lips together, allow air pressure to build up behind them, then open the lips quickly so that compressed air is released. No vocal-fold voicing is required.

Be aware:

1. Do not omit the [p], especially when it follows another consonant, in words such as *limping, gulps,* or *gasped,* or is at the end of a word, as in *weep, trap,* or *hope.*

2. Lip closure must be complete for a clear, crisp [p] sound. Lip-lazy speakers may say *ho-fully* when they mean *hopefully.*

3. Avoid substituting the voiced cognate [b] for [p], such as saying *asbirin* for *aspirin* or *camber* for *camper.*

4. Do not overexplode or pop your [p] sounds by aspirating too much air. This is especially risky when you are speaking into a microphone, for it will exaggerate the explosiveness.

POSITION

Frontal	Medial	Final, Preceded by:			
		VOWEL	[ɝ][r]	[m]	[l]
pint	grapple	polyp	warp	cramp	alp
pleasure	lapel	isotope	harp	damp	pulp
pickle	paper	strap	twerp	limp	whelp
pungent	cupid	sleep	burp	trump	yelp
periscope	expensive	tape	carp	stump	help
parsimonious	impounded	ripe			
portable	inappropriate	stoop			

[b] **Is a Voiced, Bilabial Stop-Plosive**

Production: To form [b], pull the lips together, allow air pressure to build up behind them, then open the lips quickly so that the compressed air is released. Vocal-fold vibration, or voicing, is required.

Be aware:

1. Do not omit the [b], especially when it follows another consonant, in words such as *bulbs, barbed,* or *orbs,* or is at the end of a word as in *rib, curb,* or *lobe.*

2. Voice [b] fully, for if you do not it will sound like [p]. This is especially troublesome if a voiceless sound follows the [b], in which case *mobster* might come out as *mopster* or *bobtail* as *boptail.*

3. Both [p] and [b] are frequently articulated without full aspiration (without the explosion of air that completes them) used in conversation. This occurs in rapid assimilated speech, particularly when another consonant precedes or follows them. Note that the [p] in *sport* is not as aspirated as the [p] in *port,* and the [b] in *crabgrass* does not explode as much as the [b] in *crabby.* However, do not slight the time given to the stop or closure part of these sounds, or serious distortion will result.

4. When *b* follows *m* (in orthographic spelling) at the end of a word, the *b* is not pronounced, as in *lamb, tomb, climb, dumb,* and *thumb.*

POSITION

Frontal	Medial	Final, Preceded by:		
		VOWEL		[l] [r]
boy	about	scab	slab	orb
blend	double	cob	rube	barb
bum	barbell	ebb	glib	bulb
beautiful	number	grub	bribe	
bark	tuba	vibe	babe	
belt	laboratory			
beach	dubious			

[p] *and* [b] *Paired Words*

boy—poi	bin—pin	cap—cab
belt—pelt	bare—pare	lap—lab
bike—pike	bass—pass	cop—cob
beach—peach	base—pace	cup—cub

Sentences Featuring [p] *and* [b]

1. The boy put back the pack, but leapt past the bike.
2. The lump in his blue lapel, a bruise, brought a yelp from Bud.
3. Parliament passed a bill approving the purchase of surplus barley from Nebraska's bumper crop.
4. Is it bravado, aplomb, or pluck, or is Pam just plain brash?
5. Place in Pat's lab a tube, precious herbs, barbells, plenty of paper and ballpoint pens, and a lamb-pelt lap robe.
6. Boys eat poi and peaches on beaches and at parks.
7. Thumps and gasps about the tomb made proud Bob blubber for Pop.
8. People exploit the deep blue ebb for bass, carp, bluefish, and blubber.
9. Pete the pitcher, about to bunt, drew an improbable base on balls.
10. Please prepare a papal brunch: boiled parsley, prime rib of pork, baked beets with bread crumbs, and pasta parmigiana.
11. Rob abruptly dropped the props and rubbed the lump in the magic lamp.
12. The boat swabber swapped jobs with Paula Beall, potato peeler and would-be ballplayer.
13. The pair of panda bears would be parents by now but for predictable breeding problems.
14. Prepare a paper with a carbon copy on the burden of bearing big baskets of potato blintzes.
15. Bea Peabody has made progress duplicating the broad brogue of Dubliners; she's in Prague brushing up on her Prussian.

[t] *AND* [d]

[t] Is a Voiceless, Lingua-Alveolar Stop-Plosive

Production: To form the consonant [t], press the tip of the tongue against the upper gum ridge, just behind the upper teeth, blocking the outgoing air. Then suddenly drop the tongue tip, releasing the air. No vocal-fold vibration is required.

Be aware:

1. Do not omit [t], especially at the ends of words or in consonant clusters. Avoid saying *mos'* and *jus'* for *most* and *just*, or *pain-er* and *ren-ned* for *painter* and *rented*. Such omission is especially tempting when consonants fall both before and after the [t], as in *boasts, lists,* or *wilts.*

2. Avoid substituting a glottal stop for the alveolar stop in the [t] sound. This is commonly heard in words such as *little* [lɪ ʔl] or *kettle* [kɛ ʔl].*

3. Do not use the voiced [d] in place of the voiceless [t], as in *liddle* for *little* or *preddy* for *pretty.*

POSITION

Frontal	Medial	Final, Preceded by:	
		VOWEL	*CONSONANT*
teach	laughter	diet	splint
tender	pretty	invite	melt
tube	poultry	repeat	next
taste	tartar	vote	import
trust	subtle	pout	waste
tickle	artistic	abate	adept
time	cartwheel	ought	enact

[d] Is a Voiced, Lingua-Alveolar Stop-Plosive

Production: To form [d], press the tip of the tongue against the upper gum ridge, just behind the upper teeth, blocking the outgoing airstream. Then suddenly drop the tongue tip, releasing the air. Voicing is required.

Be aware:

1. Both [d] and [t] may be made without the full explosion of air that characterizes the stop-plosives. In rapid assimilated speech, and particularly when the [t] or [d] is juxtaposed with other consonants, only the stop occurs. However, the closure for the *stop* must be completed even though the *plosive* is not. Incomplete closure will cause the sounds to be slurred and indistinct.

2. Avoid **dentalizing** either [d] or [t]. Dentalizing occurs when the tongue tip is placed on the back of the upper teeth rather than the gum ridge. Dentalizing causes [d] or [t] to sound more like fricatives than stop-plosives, for you will hear the escaping air.

3. Be sure to voice [d] fully, so that you don't substitute the cognate [t], as in *bitter* or *hurt* when you mean *bidder* or *heard.*

POSITION

Frontal	Medial	Final, Preceded by:	
		VOWEL	*CONSONANT*
dogmatic	adept	lied	bold
diaper	huddle	impede	beyond
dubious	balding	employed	land
delightful	academy	rude	loved
drip	arduous	spade	rigged
dwindle	hardly	explode	yard
daily	epidemic	blood	buzzed

*Note: [ʔ] is the IPA symbol for a glottal stop.

[t] and [d] Paired Words

drip—trip	dense—tense	dock—tock	weld—welt
dear—tear	dell—tell	wade—wait	bold—bolt
dare—tear	dart—tart	dead—debt	ode—oat
bid—bit	rude—route	bidder—bitter	bidden—bitten
need—neat	nodded—knotted	padding—patting	ladder—latter
send—sent	budded—butted	caddy—catty	bedding—betting

Avoid the influence of conventional spelling, which could cause you to write [bʌkd] for the word *bucked* when transcribing it into phonetics. Listen carefully—it is [bʌkt].

A simple rule helps to determine pronunciation of the past tense:

1. If the final sound of an original regular verb is voiceless, use the voiceless [t].
    Examples: [p]—[slæpt] slapped
    [s]—[kɪst] kissed
    [f]—[stæft] staffed

2. If the final sound of an original regular verb is voiced, use the voiced [d].
    Examples: [b]—[rʌbd] rubbed
    [z]—[bʌzd] buzzed
    [v]—[seɪvd] saved

3. If, however, the original word ends in [t] or [d], an additional syllable is required—either [ɪd] or [əd].
    Examples: [bɛd ɪd] bedded
    [speɪd ɪd] spaded
    [saɪt ɪd] sighted
    [hit ɪd] heated

Sentences Featuring [t] and [d]

1. Dot and Todd did the tune from *Deliverance* as a duet.
2. Study how to do the Howdy Doody tunes in the sand dunes.
3. The stud kicked mud on Mutt's dungarees, then strode toward the tundra.
4. The idea of a darkroom did wonders for photo development.
5. Graduate and undergraduate students attended the University of North Texas in Denton.
6. The desperate agent defused the time bomb before it ticked to its detonation deadline.
7. The dead-letter office takes hundreds of undelivered bundles to the dump each day.
8. Truman Capote told of two desperadoes in his story called *In Cold Blood.*
9. Better to put little buttons into big buttonholes than to try to force bulbous buttons into bitsy slits.
10. The rudder on the boat caught in the reeds below the water and split down the middle.
11. The Best Western Motel rented suites with double doors to traveling tourists.
12. The bride wore white as she walked beside her dad down the petal-covered aisle.
13. Doctors treat contagious diseases while dentists drill teeth to remove decay.
14. The telephone and telegraph brought together isolated cities, states, countries—even continents.
15. Dylan Thomas wrote poetry, Tennessee Williams drafted dramas, and Danny Thomas acted in *Make Room for Daddy.*

In pronouncing a double *t* or *d*, be sure to remember the phonetic spelling. *Bedding* and *betting* are [bɛdɪŋ] and [bɛtɪŋ], not [bɛd dɪŋ] and [bɛt tɪŋ]. Orthographic spelling uses the letter twice, while phonetically it occurs only once. The plosive needs to be enunciated clearly, but do not overdo it so that it sounds stilted and forced. It helps in achieving this to think of the plosive as beginning the second syllable rather than ending the first. Say [bɛ tɪŋ], not [bɛt ɪŋ].

Exercise Featuring [t] *and* [d]

Tad, a lad, and Ted, his dad
Loved food too dearly. Something had
To be done, for indeed, by fate,
Tad and Dad were a bit overweight.
Dad said "Tad, let's adopt a diet.
To this I'm devoted. Darn it, let's try it!"
Tad pouted and pleaded, with a doleful, "Oh, dear,
I'm doomed to die." There trickled a tear.
But Ted, adamant, deemed it dumb to deter.
Determined to shed, he told Tad to endure.

"No cod, no lard, avoid oats and trout;
Toddies, malteds, all drinks do without.
Tongue-taste no tarts; delight not in delis.
Drink water twice daily to dwindle our bellies.
Disdain meats and mints, delve not into dip.
Toodledoo, tenderloin! Ta-ta, beef tip!"
Tad did it quite tidily, as it turns out—
He toughened, grew sturdy, svelte, and stout.
But Dad took flight, never trimmed, never tried.
Indulgent, sated, he ate till he died.

[k] *AND* [g]

[k] **Is a Voiceless, Lingua-Velar Stop-Plosive**

Production: To form the consonant [k], press the back of the tongue against the **velum** (soft palate), allowing air pressure to build up behind the point of closure. Then suddenly lower the tongue to release the compressed air. No vocal-fold vibration is required.

Be aware:

1. It is especially tempting to omit [k], both within words and at word endings. Take care not to say *ar-tic* for *arctic*, *e-scuse* for *excuse*, or *ast* for *asked*.

2. Make full closure with [k], so that it is crisp and complete. Watch this on words such as *accessible*, *exaggerate*, and *ridiculous*. Failure to make full closure is not the same as total omission of the sound, but it comes close.

3. Don't let orthographic spelling fool you with this sound. Sometimes [k] is not pronounced at all, as in *knew*, *knife*, and *knot*. In many words, the orthographic *c* is pronounced [k]—*cool*, *include*, *case*. The orthographic *ck* is almost always [k]—*trick*, *wicket*, *backpack*. And [k] coupled with [w] is usually the phonetic equivalent of orthographic *q*, as in *quiet*, *quest*, or *queen*.

POSITION

Frontal	Medial	Final, Preceded by:	
		VOWEL	*CONSONANT*
kindle	actor	spook	arc
quick	trachea	alike	quirk
clutter	docket	artistic	plank
keen	become	squawk	embark
catchy	awkward	quack	rink
cuticle	adequate	unique	milk
quiche	increase	rhetoric	torque

[g] **Is a Voiced, Lingua-Velar Stop-Plosive**

Production: To form [g], press the back of the tongue against the velum, allowing air pressure to build up behind the point of closure. Then suddenly lower the tongue to release the compressed air. Voicing is required.

Be aware:

1. Although voicing of [g], as with [b] and [d], is less full before voiceless sounds and at sentence or phrase endings than before voiced sounds, be sure you do not eliminate the voicing entirely, or [k] will result. Be especially careful with words such as *bagful, pigskin,* and *ragtime.*

2. On the other hand, do not overvoice or aspirate [g]. While the explosion is relatively strong when [g] occurs at the beginning of words, it is usually weak in unstressed syllables or if the next sound is a voiced consonant. Avoid over-exploding on words such as *blackguard* [blæ gɚd], *shaggy,* and *rugged.* Some speakers explode [g] so heavily that you can hear a palate-grinding sound as the velum is shifted downward.

3. Do not let orthographic spelling mislead you: *ng* is seldom [n] and [g], but usually the single consonant [ŋ]. Orthographic *g* may be [dʒ] instead of [g]—*gem, gentle, gymnasium*—or it may be silent, as in *gnaw, gnome, sign,* or *champagne.*

POSITION

Frontal	Medial	Final
great	aggregate	pig
glisten	juggle	grog
garlic	diagnose	nutmeg
glutton	haggle	slug
gaudy	magazine	dialogue
guild	eggshell	fugue
gamble	pigpen	jitterbug

[k] *and* [g] *Paired Words*

pick—pig	tuck—tug	crate—grate	crow—grow
slack—slag	pluck—plug	cool—ghoul	Clyde—glide
frock—frog	leak—league	coal—goal	clean—glean
back—bag	broke—brogue	crain—grain	curl—girl

Sentences Featuring [k] *and* [g]

1. Grab the crab by the back to avoid the grip of its claw.
2. Gil haggled with the hack over the cost of a cab to Gloucester.

3.   Gullible Ken could not kill cranes with big green beaks.

4.   Frank won cups of guppies and glasses of goldfish at the carnival for guessing Gilda's weight in kilograms.

5.   Agriculture involves the difficult task of gradually cultivating good crops.

6.   Eggnog is a creamy, sugary drink heavy in caloric content.

7.   Big quarterbacks from the Cowboys, Kansas City, Green Bay, and Pittsburgh kicked pigskins across goal lines.

8.   The musical *Oklahoma!* was taken from *Green Grow the Lilacs,* a folk drama of agrarian America.

9.   Kennedy guaranteed that he could win the election from Nixon in Connecticut, Arkansas, and the Great Lakes states.

10.   Lady Godiva galloped quickly down the cobblestone pavement as the goggle-eyed folks of Coventry gawked and gazed.

11.   *Good Housekeeping, Better Homes and Gardens, Look,* and *Psychology Today* are among my selections of magazines.

12.   Grace Kelly gave up the glamour of Hollywood to become queen of Monacan society.

13.   The ox looks sick and weak as he kicks flecks of straw at the back of his cage.

14.   The Mexican cavalry galloped in expectation of encountering the Texans and Crockett's crew confined in the Alamo.

15.   Querulous quidnuncs complained that the quantity of gossip was considerably below the quarterly quota.

Read it Aloud _____

When the night wind
  howls in the chimney
  cowls, and the bat in
  the moonlight flies,
And inky clouds, like
  funeral shrouds, sail
  over the midnight
  skies,
When the footpads quail
  at the night-bird's
  wail, and black dogs
  bay at the moon,
Then is the spectres'
  holiday—then is the
  ghosts' high-noon!

—GILBERT & SULLIVAN
Ruddigore

Exercises Featuring [k] *and* [g]

"Greetings, Doc Maguirk. I'm Kim Krog. Doc, I'm all agog. Can you diagnose what I've got?"

"Okay, get on the cot, drink some apricot cocoa, and look at this cartographic magazine."

"Have I got the grippe? Am I bucking a bug?"

"Can't guess. My diagnosis requires a quick gander at your trachea."

"Am I crimped with cholera? Is it a bout with the gout?"

"Grab a clove of garlic; keep it close to your glands, on your neck."

"Come on, Doc, what gives? Are you a quack or a fluke? A clove of garlic on my neck? Cripes, what a crock!"

"You can't grok my game, Kim? I'm a fake, an actor. This medical rhetoric quickly gets awkward."

May I talk about organic gardening? Organic means carbon-based. To begin, keep your food scraps from garbage for compost. Plant carefully to avoid crowding of crops. Keep close tabs on cabbage to make kraut, cucumbers, carrots, and squash. Use a scarecrow to protect corn, rutabagas, collard greens, concord grapes, and kohlrabi. Pick the crops in August or October; bake the goodies for Thanksgiving.

EXERCISE PARAGRAPHS FOR ALL STOP-PLOSIVES

Debbie and Brad got a cabin near Penobscot for ten days of vacation. Determined to forget their debts, kids, dogs, troubles, and problems, they took off eastward in a black Studebaker on a Wednesday evening.

They had packed the auto to its peak with items picked from their plentiful kitchen cupboard: pickles, beets, Dr. Pepper, Coca-Cola, cornmeal, and blackberries. They took plenty of books, plus two bikes with which to pedal past the picturesque ponds and creeks.

But Brad and Debbie's planned adventure was a disaster from the beginning. Debbie forgot to bring the cabin key. While Brad was clumsily climbing through the window, the park sheriff approached with a gun, deputies, and dogs, demanding to see identification. Flabbergasted, Brad did some fancy explaining and managed to keep from being locked up for breaking and entering.

At last they got in and unpacked. The cabin felt cold; Brad gathered kindling and tree branches to build a blaze. Only then did Brad realize he had neglected to bring matches. Shivering, unhappy, the miserable couple kept warm by cuddling beneath a deep blue blanket.

For breakfast they had cold toast and drank chilled coffee. Brad then set out to find matches. Debbie passed the time corresponding with friends, hanging packages on the pegboard, and reading articles in the paper about Peeping Toms, Apache tee-pees, and gifted pianists.

About twelve o'clock Brad came back, wet and acting depressed and despondent. It appears he walked two to three kilometers to get matches, forgot to bring cash, and had to leave his belt as credit. But the matches got ruined when he slipped into a pond beside the steep turnpike. Amidst sneezes and shivers, Brad expressed an eager desire to go back to the Big Apple.

With bad backaches, ticks, and pneumonia, our city-bred friends Brad and Debbie drove back to Queens, where they rested within a centrally heated apartment and pledged never again to go camping near Penobscot.

FRONT VOWELS

Speak properly and in as few words as you can, but always plainly; for the end of speech is not ostentation but to be understood.

—WILLIAM PENN,
Fruits of Solitude

In Chapter 9 we described vowels as sounds that are basically free from obstruction by the articulators and that depend on resonation of the oral cavity, tongue positioning, and lip rounding for their distinctiveness. Classification of vowels as front, central, or back is based primarily on the tongue adjustment required. In addition to the placement and tension of the tongue, the extent of the mouth opening will vary with each vowel.

Front vowels are formed with the major tongue adjustment in the front of the mouth. In the IPA, these vowels are written [i], [ɪ], [e], [ɛ], and [æ]. The tongue is at its highest position for the vowel [i], as in *beat,* and at its lowest position for the vowel [æ], as in *bat.* The jaw is dropped lowest for [æ] and is raised progressively through [ɛ], [e], and [ɪ] to [i].

The lips are not usually rounded for front vowels but are slightly opened across the teeth. The highest degree of tension in the lips occurs during formation of the highest front vowel, [i].

Caution: Many dialect substitutions occur in front vowels and diphthongs. Careful attention should be paid to the execution of these sounds.

[i] **Is a Tense, High Front Vowel**

Production: To form the vowel [i], open the mouth slightly with the lips across the teeth. Arch the blade of the tongue high, nearly touching the **alveolar ridge.** Tense and point the tip of the tongue toward the lower front teeth.

Orthographic spellings:

e—ego	i—ski
ee—heed	ie—achieve
ea—each	oe—amoeba
ei—conceive	

Be aware:

1. Lack of adequate tension in the articulators will result in the highest front vowel, [i], dropping to the phoneme [ɪ]. The word *feel* [fil], for instance, becomes *fill* [fɪl].

2. When the vowel [i] is followed by the consonant [l] or [n] in the same syllable, there is a tendency to diphthongize the sound. *Feel* [fil], for example, becomes [fi əl] or [fi jəl].

POSITION

Frontal	Medial	Final
easy	spleen	she
each	repeat	plea
either	amoeba	agree
ether	antique	tree
evening	lenient	key
east	anemic	tea
easel	breeze	knee

Sentences Featuring [i]

1. People eat meat, peas, green beans, and ice cream.
2. The bleak street was free from vehicles in the evening heat.
3. Cecelia feels ill with a feverish spleen.
4. Being discreet means not revealing secrets.
5. My niece is pleased with the antique fleece.
6. Police walking the beat must keep their feet clean.
7. She feels the peaceful breeze blowing through the green trees.
8. She leaped easily over the heap of leaves that the breeze had freed from the tree.
9. A theist, a devotee of a deity, may believe in redeemed eternity.
10. Even Pete, it seems, got cold feet. The wedding vows he would not repeat.
11. The treatise deals with the theory that disease is caused by extreme heat.
12. James Dean was featured in the screen version of *East of Eden*.
13. The keen, clean stream was used by the lean, mean man to water his green beans.
14. Meet me, leaning on a street post at the pizza parlor, around three.
15. Eating cheeseburgers at convenient beaneries increases calories and obesity.

[ɪ] Is a High Front Vowel Slightly Lower Than [i]

Production: Because [ɪ] is usually shorter than [i], the lips and tongue are more relaxed. The tongue is slightly lower.

Orthographic spellings:

i—it		ea—hear	
u—busy		ie—pierce	
ui—quip		o—women	
e—here			

Be aware:

1. Lack of adequate tension in the articulators will cause [ɪ] to drop to [ɛ] or [æ]. For example, *thing* [θɪŋ] will become *thang* [θæŋ].

FYI . . .

Many phonetics textbooks do not recognize the allophone symbol [ɨ]; however, our students have found it useful in clarifying that elusive sound that occurs in the suffixes *-ing* and *-y*. For example, *singing* and *city* would be transcribed [sɪŋ ɨŋ] and [sɪ tɨ].

We recommend that this symbol be used *only* in unstressed syllables. It is a hybrid sound occurring between the phonemes [i] and [ɪ].

2. Prefixes spelled with orthographic *e* may become [ə] instead of the preferred [ɪ]. *Believe* [bɪ liv] may become *buhlieve* [bə liv].

3. Diphthongization can occur with this vowel. *Hit* [hɪt] can become [hɪ ət] or [hɪ jət].

POSITION

Frontal	Medial	Final [ɪ] *or* [ɨ]
itch	militant	pretty
illness	difficult	muddy
earphone	pickle	jolly
impetuous	billboard	happy
infection	bitter	ecology
include	still	silly
inch	whisper	truly

Minimal Pairs for [i] *and* [ɪ]

each—itch

green—grin

meet—mitt

bead—bid

ease—is

Sentences Featuring [ɪ]

1. Limpid Tim languished with wistful Jill by the silver billboard.
2. Thin pins sit in the bin on the windowsill or fill up the big tin.
3. If it fits his finger, finish this ring.
4. Billy tickles frantic fillies with little quills for thrills.
5. That quixotic individual, Rick, mirrors his own image.
6. Is Finland implicit in your definition of Scandinavia?
7. Swimming is difficult without vim and vigor.
8. A mixture of pickles and pills made him sick.
9. Tickle the silly kid in the ribs until he giggles.
10. The picture fits the image and fulfills the requisition.
11. Ripples in the Indian Ocean sink ships.
12. The physician instructed William to fill the prescription immediately.
13. The killer hid in the hills and built a cabin of hickory chips.
14. The ship served pit-cooked grits that felt like bricks.
15. The sitter picked up the pig having the fit and kissed it until it quit wiggling.

The Pure Vowel [e] Is a Mid-Front Vowel
Lower Than [ɪ] but above [ɛ]

The mid-front vowel [e] is more difficult to classify precisely, because of its almost indistinguishable closeness to the diphthong [eɪ]. Many authors do not even recognize the difference, preferring to use only [e] throughout. Since you are trying to form sounds as carefully as you can, however, you should not ignore the difference between these two phonemes.

The duration of the sound and its place in the word are the two most important determinants of when to use the pure vowel [e] and when to use the diphthong [eɪ]. Say *ape* [ep] slowly and distinctly. You will hear only a short, single sound for the vowel, with a quick move to the stop-plosive [p]. Then say *pay*, again slowly and distinctly. Note that although [p] is still short, [e] is now elongated, and you can hear a slight slide upward into the [ɪ] position. The vowel now contains two sounds—[e] and [ɪ]—and any vowelized phoneme made up of two distinct sounds is a diphthong.

Words in which [e] is in the initial position are more likely to use the pure vowel (*able, alien*), whereas [e] in the final position far more often becomes the diphthong [eɪ] (*day, play*). When [e] falls in the medial position, the pronunciation is suggested by the number of syllables and the syllabic stress. If [e] is in an unstressed syllable, it will probably remain [e] (*chaotic*), but if the syllable is stressed or accented, then [eɪ] is the preferred pronunciation (*available*). Words of one syllable with [e] in the medial position usually call for the diphthong (*rain, came, fail*), since one-syllable words are stressed when treated singly or when they appear in short phrases or sentences. Even in longer sentences in assimilated speech, one-syllable words containing [e] deserve enough time to allow for the diphthong. Many of the pronunciation problems with [e] occur when the pure vowel is substituted for the diphthong, often even sliding into the other mid-front vowel, [ɛ], so that *hailstorm* becomes *hell storm*.

We prefer to develop this sound more fully and to practice it in Chapter 13, which focuses on diphthongs, for it is as a diphthong that it presents the most problems. Here we note only a few sample words. Chapter 13 includes sample sentences and paragraphs.

POSITION

Frontal (Single-Syllable) [e] *or* [eɪ]	*Frontal (Multisyllable)* Probably [e]
Abe	April
ache	apron
ace	Asian
age	angel
ape	apex
eight	acre
aim	amiable

Medial, Unstressed or Stress Divided [e] *or* [eɪ]	*Medial, Stressed in Multisyllable Words* [e] *or* [eɪ]	*Medial, Single-syllable* [eɪ] *Preferred*
vacate	evasive	faith
maintain	nation	wave
Mayday	abrasive	raid
chaotic	labor	trace
placate	creative	graze
playmate	station	bathe
railway	relation	came

For *final* position, see Chapter 13.

[ɛ] **Is a Mid-Front Vowel**

Production: The vowel [ɛ] is a relatively short, pure phoneme. The tongue is lower and more relaxed than it is for the vowels [i] and [ɪ]. The mouth is opened wider and the jaw is dropped.

Orthographic spellings:

e—met	u—bury
ea—bread	ue—guess
ai—said	a—many
ie—friend	

Be aware:

1. In some parts of the United States, there is a tendency to nasalize this sound when it is followed by [n] in the same syllable, as in *penny* or *friendly.*

2. Substitutions occur frequently in pronunciation of words containing [ɛ]. For example, *get* [gɛt] often becomes [gɪt] and *ten* [tɛn] *tin* [tɪn].

3. Diphthongization can occur with this vowel. *Yes* [jɛs] can become [jɛ əs].

POSITION

Frontal	Medial	Final
eccentric	health	[ɛ] does not
elementary	dependent	occur in the
ever	pest	final position
extra	textile	
enter	leather	
any	many	
envy	television	

Minimal Pairs for [ɪ] *and* [ɛ]

pick—peck

tin—ten

six—sex

bit—bet

fizz—fez

Sentences Featuring [ɛ]

1. Ken sent Ben to the ten-cent store to get ten pens.
2. Get together twelve sets of leather nets.
3. The weather is best when the sun sets in the west.
4. Let feathered wrens tend to their own nests nestled in elms.
5. Perry depends on Peg to defend his eccentric friends.
6. Never let a tear in a hem go unmended.
7. Fred bet seven yen on the red thoroughbred.
8. He enclosed a fresh letter in the envelope with the message he penned yesterday.
9. The editor guessed that the text would be an indispensable reference and index.
10. The devil exacts a penalty when women and men forget the lessons of experience.
11. The pedestrian showed better sense than the fellow driving the engine.
12. Intelligence is essential in implementing medical techniques.
13. Never-ending eccentrics endure endless bending of pencils and pens.
14. Never, ever pass up the chance to engage in a clever endeavor.
15. Emma remembers the ten days in November when Kennedy's death dominated television.

[æ] Is the Lowest Front Vowel*

Production: To form the phoneme [æ], drop the jaw and open the lips wider than for any other front vowel. The tongue is slightly tensed and lies on the floor of the mouth.

*The IPA contains the phoneme [a], a sound occurring midway between [æ] and [ɑ], which is actually the lowest front vowel. However, most Standard English speakers make no distinction between [æ] as in *can* and [a] as in *can't,* or between [æ] as in *dad* and [a] as in *dance.* The major reason you need to be aware of [a] is that you will find it as the first symbol in the diphthongs [aɪ] as in *high* and [aʊ] as in *how.*

Just for Fun . . . _____

"Bobby is the sinner of my life," said Mary. Mary used [ɪ] for [ɛ], a common Southern substitution. She also omitted an internal [t]. What was Mary trying to say about Bobby?

Read it Aloud _____

**I'm very good at integral and differential calculus,
I know the scientific names of beings animalculous;
In short, in matters vegetable animal, and mineral,
I am the very model of a modern Major General.**

—GILBERT & SULLIVAN
The Pirates of Penzance

Orthographic spellings:

> a—hat
> ai—plaid
> au—laugh
> i—meringue

Be aware:

1. Too much tension in the articulators will cause [æ] to rise to [ɛ] or [e]. *Taxes* [tæk sɪz], for example, will become *Texas* [tɛk sɪs].

2. When [æ] is followed by the nasal consonants [n] and [ŋ], in words such as *can* and *sang,* nasalizing of the vowel can occur.

3. As with the other front vowels, diphthongization can occur with [æ]. *Man* can become [mæ ən] or [mæ jən].

POSITION

Frontal	Medial	Final
atlas	factory	[æ] does not
adamant	backward	occur in the
animal	damage	final position
asked	carried	
asterisk	gratitude	
ambulance	catcher	
attitude	ragged	

Minimal Pairs for [ɛ] *and* [æ]

> net—gnat
> wreck—rack
> pet—pat
> dead—dad
> mesh—mash

Sentences Featuring [æ]

1. Alan and Anne had Pat and Sam bring apples and ham last Saturday.
2. Can the stunt man span the Grand Canyon on his hands?
3. The master craftsman asked what Mack had in his backpack.
4. The quarterback sack damaged the passer's hand.
5. Grandad jams on the sax with a dixieland band.
6. Cattle stand on fallow land amid damaged plants.
7. This brand of bran crackles too fast during a repast.
8. His batting average going into the last game forced him to practice more than anticipated.
9. The pattern for the pants called for a band of tan on the back of the black slacks.
10. She pampered her family by adding linen napkins at Saturday snacks.
11. The bachelor nagged his landlady to clean up the nasty trash in the alley.
12. The faculty cabinet took action to pass on the matter of the catalog attachment.
13. The last batter took the bat and hit a fastball into the window of the flat.
14. Brad is grand at catching fat rats with his fantastic cat.
15. Ambitious Dan ran rapidly in anticipation of capturing the gangster in the alley.

FYI . . . ——————

Theater students who will be learning dialects need to distinguish [æ] from [a], since in British English [æ] becomes [ɛ]: *that* **moves toward** *thet,* **and [a] becomes [ɑ], the familiar "broad a."**

The amateur dialectician may incorrectly say [hɑv] for *have* **or [hɑt] for** *hat,* **thinking all American [æ] sounds become [ɑ] in British.**

MATERIALS FOR PRACTICING ALL FRONT VOWELS

Minimal Pairs

bead—bid	bed—bad
deed—did	said—sad
bean—bin	Ben—ban
peak—pick	peck—pack
meet—mitt	met—mat
neat—knit	net—gnat
peat—pit	pet—pat
keen—kin	Ken—can
seeks—six	sex—sacks
reek—Rick	wreck—rack
eel—ill	ell—Al
lead—lid	led—lad
Dean—din	den—Dan
seat—sit	set—sat
mead—mid	Med—mad
read—rid	red—rad(ical)
seal—sill	sell—Sal
heel—hill	hell—Hal
sleep—slip	slept—slapped
feet—fit	fête—fat

Contrasting Pairs of Front Vowels

freewheeling Fitzwilly	feeling a filling
still no steel	a frigid freeze
an inundation of enunciation	an ill eel
preen the prince	trick or treat
a fellow feeling	sell the seal
has been a bean	neatest nets
deleted letter	she says seize
anemic nemesis	equal access
fallow field	skiing scandal
mealy mallet	gravity grieves
eccentric accent	special spatula
Santa sent	backing Becky
lending land	in vast investments
bland blenders	pasteurized pests
better or bitter	impress the emperor
assemble a cymbal	insipid acceptance
blessed her blister	pensive pinstripes
strips of straps	scandalous skin
matted mittens	stacks of sticks
draft the drifter	simple sample

EXERCISES FOR CONTRASTING FRONT VOWELS

The Twelve Days of Christmas

On the first day of Christmas my true love sent to me,
A partridge in a pear tree
On the second day. . . . . two kitchen cats
On the third day. . . . . three thin hens
On the fourth day. . . . . four silly seals
On the fifth day. . . . . five bathtub rings
On the sixth day. . . . . six guests a-guessing
On the seventh day. . . . . seven sweethearts sweating
On the eighth day. . . . . eight maids a-meeting
On the ninth day. . . . . nine flappers flipping
On the tenth day. . . . . ten tellers tilling
On the eleventh day. . . . . eleven lamps a-limping
On the twelfth day. . . . . twelve leopards leaping

Sentences Contrasting [ɪ] *and* [ɛ]

1. Psychological counseling may help his public address phobia.

2. Elizabeth King thrilled the jet set with her hit that dribbled over the net in the tennis match.

3. Zazu Pitts bet ten bits that the Mets' little mitts will drop base hits.

4. Mr. Ziffel let his pet pig Bill escape from the pen as a well-intended gesture of friendship.

5. Jed says a big difference exists between Presbyterian Christianity and Zen Buddhism.

6. Mitzi met her friend Fritz in Greenwich Village and grinned in ritual recognition.

7. The billboard lettering says littering is a sin that will send the offender to finish his or her sentence in the penitentiary.

8. The bitter winter weather went on to wither the better part of seventy-seven pensive civilians' gardens.

9. His leg was injured, his eczema itched, his headache was intense, and he was generally distressed.

10. Saying Peter picked pickled peppers is plenty idiotic since everyone knows that peppers are pickled in kitchens, not in vegetable beds.

Sentences Contrasting [i] *and* [ɪ]

1. While giving his spiel, the salesman spilled the dill pickles and ruined the deal.

2. The beans in the bin were picked at their peak.

3. The dean redeemed himself by turning in his green admission ticket.

4. I would sit on the seat, but the seal on the windowsill leaks liquid.

5. If the shoes fit my feet, I feel I could climb the hill, but the heel fills me with pain—I appeal for a pill.

6. Tim joined the team; bit by bit he beat all the others. But he got sick and had to seek a surgeon to remove a splinter from his spleen.

7. The villain ate veal cutlets by lamplight. She deemed the dim light was caused by a weak wick.

8. Jean King and Tina Miller meet and knit neat mittens with three knitting needles.

9. Creativity comes easily if you'll do three things: see quickly, feel deeply, and interpret freely.

10. The seats were almost filled when we reached the theater, so it was difficult to see the picture easily.

Sentences Contrasting [i] *and* [ε]

1. His free and easy method of employing the easel helped his technique.

2. The diseased flea felt empty when it didn't eat.

3. A reasonable request should be met with an immediate effort to complete the deed.

4. Please release my friend, the gentleman seated at the end of the settee.

5. Elmer eagerly elbowed through the assemblage of people streaming endlessly along the street.

6. When his enemies destroyed his peach trees, his friends helped him reseed the eastern edge of the orchard.

7. Please pay the entrance fee; the pleasant restaurant will then greet you with pheasant, escargot, and other keen edibles.

8. The senator was unseated in an upset election after the press leaked the news that he'd been seen in police custody.

9. Each evening at the queen's request she enjoys eggs Benedict, Caesar salad, and cream cheese.

10. Steve and Eva Green asked Stephanie and Edward Gwen for an evening of entertainment at the Cedar Falls Civic Center.

Paragraphs Contrasting [ε] *and* [æ]

Did I mention the dance at the mansion on the dense land? (Annie lends it to us any Wednesday.) Dan dances in the den, and Agnes blends bland egg sandwiches and sends them to the band members, who bend over backward to beckon the dancers to edge agilely to the floor.

Dan ranted when his rented pants were locked in the penthouse, yet he met the guests with a bath mat pinned around his ample anatomy. One guest was gassed and made a pest of herself generalizing about the past. Hedda had a time telling the twins, Brent and Brant, apart. Terry tarried to meddle in the middle of a bet over who played Bat Masterson, and Pat petted the tangled terrier.

A man standing by the mantel did mental telepathy experiments for a group of men. Yet their attention was on Penny, who performed in pantomime in the shadow of a shallow shelf. Hal said it was a hell of a dance, and he was sad when it ended.

Sentences for All Front Vowels

1. Sam, meet Matt Adams, the nitwit who got wet feet when feeding figs to fat geese by the glassy little stream.

2. The tragic financial director knelt at the feet of the placid federal representative and begged for bigger dividends to prevent impending economic disaster.

3. Increasingly, sanitation engineers insist that each individual place trash in plastic bags to ensure speedy, clean collection.

4. The healthy pet should fetch a hefty sum of legal tender. Sell fast, then tell Ben that the best satin pelt is yet to be trapped.

5. It is strictly ill will that pits Mack Fitzgerald against his next of kin, the mezzo Mitzi.

6. Jan, a silly and felicitous dentist, drills for fillings for friends at less than list price. Little do they envision that she fills their cavities with an imitation doubleknit fabric that will never fit their teeth well.

7. Andy Granatelli ran the Indy derby at record speed and lived to tell of real thrills he experienced behind the wheel.

8. Seventeen Greenpeace volunteers have planned a protest demonstration on the Snake River this spring.

9. Even Pete, it seems, ate too much red meat. His dinner that evening gave him pain in his feet.

10. Whether they are needed for standing, running, depressing a gas pedal, or simply holding up a well-heeled slipper, you can depend on those flat and soleful extremities, your feet.

A Short-short Story for Practicing All Front Vowels

When did Jack and Jill flee from the hill? It is a silly tidbit, but I'll tell just the jist of the ridiculous scene.

It seems that Bill Bell bet Hal Hill, that he wouldn't risk beating Jack and Jill with his bat. Hal accepted the bet, apparently for ten pennies. With steel in his breath and stealth of step (with which he had hidden from many enemies in the past), he skillfully lifted his feet without disturbing the leaves underneath. At the crest, rapidly scanning the scene, Hal glanced to the east to see Jack and Jill sitting beneath evergreen trees, eating apples and flapjacks and drinking fizzies and milk.

This pastoral scene soon would be pestered by bad Hal, who drew a bead on the serene twins and, screaming like a banshee, ran into the pitiable pair. After that, a dreadful spectacle transpired—including fists, spills, savage attacks, threats, and plenty of thrills.

The situation appeared grim for our friends Jack and Jill, who were about to feel the wrath of Hal's best bat. Yet when misfortune seemed inevitable, a rebel yell pierced the evening air. It was Helen Dean, a free-spirited person, who ambushed Hal with fistfuls of pebbles and sand. Hal turned heel and ran down the hill. The other kids shouted insults after him: "Creep! Drip! Nasty Pest!" Hal, a mere seven years old, ran back to his aunt Tessie, who kissed his head and said he must be good.

Meanwhile, a relieved Jack and Jill went down the hill back to Philadelphia, where they live, and reflected over glasses of ginger ale on the eccentric things that people will do when it means winning a bet. Then they went to bed, thinking sleep would bring dreams to help them forget the unpleasant end to their little sortie. All slept well except Fred, the labrador retriever, who imagined cats were eating his meal; he acted a bit upset.

CROSSWORD PUZZLE
Plosive-Front Vowels

Across

1. tap lightly
3. a little one will do you
5. man's nickname
6. one of many in a strand
7. obtain
10. Richard, maybe?

11. at 4 o'clock in London
13. tam, beret
14. one over easy
15. sack, suitcase
16. proof of ownership

Down

1. don't put a round one in a square hole
2. append your list with 5 Ac. (2 wd)
3. not shallow
4. commercial (ab.)

8. clock sound
9. retain
11. you're it
12. wager
13. worthless fellow
15. *is* infinitive

PHONETICS PRACTICE: STOP-PLOSIVES AND FRONT VOWELS

Write the orthographic spelling for the following words in phonetics:

1. [pɪkt] _____

2. [dip] _____

3. [bægd] _____

4. [tik] _____

5. [bɪd] _____

6. [dɛkt] _____

7. [dɪg] _____

8. [æpt] _____

9. [æktɪd] _____

10. [i ˈgæd] _____

11. [ˈbɛ dɪd] _____

12. [pik] _____

13. [bæd] _____

14. [it] _____

15. [kæpt] _____

16. [dɛk] _____

17. [bidɨ] _____

18. [dɪtɨ] _____

19. [tæb] _____

20. [kɪkt] _____

Write the following words in phonetics:

1. pit _____

2. bead _____

3. tag _____

4. get _____

5. keep _____

6. debt _____

7. pack _____

8. gap _____

9. kept _____

10. eked _____

11. gabbed _____

12. ebbed _____

13. dead _____

14. beget _____

15. catty _____

16. petty _____

17. keyed _____

18. pig _____

19. tab _____

20. egg _____

READING FROM NOVELS THAT HAVE BEEN MADE INTO MOVIES

Note: Novels are a steady plot source for motion pictures. Some filmscripts adhere closely to the original novel, others make extensive alterations in the story and characters. Although the following paragraphs are divided by speaker sex, for the purpose of classroom practice such "casting" by sex is not necessary.

Female Speakers

Adela Quested from *A Passage to India* by E. M. Forster. Her engagement has just been broken by her fiance.

Far wiser of him. I ought to have spoken myself, but I drifted on wondering what would happen. I would willingly have gone on spoiling his life through inertia—one has nothing to do, one belongs nowhere and becomes a public nuisance without realizing it. I speak only of India. I am not astray in England. I fit in there—no, don't think I shall do harm in England. When I am forced back there, I shall settle down to some career. I have sufficient money left to start myself, and heaps of friends of my own type. I shall be quite all right. But oh, the trouble I've brought on everyone here—I can never get over it. My carefulness as to whether we should marry or not—and in the end Ronny and I part and aren't even sorry. We ought never to have thought of marriage.

Margaret Schlegel from *Howard's End* by E. M. Forster. Margaret discusses her feelings with Helen about the man she plans to marry.

In the first place, I disagree about the outer life. We've often argued that. The real point is that there is the widest gulf between my love-making and yours. Yours was romance; mine will be prose. I'm not running it down—a very good kind of prose, but well considered, well thought out. For instance, I know all Mr. Wilcox's faults. He's afraid of emotion. He cares too much about success, too little about the past. His sympathy lacks poetry, and so isn't sympathy really. I don't intend him, or any man or any woman, to be all my life—good heavens, no! There are heaps of things in me that he doesn't, and shall never, understand.

Moll Flanders from *Moll Flanders* by Daniel Defoe. Moll explains something of her own background.

I have been told that in one of our neighbor nations, they have an order from the king that when any criminal is condemned, either to die, or to the galleys, or to be transported, if they leave any children, as such are generally unprovided for by the forfeiture of their parents, so they are immediately taken into the care of the government and put into a hospital called the House of Orphans, where they are bred up, clothed, fed, taught, and when fit to go out, are placed to trades or to services, so as to be well able to provide for themselves by an honest, industrious behaviour. Had this been the custom in our country, I had not been left a poor desolate girl without friends, without clothes, without help or helper, as was my fate.

Jo from *Little Women* by Louisa May Alcott. Jo has just sold her first story and reacts to the critics' responses.

You said, mother, that criticism would help me; but how can it, when it's so contradictory that I don't know whether I have written a promising book, or broken all the ten commandments. . . . This man says "An exquisite book, full of truth, beauty, and earnestness; all is sweet, pure, and healthy." The next, "The theory of the book is bad,—full of fancies, spiritualistic ideas, and unnatural characters." Now, I had no theory of any kind, don't believe in spiritualism, and copied my characters from life. I don't see how this critic can be right. . . . Some make fun of it, some over-praise, and nearly all insist that I had a deep theory to expound, when I only wrote it for the pleasure and the money. I wish I'd printed it whole, or not at all, for I do hate to be so horridly misjudged.

Mrs. Clay from *Persuasion* by Jane Austen. She speaks to Sir Walter.

Have a little mercy on the poor men. We are not all born to be handsome. The sea is no beautifier, certainly; sailors do grow old betimes; I have often observed it; they soon lose the look of youth. But then, is not it the same with many other professions, perhaps most others? Soldiers, in active service, are not at all better off; and even in the quieter professions, there is a toil and a labour of the mind, if not of the body, which seldom leaves a man's looks to the natural effect of time. The lawyer plods, quite care-worn; the physician is up at all hours, and travelling in all weather; and even the clergyman, you know, is obliged to go into infected rooms, and expose his health and looks to all the injury of a poisonous atmosphere.

Reggie Love, a lawyer, from *The Client* by John Grisham. She talks to Mark, her young client who witnessed a murder.

It's very simple. If, and I emphasize the word *if*, Judge Roosevelt instructs you to answer certain questions, and if you refuse, then he can hold you in contempt of court for not answering, for disobeying him. Now, I've never known an eleven year old kid to be held in contempt, but if you were an adult and you refused to answer the judge's questions, then you'd go to jail for contempt. . . . I don't think he'll allow you to go free if you refuse to answer the questions. You see, Mark, the law is very clear in this area. A person who has knowledge of information crucial to a criminal investigation cannot withhold this information because he feels threatened. In other words, you can't keep quiet because you're afraid of what might happen to you or your family.

> Maggie, a middle-aged housewife, from *Breathing Lessons* by Anne Tyler. Maggie speaks to her daughter-in-law.

Oh, honey, you're just lucky they offer such things. My first pregnancy, there wasn't a course to be found, and I was scared to death. I'd have loved to take lessons! Afterward: I remember leaving the hospital with Jesse and thinking, 'Wait. Are they going to let me just walk off with him? I don't know beans about babies! I don't have a license to do this. Ira and I are just amateurs.' I mean, you're given all these lessons for the unimportant things—piano-playing, typing. But how about parenthood? Or marriage, either, come to think of it. Before you can drive a car you need a state-approved course of instruction, but driving a car is nothing, nothing, compared to living day in and day out with a husband and raising up a new human being.

> Robin's Mother, from *Waiting to Exhale* by Terry McMillan. She faces a major decision about Robin's father.

I've got to put him in a facility, Robin. I can't manage anymore. He can't pick up a fork, he can't get out of bed, and I have to turn him over every two hours. He's lost ten pounds in two weeks. . . . Your father worked very hard all his life to make sure we'd be comfortable when he retired and we were both up in age. So we've got money put away, but it'd all be gone if I were to use it to pay for a nursing home. Right after he was diagnosed, your father told me to swear I wouldn't use our savings to care for him if he became incapacitated. So the lawyer said that if I divorced your father, that would separate our assets and make it so that the state would pay for his care at the nursing home. All on his own, Fred wouldn't be able to afford it.

> Rosaura, from *Like Water for Chocolate* by Laura Esquivel. Rosaura has married her sister Tita's boyfriend.

"I'm painfully aware of the role you put me in, when everybody on the ranch saw you weeping at Pedro's side, holding his hand so lovingly. Do you know what that role is? Laughingstock! You know, you really don't deserve God's mercy! As far as I'm concerned, I couldn't care less if you and Pedro go to hell for sneaking around kissing in every corner. From now on, you can do it all you want. As long as nobody finds out about it, I don't care. Let him go to a loose woman like you for his filthy needs, but here's the thing: in this house I intend to go on being his wife. And in the eyes of everyone else, too. Because the day someone sees you two, and I end up looking ridiculous again, I swear that you are going to be very sorry."

> Hester Prynne, from *The Scarlet Letter* by Nathaniel Hawthorne. Hester tells Roger Chilingworth that she is going to reveal to the pastor, who fathered her child, that Roger is her husband whom she left years before.

I must reveal the secret. He must discern thee in thy true character. What may be the result, I know not. . . . So far as concerns the overthrow or preservation of his fair fame and his earthly state, and perchance his life, he is in thy hands. Nor do I,—whom the scarlet letter has disciplined to truth, though it be the truth of red-hot iron, entering into the soul,—nor do I perceive such advantage in his living any longer a life of ghastly emptiness, that I shall stoop to implore thy mercy. Do with him as thou wilt! There is no good for him,—no good for me,—no good for thee! There is no good for little Pearl! There is no path to guide us out of this dismal maze!

Male Speakers

Harmon Gow, a New England farmer, from *Ethan Frome* by Edith Wharton. He tells the narrator about Ethan.

When a man's been setting round like a hulk for twenty years or more, seeing things that want doing, it eats inter him, and he loses his grit. That Frome farm was always 'bout as bare's a milkpan when the cat's been round; and you know what one of them old water-mills is wuth nowadays. When Ethan could sweat over 'em both from sunup to dark he kinder choked a living out of 'em; but his folks ate up most everything, even then, and I don't see how he makes out now. Fust his father got a kick, out haying, and went soft in the brain, and gave away money like Bible texts afore he died. Then his mother got queer and dragged along for years as weak as a baby. . . . Sickness and trouble: that's what Ethan's had his plate full up with, ever since the very first helping.

Lord de Winter from *The Three Musketeers* by Alexandre Dumas. He speaks to Milady, his sister-in-law.

At present you will remain in this castle. The walls are thick, the doors are strong, the bars are massive; it is guarded, and orders have been given to fire on you should you attempt to escape. . . . The officer who commands here in my absence, you have seen him and know him already; he knows how to obey an order, as you have seen. On the way from Portsmouth you tried to make him speak; could a statue have been more mute? You have tried your seductions upon a great many men, and you have, unfortunately, always succeeded. Try them upon this man, and if you succeed, I will pronounce you to be the devil himself! . . . And now, Madam, try and make your peace with God, for you are condemned by men.

Robinson Crusoe from *Robinson Crusoe* by Daniel Defoe. He tells of his early life.

It was my lot first of all to fall into pretty good company in London, which does not always happen to such loose and unguided young fellows as I then was; the devil generally not omitting to lay some snare for them very early. But it was not so with me; I first fell acquainted with the master of a ship who had been on the coast of Guinea; and who, having had very good success there, was resolved to go again; and who, taking a fancy to my conversation, which was not at all disagreeable at that time, hearing me say I had a mind to see the world, told me, if I would go the voyage with him, I should be at no expense; I should be his messmate and companion, and if I could carry anything with me, I should have all the advantage of it that the trade would admit.. . I went on the voyage with him.

Chingachgook from *The Last of the Mohicans* by James Fenimore Cooper. The Indian speaks to the scout, Hawkeye.

A pine grew then where this chestnut now stands. The first pale-faces who came among us spoke no English. They came in a large canoe, when my fathers had buried the tomahawk with the redmen around them. Then, Hawkeye, we were one people, and we were happy. The salt lake gave us its fish, the wood its deer, and the air its birds. We took wives who bore us children; we worshipped the Great Spirit, and we kept the Maquas beyond the sound of our songs of triumph. . . . The Dutch landed, and gave my people the fire-water; they drank until the heavens and the earth seemed to meet, and they foolishly thought they had found the Great Spirit. Then they parted with their land. Foot by foot, they were driven back from the shores.

Gulliver from *Gulliver's Travels* by Jonathan Swift. Gulliver describes the Lilliputians.

As the common size of the Natives is somewhat under six inches, so there is an exact proportion in all other animals, as well as plants and trees; for instance, the tallest horses and oxen are between four and five inches in height, the sheep an inch and a half, more or less; their geese about the bigness of a sparrow; and so the several gradations downwards, till you come to the smallest, which, to my sight, were almost invisible. But nature hath adapted the eyes of the Lilliputians to all objects proper for their view. They see with great exactness, but at no great distance. . . Their tallest trees are about seven foot high, I mean some of those in the great Royal Park, the tops whereof I could but just reach with my fist clinched. The vegetables are in the same proportion.

> Mr. van der Luyden from *Age of Innocence* by Edith Wharton. As he speaks to Mrs. Archer about the newly arrived, somewhat mysterious Countess Olenska, he reveals the snobbishness of New York society in the 1870's.

You know what these English grandees are. They're all alike. Louisa and I are very fond of our cousin—but it's hopeless to expect people who are accustomed to the European courts to trouble themselves about our little republican distinctions. The Duke goes where he's amused—it seems he took her with him last night to Mrs. Lemuel Struthers. . . Louisa was rather troubled. So I thought the shortest way was to go straight to Countess Olenska and explain—by the merest hint, you know—how we feel in New York about certain things. I felt I might, without indelicacy, because the evening she dined with us she rather suggested, rather let me see that she would be grateful for guidance. And she *was*.

> Mitchell McDeere, Memphis tax attorney, from *The Firm*, by John Grisham. He talks to FBI agent Wayne Tarrance.

She knows that in the last three years the Morolto gang and its accomplices have taken over eight hundred million bucks in cash out of this country and deposited it in various banks in the Caribbean. She knows which banks, which accounts, the dates, a bunch of stuff. She knows that the Moroltos control at least three hundred and fifty companies chartered in the Caymans, and that these companies regularly send clean money back into the country. She knows the dates and amounts of the wire transfers. She knows of at least forty U.S. corporations owned by Cayman corporations owned by the Moroltos. She knows a helluva lot, Tarrance. She's a very knowledgeable woman, don't you think?

> Colin, from *The Secret Garden* by Frances Hodgson Burnett. The invalid Colin speaks to Ben Weatherstaff, Mary, and Dickon.

When Mary found this garden it looked quite dead. Then something began pushing things up out of the soil and making things out of nothing. One day things weren't there and another they were. I had never watched things before and it made me feel very curious. I keep saying to myself, 'What is it? What is it?' It's something. It can't be nothing! I don't know its name so I call it Magic. I have never seen the sun rise but Mary and Dickon have and from what they tell me, I am sure that is Magic too. Something pushes it up and draws it. . . . Everything is made out of Magic, leaves and trees, flowers and birds, badgers and foxes and squirrels and people. So it must be all around us.

> The narrator, from *A River Runs Through It,* by Norman Maclean. One of two brothers, the narrator of the story, talks of a fight they had.

I suppose it was inevitable that my brother and I would get into one big fight which also would be the last one. When it came, given our theories about street fighting, it was like the Battle Hymn, terrible and swift. There are parts of it I did not see. I did not see our mother walk between us to try to stop us. The first I saw of her was the gray top of her head, the hair tied in a big knot with a big comb in it; but what was most noticeable was that her head was so close to Paul I couldn't get a good punch at him. Then I didn't see her anymore. The fight seemed suddenly to stop itself. She was lying on the floor between us. Then we both began to cry and fight in a rage, each one shouting, 'You knocked my mother down.'

Robert Kincaid, from *The Bridges of Madison County* by Robert James Waller. He tells Francesca about himself.

There is a certain breed of man that's obsolete, or very nearly so. The world is getting organized, way too organized for me and some others. Everything in its place, a place for everything. Well, my camera equipment is pretty well organized, I admit, but I'm talking about something more than that. Rules and regulations and laws and social conventions. Hierarchies of authority, spans of control, long-range plans, and budgets. Corporate power, in 'Bud' we trust. A world of wrinkled suits and stick-on names tags. . . . We're giving up free range, getting organized, feathering our emotions. Efficiency and effectiveness and all those other pieces of intellectual artifice. And with the loss of free range the cowboy disappears, along with the mountain lion and gray wolf. There's not much room left for travelers.

CHAPTER 11

Fricative Consonants and Back Vowels

FRICATIVE CONSONANTS

Uncurbed, unfettered, controlled of speech, Unperiphrastic, bombastiloquent.

—ARISTOPHANES,
The Frogs

Fricative consonants are those phonemes produced by tensing certain articulators to narrow the passageway so that the outgoing air is emitted with friction. Phonetically, these nine phonemes are written [f], [v], [θ], [ð], [s], [z], [ʃ], [ʒ], and [h].

Fricatives are classified according to the placement of the articulators during production. For [f] and [v], the top front teeth and the bottom lip are gently pressed together. For [θ] and [ð], the tongue tip is extended between the front teeth. [s] and [z] are formed with the blade (flat front part) of the tongue pressing against the sides of the alveolar ridge. [ʃ] and [ʒ] also employ the tongue blade and the gum ridge, but the placement of the tongue is somewhat softer and slightly behind the gum ridge. The place of articulation for [h] is in or at the glottis.

Like the stop-plosives, fricatives are characterized as either *voiced* or *voiceless*. Except for [h], all the fricatives are cognate pairs, produced with the same manner of obstruction and the same positioning of the articulators but differing in phonation: [f], [θ], [s], and [ʃ] are voiceless and [v], [ð], [z], and [ʒ] are their voiced cognates. The fricative [h] is voiceless.

[f] *AND* [v]

[f] Is a Voiceless, Labio-Dental Fricative

Production: To form the consonant [f], bring the lower lip and the bottom edge of the upper teeth lightly together—not so tight as to stop the outgoing air stream, but narrowed so that the breath must be forced between them. No vocal-fold vibration is required.

Be aware:

1. Make sure your lower lip touches your upper teeth, not your upper lip. Otherwise, your [f] will take on the characteristics of a bilabial sound, resulting in distortion. Also, make sure the touching is complete, not partial, or a muffled [f] will result.

2. Avoid expelling too much air on [f] or any other fricative. Use only the amount needed for clear articulation of the sound. Too much escaping air on [f] suggests a cat fight!

3. The orthographic spelling of [f] is fairly regular, but don't "phorget" *Phillip, photographs,* and *phrases* or *cough* and *rough!* And *of* is [ɑv], not [ɑf].

POSITION

Frontal	Medial	Final
fearful	affluent	carafe
favor	conflict	cough
phantom	influence	deaf
fried	suffice	lymph
phone	soften	self
feel	comfort	turf
fair	emphasis	chief

[v] Is a Voiced, Labio-Dental Fricative

Production: To form [v], bring the lower lip and the bottom edge of the upper teeth lightly together and squeeze the breath between them. Vocal fold vibration is necessary.

Be aware:

1. Be careful not to omit [v], especially before other consonants, in words such as *evening, movement,* or *lives.* Nor should you fail to voice it fully, so that *save* becomes *safe,* or *liver* becomes *liffer.*

2. People who are not native speakers of English may substitute other sounds for [f] and [v], since these sounds are not common to all languages. Central Europeans may use [w] for [v], saying *wery much* instead of *very much.* Native speakers of Spanish may substitute [b] for [v] and [p] for [f]. This comes from closing the lips rather than the lip and upper teeth edge.

POSITION

Frontal	Medial	Final
very	clairvoyant	olive
victory	avoid	alive
voyage	survey	shelve
vanity	solvent	leave
vinegar	silver	grieve
vowel	advertise	dove
volume	eleven	nerve

[f] *and* [v] *Paired Words*

infest—invest	fairy—very	file—vile	surf—serve
first—versed	fender—vendor	awful—oval	surface—service

shelf—shelve	foist—voiced	calf—calve	leaf—leave
feel—veal	fear—veer	half—have	grief—grieve

[f] *Converts to* [v] *in the Plural of Many Words*

knife—knives	life—lives	hoof—hooves
elf—elves	loaf—loaves	self—selves
wife—wives	scarf—scarves	wolf—wolves

IN SOME WORDS, THE NOUN FORM HAS AN [f], THE VERB A [v]

Noun	Verb
strife	strive
life	live
gift	give
shelf	shelve

AND THEN, THERE ARE ALWAYS EXCEPTIONS TO EVERY RULE

waif	waifs
roof	roofs
strafe	strafes

Sentences Featuring [f] *and* [v]

1. Fervent believers in evil will never go to heaven.
2. Seven-Up is an affordable, effervescent beverage.
3. A salve of sulfur relieved the fever of the infected convict.
4. The video featured Fannie Flagg and Phil Silvers in *Vanity Fair.*
5. Chef Victor served veal fried in olive oil and covered with fresh chives.
6. The first verse refers to the adverse effects of the fruit of the vine.
7. A conference of five chiefs convened on the river rafts in the fjord.
8. The safest advice is to save, give no gifts, and avoid foolish investments.
9. Uvulas aquiver, the frightened nymphs vanished into the verdant forest.
10. Alvin, the elfin knave, gave a lofty gift to his fearful lover, Vera.
11. Even half a heifer is barely enough for Val to have for breakfast.
12. Floats are available at the fountain in seventy-five flavors, from vanilla to fresh alfalfa.
13. The Venetians' fear of television was proved valid when their first version of the fission formula was viewed in Finland.
14. *Fiddle* evokes a frame of reference significantly different from that of the more formal *violin.*
15. The Volkswagen service foreman, Vern, phoned Freda Von Cleff to inform her that foreign vermin had infiltrated her flivver's valves.

[θ] *AND* [ð]

[θ] **Is a Voiceless Lingua-Dental Fricative**

Production: To form the consonant [θ], touch the blade or flat part of the tongue (not the lip) to the edge of the upper teeth. Then squeeze air out around the teeth and tongue. [θ] is voiceless.

Be aware:

1. Omission is a particularly common problem with both [θ] and its cognate, [ð], especially when the sound occurs at the end of a phrase or sentence or is part of a consonant cluster. Watch for words such as *bath, growth,* and *truth* at phrase and sentence endings, and *fifths, widths,* and *healthful* in any position.

2. A number of substitutions for [θ] are heard in both native speakers of English and people who speak English as a second language. *Bof* for *both, wid* for *with, tanks* for *thanks, baftub* or *battub* for *bathtub*—all are commonly heard. Neither [θ] nor its cognate, [ð], occurs in most foreign languages, and therefore they are difficult sounds for nonnative speakers to acquire.

POSITION

Frontal	*Medial*	*Final, Preceded by:*	
		CONSONANT	*VOWEL*
thin	aesthetic	health	south
thunder	pithy	warmth	bath
thyroid	stethoscope	length	death
thistle	stealthy	strength	twentieth
theme	depths	tenth	wrath
thought	youthful	twelfth	breath
throw	enthrall	sixth	booth

[θ] *Followed by* [s]

fourths	sevenths	tenths	norths	breaths
fifths	eighths	births	souths	depths
sixths	ninths	deaths	earths	lengths

[ð] Is a Voiced Lingua-Dental Fricative

Production: To form [ð], touch the blade of the tongue to the edge of the upper teeth and squeeze air out around the teeth and tongue. [ð] is voiced.

Be aware:

1. [d] is a common substitution for [ð]—*dese* and *dose* for *these* and *those* or *fodder* and *mudder* for *father* and *mother.* This is a problem primarily for nonnative speakers, but it is also characteristic of some American dialects.

2. Note that the IPA symbols [θ] and [ð] differ markedly from the orthographic *th.* Orthographic spelling offers no clue as to whether these sounds are voiced or voiceless. The IPA and various diacritical marking systems provide a means to differentiate between the two sounds. Students often have problems hearing and identifying [θ] and [ð]; give these two sounds and their IPA symbols some extra attention.

3. Insufficient voicing of [ð] will cause it to sound like [θ]. Some people say [mʌθɚ] and [faθɚ] rather than [mʌðɚ] and [faðɚ]. In general, be sure to voice [ð] fully and completely.

POSITION

Frontal	*Medial*	*Final*
this	leather	writhe
that	farther	breathe
those	bother	loathe
there	mother	bathe
then	another	seethe

POSITION

Frontal	Medial	Final
though	brethren	soothe
they	either	tithe

[θ] *and* [ð] *Paired Words*

thistle—this	breath—breathe	cloth—clothes
thousand—thou	teeth—teethe	ether—either
thigh—thy	bath—bathe	moth—mother
thief—the	wrath—rather	wreath—wreathe

Sentences Featuring [θ] *and* [ð]

1. Either bequeath me the thatched wreath or throw it to Thelma Sleeth.
2. The teething puppies threw feathers hither and thither.
3. "Though thought is free," quoth Seth, "thou must do thine own thing."
4. Beth threatened to tell her mother that her brother didn't bathe.
5. "Breathe deep through the mouth," said the doctor, with stethoscope thrust athwart Mother's thyroid.
6. Arthur bothered his father with a thousand youthful ideas.
7. Is it this or that? Hither or thither? These or the others?
8. The thick-headed behemoth thundered no farther than the length and breadth of the northern heath.
9. Death might be thought of as a dearth of breath.
10. Beneath a rather thin cloth of lethargy lies a depth of loathing and wrath.
11. To shave a thrush, first bathe its feathers with a thick, frothy lather.
12. When the thermometer dips beneath thirty degrees, think about thick, thermal clothing for warmth.
13. Luther's theses delved into death and other thorny questions of theology and faith.
14. Cotton Mather taught aesthetics by tickling the youthful Puritan brethren with a long feather.
15. Thus with my thumb I crushed to death the bothersome moth.

Sentences Featuring [f], [v], [θ], *and* [ð]

1. Bathe the fevered child in soothing, reviving fluid.
2. Five relief pitchers threw in the seventh inning for the softball team.
3. Rather and Safer frequently aggravate smooth-talking, affluent government officials.
4. The *blither* is a foolish vibrating of the lips with the fingers in front of the teeth.
5. If ever this thistle seethes, then invest in vast vats of fat, with every effort to verify truths.
6. The tightfisted vicar failed to revive his rather atheistic friend.
7. Vivian's Afghan, Fifi, will faithfully retrieve anything, provided it is thrown no further than fifty feet.
8. Father will leave Duluth on the twentieth to fly south.
9. Love, life, and food are three things mothers often provide for their offspring.

10. I had as lief leave the oval office as think of myself as another Jefferson or Fillmore.

11. The villain's death was verified on the eleventh of November.

12. Arthur can vouch for the fact that Grover the tough thug writhed to ugly music played at an awful volume.

13. Three farms are full of fearful wraiths, four others farther south have evil, foul-mouthed elves.

14. If theater is the food of the gods, then this show must be a liver loaf sandwich.

15. Never define thieving Keith with the epithet "a man of steal."

[s] *AND* [z]

[s] **Is a Voiceless Lingua-Alveolar Fricative**

Production: To form the consonant [s], place the tip of the tongue just behind the teeth and force air across a groove along the top of the tongue and out between the teeth and the tongue. Some variation in the position of the tongue is possible—behind either the upper or lower gum ridge, or straight forward—without significant change in the sound produced. [s] is voiceless.

Be aware:

1. Distortions in articulating [s] exceed those of any other sound. The **sibilant** or hissing nature of [s] and [z] makes them particularly difficult to articulate clearly, crisply, and with precise control of the expelled air. A common category of [s] distortion is the **lisp,** a label frequently applied incorrectly to a number of articulation problems. The *protrusion* lisp occurs when the tongue comes too far forward between the teeth, rather than remaining behind them. Children often develop a lisp when they have lost their front baby teeth and are waiting for the permanent teeth to replace them. A protrusion lisp will cause the speaker to say *My thister things thongs* instead of *My sister sings songs.*

2. A *lateral* lisp occurs when the air escapes across the sides of the tongue, much as it does for [l], instead of forward along the groove and across the tip of the tongue. This produces a messy, sloppy-sounding [s].

3. Some speakers whistle a high-frequency sound when they produce [s]. Excessive tongue tension is usually at fault. A whistling [s] can be a real problem for anyone who uses a microphone, because electronic amplification exaggerates the whistle.

4. Excessive expulsion of air can cause a hissing [s]. It is not that the hisser overaspirates or voices the sound, which would produce a [z], but simply that too much air is allowed to escape across the tongue or the speaker holds the friction action for too long. [s] should be short and crisp.

POSITION

Frontal	Medial	Final, Preceded by:	
		CONSONANT	*VOWEL*
sand	insist	horse	loose
stipend	response	quits	crisis
snarl	missing	plaques	price
squid	precedent	fix	floss
cereal	amidst	force	fleece
scuba	closer	clocks	place
seizure	sassafras	quartz	bus

Just for Fun . . . ————

"The newly married snakes received towels marked *hiss* and *hearse."* Would this joke be funny if you could not hear or say the difference between [s] and [z]?

[z] **Is a Voiced Lingua-Alveolar Fricative**

Production: To form [z], place the tip of the tongue just behind the teeth and force air across a groove along the top of the tongue and out between the teeth and the tongue. As with [s], some variation in tongue position is possible. [z] is voiced.

Be aware:

1. Although [z] is subject to the same lisp problems as [s], they are usually not as pronounced, since full voicing tends to offset the hissing and whistling somewhat. Still, you must try to correct lateral or protrusion lisps or the [z] whistle if you have any of these problems.

2. Some speakers fail to give full voice to the sound, so that words such as *hers, cards,* and *fleas* tend to sound like *hearse, carts,* or *fleece.* [z] needs to be fully vocalized.

3. [s] and [z] are both represented by a number of orthographic spellings. Orthographic *s* (soap), *sc* (science), *sch* (schism), *ss* (miss), *c* (cease), *ce* (nice), *ps* (psalm), and *z* (pretzel) are used for [s], and *z* (zone), *zz* (buzz), *s* (ease), *ss* (scissors), *x* (xylophone), and *ts* or *cz* (tsar or czar) are used for [z]. The written spelling is not always a key to pronunciation; you need to check diacritical marks or phonetic symbols.

POSITION

Frontal	*Medial*	*Final*
zebra	resume	please
zany	hazy	froze
zygote	frozen	grows
Xerox	visible	nose
xylophone	spasmodic	gauze
zoology	easel	pins
zero	loser	eyes

[s] *and* [z] *Paired Words*

sip—zip	recent—reason	tense—tens
sewn—zone	looser—loser	force—fours
sane—zany	priced—prized	loose—lose
Sue—zoo	muscle—muzzle	peace—peas
seal—zeal	places—blazes	fierce—fears

In some words the *noun* form is pronounced [s], the *verb* [z]:

	Noun	*Verb*
house	[haʊs]	[haʊz]
excuse	[ɪk'skjus]	[ɪk'skjuz]
abuse	[ə'bjus]	[ə'bjuz]

When a final *s* is added to a word to make it plural, is it pronounced [s] or [z]? A simple rule will help you remember:

1. If the final sound of the original word is voiceless, use the voiceless [s].
    Examples: [t]—[tɛnts]
    [k]—[bʊks]
    [f]—[sɝfs]

2. If the final sound of the original word is voiced, use the voiced [z].
    Examples: [v] — [seɪvz] saves
                [d] — [bɛdz] beds
                [g] — [bægz] bags

3. If, however, the original word ends in any of the sibilants [s], [z], [ʃ], [ʒ] or either of the affricates, [tʃ] and [dʒ], an additional syllable is required—either [ɪz] or [əz].
    Examples: [glæsɪz] glasses
                [wɪʃɪz] wishes
                [kwɪzɪz] quizzes
                [hɛdʒɪz] hedges

Sentences Featuring [s] *and* [z]

1. Seize the Eskimo hunters who use harpoons to slaughter seals and whales.

2. A sneeze is a way of saying, "This dust doesn't belong in my nose."

3. Mrs. Fenster dressed busily, hastily setting a satin fez atop her curls.

4. Whose loose hose and shoes did the hostess lose?

5. It seems easier for the cosmetician to do business in his own postal zone.

6. Zeus seldom visited Greece, bypassing the peaceful East for the sizzling zones of Cypress.

7. A simple cruise missile weighs thousands of pounds and lays waste to millions of lives.

8. Gas rises through the earth's atmosphere to the ozone—I know so!

9. From Zanzibar to San Salvador, speeding cars seldom seem pleasing to police.

10. Susie's cousin missed dozens of easy questions on his sociology quiz.

11. A dozen mutinous sailors assumed control of the captain's quarters, thus committing treason.

12. Amidst gasps and hisses, the sad actor collapsed onstage, wasted by cancerous disease.

13. Through the haze, we saw the storm swirling and zooming in on us.

14. Cincinnati's citizens sometimes seemed insincere to Miss Missouri; still, they seldom seemed as false as certain natives of Kansas City.

15. Has Sampson sensed that his guests are disgusted with his excessively sophisticated ways?

[ʃ] *AND* [ʒ]

[ʃ] Is a Voiceless Lingua-Postalveolar Fricative

Production: To form the consonant [ʃ], place the blade of the tongue behind the gum ridge and push the sides of the tongue against the upper side teeth. As with [s] and [z], the air is expelled along a groove in the tongue, but it is less focused on the groove and tongue tip than on the front of the tongue in general, and the tongue is pulled more toward the back of the mouth. The lips are more rounded than for [s] and [z]—indeed, they are almost pursed or puckered.

Be aware:

1. Persons who have a lateral lisp with [s] or [z] will probably also have it with [ʃ] or [ʒ]. Again, the problem stems from air being expelled over the sides of the tongue rather than across the center front of it.

2. [ʃ] is usually represented orthographically by two letters—*sh*. But remember that phonemically it is a single sound. [ʃ] may also be spelled *si, sch, ch*, or *ci*, as in *fuchsia, schwa, quiche*, and *physician*.

3. [ʃ] and [ʒ] are subject to the same mushy production that threatens any fricative when the outgoing air does not move clearly and crisply between the narrowed articulators.

Read It Aloud _____

**When your humour they
    flout,
You can't let yourself go,
And it *does* put you out
When a person says, "Oh,
I have known that old
    joke from my cradle!"**

—GILBERT & SULLIVAN
The Yeoman of the Guard

POSITION

Frontal	Medial	Final
should	fashion	plush
shape	fuchsia	quiche
shine	shish kebab	brash
schwa	cashew	dish
show	nation	fresh
shell	freshman	squash
shawl	lotion	marsh

[ʒ] Is a Voiced Lingua-Postalveolar Fricative

Production: To form [ʒ], place the blade of the tongue in back of the gum ridge and push the sides of the tongue against the upper side teeth. The tongue is somewhat retracted in the mouth and the lips are rounded. [ʒ] is voiced.

Be aware:

1. It may seem that [ʒ] occurs infrequently in English because there are only a few words—and most of those adopted from French—that begin with [ʒ]. It is heard more frequently in other Indo-European languages. However, [ʒ] intrudes itself into a number of words, such as *treasure, leisure, inclusion*, and *illusion*. Be on guard for it.

2. As with any voiced cognate, the speaker may fail to initiate sufficient vocal fold vibration, thereby causing a shift to the voiceless version of the pair. The final syllable of *occasion* is not *shun*, nor does *pleasure* end with *sure*, nor *allusion* end as *Aleutian*. Fully vocalize [ʒ].

3. We prefer [ʒ] as the pronunciation of the final sound in words such as *beige, rouge, garage, mirage*, or *corsage*, although a number of contemporary dictionaries offer the consonant [dʒ] as an acceptable alternate. (We admit the inconsistency of *huge* [hjudʒ] and *luge* [luʒ] or of *loge* [louʒ] and *doge* [doudʒ]—but whoever said the English spelling system makes sense?)

POSITION

Frontal	Medial	Final
genre	azure	beige
Zhivago	Asia	rouge
Zsa Zsa	measure	garage
	leisure	massage
	lesion	corsage
	confusion	entourage
	vision	camouflage

Words Contrasting [s], [z], [ʃ], *and* [ʒ]

lesser—buzzer—pressure—measure

passer—jazzer—masher—azure

lease—lees—leash—lesion
base—bays—bash—beige
closer—dozer—kosher—closure

Sentences Featuring [ʃ] and [ʒ]

1. A shimmering vision of Krishna arose from the marshes.
2. A foolish shout of "fire" caused a crush of confusion at the Bijou.
3. Sharon O'Shea wore a plush beige negligee.
4. That Russian said Brezhnev ate a fresh dish of quiche once in Central Asia.
5. Measure by measure the brash soloist played a wishful, wistful adagio.
6. Persian fashion calls for a fusion of fuchsia leisure suits and shiny gumshoes.
7. A sure sign of diminishing vision is difficulty distinguishing Zsa Zsa from Sha Na Na.
8. Sheets of shiny snow diminished Zhivago's vision.
9. Flashy fashion models take pleasure in showing their sharp-looking leisure suits.
10. Sure-handed nurses should establish a triage to treat soldiers shot with shrapnel.
11. A sharp flash of sunshine gave full disclosure to Shawn's camouflaged position.
12. Six patient Hoosiers shared toothbrushes on a pleasure cruise to Chicago.
13. Gigi washed the rouge off with dishwashing lotion.
14. Marsha Pershing's treasure chest should contain a splashy collage.
15. When the sheriff fired three shots, Portia stopped her shameless seizure of buried treasure.

[h]

[h] Is a Voiceless Glottal Fricative

Production: To form the consonant [h], the last of the nine fricatives, forget about your mouth except to keep the soft palate sufficiently raised so that air will not be expelled through the nose. The position of the tongue and lips is relatively unimportant—in fact, they will assume the position for the adjacent phoneme in the word. [h] is the only American English sound legitimately articulated in the glottis. The vocal folds are brought together to form the narrowed opening required for friction, and the air escapes in a puffing action. [h] is voiceless and has no cognate voiced sound.

Be aware:

1. Do not omit [h] at the beginning of words such as *hook, horse,* and *hot*. English people with cockney dialects, some Australians, and certain speakers who learned English as a second language will often omit [h] in the initial position. In *My Fair Lady,* for example, Eliza called the professor "'enry 'iggins" instead of "Henry Higgins."
2. Many words spelled with an initial *h* do not include [h]—*heir, honor,* and *hour,* for instance. A few others are considered acceptable either with or without [h]—*herb, homage,* and *humble,* for instance. And there is no [h] at the end of words such as *rah, blah, ooh,* and *oh.*
3. Be careful not to overaspirate [h] so that it becomes excessively breathy. We should hear the sound that is produced by the expelled air, but not the sound of the escaping air itself.

POSITION

Frontal	Medial	Final
hello	sweetheart	[h] does not
who	inhale	occur in the
horror	inhuman	final position
human	brouhaha	
highway	molehill	
haughty	mishap	
halibut	foxhole	

In most words beginning with orthographic *wh*, the *h* is pronounced before the w: [hw]. We discuss this sound in more detail in Chapter 13.

what	while
when	which
where	whet
why	whether

In certain other words, however, only the *h* is pronounced and the *w* is silent—for example, *whom*, *who*, and *whole*.

Sentences Featuring [h]

1. Hannah fixed hearty hero sandwiches for the hungry hydraulic engineers.
2. I hiccuped during hide-and-seek, enabling Henry to find where I had hidden.
3. Get off your high horse—your high-hat, headstrong habits are humiliating.
4. The hayseed harvested hawthorn branches and hollyhock blossoms along with the hay.
5. Harmonious and healthful living is less hazardous to your health than horseplay and high jinks.
6. The haberdasher sold hats, riding habits, hip-huggers, hosiery, hoods, high-topped shoes, and other habiliments.
7. My hamburger was a humdinger, but Harriet said hers was only ho-hum and hardly a hearty meal.
8. The hills harbor hickory, hazelnut, and holly trees, while the highlands have huckleberries and heather.
9. He who hesitates may be here longer than he who is pigheaded, bullheaded, or hard-nosed.
10. Hubert fell head over heels in love with Helen, but she had no heart for him.
11. A hamster named Horace sometimes rode on the back of Harry the horse, sometimes on Horatio the hog, and sometimes on Harvey the hippopotamus.
12. I have heard the music of Hindemith, and its harmonics are hardly in the hit-parade style of the happy tunes of Victor Herbert.
13. Is it heresy to suggest that heathens may find a home and happiness in heaven?
14. Hercules heaved the huge hammerstone into the harbor, upholding his heroic image.
15. Hurricanes do happen in Hereford and Hampshire, as well as Hong Kong, Honolulu, and Hackensack.

Sentences Featuring [s], [z], [ʃ], [ʒ], *and* [h]

1. Julius Caesar was sometimes paralyzed by harsh seizures.
2. Confusion muzzled the muscled denizens at the Disco when a short fuse blew, shooting a shower of sparks.
3. "Ou sont les neiges d'antan?" means "Where are the snows of yesteryear?"

4. Aphasia, a partial or total loss of one's capacity to express ideas, results from brain damage.

5. Those exhausted lumberjacks hope to shear the frozen bushes with buzz saws.

6. It was the squid's chic galoshes that hastened his swift demise.

7. The haphazard chef splashed sponges and suds into the hash.

8. "Pass the keys to the Porsche," said Xavier, finishing his spinach quiche.

9. Amidst confusion, smoke, and shrapnel, the sailor observed dozens of sinking ships.

10. She sees policemen sneeze when they eat cheese in the sixth precinct.

11. We saw the Bahamas and Cozumel on a six-day ocean pleasure cruise.

12. The sheep's fleece serves as a treasure chest for hordes of fleas.

13. Tinsel dishes are showy, but easily the most haphazard of all serving possibilities.

14. Shunning the sun for the safety of shady forests, seven thousand Huns shook western Asia.

15. Some heroes say the sweetest mysteries of life are shown through the misery of harsh exercise and discipline.

EXERCISES FOR FRICATIVES

Let's pack up our fricative-mobile and see America! This is a geographic journey through place names full of fricatives. We begin in western Canada and end in eastern Canada, but spend the rest of the time in the United States. Repeat the following:

Vancouver, British Columbia	Fort Smith
Salem	Kansas City, Missouri
Mount Shasta, California	Chicago
San Francisco	Memphis
San Jose	Nashville
Thousand Oaks	Frankfort
Las Vegas	Cincinnati
Southern Nevada	Harrisburg
Hoover Dam	Philadelphia
Phoenix, Arizona	Elizabeth, New Jersey
Santa Fe	East Rutherford
Fort Worth	New Haven
Houston	Framingham, Massachusetts
Baton Rouge	Plymouth Rock
Shreveport	Halifax, Nova Scotia

Now let's go around the world! Your passport to pronunciation begins and ends in England.

Portsmouth	Himalayas
Belfast	Kashmir
Netherlands	Southeast Asia
Switzerland	Philippines
Vesuvius	Shanghai
Tunisia	Northern Mariana Islands
Sahara Desert	Hawaii
Marrakesh	Honduras
Ethiopia	Venezuela
Zimbabwe	Gulf of Mexico
Indian Ocean	North Atlantic Ocean
Afghanistan	Southampton

BACK VOWELS

"Everybody says words different," said Ivy. "Arkansas folks says 'em different, and Oklahomy folks say 'em different. And we seen a lady from Massachusetts, an' she said 'em differentest of all. Couldn't hardly make out what she was sayin'."

—John Steinbeck,
The Grapes of Wrath

Back vowels are formed with the major tongue adjustment occurring in the back of the mouth. Phonetically these vowels are written [ɑ], [ɔ], [o], [ʊ], and [u]. The back of the tongue is at its highest toward the velum (soft palate) for [u], as in *food,* and at its lowest for [ɑ], as in *fob.* Lip rounding is important in the proper formation for all but one of the back vowels. Lip rounding is greatest with [u] and decreases for [ʊ], [o], and [ɔ]. There is virtually no lip rounding for the most relaxed sound we make, [ɑ].

[ɑ] **Is the Lowest Back Vowel**

Production: To form the phoneme [ɑ], drop the jaw to its lowest position. Open the mouth wide and slightly tense the back of the tongue. (In changing from the lowest front vowel, [æ], to the back vowel [ɑ], the tongue arch moves from front to back.)

Orthographic spellings:

> a—charm
>
> o—hot
>
> e—sergeant
>
> ua—guard
>
> ea—hearth

Be aware:

1. If the arch of the tongue is moved forward, [ɑ] will become [æ]. For example, *stop* [stɑp] will become *stap* [stæp].
2. Too much tension in the back of the tongue will cause [ɑ] to rise to [ɔ]. The word *are* [ɑr] will become *or* [ɔr].

Many speakers use a variant sound [ɒ] that occurs between the pure vowels [ɑ] and [ɔ]. The sound is heard most frequently in "short o" words, such as *hot, dog, moth,* and *frog.* The use of this variant is acceptable providing it does not impair clarity. [ɑ], [ɒ], and [ɔ] can be used interchangeably in certain words, such as *fog, office,* and *mosque.*

POSITION

Frontal	Medial	Final
ominous	job	la
oxen	prompt	spa
aria	watch	shah
opposite	philosophy	blah
opera	cobbler	fa
odd	beyond	ha
oxygen	father	hurrah

Sentences Featuring [ɑ]:

1. That obstinate clod Ron is fond of pop philosophy.
2. When golfing, the odds of swatting a dirt clod are obvious.
3. Through the swamp hopped an ominous fox.

4. Blond Bob Mackintosh chops on a top-notch chopping block.

5. There was not a spot on the posh Dodge in the garage.

6. A mob fills the synagogue to honor Rosh Hashanah.

7. Spot, the watchdog, trod through a kumquat plot in Oshkosh.

8. An ad hoc mob of vagabonds slopped water on top of the yacht.

9. Drop a lot of coins in the slot of the kiosk.

10. If you don't want a response from Tom, watch out for orthodox paradoxes.

11. The bomb shot boxes of eggnog across the block.

12. A colossal rhinoceros threw bottles of pop at Wanda Dobson.

13. His odd obsession with an albatross gave fodder for many sonnets.

14. Was *A Clockwork Orange* a box office flop?

15. Ah! I dropped a squash bonbon on my watch fob.

[ɔ] **Is a Low Back Vowel**

Production: To form the phoneme [ɔ], raise the back of the tongue toward the soft palate slightly more than for [ɑ]. There is minor tension in the tongue and a beginning of lip rounding.

Orthographic spellings:

> a — fall
> aw — crawl
> au — taught
> ou — ought
> o — cost
> oa — broad

Be aware:

1. Too much tension in the jaw or excessive puckering of the lips will cause the tongue to be pulled back in the mouth. The sounds that occur will be "dark" and muffled.

2. Diphthongization can occur with this vowel. *Dog* [dɔg] can become *daw-ug* [dɔ əg].

3. In certain areas of the United States, there is a tendency to substitute the middle back vowel [o] for the more lax [ɔ]. In this case, *dog* [dɔg] will be pronounced *doe-ug* [do əg].

POSITION

Frontal	Medial	Final
auburn	balk	jaw
awning	false	claw
automobile	waltz	straw
autumn	haul	law
ought	appall	draw
auction	launch	flaw
author	exhaust	withdraw

Sentences Featuring [ɔ]

1. A thought dawned on the astronaut—there is no such thing as a free launch.

2. Awestruck Mr. Micawber applauded the marauders' so-called assault.

3. I saw a tall bald man covered with straw from his jaws to his paunch.

4. They ought to recall all autos that stall.
5. A squall left Mt. Auburn covered in an awful snowfall.
6. Chalky, gaunt Paul waltzed with his mother-in-law.
7. The Hawks' hard-fought football game was broadcast as an afterthought.
8. With a tomahawk a squaw caught prawns in the waterfall.
9. You ought not to have gawked as I bound the growling dog's paw with gauze.
10. I'll have crab claws in sauce, a malt, and some salt.
11. A faulty pratfall caused Dawn's broken collarbone.
12. The thought of hearing Audrey's maudlin talk on the Falklands makes me yawn.
13. I thought the brawny outlaws were too exhausted to brawl.
14. A gnawing autumn feeling haunts August in Catawba.
15. You ought to breathe from the craw and talk with the jaw.

Sentences Featuring [ɑ] and [ɔ]

1. You ought to have caught and bottled the otter.
2. Pshaw! Boston hardly got hot in August.
3. The popular politician, never pausing, doggedly sought lawful contributions.
4. Paul Oliver wore an awful, off-color collar.
5. Maude Cox showed off her body in her orange jogging togs.
6. Do cod spawn in Austin and Wichita Falls, or farther north in Bar Harbor?
7. Solid globs of straw dotted the lawns of squalid Providence.
8. John Cobb hobnobs with cops, paupers, and Harvard law profs.
9. Stop those moss-covered hogs from fulfilling their awesome promise.
10. In the calm waters, Sergeant Dawn Carter fought a tawdry shark.
11. Don was wrong: the awning was not strong enough to hold the fawn.
12. A honking swan startled Bob; he bawled all day long.
13. Paupers bought lots of psalms from Saul Thompson for a paltry cost.
14. A columnist from Catawba auctioned off all the raw walnuts.
15. At dawn Lon donned his long johns for a jaunty trot across the forest.

The Pure Vowel [o] Is a Middle Back Vowel

The difference between the pure vowel [e] and the diphthong [eɪ] was discussed in Chapter 10. One other comparable pair of phonemes is found in Standard American English—[o] and [oʊ]. The [o] sound occurs as a pure vowel, and with the addition of a slight slide upward into the [ʊ] position it is elongated into a diphthong. Again, the relationship between stress and duration determines the outcome. Duration is a method of achieving stress: to stress a syllable or word, hold onto it longer. The pure vowel [o] is difficult if not impossible to hold, so we slide into [ʊ] when stress is required, thus creating the diphthong [oʊ].

Chapter 13 offers sentences and drills for [oʊ]. For now, try to hear the difference between the two sounds in the following words.

INITIAL POSITION

Unstressed [o] Preferred		Stressed [o] or [oʊ]	
obey	omit	old	open
okay	ovation	oak	over
opaque	overrate	oar	only
oasis	overseas	oath	ocean

MEDIAL POSITION

Unstressed		*Stressed*	
[o] *Preferred*		[oʊ] *Preferred*	
hotel	notation	motion	ptomaine
rotation	totalitarian	coping	oppose
domain	ingrown	portable	phonograph
phonetic	vocation	coldhearted	lowered

FINAL POSITION

[o] *Preferred, but Avoid*
[ɑ] *and* [ə]

swallow	Othello
vertigo	yellow
Jello	pillow
fellow	window

Note the difference between *Jello* and *hello:* when the accent is on the first syllable, as in *Jello,* [o] is preferable. But when the accent is on the second syllable, as in *hello,* [oʊ] is used.

[ʊ] **Is a High Back Vowel**

Production: To form the phoneme [ʊ], arch the back of the tongue high toward the soft palate. The lips are rounded, but slightly less than for the highest back vowel, [u].

Orthographic spellings:

u—pull

oo—cook

ou—should

o—wolf

Be aware:

1. Diphthongization can occur with this vowel. *Pull* [pʊl] can become *poo-wel* [pu wəl].
2. Substitutions occur frequently when words containing [ʊ] are pronounced. For example, *cookie* [kʊkɪ] becomes *kooky* [kukɪ], *look* [lʊk] becomes *luck* [lʌk], and *your* [jʊr] becomes *yore* [jor].

Notice that [ʊ] does not appear in the frontal position nor the final position.

POSITION

Frontal	*Medial*	*Final*
[ʊ] does not occur in the frontal position	full	[ʊ] does not occur in the final position
	should	
	bulletin	
	couldn't	
	pudding	
	rookie	
	sugar	

Sentences Featuring [ʊ]

1. A book comparing the hoof to the foot could win the Pulitzer Prize.
2. Mr. Booker looked around the bush for some good wood to burn.

3. I mistook her putting her foot down for an attempt to boogie-woogie.

4. Buy a bushel of sugar to make cookies for the neighborhood.

5. The bookie took a loss betting the Bulls wouldn't pull out a victory.

6. Giving me only a cursory look, pushy Beth Shultz took my rook.

7. She should be full; she forsook her cookies.

8. The good-looking wool pullover was ruined by soot.

9. By hook or by crook, Wood took chances he shouldn't.

10. The rookie put a live bull in the breakfast nook.

11. In winter, put a good hood fully over your head.

12. A wicked-looking crook pushed John Hood and called him a "no-good sourpuss."

13. The jury noted that the woman shot the bullet at the hood.

14. She shook a crooked cane and took me through the looking glass.

15. Look—cook by the book, as you should, toots!

[u] **Is the Highest Back Vowel**

Production: To form the phoneme [u], open the mouth slightly, round the lips as much as possible, and arch the back of the tongue high, nearly touching the soft palate.

Orthographic spellings:

oo—pool	ough—through
o—do	ous—rendezvous
oe—shoe	ui—fruit
ou—soup	wo—two
ew—grew	u—gnu
ue—due	eu—bleu cheese

Be aware:

1. Inadequate tension in the tongue and insufficient lip rounding will cause [u] to drop to [ʊ]. The word *pool* [pul] will become *pull* [pʊl].

2. When [u] is followed by the consonants [l] or [n] in the same syllable, there is a tendency to diphthongize the sound. In addition, an extra consonant is frequently inserted. Words such as *cool* [kul] become *koo-wel* [ku wəl].

3. In affected speech, [j] is often added to [u], producing words such as [sjut] and [sju] for the more standard *suit* [sut] and *Sue* [su]; *liqueur* [lɪ kɝ'] becomes the British [lɪ kjuə(r)].

The phoneme [u] infrequently appears in the frontal position unless it is preceded by [j]. There are a number of words in Standard American English where it is desirable to include [j] before [u]. These words will be discussed in Chapter 13.

POSITION

Frontal	*Medial*	*Final*
ooze	gloomy	who
oops	fool	shoe
oolong	roof	threw
umlaut	suit	bayou
umiak	school	bamboo
oodles	prune	undo
	truth	ballyhoo

There is occasionally debate over the "correct" pronunciation of words such as *roof, room,* and *hoof.* [u] and [ʊ] are interchangeable in these instances. A rule of thumb would be to follow the practice of educated speakers in your geographic area.

Sentences Featuring [u]

1. What unruly ghoul threw plumes through the roof?
2. Lou wore her new blue suit to school.
3. In truth, you knew who renewed her dues in June.
4. Bamboo is useless on the roof of an igloo.
5. He threw his tools in the blue pool.
6. Sue Lewis was too cool to root for New York University.
7. The group saw goofy loons, cougars who cooed, and pumas who mooed at the zoo.
8. Youth consume Fruit Loops with spoons en route to the moon.
9. Two rude dudes practiced voodoo while watching "Looney Tunes" cartoons.
10. Who'll snoop on Mary Lou—you or foolish Duke Boone?
11. As the moon loomed large that gloomy June night, the doomed loon swooned, soon to be food for the racoon.
12. Groups of goons goose-stepped through the moonlit streets of Cancun.
13. Juvenile students used tools to bind school books to their stools with glue.
14. Poof! The Who issued two new tunes, then faded from view.
15. The new thruway will soon prove a boon to Liverpool.

MINIMAL TRIPLETS FOR [u], [ʊ], AND [o]

[u]	[ʊ]	[o]	Phrases
pool	pull	pole	Pull the pole through the pool.
fool	full	foal	Fool the full foal.
gouda	good	goad	Goaded by good gouda.
shooed	should	showed	She showed how he should have shooed.
crew cut	crook	croak	"Cripes!" croaked the crew cut crook.
wooed	would	woe	He wooed; she wouldn't; oh, woe!
suit	soot	sote	Creosoted soot coated the suit.
Luke	look	local	Luke looks like a local.
who'd	hood	hoed	The hood who'd hoed the garden was old.
cooed	could	code	The pigeon could have cooed the code.
boola	bull	bowl	Boola-boola! The Bulls are in the Hula Bowl.
pewter	put	potato	Put on a pewter potato.

Sentences for All Back Vowels

1. A good smart dog could have caught the oblong ball.
2. What do you do to make poppies bloom in Altoona sooner than June?
3. Toss the soggy cookies along with that awful gouda.
4. Mohammed sought to water his camels under a palm tree at a calm oasis.
5. Politicians who are pursuing possible office should test the waters with a straw vote.
6. During June, July, and August, the neighborhood lawns are watered only in the mornings.

Read It Aloud _____

**For he can prophesy
With a wink of his eye,
Peep with security
Into futurity,
Sum up your history,
Clear up a mystery,
Humour proclivity
For a nativity—for a
  nativity;
With mirrors so magical,
Tetrapods tragical,
Bogies spectacular,
Answers oracular,
Facts astronomical,
Solemn or comical,
And, if you want it, he
Makes a reduction on
  taking a quantity!**

—GILBERT & SULLIVAN
The Sorcerer

7. Occasionally, a good tutor swaps a stock of books for a costly domicile.

8. Remove the official rule book, and you'll hear the applause of numerous students.

9. Coco is through with hot spots, honky-tonks, and all haunts of bookies and notorious folks.

10. Jo's portfolio is full of good mutual funds and common stocks; still, her mood is gloomy and she puts most of her deposits in a vault.

11. Okra casserole, rutabaga pudding, and almond soup—there's food for thought.

12. The tropical youth couldn't toss large coconuts; he was too exhausted.

13. Look—you misunderstood, and that colossal goof is your fault.

14. If I were you, I would fix the roof and unclog the faucet before Pa gets home.

15. Barbara wants a forty-foot yacht—or schooner—to sail slowly across Boston Harbor.

Sentences Contrasting [æ], [ɑ],
[ɔ], [o], *and* [oʊ]

1. Dan and Don don't get up before dawn.

2. I caught the cat asleep on the coat I'd thrown on the cot.

3. We sowed the sod with seed and sawed arms for a scarecrow.

4. The hockey team—the Philadelphia Hawks—looked hokey as they hacked at the puck.

5. I taught the girl to tat when she was a small tot; she made a tote bag.

6. It means naught to a gnat if you do not write it a note.

7. A rat took the letter I wrote you, carried it under the wrought-iron sofa, and left it to rot.

8. Although the hotel room was hot, the haughty lady would not take off her hat.

9. Do not shock Shaw by showing him the shack.

10. Maw mopped the floor while Paw moped because he lost his map.

11. The politician was appalled to find that his pals did not vote for him at the polls.

12. The loan of some artificial lawn made of nylon helped the lawyer sell the land.

13. On the bottom of the boat Lottie bought were boxes of baseball bats.

14. Hal found a hole at the end of the empty, hollow hall.

15. I woke up early, walked to the Oriental restaurant, and had breakfast cooked in a wok.

A NEWS BROADCAST FOR PRACTICING ALL BACK VOWELS

Our top story tonight:

A Trojan poultry farmer remains in a coma following an awful fall this morning in Woodstock. His puny pony lost her footing on awful old Sawville Road—it is reported she was startled by an auto or a mule and couldn't be calmed. The farmer is now in Johns Hopkins Hospital, where the prognosis is good for a full recovery. Stay tuned for more news on this important story.

The university neighborhood has been bothered recently by wolves and dogs running loose through homes, cottages, and schoolyards. The dogs strew bones along the boulevards, gnaw and pull at the pants legs of unfortunate postmen, crawl through sewers, and often just get underfoot. Those owners of the unruly four-pawed marauders ought to call them home soon—for all dogs loose on the streets will be caught. I suppose one could call this new law a *cur*-few.

Noted doctor Luther Foothall of the medical college boasts of a new solution for the common cold. Foothall, a pathologist who taught audiology at Antioch last fall, says a prudent program of cold okra pudding every afternoon will stop a cough, soothe a raw throat, and provide an ongoing duel with the blahs. The truth of his ludicrous offering wants proof.

And now for our on-the-spot weather report:

An ominous cold front is pushing its way toward us from Montana. There, raw grueling winds and snow dropped temperatures below zero. The blue norther should fall upon our area beginning after ten o'clock tonight and continue through tomorrow. Look for gloomy, overcast skies, a good chance of frozen roads, and accumulated snowfalls of two to four inches. Our low tonight—fourteen degrees, with strong north winds. Tomorrow's high—only twenty-two or so. So—I think you ought to lock the doors, pull out the wool socks and long johns, fix hot chocolate or coffee—and stay cozy!

And now for the sports news:

In football, Oakland lost to Los Angeles; Auburn stomped Wisconsin; and Washington demolished Chicago.

In basketball, North Carolina, led by youthful sophomore Paul Cook, withstood a furious onslaught to post a 74 to 72 win over Boston College. Other games: Loyola rolled over St. Johns; New York University bulled past Old Dominion; and Oregon stomped on the Georgia Bulldogs.

Finally, coach Sondra Logan has chosen rookie guard Ruth Austin as captain of the U.S. Olympic volleyball team. Austin, of Tucson, Arizona, will call the shots as the team tries to pull off a long-shot upset against strong competition next June in Innsbruck, Austria.

That's tonight's news. Stay tuned for a special report by correspondent Paula Osgood on "The Fall of the Family," featuring interviews with bully nephews and frosty mothers-in-law, plus stories of false brotherhood. That important show will be followed by the rollicking comedy "All My Poodles."

Good night to you all!

PHONETICS PRACTICE 1: FRICATIVES AND BACK VOWELS

Write the following words in phonetics:

1. sues _____
2. thaw _____
3. Oz _____
4. of _____
5. shah _____
6. haws _____
7. hoof _____
8. pshaw _____
9. soothe _____
10. off _____

11. hooves _____
12. sooth _____
13. shoes _____
14. who _____
15. zoo _____
16. whose _____
17. ooze _____
18. behoove _____
19. (r)ouge _____
20. soph(omore) _____

CROSSWORD PUZZLE
Plosive, Fricative, Front and Back Vowels

Across

1. telephone or voting
4. a dandy
7. fixation
10. aspirate
11. large keg or container
13. person or thing present
15. not hard
16. seep out
18. 12 inches
19. Quaker second person
20. female sibling
21. Wizard's land

Down

1. where cranberries are grown
2. _____ and ah
3. robber
4. battled
5. ooh and ____
6. shove
8. hen fruit
9. _____ bitty, teeny-weeny bikini
10. a _____ been (over the hill)
11. several vice presidents
12. minor fights
13. Marlo Thomas was _____ girl
14. relieves, placates
17. Zuider _____
21. the doctor's sound

PHONETICS PRACTICE 2: STOP-PLOSIVES, FRICATIVES, AND FRONT AND BACK VOWELS

Write the orthographic spelling for the following words:

1. [fʊt] _____
2. [gɪv] _____
3. [θɔt] _____
4. [ðiz] _____
5. [sæʃ] _____
6. [zut sut] _____
7. [ʃɑk] _____
8. [ʒɑʒɑ] _____
9. [hɔtɪ] _____
10. [θɛft] _____
11. [væ pɪd] _____
12. [tiθ] _____
13. [ðɪs] _____
14. [fiz] _____
15. [sɑgɪ] _____
16. [ʃɑp] _____
17. [sutɪd] _____
18. [hɑpt] _____
19. [bʊkt] _____
20. [pɑts] _____

Write the following words in phonetics:

1. gaff _____
2. vest _____
3. booth _____
4. teethe _____
5. hoops _____
6. gods _____
7. push _____
8. behoove _____
9. foggy _____
10. heavy _____
11. thick _____
12. gasses _____
13. seethe _____
14. zigzag _____
15. bushes _____
16. behead _____
17. kooky _____
18. fought _____
19. opt _____
20. (dé)jà vu _____

MONOLOGUES FOR PRACTICE

Male Speakers

MANFRED: It is so beautiful. You can see everything. Like the clouds. When I was a child, I would stare up at the clouds and try to decide what they were shaped like. I never came up with anything. My brother, Lothar, could see a thousand creatures in one cloud; I saw only a cloud. In pilot training school, I began looking at the clouds from above. I would fly over a cloud and stare at it until my eyes hurt. They still looked like clouds to me. One day a new instructor arrived at the field; he was replacing our old instructor who had been killed the week before. Anyway, he had an enormous bulbous nose, and when he put on his flight cap, he looked like a cloud. I saw him in every cloud I flew over. Now I see twisted faces and broken planes in the clouds. If I could just see that instructor, or even a plain old cloud again, I think I would be all right.

—KEN JONES,
A Red Eagle Falling

WILL (O. Henry): I will try and give you a truthful and correct account in a brief and condensed manner of some of the wonderful things to be seen and heard in this country. The people of the state of Texas consist principally of men, women, and children, with a sprinkling of cowboys. The weather is very good, thermometer rarely rising above 2,500 degrees in the shade and hardly ever below 212 degrees. There is a very pleasant little phase in the weather called a "Norther" by the natives. You are riding along on a boiling day in September, watching the fish trying to climb out of the pools of boiling water along the way, when a wind as cold as the icy hand of death swoops down on you from the north, and the "norther" is upon you. Where do you go? If you are far from home it depends entirely upon what kind of life you have led previous to this time as to where you go. Some people go straight to heaven, while others experience a change of temperature by the transition. "Northers" are very useful in killing off the surplus population.

—JOSEPH HOESL,
What's Around the Corner

STEVE: I studied dance for quite a while. When I was two, my dream was to dance for the Bolshoi Ballet company, but at my preschool dance recital, I pulled a hamstring. I had to sit out for a year. It really hurt my technique. During that year, I took voice. I toured with *Sugar Babies,* until I had to start school. So it wasn't until the summer after first grade that I got my big break. I did *A Chorus Line.* I was tall for my age. I stayed with it, until my voice changed. Then I understudied Carol Channing for a year. Goals? Well, I joined the Peace Corps and started a dance company for third world nations, but the injury rate was high. And the dances never seemed to have any energy. I'm also not a big fan of rice dishes. Is shopping a good goal?

—KEN JONES,
The Big One

DON: I don't know why, but I can't seem to stop stuffing my face. No matter how much I eat, I'm ravenous a little while later. I eat snacks between my snacks and snacks between my meals and dessert after my meals and dessert after my dessert—or is that considered another snack? At any rate, I guess I'm pretty much a pig. I'm starting to look the role, too. And speaking of rolls—sorry, just a little hunger humor. But I don't care too much anymore, really. All I know is that I'm getting hungry again. Maybe I'll eat that big chocolate Frankenstein head I got for Halloween. Then again, a big four-foot pizza doesn't sound half bad either.

—KYLE KINZER

IRWIN: I am an electrical by-circuit, interphase coordinating engineer. I love my job. I have my own office. Office cubicle. It's almost like an office. There are no walls, but there are partitions which go close to the ceiling. I have a desk, and a spine-supporting, state-of-the-art desk stool. Oh, and a computer. A Grody 9000. Grody's are the best computers on the market for electrical by-circuitry, interphase coordination. The company supplies our lunches. Which I don't have to tell you, is a real perk. They deliver our lunches right to our doors. If we had doors, I mean. I suppose they really deliver our lunches to our archways. It saves the company lost work time, and it saves me a lot of money. Money that I tunnel into the dating scene. Two dates each within a month of each other. They never knew. Poor girls. Never knew that I was seeing the other woman. I was nervous, but it was worth it

—Ken Jones,
Lifelines

ALEX: I have two girls. Babies really. I rush home from the job to be with them as much as I possibly can. I love them, and I do what I think is best for them. But is it enough? Will they grow up knowing what they need to know? How to share with others, and how to do for themselves. Will they remember the good times? Laughing. Playing. Or will they dwell on the bad? Crying. Hiding. (pause) My youngest pushed me to my limit the other day. Grabbing everything in sight. Throwing her food. Demanding attention. And, finally, she accidentally knocked over a small table in the living room and broke this tiny ceramic house I had bought in New England. I blew up. I was furious. I had been pushed too far. I charged into the room, and I was met by a tiny, crying face. A little face was saying, "I sorry, I sorry," over and over again. I was dumbfounded. This child had been terrified by my rage, and it scared me. Would she be haunted by that one image of me? Angry me? And the ceramic house was saved. I glued the broken gable and put it away. The house was fine, but I wasn't sure the baby was.

—Ken Jones,
Inside a Paper House

HERB (male college student): Okay, I'll bug out and let you alone. But let me tell you one thing first. This is just between you and me—I really shouldn't tell you. But my fraternity has had an eye on you—some of the guys think you'd make a good brother. But there are others who think you're too square, that you stick to yourself too much. You know, it's important that you get in on some of the rap sessions or card games. You seem so uptight about everything. You need to relax once in a while. I know you're gonna do what you want, but I'm telling you for your own good. If you want to get anywhere on the campus, you've got to socialize some. Just studying and getting a degree isn't all there is to college. A fraternity can be mighty important to a man—a lot of social and business contacts are made by the brothers. You need to look to the future in more ways than one.

—Ethel Glenn,
Where Do You Go From Here

SAMMY: So I like laying around my sardine can room listening to music or punching away at the computer. Big deal! I always say, go ahead and take time to do stuff you like. Does she? Of course not. What kind of stupid question is that? I'm sorry if I do things without her, but I'm at a point in my life where I think we need space. And before I'm called a pig by you women, let me explain something. I'm not saying I want to break up or even separate. It's just that with going to school, work, and spending a lot of time with her, I have no time for myself. Relationships are a dangerous thing. Even when you think it's a sure thing, problems arise. I can't say I will change into the person she wants me to be. I won't surrender. I would be miserable. She would be miserable. I wouldn't blame her for leaving me. I want her to be happy, but if she can't find happiness with me, then I would rather she find it with someone else. Relationships. It's "I said I love you first." Or "I spent more money on your Christmas gift." You've done it. I've done it. I just don't understand why we do it.

—Jeff Nagel

WILLIAM: Parades. A natural by-product of being a celebrity. A hundred parades in a hundred towns. Faceless people waving from a faceless crowd. And I wave. And they wave. My doctor says that I am developing parade elbow. Today is different. This is my hometown. One of my hometowns. I actually had quite a few. My parents moved us around a lot. They said it was the job, but I always believed that they were just trying to escape the friends they had accumulated. Friends who could only speak of oil changes, P.T.A., and tax increases. So, in our nomadic tradition, we moved here. I wanted to play the saxophone in the high school band, but the band director died and the program crumbled. So in an effort to alleviate my artistic frustrations, I joined the drama department. I became an actor. I trained as an actor. And like all well-trained, non-working actors I became a writer . . . and a director. So you can see why I call this town my hometown. That is, if I am where I think I am.

—KEN JONES,
Lifelines

AL (male college student): So I cornered the freshman outside the cafeteria and said, "Man, you can't eat in here. Don't you know this cafeteria's only for upperclassmen?" He looks kinda pitiful for a minute, then says, "Where do the freshmen eat?" So I frown up like I'm real concerned and say, "Man, that is a real problem around this place—unless, of course, you've got a car. Have you got a car?" "No," he says, really starting to look scared. "Well," I said, "the nearest decent place to eat is about five miles from here. It only takes about an hour—each way—to walk it." "Three times a day?" he says. "Well, there is a way," I say, like it's a big secret. "Talk to Luther, the guy behind the grill—the sort of fat one—if you'll give him ten dollars, he'll pretend you're a transfer student, then you can eat in the snack bar." He went right in and forked over the ten. Luther gave me my five later on!

—ETHEL GLENN,
Where Do You Go From Here

Female Speakers

SALLY: I am a phone operator for *Time/Life* Books. I'm actually a model-slash-actress. Really. I've been on a soap opera, or daytime drama as we like to call it in the business. I carried a punch bowl during a wedding scene. Maybe you saw it? Jeanette and Nathaniel's wedding on *Wisdom's Crest*. I came on right after Jeanette had the affair with the Lutheran minister who had given the last rites to her Uncle Toliver. Nathaniel was dipping Caitlin Crandall's ballet slipper into the punch when the cyclone tore down the rose archway. I said the line, "looks like a Nor-easter." Remember? (Pause) I work at *Time/Life* just for the experience. And the money. If you order the Photographic History of Primitive Man, more than likely you are speaking with me. It's a wonderful set of books. There have been complaints that the photos are a bit grainy, but I figure pictures that old, we're darn lucky to even have them. Nineteen-ninety-five per book. Mastercard or Visa. Just call 1-800-Dawn of Man.

—KEN JONES,
Lifelines

JENNIFER: I wish my life was like a bird. So I could fly all over and see the world. That would be so cool, to fly all over. I'd go to Europe and Asia and—if I had an airplane, I would be fine. Okay, so all I need to do is find someone rich and marry him. We wouldn't have to be happily married or anything. I just want to travel. His money would then be my money. Oh, how wonderful life would be. "There's always a pile of money at the end of the rainbow." That would be my motto! Money isn't everything, although it is better than this love and suffering "thing." Can't you have both love and money? I guess if you have love you can't really fly like a bird. You know that freedom thing. So, don't tell me to forget money anymore. It's much better than love. Money can't buy me love, I know, but it can buy me freedom.

—LAURA BURKE

A RAPE VICTIM (female): . . . down where they scribble obscenities under the bridge. That's where I had this dream. They . . . you could hear the words laughing as they cursed. They weren't spray paint, at all. They were alive, like demon voices that ripped at your clothes and slapped your face until it was black and blue. And I saw something awful happening, so I ran away.

It wasn't me. It was someone else. It was someone else, but I recognized her voice, as I hid in the bushes and didn't make a sound. I listened to her cries and whimpers for over an hour before it was safe to come out. And, when I did, the voices had written themselves back on the concrete columns, in purple spray paint. I looked around for her, but I couldn't find her. I cut my feet on the broken glass, looking for her. I turned, every time I heard her cry, but she was gone. And I was naked and shivering, when the patrol car drove up.

It wasn't me. It was somebody else.

—Lawrence M. Fogelberg,
Essences

WENDY: If I had a teddy bear like the one I had when I was little, I'd be fine. I could talk to it, tell it all my secrets that no one else would know. I could hold it when I'm scared. It would always be there for me. It wouldn't leave me like everyone else does. Yeah, I wish my life was like a little kid's life. No worries, your parents take care of everything. When you're a little kid all you are required to do is play. When you grow up, life stinks—there are so many problems. I've discovered that there's always a big dark cloud waiting to smother you at the end of the rainbow. Adults don't have any fun. It's all work, work, work. Well, not me. I refuse! So don't tell me to grow up anymore. I'm not going to—I'd rather play with my teddy bear.

—Julie Vance

ELIZABETH BLACKWELL: Dear Family: I must tell you what I experienced. I was filled with such terrible sadness and loneliness. But what was worse, I began to be overwhelmed with terror and grave doubts about what I was undertaking.

Suddenly I was filled with a powerful joyous presence which vanquished all the despair which had so overwhelmed me. All doubt about my future vanished. All hesitation as to the rightfulness of my purpose left me, and I know that I shall never be uncertain again. It is a right direction, and God's steadying hand will never leave me.

—Anthony N. Fragola,
A Test of Integrity

HEATHER: Dick sells stock. I deal in commodities. Double income. We really couldn't get by on just what he makes. And besides, I love buying and selling. More buying than selling. Buying reaffirms my power over material objects. I have always been afraid that a thing could take me over. Mind and body. Like a car. A Porsche, for example. A Porsche could really haunt me. Entice me. Lure me. Seduce me. But not if I buy it. Then I own it. It can't get to me. No, buying is a healthy thing. The only problem is finding places to put all the stuff. But that's exactly why God invented the Real Estate market. Places to put stuff.

—Ken Jones,
Lifelines

CORIE: I have never been so embarrassed in my life as I was last month in the school play. I worked so hard to get that part. The part of a lifetime. I was Martha Washington in the greatest American play written by the greatest American playwright, *Take Out Those Wooden Teeth and Kiss Me, Dear* by Giovanni Wilhelm Jones. I was the leading lady. I had over two thousand and six lines! Even more lines than Dirk Kirby who was playing George. I was going to be a star. Rehearsal after rehearsal, beautiful, big Dirk Kirby alias George Washington would pop out those brown wooden teeth at the climax of the second act, take me in his large round arms, and plant a big wet one right on my mouth. Then, with an unabashed dignity, I would push him away from my quivering body and say, "I know you never tell a lie, George, but as sure as the hair on my head I don't believe you when you say the war can wait until we make love! We can wait for our moment of whoopee! It's time now for our country's moment of whoopee!" Wow! What a great line! Then Dirk, I mean George, trudges off to win our freedom and to establish our independence.

—KEN JONES,
*Space Between Monday
and Tuesday*

MARTHA: Where the dickens are my new glasses? I can't find anything in this house anymore. I just had them when I went down to the Piggly Wiggly this morning—hummm—I came home, I unpacked the groceries, fed the fish, ate some yogurt, watched my soaps (sees herself in the mirror). Oh dear, here they are right on my block head! Oh, good gracious, has my hair looked like this all day? I look like the Bride of Frankenstein! Or like Mrs. Fitzpatrick next door the week her husband left her—she was a sight! Oh well, I guess I'll fix up after supper. Let me see, what would the boys eat after baseball practice—Ah Hah! Frozen pizza, always a winner. Now where did I put that pizza pan?

—ERIN SHULL

MISS LINA (O. Henry's aunt): Dear Will and Athol: Spring is upon us and as you know, there is no prettier place than North Carolina in the spring. You may not have heard it, so let me be the first to tell you. The Vanderbilts are building a mansion in Asheville, with 250 rooms. It will be the largest home in America. I don't know what they're going to do with that many rooms. I certainly wouldn't want them. I keep thinking who's going to clean all those rooms. But it's a problem I don't have to worry about. . . . Will, I just don't understand the many jobs that you have had. Let me see if I remember. You worked on the ranch, and then in the real estate firm, then as a draftsman in the Texas Land Office and now at a big bank. I can see you are still "looking round the corner." I will say a prayer that one of your stories is published because, I believe, that's where your real interest lies.

—JOSEPH HOESL,
What's Around the Corner

HOLLY: I have seen the eruption of the great volcanoes, and the death of my kind. I, Anatosaurus, am the last of the duck-billed dinosaurs. I am old and weary. My mouth once filled with crushing, lozenge-shaped teeth is now bare, and I am only able to gum my prey and various sources of vegetation. I am tired. I sleep. (*She gracefully descends to the floor in a swan-like death*). Thank you. Thank you. I don't . . . well . . . it's just that I have never felt such a bond with a character before this moment. I feel that lizard's pain. I truly feel the Anatosaurus and I . . . well . . . we're sisters. Thank you for allowing me this opportunity to live, even for a moment, this reptiles' life. (*She begins to exit, but turns back suddenly*) Oh, I almost forgot. I tap dance. Single-, double-, and triple-time step. And I will appear nude on stage.

—KEN JONES,
The Big One

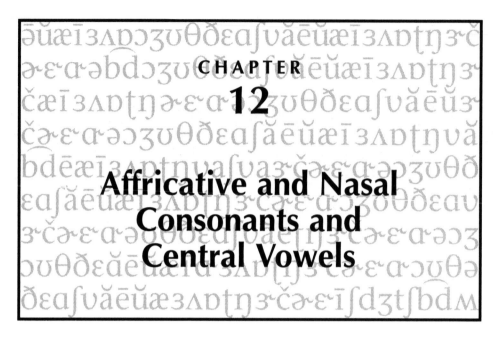

Affricative and Nasal Consonants and Central Vowels

And it is so plain to me that eloquence, like swimming, is an art which all men might learn, though so few do.

—RALPH WALDO EMERSON

THE AFFRICATIVE CONSONANTS

A **digraph** is a union of two separate symbols that represent a single sound. The affricates [tʃ] and [dʒ] are digraphs. Although each uses phonetic symbols for both a stop and a fricative, they do not represent two separate sounds. These two phonemes are physiologically distinct, not blends. They cannot be divided. They are, however, articulated in part as stops (full closure) and in part as fricatives (narrowed opening)—hence the concept of two modes of articulation in a single sound. Remember—[tʃ] and [dʒ] are single phonemes, not consonant clusters.

[tʃ] Is a Voiceless Lingua-Palatal-Alveolar Affricate

Production: The tip and blade of the tongue are in broad, firm contact with the gum ridge. When air pressure is built up, the tongue is lowered, releasing the air in such a way as to create a fricative-like sound. [tʃ] is voiceless.

Be aware:

1. Because of the **sibilant** nature of [tʃ] and [dʒ], lisping may occur if the tongue is allowed to protrude between the teeth or if air is allowed to escape over the sides of the tongue. Proper closure at the beginning of these two phonemes is imperative; otherwise words such as *much* [mʌtʃ] and *huge* [hjudʒ] might sound like *mush* [mʌʃ] and *hues* [hjuz].

188

2. Be sure the tongue is on the gum ridge at the beginning of [tʃ] and [dʒ], not on the teeth. Some speakers tend to dentalize the alveolar (gum ridge) sounds ([t], [d], [s], [z], [ʃ], [ʒ]) and [tʃ] and [dʒ] by touching the teeth instead of the gum ridge. Try it and you will hear the obvious distortion.

POSITION		
Frontal	*Medial*	*Final*
chair	lecture	birch
cello	pitcher	lunch
charm	picture	research
chocolate	suture	inch
chirp	satchel	munch
cherish	searching	couch
child	inchworm	torch

Sentences Featuring [tʃ]

1. Charles's charm school did not teach him to chew loudly or belch.
2. I have searched each orchard for the juiciest peaches.
3. She carries her lunch in her satchel.
4. Given a choice, I'd choose rich chocolate over cheese.
5. I have seen the future, and it presents a challenging picture.
6. Cheech and Chong performed catchy, raunchy routines.
7. Marching to the sound of cellos, the hunchback archers charged.
8. Chad reached for the matches, only to touch the chimney.
9. Blanche baked a batch of cherry cheesecakes.
10. The rich man's henchmen watched the ranch to catch horse snatchers.
11. The catcher chided the pitcher to pitch a championship match.
12. A crab munched on an inchworm, holding it in its pincer.
13. The crotchety chief chortled, watching his children chase each other.
14. Treat the punctured cheek judiciously, with tincture of iodine.
15. Archie had brunch with a cheetah on the beach.

[dʒ] Is a Voiced Lingua-Palatal-Alveolar Affricate

Production: The tip and blade of the tongue are in broad, firm contact with the gum ridge. When air pressure is built up, the tongue is lowered, releasing the air in such a way as to create a fricative-like sound. [dʒ] is voiced.

Be aware:

1. If you are learning the IPA, the affricates are the first phonemes you have encountered that have two symbols instead of one. Do not let this confuse you. They are the only consonants that do not use a single symbol. Most diacritical systems use *ch* and *j* for these two sounds. Orthographic spellings vary. Consider *watch, reach, suggestion,* and *factual* (*tch, ch, ti,* and *tu*) as orthographic representations of [tʃ], and *just, fudge, gem,* and *gradual* (*j, dge, g,* and *d*) as some of the ways [dʒ] may be spelled.

2. Just as with the fricatives and stops, there is the problem of insufficient voicing of the voiced member of any cognate pair. Because not as much voicing is used at phrase endings or before unvoiced sounds as in more stressed positions, we tend to let the voicing slide, even when the sound should be stressed. If

[dʒ] is not fully voiced, *gyp* might sound like *chip, Jane* like *chain,* and *edge* like *etch*. Voice [dʒ] fully

POSITION

Frontal	Medial	Final
journey	subject	fringe
genius	gorgeous	budge
juvenile	dungeon	stage
gentle	soldier	pledge
jacket	logic	cartridge
juicy	surgeon	strange
joke	major	large

Sentences Featuring [dʒ]

1. Judy called George a gorgeous jock.
2. A soldier threw the perjuring defendant into the dungeon.
3. John joined the others in the gym adjacent to the stage.
4. The strange juggler's silly jig was just a joke.
5. The junk arrived laden with jade and other jewels.
6. A skilled surgeon repaired my fragile jaw.
7. She made a huge pledge to the Jewish Home for the Aged.
8. The proud major general wore his jacket even in July.
9. The prejudiced agitator engaged in exchanging juicy gossip.
10. His jaundice was caused by germs in the jugular vein.
11. The jolly jester told jokes, juggled, and danced a jig.
12. Those jarring jumping jacks reinjured his knee.
13. Jonas objected to the genuine rejoicing seen at the Cajun jamboree.
14. The enraged judge, refusing to budge, rejected her plea.
15. I sometimes cringe at the juvenile jive from the jukebox.

Words Contrasting [dʒ], [tʃ], [ʃ], and [s]

gin	chin	shin	sin
Joe	Cho	show	sow
Jews	choose	shoes	sues
jaw	chaw	shaw	saw
jock	chock	shock	sock
jowl	chow	shower	sour
jot	chop	shop	sop
Jill	chill	shill	sill
jell	cello	shell	sell
gyp	chip	ship	sip

Sentences Featuring [tʃ] and [dʒ]

1. A jury of teachers watched pictures to reach their objective decision.
2. A batch of French hens and a partridge from a birch tree branch edged near a large archery range.
3. The pudgy rancher kept his general ledger near his cherished armchair.
4. Major Archie Birch arched his jaundiced brows with jovial agility.

5. Blanche is justly famous for her bland, cheesy brunch flapjacks.

6. Rejected Richard searched each wall for a breach in the dingy dungeon.

7. Cheers turned to jeers when the chess champion rejected the challenger's invitation to a rematch.

8. Chester Jones chided his future bride for mentioning their nuptial to Jan.

9. Jump into a chair and chow down with your jowls on some Cambridge chowder.

10. Roger the rich surgeon will not budge an inch from his rigid judgments.

11. Dangerous changes in major legislation left Georgia on the verge of tragedy.

12. Judges searched for chalk marks on the jockey's serge slacks.

13. Such a suggestion abjures logic in favor of childishly charging ahead.

14. Marching soldiers chatted jovially in *The Red Badge of Courage.*

15. Crotchety John Charles crouches behind chutney jars, ready to lunge at each stranger.

THE NASAL CONSONANTS

Except for three phonemes, all sounds in Standard American English are formed with the velum (soft palate) in a raised position to allow the breath stream to resonate through the mouth. When the soft palate is relaxed and lowered, the breath stream is directed through the nose. The term *nasal consonant* is used to characterize these three sounds. In the IPA, they are written [m], [n], and [ŋ].

Although air is emitted through the nose and the primary resonance occurs in the nasal cavity, the place of articulation of these three phonemes is the oral cavity. All three sounds are voiced. Proper placement of the articulators and good nasal resonance in providing these sounds give fullness and carrying power to the voice. Nasal consonants have much potential resonance that the speaker should use advantageously.

[m] **Is a Voiced, Bilabial Nasal**

Production: To form the consonant [m], lower the soft palate so that air can move freely through the nasal passage. Bring the lips firmly together as for the stops [p] and [b], and expel air through the nose. [m] is voiced.

Be aware:

1. The three nasal consonants share a common problem, for if you have difficulty with one of these sounds, you probably have it with the other two. The problem stems from the degree to which the soft palate is lowered, and hence from the amount of air directed through the nose. If the palate is lowered too far and for too long, too much air will move through the nasal passages, resulting in one form of nasality. If insufficient palatal lowering occurs, with subsequent insufficient air, the sound will be denasalized. (Nasality and denasality were discussed in detail in Chapter 8). As you practice the nasal consonants be sensitive to the need for balanced nasal resonance.

2. A related problem with nasal consonants is the time given to lowering the palate. If the lowering significantly precedes or follows the production of the consonant, a form of assimilation nasality will result—that is, the sounds that occur before or after the nasal sound will be nasalized.

3. On the opposite end, failure to allow sufficient time for the full development of the nasal consonants results in skimpily articulated sounds that are weak on resonance and hence flat and colorless. [m] should have a rich, humming quality when it is produced with balanced palatal tension.

POSITION

Frontal	Medial	Final	Followed by p	Followed by s [z]
music	army	palm	empire	rhymes
mast	number	alarm	jump	worms
mule	immense	some	lamp	harms
motor	moment	worm	clamp	forums
mend	warmth	beam	blimp	themes
masked	permit	gloom	camper	names
moving	tumble	lime	hamper	seems

As mentioned in Chapter 10, when *b* follows *m* in the same syllable in orthographic spelling, the *b* is usually silent. The same rule applies to words in which *n* follows *m:*

aplomb	thumb	condemn	autumn
lamb	dumb	solemn	column
climb	limb	hymn	damn

When *l* precedes *m* in orthographic spellings, the *l* is silent.

calm	alms
embalm	qualm
psalm	palm

Sentences Featuring [m]

1. Meet Millie Mamet, matchmaker of mirthful maidens and gloomy grooms.
2. I almost forgot to mention Birmingham, home to mayonnaise manufacturing magnate Marvin Mueller.
3. For months the mother Brahmans mooed mournfully at the moon.
4. A masque is a medieval form of formal movement performed to music.
5. Calmly palming a megaton bomb, the mad Marxist solemnly removed the military regime from office.
6. Only a maniacal mermaid might embrace the llama, a multi-humped mammal.
7. Diminutive, myopic Myron is squeamish, asthmatic, and morbid.
8. Our minister welcomed a multitude of unassimilated immigrants into her home.
9. Lambda Chi alumni automatically make amends for a myriad of mistakes by donating money.
10. "She's a mean mother" may have a number of meanings; one must make some assumptions.
11. Lambs gambol in misty meadows; men and women gamble in musty meetings.
12. Don't blame the remodeled motor for the dim beam emitted from the mouth of the mobile home.
13. All humans should embrace the theme of tomorrow, or *mañana,* as the Mexicans might say.
14. Mums bloom in May, emitting a musky, primitive perfume.
15. If you must know the outcome of the murder mystery, the maid committed the morbid crime in the master bedroom of Biltmore Mansion.

[n] Is a Voiced Lingua-Alveolar Nasal

Production: To form [n], lower the soft palate so that air can move freely through the nasal passages. Press the tip of the tongue against the gum ridge as in the formation of [d] and [t], and expel air through the nose. The sound is voiced.

Be aware:

1. [n] suffers from the problems of excessive nasality, denasality, and assimilation nasality described for [m]. If you have such a problem, work carefully on the corresponding exercises in Chapter 8.

2. Some speakers tend to dentalize [n] by pressing the tip of the tongue to the teeth instead of the gum ridge. Watch this placement as you practice the words that follow.

3. Some substitutions for [n] are fairly common. [m] is sometimes substituted, especially before [f] or [v], as in *imfer, umveil,* and *comfuse,* instead of *infer, unveil,* and *confuse.* Some speakers substitute a slight [ŋ] for [n] in words such as *unclear, consider,* and *ingrown.* These are closely related to words such as *hunger, banker,* and *anchor,* which do contain [ŋ], so the substitution is understandable. Still, it should be avoided.

POSITION

Frontal	Medial	Final
knowledge	furnish	nation
pneumonia	vanish	return
night	intend	driven
noise	uneasy	region
kneel	panic	lone
gnash	manage	town
nuisance	original	condone

Words Contrasting [m] *and* [n]

mother—another	adamant—adenoid	room—rune
term—turn	gum—gun	cream—green
skimmer—skinner	same—sane	gym—gin
prism—prison	firm—fern	moist—noise

Sentences Featuring [n]

1. Nellie, an obnoxious nincompoop, nearly won the affections of that pinheaded nerd Ned Manning.

2. It is no news that Nanook lives near the North Pole.

3. Confused and forlorn, the frightened ponies neighed at the distant carnival sounds.

4. Seven mean men noiselessly kneeled in the darkness of night, listening on stolen telephones.

5. Uncle John's pancakes are neither renowned nor sensational; no, they are only nice nonentities.

6. A retinue of agents from the Internal Revenue surrendered their tax returns to government investigators.

7. In the finals, a panel of nine men and women examine all the evidence.

8. "Send in the clones" is a slogan for modern genetic scientists.

9. In the Niger basin near Nairobi, nominal herds of bison wander over the dunes.

10. A broken ulna means no tennis for many months.

11. Agnew did not nominate Nixon for president in 1969.

12. Have an annual examination by a physician, and you may not necessarily need to surrender your original adenoids.

13. Fine-tuned adrenal glands invariably will respond to the most minute excitement.

14. Aunts and uncles tend to know the names of many distant nieces and nephews.
15. This manual transmission engine should run about twenty-nine miles per gallon in town.

[ŋ] Is a Voiced Lingua-Velar Nasal

Production: To form [ŋ], lower the soft palate so that air can move freely through the nasal passages. While the air is passing through the nose, the back of the tongue and the lowered soft palate meet to articulate the sound within the mouth. The sound is voiced.

Be aware:

1. When added to a word, the suffix *ing* is pronounced [ɪn] instead of [ɪŋ] by so many people that the former pronunciation would seldom be viewed as non standard. Yet in polished speech *going, running,* and *jumping* continue to be more acceptable than *goin', runnin',* and *jumpin'.*

2. Usually the orthographic spelling *ng* is associated with the single phoneme [ŋ]. When *ng* appears in the medial position, however, the stop [g] is sometimes articulated as well. Consider the difference between *singer, ringer,* and *swinger,* in which only the [ŋ] is pronounced, and *finger, linger,* and *anger,* in which a [g] follows the [ŋ]. Unfortunately, there is no clear-cut rule for determining when to use [ŋ] and when to use [ŋg]. Let a standard dictionary be your guide. Do try, however, to avoid using [ŋg] when it is not called for. [sɪŋgɚ] and [lɔŋ gaɪlnd] are strictly New York City pronunciations.

3. Note that [ŋ] can be spelled *n,* as in *uncle, bank,* and *larynx,* rather than the customary *ng.* If you try to say these words using [n], you will easily see that [ŋ] is called for.

POSITION		
Frontal	*Medial*	*Final*
[ŋ] does not appear in the frontal position	strength	doing
	anger	rang
	jungle	tiring
	uncle	following
	trinket	ping pong
	distinguish	string
	donkey	training

Sentences Featuring [ŋ]

1. It was Ringo's thing to sing along with any recording.
2. A lingering feeling of anguish strengthens her long-standing anger.
3. I think English is a distinctively alluring language.
4. Uncle Ben longed for the stirring sound of diving pigs and honking geese.
5. The old king had a string of trinkets dangling from his finger.
6. You're saying I should be flinging mangoes into the jungle? Nothing doing!
7. The jingle-jangle of spurs is a sound belonging to the riding cowboy.
8. A strong mothering instinct caused the rapidly tiring starling to ignore her own hunger.
9. Engles brings me a sarong each spring from Hong Kong or Singapore.
10. With an insulting remark the rough-looking punk stung the feelings of Jinx Pringle.

11. The sailors sank anchor in Bangkok harbor, disembarking for a brief fling.
12. Frank gave Inga a sparkling ingot wedding ring.
13. The rinky-dink skating rink is teeming with throngs of long-legged teens.
14. In hang gliding, experts think, timing is everything.
15. After pouring a refreshing drink, Buckingham spent a long time doing nothing.

Words Contrasting [k], [ŋ], and [ŋk]

pick—ping—pink	sack—sang—sank
thick—thing—think	tickle—tingle—tinkle
Rick—ring—rink	brick—bring—brink
rack—rang—rank	sick—sing—sink
sticker—stinger—stinker	suck—sung—sunk
huck—hung—hunk	hacker—hanger—hanker

Words Contrasting [g] and [ŋ]

wig—wing	league—linger
bag—bang	hog—Hong
hug—hung	toggle—tong
lug—lung	rig—ring
log—long	rug—rung
Hague—hang	sprig—spring

Words Contrasting [n] and [ŋ]

sin—sing	done—dung
win—wing	hun—hung
kin—king	sun—sung
pin—ping	stun—stung
ton—tongue	tan—tang
run—rung	ban—bang

Phrases for Practice

ring around the rosy	and Bingo was his name
manna from heaven	thunder and lightning
the damp, dank ground	name, rank, and serial number
momma, nanna, and grandma	England invading France
solemn monkeys in the jungle	armed marauders pillaging Poland
a lane goer in languor	remember the Alamo
I'm not coming home tomorrow	pneumatic sounds emanating from inside

SINGING EXERCISE FOR NASALS

Sing the following to the tune of the *William Tell Overture*. Begin slowly and increase the rate gradually while maintaining clear articulation.

Many men many men many men men men
Many men many men many men men men
Many men many men many men men men
Many men, many men men men

Bridge: Many men many men many men men men men men men men men men
Many men many men many men men men men men men men
Many men, many men, many men, many men, many men, many men,
many men . . . (repeat)

Sentences Featuring [m], [n], *and* [ŋ]

1. Tomorrow is an immensely long time from now.
2. Immerse nervous nerds in boiling cauldrons of molten ink.
3. Pringle seems to be moving minute to minute, moment by moment.
4. Mouth the sounds, feeling the formation of the English language.
5. Do not mix ammonia molecules among the manicotti.
6. *Mending, minding,* and *knowing* are not proper nouns: *New England* is.
7. "What's new?" mumbled the gnu as the gnome from Nome meandered home.
8. A malingerer imagines ill feelings in an attempt to shun unpleasant things.
9. Strip mining lingers as a major environmental issue from Montana to Pennsylvania.
10. Manuel knew Nancy would enamel everything, including the kitchen sink.
11. I never met a man named Naomi in North America.
12. Pandas are mammals hailing from the mountains near Nanking.
13. In anger the monkey mangled my ankle, bringing me pain.
14. *Uncommon Women* is a compelling contemporary drama.
15. Many moons ago, when hungry animals roamed the swamplands, there came a stumbling, grinning primate with a penchant for thinking: the human being.

CENTRAL VOWELS

In general those who nothing have to say
  Contrive to spend the longest time in doing it;
They turn and vary it in every way,
  Hashing it, stewing it, mincing it, ragouting it.

—J. R. LOWELL

As we have seen, front and back vowels require major adjustments and tension in the front and back of the tongue, respectively. Central vowels are somewhat more difficult to explain. **Stress** is the most important element in defining the central vowels. Although there are four symbols for these vowels—[ɝ], [ɚ], [ʌ], and [ə]—they represent only two specific sounds. [ɝ] and [ʌ] are found primarily in *stressed* syllables, [ɚ] and [ə] in *unstressed* syllables. In this chapter, you will see that there is enough differentiation among the four to warrant a separate phonetic symbol for each.

Production of the central vowels is also characterized by a major adjustment in the central portion of the tongue. A third consideration is the presence or absence of *r-coloring*. R-coloring suggests that the articulators move as if [r] were going to follow the vowel, but the lip rounding of [r] is not completed. Finally, there is no significant lip rounding.

[ɝ] Is a *Stressed* Midcentral Vowel

Production: To form the phoneme [ɝ], press the blade of the tongue firmly against the alveolar ridge. The tip of the tongue may be either pointed or slightly curled back. There is little lip rounding and the jaw is moderately open.

Orthographic spellings include:

er — terse	ear — heard
ir — thirst	our — courage
ur — absurd	yr — myrrh
or — word	olo — colonel

Be aware:

1. Excessive tension in the tongue can cause too much r-coloring. A harsh, sometimes nasalized vocal quality will result.

2. Too little r-coloring can cause [ɝ] to sound like the British central vowel [ɜ], in which case *bird* [bɝd] would sound more like *bud* [bɜd].

3. In some areas of the United States, there is a tendency to add the consonant [r] after [ɝ]. The result is an additional syllable. *Fir trees* [fɝ triz] will sound like *firuh trees* [fɝr triz].

4. Speakers of words in which the front vowel [ɪ] or [ɛ] is followed by the consonant [r] sometimes retract this combination to the central vowel [ɝ]. For example, *here* [hɪr] becomes *her* [hɝ]; *there* [ðɛr] becomes *thur* [ðɝ].

POSITION

Frontal	Medial	Final
urgent	colonel	recur
earnest	curtains	spur
urban	thorough	occur
urge	firm	were
ermine	third	purr
early	perfect	fir
earning	determine	her

Sentences Featuring [ɝ]

1. Churn the urn thoroughly to separate the curds.
2. Irma, the stern attorney, turned into a worm-eating ermine.
3. A nurse removed the burr from the hurt bird.
4. Her wide girth could be curtailed with a firm girdle.
5. First, stir the burning coal in the furnace.
6. Myrna, a perky girl, flirted with Herman, an irksome nerd.
7. A herd of urban horses converged in New Jersey.
8. Colonel Kurtz stood on the verge of entering the Third World.
9. "Make her hurry," urged Percy, speaking in the third person.
10. Be on alert—germs occur in dirt and fertilizer.
11. Al Hirt yearned for a seldom heard, mirthful dirge.
12. The early hours were a blur—Pearl's urban cowboy had deserted her.
13. Irving the erstwhile earl alertly swerved to avert a certain hurt.
14. The inert cat purred luxuriously on our thermal furniture.
15. The serfs laid thirteen purple furs in a perfect circle.

[ɚ] Is an *Unstressed* Midcentral Vowel

Production: [ɚ] sometimes called the *hooked schwa*, is produced in approximately the same manner as [ɝ]. However, the tongue is slightly lower and more relaxed. [ɚ] is articulated with less *force* than [ɝ]. It is found *only* in unstressed syllables.

Orthographic spellings include:

er—mot<u>he</u>r

ur—mixt<u>ure</u>

or—col<u>or</u>

ar—doll<u>ar</u>

Be aware:

1. If there is too much tension in the tongue, [ɚ] will take on the character of [ɝ] and a harsh vocal quality will result. This is especially evident when [ɚ] occurs in the final position.

2. In certain eastern and southern dialects, [ɚ] is *under*stressed. Words such as *mother* [mʌðɚ] and *father* [fɑðɚ] sound like *motha* [mʌðə] and *fatha* [fɑðə]; a schwa [ə] is substituted for the hooked schwa (the schwa with r-coloring).

POSITION		
Frontal	*Medial*	*Final*
ergosterol	covered	lawyer
	opportunity	doctor
(otherwise rarely	surmise	owner
found in the	engendered	recorder
frontal position)	tenderly	smarter
	repercussions	nuclear
	reservation	picture

Sentences Featuring [ɚ]

1. The surveyor discovered an error in her information.
2. The malingerer made a concerted effort to exacerbate his condition.
3. Remember "The Purloined Letter" by Edgar Allan Poe?
4. Thousands of Confederate soldiers surrendered to the Federals in northern Virginia.
5. Bernice's broker never broke her of overspending.
6. Given other opportunities, most followers go forward behind leaders.
7. The perfection of the hamburger on pumpernickel has serious repercussions for the Germans.
8. Booker T. Washington never encountered a nuclear disaster.
9. A curvaceous dancer is wiser to live her life with her liver intact.
10. Walter's persistent urbanity makes him a better waiter.
11. Our minister offered a prayer for all endangered parishioners.
12. Doctor Roberts tenderly operated an aspirator on the suffering worker.
13. The mother superior always maintains a reverent persona.
14. Culture can mean pictures, theaters, or even cheeseburgers and collard greens
15. You can't ever expectorate in society if you ever expect to rate in society!

[ʌ] Is a *Stressed* Lower Midcentral Vowel

Production: To form the phoneme [ʌ], lay the front of the tongue on the floor of the mouth and make it relatively relaxed. The middle of the tongue is moderately tense where it rises slightly. The jaw is also relaxed and there is no lip rounding.

Orthographic spellings include:

u—h<u>u</u>ndred

o—c<u>o</u>ver

ou—double

oe—does

oo—blood

Be aware: The primary problem with [ʌ] is the tendency to substitute the front vowel [ɛ] or [ɪ] for it. Words like *such* [sʌtʃ] may be pronounced *sech* [sɛtʃ], or *just* [dʒʌst] may sound like *jist* [dʒɪst].

POSITION

Frontal	Medial	Final
uncle	flutter	[ʌ] does not
under	cunning	appear in the
upward	buzz	final position
oven	jugular	
umpire	husband	
uproar	alumnus	
ultimate	conjunction	

Sentences Featuring [ʌ]

1. Under the cover is a cup of butternut fudge.

2. A gruff old humbug secretly hummed while hugging a cuddly puppy.

3. Give the hungry mutt a chunk of peanut butter for its supper.

4. The Hungarian army could muster up nothing but muskets.

5. A reluctant umpire stood in the mud with an umbrella—a true glutton for punishment.

6. Her ho-hum husband is just an old fuddy-duddy.

7. Mother Hubbard served overtoasted buns with mulligan stew.

8. Uncle Gus must not give up so suddenly on his luck.

9. The governor will provide public funds to clean up rubbish from the slums.

10. An usher suggested to the fussy troublemaker that she shut up.

11. Doug must be underwhelmed by my utter profundity.

12. Two dozen double-decker buses were stuck in rush hour traffic.

13. An unusual juxtaposition of puns brought groans of utter disgust.

14. Muscle men and their buxom honeys had fun in the sun in *Love's Labors Lust.*

15. Chuck unloaded a truckful of mukluks in Thunder Bay.

[ə], Commonly Called a *Schwa,* Is an *Unstressed* Lower Midcentral Vowel

Production: Sometimes called a "neutral" sound, the schwa is formed in the same way as [ʌ], but is shorter and weaker. The schwa is the most commonly used phoneme in the English language.

Orthographic spellings include:

a—sofa	ai—fountain	ou—dubious
e—benefit	ia—official	he—vehement
i—April	ie—efficient	
o—occur	eo—dungeon	
u—upon	oi—porpoise	

Be aware: The schwa is an unstressed sound whose appearance varies with the relationship of the words within a phrase or sentence. For a fuller discussion of sound length and stress, see Chapter 7.

POSITION

Frontal	*Medial*	*Final*
another	television	sofa
abrupt	stricken	idea
asparagus	satellite	cornea
affirmative	machine	asthma
alliance	permanent	gladiola
apparent	capable	dilemma
attempt	dialogue	enchilada

Sentences Featuring [ə]

1. The psychotherapist experimented with mental telepathy on her patients.
2. What percentage of Alabama's citizens are residents of Montgomery or Selma?
3. I couldn't envision a more capable or formidable opponent.
4. The region of America known as the Southwest extends from California to Louisiana.
5. Children shouldn't abandon their natural ancestral heritage.
6. Apparently the physician's assumption was that this is a case of pulmonary edema.
7. I assure you the latest technological methods have been applied to your situation.
8. At present are you able to envision providing assistance to more than seventeen orphans?
9. Elementary students of tomorrow will receive substantial education from cable television.
10. No reservations are necessary to attend a performance at the theater festival.
11. Eva indicated her affinity for adult condominiums.
12. The vagabond fell asleep in the Union Station terminal.
13. On behalf of the municipal council, I want to welcome all rational, alert citizens.
14. The presentation was decidedly humorous; in fact, it was magnificently comical.
15. In this apparent emergency, all perishables, including your lotion, must be carefully rationed.

Note: The [ə] sounds are underlined in the preceding sentences to indicate a conversational reading. A word-by-word reading will bring emphasis to some sounds, in words such as *the* and *a*, changing the pronunciation of their vowels from [ə] to [i] and [eɪ].

Sentences Featuring [ɝ], [ɚ], [ʌ], *and* [ə]

1. The doctor, a young neurosurgeon, had his medical insurance docked by deterring an unjust claim.
2. The National Council of Churches furnishes judgments on major moral dilemmas.
3. The early bird gets the worm; the suburban bird gets the perm.
4. In a verdant jungle I encountered muskrats, mynah birds, and mallard ducks.
5. I had no idea hush puppies were considered a luxury in northern Iowa.
6. Merlin suggested we attend a performance of the contemporary drama, *The Runner Stumbles.*
7. Gussie's shirt got stuck in the turnstile in front of the public facility, Municipal Stadium.

8. Unable to sustain pennant fever, the struggling Cubs fell even further from first place.

9. Wyatt Earp is featured in another western television special.

10. Conjunctions are not generally considered to be as humorous or funny as verbs.

11. Divers have discovered a buried treasure where once a disaster occurred just off of Bermuda.

12. Mums, petunias, and some other flowers must grow better in sunny southern California than in Russia.

13. Serve pumpernickel buns fresh from the oven for an early supper.

14. If Virginia appears jumpy, just remember that she suffers from a nervous disorder.

15. Unencumbered by any other blockers, a tough tackle tenderly crushed the hurt quarterback into the dirt.

PHONETICS PRACTICE 1: AFFRICATES, NASALS, AND CENTRAL VOWELS

Write the following words in phonetics:

1. chum _____
2. church _____
3. judge _____
4. churn _____
5. numb _____
6. among _____
7. much _____
8. nudge _____
9. nurture _____
10. munch _____

11. merge _____
12. urge _____
13. germ _____
14. churner _____
15. merger _____
16. Irma _____
17. Myrna _____
18. Chung _____
19. Chun _____
20. murmur _____

PHONETICS PRACTICE 2: STOP-PLOSIVES, FRICATIVES, AFFRICATES, NASALS, AND ALL THE PURE VOWELS

Write the orthographic spelling for the following words:

1. [væk sin] _____
2. [stitʃ ɪŋ] _____
3. [θæŋk] _____
4. [dʒɝk] _____
5. [tʃɛ ʃɚ] _____
6. [vɝdʒ] _____
7. [mʌtɚ] _____
8. [ʌpɚ] _____
9. [hæŋɚ] _____
10. [nɝvəs] _____

11. [ɪ mɝ dʒən si] _____
12. [bæd ən ɑʒ] _____
13. [tʃɔk] _____
14. [dʒɛn dɚ] _____
15. [θɝ tɪ] _____
16. [si ʒɚ] _____
17. [ə gɛn] _____
18. [hɪtʃ] _____
19. [sɪŋ ɚ] _____
20. [dʒɝ nɪ] _____

Write the following words in phonetics:

1. avert _____
2. chatter _____
3. zither _____
4. azure _____
5. hatchet _____
6. urgent _____
7. thunder _____
8. bummer _____
9. hanker _____
10. turnip _____

11. thus _____
12. peach _____
13. stodgy _____
14. fern _____
15. them _____
16. huffy _____
17. shirk _____
18. thong _____
19. number _____
20. jesting _____

CROSSWORD PUZZLE 12–1

Across

1. stroke
4. instruct
7. entreats, solicits
9. knowledge
11. midday
13. title for a knight
14. stick out
16. you and me
18. Wyatt _____
19. subject or topic
22. question to which "it is" might be the response (2 words)
23. wasps and bees have them

Down

1. contented cat sound
2. rim, border
3. color
5. barely get by
6. a game for kings & queens
8. where animals are kept
10. daring, courage
12. of no value or consequence
14. pull, tug
15. toward a higher point
17. Roman emperor
20. MS
21. by or near

CROSSWORD PUZZLE 12–2

Across

1. insect attracted to light
4. obliged to
6. a little orphan
7. knob or lump
9. below your mouth
10. dog
11. form of "to be"
13. article
14. that lady
16. No more left!
19. horn sound
20. pecan
21. unusual
22. noise
24. one by one

Down

1. a striking object
2. canvas roof
3. not fat
4. not off
5. pleat or fold
8. Aaron _____
11. picnic intruder
12. airplane
13. likely to
14. aspirate
15. annoyed
17. picture show
18. in fact; truly
21. laryngologist's sound
22. perform, accomplish
23. chew a bone

PHILOSOPHICAL AND RELIGIOUS READINGS FOR PRACTICE

Some of the finest literature is found in religious and philosophic writing. The contemplative nature of the content requires careful, thoughtful interpretation on the part of the reader. Concentrate on the depth of meaning as you read the following passages.

To every thing there is a season, and a time to every purpose under heaven:
A time to be born, and a time to die; a time to plant, and a time to pluck up
    that which is planted;
A time to kill, and a time to heal; a time to break down, and a time to build up;
A time to weep, and a time to laugh; a time to mourn, and a time to dance;
A time to cast away stones, and a time to gather stones together; a time to em-
    brace, and a time to refrain from embracing;
A time to get, and a time to lose; a time to keep, and a time to cast away;
A time to rend, and a time to sew; a time to keep silence, and a time to speak;
A time to love, and a time to hate; a time of war, and a time of peace.
. . . every man should eat and drink, and enjoy the good of all his labor, it is
    the gift of God.

—Ecclesiastes 3:1–8, 13

Highest good is like water, Because water excels in benefiting the myriad creatures without contending with them and settles where none would like to be, it
comes close to the way.
    In a home it is the site that matters;
    In quality of mind it is depth that matters;
    In an ally it is benevolence that matters;
    In speech it is good faith that matters;
    In government it is order that matters;
    In affairs it is ability that matters;
    In action it is timeliness that matters.
It is because it does not contend that it is never at fault.

—Lao Tzu,
Tao Te Ching,
Fourth century B.C.E.

When the sun shall be folded up,
And when the star shall fall,
And when the mountains shall be set in motion,
And when the she-camels shall be abandoned,
And when the wild beasts shall be gathered together,
And when the seas shall boil,
And when souls shall be paired with their bodies,
And when the female child that had been buried alive shall be asked
For what crime she was put to death,
And when the leaves of the Book shall be unrolled,
And when the Heaven shall be stripped away,
And when Hell shall be made to blaze,
And when Paradise shall be brought near,
Every soul shall know what it hath produced.

—*The Koran,*
Sura LXXXI, Mecca

To evoke in oneself a feeling one has once experienced, and having evoked it in
oneself, then, by means of movement, lines, colors, sounds, or forms expressed
in words, so to transmit that feeling that others may experience the same feeling—this is the activity of art.

Art is a human activity, consisting in this, that one man consciously, by means of certain external signs, hands on to others feelings he has lived through, and that other people are infected by these feelings, and also experience them.

—Leo Tolstoy,
*Art as Emotional
Communication*

Blessed are the poor in spirit: for theirs is the kingdom of heaven.
Blessed are they that mourn: for they shall be comforted.
Blessed are the meek: for they shall inherit the earth.
Blessed are they which do hunger and thirst after righteousness: for they shall
    be filled.
Blessed are the merciful: for they shall obtain mercy.
Blessed are the pure in heart: for they shall see God.
Blessed are the peacemakers: for they shall be called the children of God.
Blessed are they which are persecuted for righteousness' sake: for theirs is the
    kingdom of heaven.

—Matthew 5:3–10

Who is wise?
The man who can learn something from every man.
Who is strong?
The man who overcomes his passion.
Who is rich?
The man who is content with his fate.
Whom do men honor?
The man who honors his fellow men.

—*Sayings of the Fathers*

Music is harmony of being; but the music of Soul affords the only strains that thrill the chords of feeling and awaken the heart's harpstrings. Moved by mind, your many-throated organ, in imitative tones of many instruments, praises Him; but even the sweetness and beauty in and of this temple that praise Him, are earth's accents, and must not be mistaken for the oracles of God. Art must not prevail over Science. Christianity is not superfluous. Its redemptive power is seen in sore trials, self-denials, and crucifixions of the flesh. But these come to the rescue of mortals, to admonish them, and plant the feet steadfastly in Christ. As we rise about the seeming mists of sense, we behold more clearly that all the heart's homage belongs to God.

—Mary Baker Eddy,
May 26, 1895

Though I speak with the tongues of men and of angels, and have not charity, I am become as sounding brass, or a tinkling cymbal.

And though I have the gift of prophecy, and understand all mysteries, and all knowledge; and though I have all faith, so that I could remove mountains, and have not charity, I am nothing.

And though I bestow all my goods to feed the poor, and though I give my body to be burned; and have not charity, it profiteth me nothing.

Charity suffereth long, and is kind; charity envieth not; charity vaunteth not itself, is not puffed up,

Doth not behave itself unseemly, seeketh not her own, is not easily provoked, thinketh no evil;

Rejoiceth not in inquity, but rejoiceth in the truth;

Beareth all things, believeth all things, hopeth all things, endureth all things.

Charity never faileth: but whether there be prophecies, they shall fail; whether there be tongues, they shall cease; whether there be knowledge, it shall vanish away.

For we know in part, and we prophesy in part.

But when that which is perfect is come, then that which is in part shall be done away.

When I was a child, I spake as a child, I understood as a child, I thought as a child: but when I became a man, I put away childish things.

For now we see through a glass, darkly; but then face to face: now I know in part; but then I shall know even as I am known.

And now abideth faith, hope, charity, these three; but the greatest of these is charity.

—I Corinthians 13

To appreciate a landscape, we must be in tune with it. To understand the sunbeam, we must vibrate with it; we must quiver with the moonbeam in the evening darkness; and we must sparkle with the blue or golden stars; to understand the night we must feel the shudder of dark spaces, of that vague and unknown vastness passing through us. To feel spring we must have in our hearts some of the lightness of a butterfly's wings, the fine dust of which we breathe as it is widely scattered through the vernal air.

—Jean Marie Guyau,
Art and Social Solidarity

Avoid late and unseasonable Studies, for they murder Wit, and are very prejudicial to Health. The Muses love the Morning, and that is a fit Time for Study. After you have din'd, either divert yourself at some Exercise, or take a Walk, and discourse merrily, and Study between whiles. As for Diet, eat only as much as shall be sufficient to preserve Health, and not as much or more than the Appetite may crave. Before Supper, take a little Walk, and do the same after Supper. A little before you go to sleep read something that is exquisite, and worth remembering; and contemplate upon it till you fall asleep; and when you awake in the Morning, call yourself to an Account for it.

—Desiderius Erasmus

My soul preached to me and showed me that I am neither more than the pygmy nor less than the giant.

Ere my soul preached to me, I looked upon humanity as two men: one weak, whom I pitied, and the other strong, whom I followed or resisted in defiance.

But now I have learned that I was as both are and made from the same elements. My origin is their origin, my conscience is their conscience, my contention is their contention, and my pilgrimage is their pilgrimage.

If they sin, I am also a sinner. If they do well, I take pride in their well-doing. If they rise, I rise with them. If they stay inert, I share their slothfulness.

—Kahlil Gibran

In order to cure most of the ills of human life, I require not that man should have the wings of the eagle, the swiftness of the stag, the force of the ox, the arms of the lion, the scales of the crocodile or rhinoceros; much less do I demand the sagacity of an angel or cherubim. I am contented to take an increase in one single power of faculty of his soul. Let him be endowed with a greater propensity to industry and labour; a more vigorous spring and activity in mind; a more constant bent to business and application. . . . Almost all the moral, as well as natural evils of human life arise from idleness; and were our species by the original constitution of their frame, exempt from this vice or infirmity, the perfect cultivation of land, the improvement of arts and manufactures, and exact execution of every office and duty, immediately follow; and men at once may fully reach that state of society, which is so imperfectly attained by the best-regulated government.

—DAVID HUME,
*Dialogues Concerning
Natural Religion*

Of whom and of what indeed can I say: "I know that!" This heart within me I can feel, and I judge that it exists. This world I can touch, and I likewise judge that it exists. There ends all my knowledge, and the rest is construction. For if I try to seize this self of which I feel sure, if I try to define and to summarize it, it is nothing but water slipping through my fingers. I can sketch one by one all the aspects it is able to assume, all those likewise that have been attributed to it, this upbringing, this origin, this ardor or these silences, this nobility or this vileness. But aspects cannot be added up. This very heart which is mine will forever remain indefinable to me. Between the certainty I have of my existence and the content I try to give to that assurance, the gap will never be filled. Forever I shall be a stranger to myself.

—ALBERT CAMUS,
The Myth of Sisyphus

My silence, like an expanding sphere, spreads everywhere.

My silence spreads like a radio song, above, beneath, left and right, within and without.

My silence spreads like a wildfire of bliss; the dark thickets of sorrow and the tall oaks of pride are all burning up.

My silence, like the ether, passes through everything, carrying the songs of earth, atoms, and stars into the halls of His infinite mansion.

—PARAMAHANSA YOGANANDA,
Metaphysical Meditations

A foolish consistency is the hobgoblin of little minds, adored by little statesmen and philosophers and divines. With consistency a great soul has simply nothing to do. He may as well concern himself with his shadow on the wall. Speak what you think now in hard words and to-morrow speak what to-morrow thinks in hard words again, though it contradict every thing you said to-day.—"Ah, so you shall be sure to be misunderstood."—Is it so bad then to be misunderstood? Pythagoras was misunderstood, and Socrates, and Jesus, and Luther, and Copernicus, and Galileo, and Newton, and every pure and wise spirit that ever took flesh. To be great is to be misunderstood.

—RALPH WALDO EMERSON,
"Self-Reliance"

Condemn no man and consider nothing impossible, for there is no man who does not have a future, and there is nothing that does not have its hour.

Why was man created on the last day? So that he can be told when pride takes hold of him: God created the gnat before thee.

God did not create woman from man's head, that he should command her, nor from his feet, that she should be his slave, but rather from his side, that she should be near his heart.

—*The Talmud*

The eye, which is called the window of the soul, is the chief means whereby the understanding may most fully and abundantly appreciate the infinite works of Nature; and the ear is the second, inasmuch as it acquires its importance from the fact that it hears the things which the eye has seen. If you historians, or poets, or mathematicians had never seen things with your eyes, you would be ill able to describe them in your writings. And if you, O poet, represent a story by depicting it with your pen, the painter with his brush will so render it as to be more easily satisfying and less tedious to understand. If you call painting "dumb poetry," then the painter may say of the poet that his art is "blind painting." Consider then which is the more grievous affliction, to be blind or to be dumb!

—Leonardo Da Vinci

The Lord is my shepherd,
I shall not want;
He makes me lie down in green pastures.
He leads me beside still waters;
He restores my soul.
He leads me in paths of righteousness
for his name's sake.

Even though I walk through the
valley of the shadow of death,
I fear no evil;
for thou art with me;
thy rod and thy staff,
they comfort me.
Thou preparest a table before me
in the presence of my enemies;
thou anointest my head with oil,
my cup overflows.
Surely goodness and mercy shall follow me
all the days of my life;
and I shall dwell in the house of the Lord
forever.

—Psalm 23

PHILOSOPHICAL AND RELIGIOUS READINGS ACKNOWLEDGMENTS

Metaphysical Meditations by Paramahansa Yogananda. Copyright © 1964 Self-Realization Fellowship.
The Wisdom of Gibran: Aphorisms and Maxims by Kahlil Gibran, Joseph Sheban, Ed. Permission of Philosophical Library.
The Myth of Sisyphus and Other Essays by Albert Camus, translated by Justin O'Brien. Permission of Alfred A. Knopf, Inc.

Glides (Semivowels) and Diphthongs

Nothing is more useful to man than to speak correctly.

—PHAEDRUS
Fables

GLIDE CONSONANTS

In Chapter 9, consonants were defined as sounds that result from a significant degree of obstruction of the outgoing breath stream by the articulators, whereas vowels are basically *free* from obstruction. Five consonants in Standard American English are relatively "open," or free from articulatory obstruction, much like the vowels. Phonetically, they are written [ʍ], [w], [j], [r], and [l]. The term **semivowel** is often applied to these phonemes; however, **glide** is more accurate. Stop-plosives, fricatives, affricates, and nasals are essentially stationary in production. Glides are produced through sustained motion of the articulators from one position to another. This movement produces a change in resonance that is also a characteristic of these five sounds.

[ʍ] Is a Voiceless Bilabial Glide

Production: To form the consonant [ʍ], round the lips almost into a pucker and blow air through them in a fricative action that approximates [h]. Then glide the lips into the [w] position while moving the tongue and other articulators toward the subsequent vowel sound. [ʍ] is voiceless.

[ʍ] is described differently by different authors. Some call it a bilabial fricative instead of a bilabial glide. The first movement of the sound is closely related to the glottal fricative [h], yet the friction is created on the lips instead of in the glottis.

Other authors call it a combination fricative-glide, in recognition of the two distinct parts of the sound—the friction [h] and the glide [w]. In fact, the IPA recognizes [hw] as well as [ʍ] as a symbol for this sound.

We classify the sound as the voiceless cognate of the bilabial glide [w], though we understand that this classification slights the obvious fricative action at the beginning of the sound.

Perhaps [ʍ] needs a category all its own!

Be aware: [w] is substituted for [ʍ] quite commonly in everyday speech and with no loss of meaning. If you said, "*Wear* did you go?" most people would doubtless think you meant "*Where* did you go?" Many authors argue that [ʍ] is dying out as a standard English phoneme, and it may well be. But until it does, we hope you will try to distinguish between the two sounds. We believe enough useful discrimination exists between *which* and *witch* that we would see them become homophones only reluctantly!

POSITION

Frontal	Medial	Final
wheel	overwhelm	[ʍ] does not
whey	nowhere	appear in the
which	somewhat	final position
whirl	cartwheel	
whisker	bobwhite	
while	tilt-a-whirl	
where	meanwhile	

Sentences Featuring [ʍ]

1. The whippoorwill whistled from where he perched in the whiffletrees.
2. Why did Wally Whitesides whip the whining whippet and her whelps?
3. Where do the whales go when they are nowhere to be seen?
4. Alice Whitlock and Anna Wharton had a whopping good time riding the tilt-a-whirl and the whirligig.
5. I got a whiff of an overwhelming, somewhat rancid, pile of wheat.
6. Walt Whitman is often pictured with long white whiskers, which somewhat hide his face.
7. *Whomp, whack, wham,* and *whang* all mean "to hit or beat," but a *whump* is only a thump or bang.
8. Did James Whitmore's portrayal of Harry Truman show his whirlwind of campaign whistle-stops?
9. Sam Wheeler horsewhipped Whitey Whitaker with a bullwhip, which is why Whitey is in a wheelchair.
10. Golly gee whizbang! I'm so happy I could turn cartwheels and yell "Whoopee!"
11. Eli Whitney invented the cotton gin, which is not a type of whiskey.
12. The bobwhite whizzed through the air bringing worms from somewhere to whet the appetites of her new-hatched chicks.
13. *Whistler's Mother* is a whimsical, somewhat nostalgic portrait painted while Whistler was in London.
14. Will Whitworth, a young whippersnapper if I ever saw one, whimpered when his asthma made him wheeze and whine.
15. Why use archaic words such as *whilst, whence, whither,* and *whilom* when you can say *while, from where, to where,* and *formerly*?

[w] **Is a Voiced Bilabial Glide**

Production: To form the consonant [w], round the lips into a pucker and begin vocal fold vibration. Then glide the lips while moving the tongue and other articulators toward the position of whatever vowel follows. [w] is voiced.

Be aware:

1. The bilabial articulation required to form [w] demands the same precision of lip movement as the other bilabials—[p], [b], and [m]. *Lip-lazy* is a term that has been applied to speakers who do not use their lip muscles as fully as crisp enunciation requires. Watch yourself in the mirror to see that your lips make full closure or firm rounding on all bilabial consonants.

2. [w] occurs in words that have no orthographic *w*. Most words spelled *qu* are pronounced [kw]—*quick, queen, quiet,* and *quest,* for instance—and *choir* is plainly [kwaɪr].

3. A tendency exists to omit [w] when it begins the second syllable of a word. *Forward, woodwork, housewife,* and *railway* need fully developed, fully voiced [w] sounds.

POSITION

Frontal	Medial	Final
want	unaware	[w] does not
weigh	coward	appear in the
weed	unwind	final position
wizard	hallway	
woven	swear	
once	between	
worse	quote	

Sentences Featuring [w]

1. Wendell Wilkie won in Wisconsin and Wyoming; otherwise his defeat was widespread.
2. A loquacious squid waxed eloquent in the liquid waters.
3. Drive quickly westward on the thruway to Walla Walla, Washington.
4. A wizard waved his wand, and a quivering quidnunc appeared.
5. Some inward power is required to acquire personal wealth.
6. Captain Queeg wandered inquisitively over the wide world.
7. "Waste not, want not" is not an unwise way to live.
8. The Weight Watchers' waist-reduction plan requires quiet willpower.
9. For a quarter, Dr. Quince will make warts wilt with a liquid wax.
10. One swearing woman quibbled with twelve cowering clerks in Warsaw.
11. Twenty-one woolen towels were woven into quilts in Quincy.
12. Squire Wilson wavered; now he must wend his way back to square one.
13. Wanda is unaware of her powerful, winning ways of wooing.
14. Pickwick, who has a way with words, is always being quoted.
15. Wintry showers help the weeds grow wildly skyward.

Words Contrasting [ʍ], [w], *and* [h]

what—watt—hot	which—witch—hitch
whet—wet—head	whirled—world—hurled
when—wen—hen	whit—wit—hit
wheel—weal—heal	whether—weather—heather
where—wear—hair	whale—wail—hail
whey—way—hay	whine—wine—hind

Sentences Featuring [ʍ] *and* [w]

1. William Wheeler wafted his wobbly canoe over the wild white waters of Wichita Falls.
2. Which do you wish—warm cream of wheat or curds and whey?
3. I'm aware that whiskey may come from wheat, but whence comes wine?
4. The quick wild stallion was horsewhipped, whereupon he whinnied woefully.
5. Walter whispered sweet nothings to his inquisitive wife.
6. I would not wish to quibble with a woolly whiskered whippet.
7. Quasars are somewhere between our world and the rest of the Milky Way.
8. I wish I knew which sandwich Wilma switched.
9. Wanda White wandered down the midway while we rode the tilt-a-whirl.
10. I swear I was nowhere near the town square last Wednesday.
11. Whew! We were worn out from whooping it up following our win.
12. The wobbly kneed squirt wheedled his way out of a whipping by whimpering persuasively.
13. When women whisper in Wales, men wonder what Welsh words mean.
14. A school of squid watched twenty whales swimming near the western shore of Ecuador.
15. The stairway to the squire's tower winds in a clockwise pinwheel around the west wing.

DRAMATIC SCENE FEATURING [ʍ] AND [w]

Wicker World
SHARON THOMAS

Voice 1:   Mr. Wiggins, proprietor
Voice 2:   first customer
Voice 3:   second customer

1: Welcome to Wiggins Wicker World.
2: Yes, well, I'm Mrs. Rickard. I called about a white wicker for my window.
1: Oh, Mrs. Rickard, I'm Willard Wiggins. I talked with you about the white wicker for your window. We have a wide selection of wickers. These are our white wickers. Which white wicker do you want?
2: The white wicker with the weeping willow design. Let me see that one.
1: What a wonderful wicker!
2: Oh, this wicker is thicker than I wanted.
1: Too thick of a wicker? Let's switch wickers. Pick a white wicker that suits you.
2: The white wicker with the whippoorwills stitched on it.
1: The whippoorwill wicker. Wonderful!
2: This wicker is slicker than the first one.
1: Well, which wicker would you like? The weeping willow wicker that is thicker, or the whippoorwill wicker that is slicker?
2: I want a wicker that is neither thicker nor slicker.
3: Wow! What a whale of wicker.
1: I'll be with you in a moment, miss.
3: I'm wild about wicker!

1: (*to first customer*) Would you like to wander through the wicker while I wait on this woman?

2: Well, I suppose so.

1: (*to second customer*) Welcome to Wiggins Wicker World. What kind of wicker would you want?

3: Something warm, wicked, wild . . . white! Yes, white wicker is wild!

1: And which white wicker would you want?

3: The white wicker with the weeping willow is weird.

2: I'll take the weeping willow wicker.

3: Excuse me, but I want the weeping willow wicker.

2: Young lady, I was here first. The weeping willow wicker is what I want, Mr. Wiggins.

3: But you were wandering through the wicker . . .

1: Please, ladies . . . let's not bicker about the wicker. There's enough wicker for you both.

2: But this is the only weeping willow white wicker.

1: Mrs. Rickard, you just said the weeping willow white wicker was thicker than you wanted.

2: I've changed my mind.

1: Miss, perhaps you'll consider another weird wicker. We have many other twenty-dollar pieces . . .

3: Twenty dollars! That little wiry wimp of white wicker is twenty dollars? It's yours, lady.

2: Thank you.

3: How much is the whippoorwill white wicker?

1: The whippoorwill white wicker is twelve dollars.

3: What a weird white wicker. I'll take it.

1: Wonderful! Shall I wrap your white wickets, ladies?

2 and 3:   No, thank you.

3: Wow! What a wicked weave on this weird white wicker . . . wild!

1: Here you are ladies. I hope you enjoy your weeping willow and whippoorwill white wickers. And thank you for shopping Wiggins Wicker World. Do come again!

[j] **Is a Voiced Lingua-Velar Guide**

Production: The high front glide [j] is produced by raising the front of the tongue toward the hard palate and pressing the blades of the tongue against the alveolar ridge. Like [ʍ] and [w], the tongue then moves toward the position for the sound that is to follow. [j] is voiced.

Be aware:

1. Although [ʍ] may be disappearing from standard American English, [j] is in no such danger. It is firmly entrenched in many words—*young, beyond, cute*—but it has been optional in a number of words that contain the vowel [u], particularly when [u] follows [t], [d], or [n]. Words such as *student, Tuesday, duty,* or *news* can be pronounced with either a [u] or a [ju]. By now you should have realized that we tend to be sticklers for precise pronunciation, so you will probably not be surprised to learn that we prefer [ju]. The distinction between *do* and *due, moos* and *mews, cootie* and *cutie,* and *two lips* and *tulips* may be obvious from context, but why not give the listener the added benefit of a difference in sound?

2. We are so accustomed to substituting [tʃə] or [dʒə] for [u] or [ju]—compare *nature* and *injure* with *mature* and *procure*—that we accept these substitutions

as standard in many phrases, such as *would you* or *did you* ([wʊ dʒə] or [dɪ dʒə]) rather than [wʊd ju] or [dɪd ju]). There is, however, a halfway point between the overprecision of [wʊd ju] and the total slurring of [wʊ dʒə] that is more effective articulation. No one wants to sound pedantically stiff, yet excessive assimilation can sound slovenly.

POSITION

Frontal	*Medial*	*Final*
young	news	[j] does not
yesterday	cute	appear in the
yacht	reputation	final position
unique	human	
utilize	music	
euphemism	funeral	
unicorn	beauty	

Sentences Featuring [j]

1. You should utilize your uvula every Tuesday.
2. Few students assume any unusual duties.
3. More than a few humans speak Yiddish in New York.
4. Cuba refused to get into a dispute with the United States.
5. A Yugoslavian refugee rode a huge yacht to Yalta.
6. "Y'all" is a contraction often used in Houston.
7. If you have a yen, you either yearn or you have valuable money.
8. The Reverend Hughes gave a humorous eulogy at the funeral.
9. I assume the *New Orleans Times Picayune* has a good reputation.
10. Is *beautiful* sometimes used as a euphemism for *cute?*
11. Yes, there are few fumes blocking the view in Butte.
12. A pugilistic yak yodeled at the dewy unicorn in his yard.
13. The tutor reviewed the Tudor kings for an entire year with her pupils.
14. A yell is one useful form of human communication.
15. After communion, the pew over yonder was covered with moisture.

[r] **Is a Voiced Lingua-Postalveolar Glide**

Production: [r] is formed in different ways by different speakers; therefore it is hard to describe its production precisely. In general, the tongue is raised toward the front of the hard palate and the lips and teeth are brought close together. Phonation is begun, and the articulators begin the characteristic glide toward the vowel that follows the [r]. [r] is voiced.

Be aware:

1. As the tongue tip rises it should not be retracted toward the palate. Retraction can cause a fuzzy or muffled [r] that distorts the vowel that precedes or follows it. For example, *Frrush urr* instead of *fresh air* might result from a retracted tongue. When coupled with palatal-tension nasality, a Midwestern or East Texas twang may result.

2. If, however, the tongue stays too far forward in the mouth without being retracted toward the palate, [w] will replace [r]. This may sound humorous, as when Elmer Fudd calls Bugs Bunny "that wascally wabbit," but it is a serious

articulation impediment for a number of speakers, many of whom must seek out a speech therapist. Self-help here is almost impossible.

3. Avoid the "intrusive r"—an [r] that does not belong. Did you ever hear anyone say, "I sawr an angel," "Hawaiier is an island," or "I had no idear it was so late"? The speaker has inserted [r] between two vowel sounds to make it easier to assimilate them. It is much better to take the slight articulation break that is needed when two vowels are adjacent than to insert an inappropriate [r] or any other sound.

POSITION

Frontal	Medial, Preceded by:		Final
	VOWEL	*CONSONANT*	
receive	cheerleader	brought	care
rebel	chorus	abrupt	floor
referee	parcel	draft	career
rhinoceros	pyromaniac	friend	poor
roll	hoard	already	rare
rover	zero	approve	where
rough	wary	truth	sheer
ruthless			

VOWELS FOLLOWED BY [r]

[ɪr]	[ɛr]	[ɑr]	[ɔr]
pierce	error	chart	storm
fierce	bearing	charm	warn
beard	dare	alarm	absorb
seared	fair	ark	fork
dear	their	artist	swarm
hear	lair	farm	north
fear	where	smart	York

[or]	[aɪr]	[ʊr]	[aʊr]
port	wired	sure	our, hour
pork	tired	pure	flower
forth	liar	tour	power
mourn	hire	moor	tower
torn	fire	endure	shower
more	admire		
core	attire		

Sentences Featuring [r]

1. Randolph ran rapidly around the entire perimeter of Grand Rapids.

2. "My nose is like a red, red rose," said Rudolph the reindeer.

3. Vera poured a reservoir of syrup over the four French party crepes.

4. Prisons are for hard-core criminals, not for pranksterish children.

5. Only Prudence Henderson wore a strapless dress to the reception in February.

6. Reading articles in periodicals helps keep one aware of internal and foreign governmental affairs.

7. Harold repeated the same ridiculous rhyme three times in a row.

8. Rabbis and priests have the right to pray for more contributions from their parishioners.

9. Just recently that rogue cornered forty weary rats on the roof.

10. We're rappelling from a ridge with a three-hundred-yard sheer drop.

11. An irritating virus spread throughout the grade school.

12. Rhonda threw a bearskin rug on the living room floor near the front door.

13. I am frequently reminded to try to separate right from wrong.

14. Orville arose promptly for an early breakfast, then rode his horse en route to the rodeo.

15. Bring a sturdy rubber raft to run the rough Red River rapids.

Sentences Featuring [r] *Preceded by Vowels*

1. Did the pair from Newark carve the warm pork?

2. The bear felt fear in his heart when he faced the barn door.

3. You cannot wear your fire-colored beard any more this year.

4. The worn gear fell into the moor near the tar pit.

5. The fire near the wire chair was put out by a warm shower.

6. The fierce boar neared the deer's lair.

7. They wore clear, rare earrings in their pierced ears.

8. I fear the fair-haired dear will sear his beard if he dares the air.

9. Fill out the part of the form that allows the import of pork from the farm.

10. Park the car at the hardware store where hordes of stars pour forth.

11. I cannot bear a boorish bore who cares not for art.

12. The scary bear was an orphan named Marvin from Yorkshire.

13. A smart, charming artist is a sure cure for a forlorn dormitory.

14. Be sure to sear the pork before you roast it, then check it with a fork about four o'clock.

15. It was a dark and stormy night when the farmer made his way across the moor on his gray mare.

[l] **Is a Voiced Lingua-Alveolar Glide**

Production: To form the consonant [l], curl the tongue tip and press it against the alveolar ridge. Lower the sides of the tongue to allow the breath stream to escape laterally rather than across the front of the tongue. This is why [l] is classified as a lateral as well as a glide. The resonant quality of [l] changes considerably depending upon where the sound occurs in the word, since the position of the articulators moves to adjust to the preceding or following sound. [l] is voiced.

Be aware:

1. [l] has two varieties—light or front [l], produced with the back of the tongue lower, and dark [l], produced with the back of the tongue raised somewhat. Light [l] is usually found toward the beginning of words, as in *look, clear,* and *fleet,* whereas dark [l] occurs near the end of a word, as in *tell, felt,* and *hold.* Some speakers—especially those who learned English as a second language—tend to use the light [l] in all positions. Other speakers, more often natives, make all [l] sounds with the tongue raised, making them overly dark. To experience this, say *fall,* sustain the [l] placement, and use it to begin the word *lawn.* Hear the retracted, muffled quality of the initial [l] in *lawn?* That should be avoided.

2. [l] is often omitted, especially when it occurs before another consonant. Be careful not to omit the [l] from words such as *help, helm, million, stallion, film, twelve,* and *railroad* and phrases such as *all right* and *all gone.*

3. Many children have problems with [l], some that carry over into adulthood. One is using the lips instead of the tip of the tongue to articulate the sound, resulting in a [w] substitution—*pwease* for *please* or *wittle* for *little*. Failure to lift the front of the tongue, combined with an absence of lip articulation, will cause a [j] for [l] substitution—*yake* for *lake* or *yight* for *light*. Persons of Asian background sometimes reverse [r] and [l]—*prease* and *blight* for *please* and *bright*.

	POSITION		
Frontal	*Medial, Preceded by:*		*Final*
	VOWEL	*CONSONANT*	
laboratory	alliteration	England	jungle
laugh	almost	plant	missile
library	elbow	flat	sale
little	island	flirt	wheel
lobster	pulled	plunder	boil
love	ability	mistletoe	startle
luck	early	chloroform	smile

Sentences Featuring [l]

1. Simultaneously on television are "The Eleven O'Clock Late Movie" and the play *Love's Labors Lost*.
2. Legions of yellow-bellied soldiers fled the battlefield.
3. In the fall large leaves flutter from tall elm limbs onto the fallow soil.
4. You can't always believe a tale told by a pathological liar.
5. Luke modeled a bold, startling new look in children's clothing.
6. In a flash the tadpole's tongue pulled in a fly for lunch.
7. The islanders grilled a luscious lobster for the holiday season.
8. Cleo got involved in a little altercation with the class bully after school.
9. I had to laugh at that silly fellow's pratfalls and slapstick clowning.
10. Albert played follow-the-leader with his pal Lloyd all over the Loop.
11. Lance led eleven lovely lasses in an elaborate Highland fling.
12. Greenland is the least livable place listed in our library's geographical atlas.
13. Allen always allowed Algernon to allude to the alphabet in all his alliterations.
14. The piglet squealed with delight while licking his lips over his smelly slop.
15. Bill dislodged Laura and Lewis, then pulled livid Jill under the mistletoe.

Words Contrasting [w], [r], and [l]

weep—reap—leap		weave—Reeve—leave	
wine—Rhine—line		wave—rave—lave	
woe—row—low		wight—right—light	
wore—roar—lore		went—rent—lent	
wed—red—led		quick—crick—click	
quip—crip—clip		queer—career—clear	

Sentences Featuring [r] and [l]

1. The Rolling Stones are a world-renowned rock-and-roll group.
2. The French Revolution forever altered the course of European history.

3. Latin is the original tongue from which sprang all the Romance languages.

4. Rocky locked his fiddle in an unbreakable violin case.

5. The leaders of the English people rule Great Britain from the Houses of Parliament.

6. For lunch we had shrimp egg rolls, french fries, and cole slaw.

7. "Eleven lords-a-leaping" is a silly line from a popular Christmas melody.

8. Laura strolled down the hill, calling for her Labrador retriever.

9. Mushrooms are delicious fried in golden olive oil.

10. Just below your elbow in your arm are your radius and ulna.

11. A terrible legend tells of evil warlocks casting ludicrous spells on helpless librarians.

12. The gullible retirees bought twelve parcels of worthless swampland in Florida.

13. Rebel soldiers were successful at the Civil War battle of Chancellorsville.

14. With a flick of his wrist, the freak wrote out a list of places to visit along the old road.

15. An ugly radiologist ran a classified singles ad looking for a pretty lady with long blond hair.

Sentences Featuring [ʍ], [w], [j], [r], and [l]

1. The Prince of Wales's ailing white horse rides the rail from Vail to Yale University.

2. The whetstone was wet, yet Rhett let me borrow it.

3. What Eunice installed on her rotting yacht was a fifty-watt lamp.

4. In broad daylight they drifted near the Isle of Wight, in a dispute over whaling rights.

5. In lieu of being able to woo Koo, he ruefully warbled "I love you."

6. A wan, shipwrecked Ron awoke on a manicured front lawn in Ireland.

7. The whiny steward served white wine and watermelon rinds.

8. Lynn began to grin at the whinny of the winning horse in the race at Baltimore.

9. When his friend lends enough yen, Roland will rent a vessel to wend his way across the Atlantic.

10. She wanted to know what fool drew those unique, loony runes.

11. Sheila whipped a yipping wimp, bloodying his lip and ripping his clothes.

12. "Yare," yelled the admiral from his private lair, where he wore a rare uniform.

13. The young leader tries to rise above the lies by asking herself the proper whos and whys.

14. With a whack on the back of the black yak, Jethro saddled the yoke to the rack.

15. Now that I have finished this wistful epistle, I will play a few useless rounds of whist or bridge.

DIPHTHONGS

Speech is the image of life.

—DEMOCRITUS

The word *diphthong* comes from the Greek *di*, "twice," and *phthongos*, "sound." Diphthongs, then, combine two pure vowels into a single distinguishable phoneme. In phonetics, the five diphthongs in Standard American English are [eɪ], [aɪ], [ɔɪ], [aʊ], and [oʊ].

Diphthongs are characterized by the movement of the articulators upward from one vowel position to a higher vowel position; the primary stress is on the initial part of the sound. Another feature of these phonemes is the change in resonance that occurs within the sound.

Technically, the diphthongs [eɪ] and [oʊ] are considered *nonphonemic,* in that the meaning of words such as *labor* and *oath* will be clear whether the speaker uses [eɪ] and [oʊ] or the pure vowels [e] and [o]. You will recall that we discussed the difference in Chapters 10 and 11, suggesting when the diphthong might be preferred to the pure vowel. Remember that many speakers do not make this fine distinction, yet are easily understood. On the other hand, the diphthongs [aɪ], [ɔɪ], and [aʊ] are distinctly *phonemic,* in that any pure vowel substitution will alter the meaning of the words in which they occur. For example, *oil* [ɔɪl] will become *all* [ɔl] and *mice* [maɪs] will become *mass* [mas] if the pure vowel is used.

The majority of dialect substitutions occur in front vowels and diphthongs. Therefore, careful attention should be paid to these sounds.

[eɪ]

Production: To form the diphthong [eɪ], open the jaw, relax the lips, and moderately tense the tongue. Close the jaw slightly as the tongue glides up from the midfront position for [e] to the high position for [ɪ].

Orthographic spellings include:

a — paper	ey — prey
ea — yea	ai — bail
ay — bay	ei — heinous
eigh — weigh	e — crepe

Be aware:

1. Lack of adequate tension in the tongue will distort [eɪ] toward the lower front vowels [ɛ] and [æ]. Words such as *sale* [seɪl] will sound like *sell* [sɛl] or *sal* [sæl].

2. Take care not to *triphthongize* this sound, especially in words where [eɪ] precedes the consonant [l]. If you do, *pale, wail,* and *nail* will sound like [peɪ əl], [weɪ əl], and [neɪ əl].

POSITION

Frontal	*Medial*		*Final*
[eɪ] *or* [e]	[eɪ]	[e]	[eɪ]
age	bake	decade	display
able	parade	tirade	sway
acre	crazy	inlaid	essay
ache	fade	chaotic	gray
alien	phase	cremated	may
aim	gauge	capon	sleigh
eight	mail		clay

Sentences Featuring [eɪ] *and* [e]

1. Gail made a great cake for the seventh-grade bake sale.
2. When asked to state his birthplace, the alien from space hastily named his favorite crater.
3. Yesterday at eight my neighbor watched the Blue Jays play major league baseball.
4. The blank-faced bass player kept an easy-paced cadence.
5. Pay attention while I regale you with strange tales of papal regalia.

6. Lazy Jane lay in the lane all day, creating a chain of daisies.

7. I hate to mail pastries and crepes to Ray Brady.

8. James gave fake papers to his state navy agent.

9. Eight patient natives serenaded the angry apes.

10. Kane hastily disobeyed, using profane language.

11. Jay took Nate, the great dane, out Tuesday to chase quail.

12. Maybe if I gave away my pay, I might gain nationwide fame.

13. "When I pass away, I may be cremated," said Jason, gazing at the grave.

14. Fay and Luray Major saw an array of Broadway plays ranging from *Dames at Bay* to *Babes in Norway.*

15. Who came from the Quaker State, Pennsylvania—Tom Paine or Nathan Hale?

[aɪ]

Production: To form the diphthong [aɪ], open the jaw; keep the lips unrounded and the tongue low and flat in the mouth. The articulators glide upward from the low position [ɑ] or [a] to the high front position for [ɪ].

Orthographic spellings include:

i—bright	uy—buy	oi—choir
igh—sigh	ai—Cairo	is—isle
y—try	ei—heist	ui—guide
eye—eye	ie—hieroglyphics	

Be aware:

1. Too much tension in the back of the tongue will result in the initial [aɪ] rising to [ɔ]. *Tie* will become *taw.*

2. Not completing the diphthong or omitting the second vowel, [ɪ], will result in a "flat" sound. *Fire* will become either *far* [fɑr] or *far* [fær].

3. Occasionally, in assimilated speech, the first-person pronoun *I* may become a schwa [ə]. *I'm* will sound like *um.*

POSITION

Frontal	Medial	Final
idle	mind	defy
aisle	stripe	high
Ireland	virus	dry
iron	white	apply
island	disguise	rely
I've	library	indemnify
ivory	decline	why

Sentences Featuring [aɪ]

1. I spy a fly on the side of your tie.

2. Might Mike be obliged to try smiling awhile?

3. March is an ideal time to refine kite-flying styles.

4. A fine gynecologist cried at the sight of the senile bison.

5. While on the island, pirates must decipher a diverse group of signs.

6. The diver climbed high for another death-defying try.

7. Hines, the benign librarian, hides classified items in aisle five.
8. The smiling dinosaur climbed over Ireland, disguised as a poltergeist.
9. Ivan might like to buy a nice high-rise condominium.
10. Simon apprised his client of the likelihood that the writer might file for libel.
11. The line "pie-in-the-sky idea" is a fine example of the use of hyphens.
12. A cry of sirens on Highland Drive pierced the quiet nighttime sky.
13. That refined fighter pilot likes to dine with a fine wine on the side.
14. McBride is trying not to cry about the final demise of the Flying Tigers.
15. A scientist took a midnight flight to Cairo to try to decipher the disguised hieroglyphics.

Minimal Pairs Contrasting [aɪ] *and* [eɪ]

by the bay	mail a mile
bite the bait	the Dane dined
fight the fate	tale of a tile
right the rate	stale turnstile
pile the pale	prayed for pride
tried the trade	a vain vine
might the mate	inane in nine
the bride brayed	pay for a pie
sign for the sane	rain on the Rhine
type on tape	fail the file
liars in layers	the player's pliars
fries the phrase	claim the climb

MINIMAL TRIPLETS FOR [eɪ], [aɪ], and [ɑ]

[eɪ]	[aɪ]	[ɑ]	*Phrases*
bate	bite	bottle	I bought a bottle of bite-sized bait.
Kate	kite	cot	Kate caught her kite on the cot.
spate	spite	spot	In spite of sports, I spied a spate of spots.
late	light	lot	It's late—light the little lot.
plate	plight	plot	We plotted the plate's plight.
rate	right	rot	The right rate to rot a wrought-iron gate.
sate	sight	sot	I sought sight of a sated sot.
raid	ride	rod	Raiders took the hot rod for a raw deal of a ride.
prayed	pride	prod	When prodded, I prayed with pride.
trade	tried	trod	The trawler trader trod over tried and true trails.
lake	like	lock	I'd like the law to lock up the lake.
make	Mike	mock	Make mockery of mawkish Mike.
pain	pine	upon	Upon my word—a painful, pining pawn.
race	rice	Ross	Race Ross to the raw rice.
wade	wide	wad	Wade through a wide wad of ones.

[ɔɪ]

Production: To form the diphthong [ɔɪ], open the jaw, slightly round the lips, and tense the tongue for the back vowel [ɔ]. Then close the jaw slightly and unround the lips as the tongue shifts forward to the high front position for [ɪ].

Orthographic spellings include:

oi—boil	eu—Freud
oy—oyster	aw—lawyer (also pronounced [lɔ jɚ]

Be aware:

1. In certain parts of the United States, there is a tendency to distort [ɔɪ] so that it sounds like the pure vowels [ɝ] and [ɔ] or the diphthong [aɪ]. *Oil* will sound like *earl* or *all; boil* will sound like *bile.*

2. As with [eɪ], do not triphthongize [ɔɪ], especially when it is followed by the consonant [l]. In this case, *boil* will sound like [bɔɪjəl], *oil* [ɔɪjəl].

POSITION

Frontal (rare)	Medial	Final
oyster	boisterous	boy
oil	recoil	alloy
oink	rejoin	decoy
	appoint	annoy
	poise	toy
	invoice	convoy
	voyage	ploy

Sentences Featuring [ɔɪ]

1. Count Tolstoy planned a long voyage to Troy.
2. A court-appointed lawyer was foisted on Portnoy.
3. The boisterous boys' chorus made a joyful noise.
4. The moist soybean was a Freudian decoy to Roy.
5. By choice, Joyce proposed a royal toast.
6. A convoy of voyeurs covered Des Moines with boiling poison.
7. The young boy avoided pointing with his new toy.
8. One of Doyle's choicest foibles is his tendency to oink loudly.
9. The envoy's proposal was a ploy to foil the loyalists.
10. Please have Floyd Poindexter void my old invoice.
11. The royalty eat poi and cover their groins with loincloths.
12. Sister Joyce was anointed with oil in the cloister.
13. Leroy seems to enjoy being cloyed with oysters.
14. Please avoid tracking muddy soil into the foyer.
15. Which did Lloyd Sawyer most enjoy—D'Oyly Carte or the Bolshoi Ballet?

Words Contrasting [ɔɪ] and [ɝ]

toys—terse	adjoin—adjourn	avoid—averred
poise—purrs	loin—learn	oil—earl
poison—person	coil—curl	coy—cur
moist—immersed	foist—first	voice—verse

[aʊ]

Production: To form [aʊ], open the jaw, relax the lips, and keep the tongue low and flat as for the low vowels [ɑ] and [a]. Then close the jaw and tense and round the lips as the tongue glides upward to the high back vowel [ʊ].

Orthographic spellings include:

ow—how	ough—drought
ou—rout	au—sauerkraut

Be aware:

1. Not completing the diphthong or omitting the second sound, [ʊ], will result in the same "flat" quality that occurs with [aɪ]. *Sour* [saʊr] will sound like *saar* [sar].

2. Too much tension in the back of the tongue will cause the diphthong to rise to [oʊ] or [u]. For example, *about* [ə ˈbaʊt] will become *aboat* [ə ˈboʊt] or *aboot* [ə ˈbut].

POSITION

Frontal	Medial	Final
owl	flower	bow (bough)
our (hour)	crown	allow
hourly	trout	cow
ourselves	shower	brow
outside	prowler	plow
oust	ground	avow
outer	pounce	meow

Sentences Featuring [aʊ]

1. The renowned socialite went out and about the town.
2. News of the lousy movie spread by word of mouth throughout the crowd.
3. Thou shalt not shout at a Mau-Mau luau.
4. Powell encountered a dour, frowning owl.
5. Buy some towels, a pound of flour, and eight ounces of sauerkraut.
6. The trout-fishing boat traveled around Puget Sound.
7. A prowler might encounter the loud meow of a stout mouser.
8. Now shower, put on your gown, and expound about vowels.
9. A growling Bowser pounced on an unsuspecting grouse.
10. How could she be allowed to take her vows without powdering her nose?
11. After carousing for hours, they headed south toward the Bowery.
12. Those who doubt the crown's power may spend time impounded in the tower.
13. Even sows and cows wore down-filled gowns outside.
14. "Howdy" might be shouted in a town down in the South.
15. We are allowed to mouth our sounds out loud.

[oʊ]

Production: To form [oʊ], open the jaw, round the lips, and moderately tense the tongue in the midback position for [o]. The jaw then closes and the lips tense and become more rounded as the tongue moves upward to the high back vowel [ʊ].

Orthographic spellings include:

o—go

oa—oat

oe—doe

ough—dough

eau—beau

ow—know

ou—soul

Be aware:

1. [oʊ] can be distorted to the schwa [ə] or the hooked schwa [ɚ], especially when it appears in the final position of a word. *Piano* [pɪˈænoʊ] may sound like *piana* [pɪˈænə] or *pianer* [pɪˈænɚ]; *yellow* [jɛloʊ] may sound like *yella* [jɛlə] or *yeller* [jɛlɚ].

2. Triphthongizing [oʊ] words that end in [l] can occur. For example, *coal* [koʊl] will sound like *co-well* [koʊ wəl].

POSITION

Frontal	Medial	Final
old	broken	minnow
only	poultry	rodeo
open	gnome	banjo
ozone	frozen	chateau
oval	cloak	window
okra	coma	buffalo
Oklahoma	phoneme	although

Sentences Featuring [oʊ] and [o]

1. Oh, no! Don't go home before tomorrow.
2. Hope and Lamour took the road to Morocco.
3. Nero boasted that his home was the most cozy domicile in Rome.
4. An old polar bear rode a porcelain pony in the rodeo.
5. Nora wore a polo shirt with a logo of a Trojan horse.
6. Four Cosa Nostra Romeos danced the bossa nova at a local disco.
7. "Thanks to bowling," said Homer Jones, blowing his nose, "there is hope for tomorrow."
8. The orderly dozed on the orthopedic ward sofa.
9. A mezzo-soprano closed the show with a low, melodious solo.
10. Jethro Holt, the mobile-home owner, is a notorious bozo.
11. Those Dobermans dug holes in which to stow their quota of bones.
12. Moans and groans are the known tones in an old boneyard full of tombstones.
13. Lola snored through a virtuoso performance of Mozart's oboe concerto.
14. Only in October do Holy Rollers stroll on the Kokomo.
15. Bo Olson poured oleo over Post Toasties in oaken bowls.

Sentences Featuring [aʊ], [oʊ], [ɔɪ] and [eɪ]

1. Bow lowly to the boiling bowl of bouncing balls.
2. Stand the towel tall lest toil take its toll.
3. The foul fall failed to foil the foal.
4. Doyle's doll installed Dole's doweling rods.
5. Roy rested his royal roll on Ralph's round rail.
6. Scowling Sol softly soils the sallow soulful soil.
7. The concentrating cow never could con a coin for a cone.

8.   Now zoo noise gnaws at my nose.

9.   Foolish folderol fouled the folded foil dinner.

10. Hoist up the ousted, hostile host.

11. Baugh's beau bowed to her boyfriend.

12. So, you saw a sow eat soybeans.

13. Lloyd lauded his leader's load aloud.

14. The mouse trembled most in the moist, deep moss.

15. Forced austerity fostered the ouster of all of our oysters.

Sentences Featuring All Diphthongs

1.   Time and tide are known quantities that are bound to change.

2.   The round royalty tried all kinds of dieting, to no avail.

3.   Five players posed, poised and ready to shout out loud.

4.   Invite the cowboy to tape a toaster to his eyelash hourly.

5.   I know that Boyce's renowned sinus problem most likely originates in his brain.

6.   No one is afflicted with goiter in the famous play *Our Town* by Thornton Wilder.

7.   O say, you can sigh—Blake may have found those lousy soybean-flavored sundaes.

8.   Oily Joe told a tasteless joke about fried pies to his pouting spouse.

9.   How did Goya paint such bold, bright portraits?

10. Nine thousand houses employ maids who mistakenly bake the daily paper while reading a soufflé.

11. The Boy Scouts loaned their adenoids to a nice old lady.

12. For safety's sake, allow the coiled snake to lay outside in the dry soil all night.

13. I do so enjoy pointing out the foibles of those less capable than I.

14. In an orgy of noise and violence, a dangerous crowd of bikers destroyed the South Side Polo Lounge.

15. Miles Morgan, a mild-mannered lawyer, was appointed as counsel to both the mayor and the town council of Ames, Iowa.

PHONETICS PRACTICE 1: GLIDES AND DIPHTHONGS

Write the following words in phonetics:

1. weigh _____

2. woe _____

3. lore _____

4. yea _____

5. roll _____

6. wow _____

7. Yale _____

8. lay _____

9. lisle _____

10. loyal _____

11. while _____

12. whale _____

13. oil _____

14. yore _____

15. rail _____

16. owl _____

17. wire _____

18. why _____

19. ale _____

20. royal _____

PHONETICS PRACTICE 2: WORDS CONTAINING ALL THE SOUNDS AND PHONETIC SYMBOLS

Write the orthographic spelling for the following words written in phonetics:

1. [ʍɝˈl] _____
2. [lɔjɚ] _____
3. [ruʒ] _____
4. [trɛʒɚ] _____
5. [juθfl] _____
6. [kritʃɚ] _____
7. [ɛndʒɔɪ] _____
8. [ɝθlɪ] _____
9. [teɪ blɪŋ] _____
10. [wɪθhoʊld] _____
11. [ɔl ðoʊ] _____
12. [feɪvɚɪt] _____
13. [laɪk lɪ] _____
14. [fɔɪbl] _____
15. [maʊn tn] _____
16. [hoʊp ləs] _____
17. [vɔɪ sɪz] _____
18. [jɛl oʊ] _____
19. [ʍɪp læʃ] _____
20. [ʌn wɪ tɪŋ] _____

Write the following words in phonetics:

1. leisure _____
2. shapely _____
3. rhyming _____
4. joint _____
5. round _____
6. opening _____
7. couldn't _____
8. chutney _____
9. resist _____
10. usual _____
11. violent _____
12. hoist _____
13. louder _____
14. zoned _____
15. shirked _____
16. rajah _____
17. warming _____
18. chain _____
19. together _____
20. couples _____

CROSSWORD PUZZLE 13–1
All Sounds

Across

1. beat, pulsate
5. enemy
7. rundown, shabby; rodent-like
8. third person (feminine pronoun)
9. totally, completely
11. perceive with the eyes
12. kind of fresh water fish
14. casette or adhesive
17. Einstein's given name (abbr.)
18. first person pronoun
19. feminine parent
20. petroleum

Down

1. in fencing: parry and _____
2. rodent
3. playful aquatic mammal
4. made, constructed
5. large, elegant meal
6. exclamation!
10. formerly Persia
13. nocturnal bird with large eyes
15. goal, desire
16. masculine parent
18. _____ of Capri

CROSSWORD PUZZLE 13–2
All Sounds

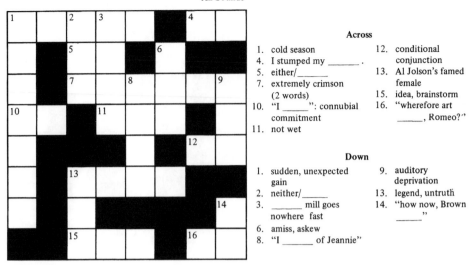

Across

1. cold season
4. I stumped my _____ .
5. either/_____
7. extremely crimson (2 words)
10. "I _____": connubial commitment
11. not wet
12. conditional conjunction
13. Al Jolson's famed female
15. idea, brainstorm
16. "wherefore art _____, Romeo?"

Down

1. sudden, unexpected gain
2. neither/_____
3. _____ mill goes nowhere fast
6. amiss, askew
8. "I _____ of Jeannie"
9. auditory deprivation
13. legend, untruth
14. "how now, Brown _____"

CROSSWORD PUZZLE 13–3
All Sounds

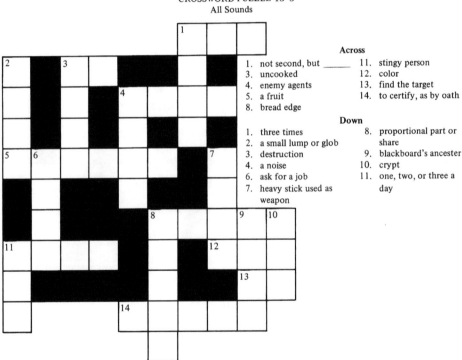

Across

1. not second, but _____
3. uncooked
4. enemy agents
5. a fruit
8. bread edge
11. stingy person
12. color
13. find the target
14. to certify, as by oath

Down

1. three times
2. a small lump or glob
3. destruction
4. a noise
6. ask for a job
7. heavy stick used as weapon
8. proportional part or share
9. blackboard's ancester
10. crypt
11. one, two, or three a day

POETRY AND SHAKESPEARE FOR PRACTICE

This final chapter offers you the most difficult oral reading practice material in the book—poetry and passages from Shakespeare. As mentioned in Chapter 7, poetry challenges the reader in phrasing, for the line layout on the page often does not coincide with natural pauses. Beginning readers have a tendency to break the thought at the end of the line rather than pausing where it makes sense. Poetry is also more compact than prose, so the language needs to be savored at a careful tempo to keep the meaning clear. Shakespeare is often in verse, and the sentence structure may be complex. Vocabulary can present a problem, as some words that Shakespeare used are no longer commonplace. Practice carefully to bring all the elements of rate, rhythm, and vocal color together to help you communicate the meaning of these poems and Shakespearian passages.

Poetry

"Martin Luther King, Jr."
GWENDOLYN BROOKS

A man went forth with gifts.

He was a prose poem.
He was a tragic grace.
He was a warm music.

He tried to heal the vivid volcanoes.
His ashes are
    reading the world,

His Dream still wishes to anoint
    the barricades of faith and of control.

His word still burns the center of the sun,
    above the thousands and the
    hundred thousands.

The word was Justice. It was spoken.

So it shall be spoken.
So it shall be done.

"The Wind Tapped Like a Tired Man"
EMILY DICKINSON

The wind tapped like a tired man,
And like a host, "Come in,"
I boldly answered; entered then
My residence within

A rapid, footless guest,
To offer whom a chair
Were as impossible as hand
A sofa to the air.

No bone had he to bind him,
His speech was like the push
Of numerous humming-birds at once
From a superior bush.

His countenance a billow,
His fingers, if he pass,
Let go a music, as of tunes
Blown tremulous in glass.

He visited, still flitting;
Then, like a timid man,
Again he tapped—'twas flurriedly—
And I became alone.

"Ozymandias"
PERCY BYSSHE SHELLEY

I met a traveler from an antique land
Who said: Two vast and trunkless legs of stone

Stand in the desert. Near them, on the sand,
Half sunk, a shattered visage lies, whose frown,
And wrinkled lip, and sneer of cold command,
Tell that its sculptor well those passions read
Which yet survive, stamped on these lifeless things,
The hand that mocked them and the heart that fed;
And on the pedestal these words appear:
"My name is Ozymandias, king of kings:
Look on my works, ye Mighty, and despair!"
Nothing beside remains. Round the decay
Of that colossal wreck, boundless and bare
The lone and level sands stretch far away.

"Composed upon Westminister Bridge, Sept. 3, 1802"
WILLIAM WORDSWORTH

Earth has not anything to show more fair:
Dull would he be of soul who could pass by
A sight so touching in its majesty:
This city now doth like a garment wear
The beauty of the morning; silent, bare,
Ships, towers, domes, theaters, and temples lie
Open until the fields, and to the sky;
All bright and glittering in the smokeless air.
Never did sun more beautifully steep
In his first splendor, valley, rock, or hill;
Ne'er saw I, never felt, a calm so deep!
The river glideth at his own sweet will:
Dear God! the very houses seem asleep;
and all that mighty heart is lying still!

"Eldorado"
EDGAR ALLAN POE

Gaily bedight,
A gallant knight,
In sunshine and in shadow,
Had journeyed long,
Singing a song,
In search of Eldorado.

But he grew old—
This knight so bold—
And o'er his heart a shadow
Fell as he found
No spot of ground
That looked like Eldorado.

And, as his strength
Failed him at length,
He met a pilgrim shadow—
"Shadow," said he,
"Where can it be—
This land of Eldorado?"

"Over the Mountains
Of the Moon,
Down the Valley of the Shadow,
Ride, boldly ride,"
The shade replied,—
"If you seek for Eldorado!"

"Spring Comes Dancing"
PEARL W. CHAPPELL

A deep well lies in the palm of my hand;
    I cup my ear
    That I may hear and understand.
Winds make love to the sea,
Waves clap hands with the shore
    In ancient rhythms of old folklore.

Tomtoms beat
While unslippered feet
    Dance with a soft tap tap.
    Trees hum low familiar tunes,
  Reviving old runes of the rising sap.
Rains play staccato upon dead leaves.
Birds talk quietly under the eaves.

    All earth is advancing
    As Spring comes dancing
To the lilting treble of laughing streams.
Waking songs of yesterday's dreams.

"Prospice"
ROBERT BROWNING

Fear death?—to feel the fog in my throat,
    The mist in my face,
When the snows begin, and the blasts denote
    I am nearing the place,
The power of the night, the press of the storm,
    The post of the foe;
Where he stands, the Arch Fear in a visible form,
    Yet the strong man must go:
For the journey is done and the summit attained,
    And the barriers fall,
Though a battle's to fight ere the guerdon be gained,
    The reward of it all.
I was ever a fighter, so—one fight more,
    The best and the last!
I would hate that death bandaged my eyes, and forbore,
    And bade me creep past.
No! let me taste the whole of it, fare like my peers
    The heroes of old,
Bear the brunt, in a minute pay glad life's arrears
    Of pain, darkness and cold.
For sudden the worst turns the best to the brave,
    The black minute's at end,
And the elements' rage, the fiend-voices that rave,
    Shall dwindle, shall blend,
Shall change, shall become first a peace out of pain,
    Then a light, then thy breast,
O thou soul of my soul! I shall clasp thee again,
    And with God be the rest!

"Invictus"
WILLIAM ERNEST HENLEY

Out of the night that covers me,
    Black as the Pit from pole to pole,
I thank whatever gods may be
    For my unconquerable soul.

In the fell clutch of circumstance
   I have not winced nor cried aloud.
Under the bludgeonings of chance
   My head is bloody, but unbowed.

Beyond this place of wrath and tears
   Looms but the Horror of the shade,
And yet the menace of the years
   Finds, and shall find, me unafraid.

It matters not how strait the gate,
   How charged with punishments the scroll,
I am the master of my fate:
   I am the captain of my soul.

"I Hear America Singing"
WALT WHITMAN

I hear America singing, the varied carols I hear,
Those of mechanics, each one singing his as it should be blithe and strong,
The carpenter singing his as he measures his plank or beam,
The mason singing his as he makes ready for work, or leaves off work,
The boatman singing what belongs to him in his boat, the deckhand singing
   on the steamboat deck,
The shoemaker singing as he sits on his bench, the hatter singing as he stands,
The wood-cutter's song, the ploughboy's on his way in the morning, or at
   noon intermission or at sundown.
The delicious singing of the mother, or of the young wife at work, or of the girl
   sewing or washing,
Each singing what belongs to him or her and to none else.
The day what belongs to the day—at night the party of young fellows, robust,
   friendly,
Singing with open mouths their strong melodious songs.

"A Curiosity"
KARL SHAPIRO

Tiny bees come to see what I am,
Lying in the sun at summer's end,
Writing a poem on a reclining chair.
A butterfly approaches and retreats;
Flies bang into my body by mistake,
And tinier things I can't identify;
And now and then a slow gigantic wasp
Rows on its stately voyage to the fence.
The trees are still too little to have birds;
Besides, the neighbors all have special cats
Bred for their oddity or arrogance.
A dragonfly sips at a lemon twig
After a helicopter landing. It
Appears that I am a curiosity
In my own backyard.
The dog of doubtful breed
Sleeps on the carpet of the sod,
And a bee necks with a rose.

Shakespeare for Practice

No other playwright or poet in the history of the English language has offered so many excellent, challenging lines of prose and poetry as has William Shakespeare. Not only actors but readers and public speakers profit from interpreting and reading Shakespeare aloud.

JAQUES: All the world's a stage
And all the men and women merely players.
They have their exits and their entrances,
And one man in his time plays many parts,
His acts being seven ages. At first the infant,
Mewling, and puking in the nurse's arms.
Then the whining schoolboy with his satchel
And shining morning face, creeping like snail
Unwillingly to school. And then the lover,
Sighing like furnace, with a woeful ballad
Made to his mistress' eyebrow. Then, a soldier,
Full of strange oaths, and bearded like the pard,
Jealous in honour, sudden and quick in quarrel,
Seeking the bubble reputation
Even in the cannon's mouth. And then, the justice,
In fair round belly, with good capon lined,
With eyes severe, and beard of formal cut,
Full of wise saws and modern instances,
And so he plays his part. The sixth age shifts
Into the lean and slippered pantaloon,
With spectacles on nose, and pouch on side,
His youthful hose well saved, a world too wide
For his shrunk shank, and his big manly voice,
Turning again toward childish treble pipes
And whistles in his sound. Last scene of all,
That ends this strange eventful history,
Is second childishness and mere oblivion,
Sans teeth, sans eyes, sans taste, sans every thing.

—As You Like It

KING RICHARD THE SECOND: For God's sake let us sit upon the ground,
And tell sad stories of the death of kings,
How some have been deposed, some slain in war,
Some haunted by the ghosts they have deposed,
Some poisoned by their wives, some sleeping killed,
All murdered. For within the hollow crown
That rounds the mortal temples of a king
Keeps Death his court, and there the antic sits,
Scoffing his state and grinning at his pomp,
Allowing him a breath, a little scene,
To monarchize, be feared, and kill with looks,
Infusing him with self and vain conceit,
As if this flesh which walls about our life,
Were brass impregnable; and humoured thus,
Comes at the last and with a little pin
Bores through his castle wall, and farewell king.

—King Richard the Second

QUEEN KATHERINE: I have been to you a true and humble wife,
At all times to your will conformable,
Ever in fear to kindle your dislike,
Yea, subject to your countenance—glad or sorry
As I saw it inclin'd. When was the hour
I ever contradicted your desire
Or made it not mine too? Or which of your friends
Have I not strove to love, although I knew
He were mine enemy? What friend of mine
That had to him deriv'd your anger did I
Continue in my liking? Nay, gave notice

He was from thence discharg'd? Sir, call to mind
That I have been your wife in this obedience
Upward of twenty years, and have been blest
With many children by you. If, in the course
And process of this time, you can report,
And prove it too against mine honour, aught,
My bond to wedlock or my love and duty,
Against your sacred person, in God's name,
Turn me away and let the foul'st contempt
Shut door upon me, and so give me up
To the sharp'st kind of justice.

—King Henry the Eighth

MACBETH: She should have died hereafter;
There would have been a time for such a word.
To-morrow, and to-morrow, and to-morrow,
Creeps in this petty pace from day to day,
To the last syllable of recorded time;
And all our yesterdays have lighted fools
The way to dusty death. Out, out, brief candle.
Life's but a walking shadow, a poor player,
That struts and frets his hour upon the stage,
And then is heard no more. It is a tale
Told by an idiot, full of sound and fury
Signifying nothing.

—Macbeth

RICHARD: Now is the winter of our discontent
Made glorious summer by this son of York;
And all the clouds that loured upon our house
In the deep bosom of the ocean buried.
Now are our brows bound with victorious wreathes,
Our bruised arms hung up for monuments,
Our stern alarums changed to merry meetings,
Our dreadful marches to delightful measures.
Grim-visaged war hath smoothed his wrinkled front;
And now, instead of mounting barbed steeds,
To fright the souls of fearful adversaries,
He capers nimbly in a lady's chamber,
To the lascivious pleasing of a lute.

—King Richard the Third

LEAR: Blow, winds, and crack your cheeks! rage! blow!
You cataracts and hurricanoes, spout
Till you have drenched our steeples, drowned the
        cocks.
You sulphurous and thought-executing fires,
Vaunt-couriers of oak-cleaving thunderbolts,
Singe my white head. And thou all-shaking thunder,
Strike flat the thick rotundity o' th' world,
Crack nature's moulds, all germens spill at once,
That makes ingrateful man.

—King Lear

KATE: I am ashamed that women are so simple
To offer war, where they should kneel for peace;
Or seek for rule, supremacy, and sway,

When they are bound to serve, love, and obey.
Why are our bodies soft, and weak, and smooth,
Unapt to toil and trouble in the world,
But that our soft conditions, and our hearts,
Should well agree with our external parts?
Come, come, you froward and unable worms,
My mind hath been as big as one of yours,
My heart as great, my reason haply more,
To bandy word for word, and frown for frown.
But now I see our lances are but straws;
Our strength as weak, our weakness past compare,
That seeming to be most, which we indeed least are.

—The Taming of the Shrew

PROSPERO: Our revels now are ended. These our actors,
As I foretold you, were all spirits, and
Are melted into air, into thin air,
And like the baseless fabric of this vision
The cloud-capped towers, the gorgeous palaces,
The solemn temples, the great globe itself,
Yea, all which it inherit, shall dissolve,
And like this insubstantial pageant faded
Leave not a rack behind. We are such stuff
As dreams are made on; and our little life
Is rounded with a sleep.

—The Tempest

JOHN OF GAUNT: This royal throne of kings, this scept'red isle,
This earth of majesty, this seat of Mars,
This other Eden, demi-Paradise,
This fortress built by Nature for herself
Against infection and the hand of war,
This happy breed of men, this little world,
This precious stone set in the silver sea,
Which serves it in the office of a wall,
Or as a moat defensive to a house,
Against the envy of less happier lands;
This blessed plot, this earth, this realm, this England,
This nurse, this teeming womb of royal kings,
Feared by their breed, and famous by their birth,
Renowned for their deeds as far from home,
For Christian service, and true chivalry,
As is the sepulchre in stubborn Jewry,
Of the world's ransom, blessed Mary's Son;
This land of such dear souls, this dear dear land,
Dear for her reputation through the world,
Is now leased out—I die pronouncing it—
Like to a tenement or pelting farm.
England bound in with the triumphant sea,
Whose rocky shore beats back the envious siege
Of watery Neptune, is now bound in with shame,
With inky blots, and rotten parchment bonds.
That England that was wont to conquer others,
Hath made a shameful conquest of itself.

—King Richard the Second

PORTIA: The quality of mercy is not strained,
It droppeth as the gentle rain from heaven

Upon the place beneath. It is twice blest:
It blesseth him that gives, and him that takes.
'Tis mightiest in the mightiest, it becomes
The throned monarch better than his crown.
His sceptre shows the force of temporal power,
The attribute to awe and majesty,
Wherein doth sit the dread and fear of kings.
But mercy is above this sceptred sway,
It is enthroned in the hearts of kings,
It is an attribute to God himself;
An earthly power doth then show likest God's
When mercy seasons justice.

—*The Merchant of Venice*

POETRY ACKNOWLEDGMENTS

"Martin Luther King, Jr." by Gwendolyn Brooks. By permission of Broadside Press.
"The Wind Tapped Like a Tired Man" by Emily Dickinson. Reprinted by permission of the publishers and the Trustees of Amherst College from *The Poems of Emily Dickinson,* edited by Thomas H. Johnson. Cambridge, Mass.: The Belknap Press of Harvard University Press, Copyright © 1951, 1955, 1979, 1983 by The President and Fellows of Harvard College.
"A Curiosity" by Karl Shapiro. By permission of Random House, Inc.

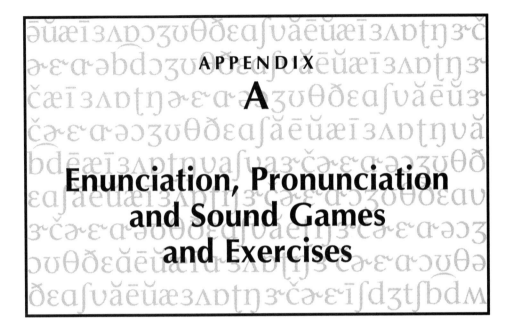

APPENDIX A

Enunciation, Pronunciation and Sound Games and Exercises

SOUND ASSIMILATION

Practice the following sentences for accurate assimilation of the underlined paired sounds. For a classroom exercise, one of the two underlined phrases in each pair can be placed on a card. One student reads from the card and the listeners determine which of the two sentences contain the phrase as pronounced.

1. (a) Nancy <u>Green's table</u> is always covered with food.
   (b) They kept the horse in the <u>green stable</u>.

2. (a) <u>Nixon cuts</u> segments from unwanted tape recordings.
   (b) He had <u>nicks and cuts</u> on his face after he shaved in the dark.

3. (a) I like to wear a halter as a <u>short's top</u> when I play tennis.
   (b) Charlie plays <u>short stop</u> for the little league team.

4. (a) I <u>heard rum</u>-runners as their ships slipped into the harbor.
   (b) <u>Her drum</u> is painted red, white, and blue.

5. (a) We went to the race at <u>Upson Downs</u>.
   (b) My life has been a series of <u>ups and downs</u>.

6. (a) Over the <u>lawn gloom</u> fell like a foliaged shadow.
   (b) The shuttle whirred noisily across the <u>long loom</u>.

7. (a) The dream was <u>so real</u> that I thought it had really happened.
   (b) The ichthyologist gave treatment to the <u>sore eel</u> at the aquarium.

8. (a) We <u>were cold</u> as we huddled around the meager fire.
   (b) Do you ever <u>work old</u> crossword puzzles in the *New York Times*?

9. (a) When they make these treats, do they have a special donut <u>hole dough</u>?
   (b) When you repeat the diphthongs, <u>hold o</u> longer than the other sounds.

10. (a) <u>I leak</u> information and gossip to my boss anytime I hear it.
    (b) <u>I'll eke</u> out an existence on my allotment, but it will be hard to do.

11. (a) Did you buy a <u>colored ream</u> of paper for the Xerox machine?
    (b) I had a techni<u>color dream</u> last night.

12. (a) <u>Grass spins</u> through my power mower and blows out all over the sidewalk.
    (b) <u>Grasp pins</u>, patterns, and scissors, and let's cut out the costume.

13. (a) I asked him, "<u>Why toil</u> your life away and never have any fun?"
    (b) I asked for <u>white oil</u> to burn in my clear crystal oil lamp.

14. (a) <u>Leap—I'll</u> catch you if you fall.
    (b) <u>Lee, pile</u> the leaves next to the curb.

15. (a) A <u>wish is</u> a sign of hope and optimism for the future.
    (b) He <u>wishes</u> they would call and tell him he got the job.

NONSENSE SENTENCES

Practice the following nonsense sentences. In nonsense sentences, contextual clues to meaning are not available. Careful enunciation is necessary. Classmates listen to one another without looking at the written sentences to check for understanding.

1. The napkin slept and the butterfly glided along during the lengthy grill.
2. Gardens of cement-grown wrought iron fences bloom in anthem-filled hospitals.
3. Whistles on swans filled whale flubber noses through woodcutters' hands in Chinese woks.
4. The contemplating fleas shocked horns with misty grass and stale bread mold.
5. Millions softly swarmed toward Edgar, billowing Manilla hats in grassy elephants.
6. A purple friendly city looked about the chair and trucked the wet log as carpets smelled cheaply.
7. The mushy pink wall washed between the table and the snow when fat, stupid bathtubs baked above sticky trees.
8. The absurd chocolate cake executive enticed a tranquilizing modification upon disjointed ant vehicle tongue twisters.
9. At the knock, mow the paper and blow the tree while sneezing hummingly.
10. The sweet concluding can working on a catalog sneezed slowly when an ugly rain walked to the sad shoe.
11. He who peels parsnips today will eulogize a snaredrum tomorrow.
12. Archibald, the crimson critique, seriously secluded the marbled denim stocking above the nine-tiered bunker abodes.
13. Catch cream puff icicles and grind rigid lepidopterists into sky-blue perambulators.
14. Isolate your eyelashes as you idle your engine on eggplant arteries purified with ambition.
15. The open mattress pad stomped bricks and tinder boxes in its highland fling down artificial philosophers.

TONGUE TWISTERS

Tongue twisters are excellent practice for achieving distinct enunciation. The secret to handling tongue twisters without stumbling is to complete all final consonants carefully—almost exaggerate them. Repeat each of the following tongue twisters five times rapidly.

1. Sheila studied statistical strategies using strange strategic statistics.
2. The white whale wailed while Wes Washington watched his washed watch whirling.
3. Ship the sheepskin sleepers and the shotsilk slippers to the sleepy sheep-shearers.
4. Pete replies, "My plate is replete with pot pies; please, don't repeat peas and plum pops."
5. The hoarse farmer forswore his first-born to force no harm on the horse barn.
6. Chunk Chuck the matched M*A*S*H crushed chin splints.
7. Brady Beatty was a blameless bigamist.
8. Sue shipped the shoe and simple zipper to the sloppy slipped shoe and zipper shop.
9. Grab crab crepes and grape cakes from the cracked case.
10. Sue and Hugh Gnu knew that a new gnu was due at two on Tuesday.

The following tongue twisters have been around so long and are so well-known that we do not know who to credit with original authorship.

11. Shave a cedar shingle thick.
12. A big black bear bit a big black bug.
      or
   A big black bug bit a big black bear.
13. Red leather, yellow leather.
14. The sixth sheik's sixth sheep's sick.
15. Blue broadloom rug.
16. Tie twine to three tree twigs.
17. A fat-free fruit float
18. Bring the brown baked bread back.
19. Real wristwatch straps.
20. Long, slim, slick sycamore saplings.

CHANGE THE PHONEME GAME

Word games are a wonderful way for speech students to learn more about language—sounds, word meanings, any aspect that helps us handle the language more effectively.

Begin the round with words that contain only three phonemes. In this example, we use *bat, word, nick,* and *coat.* If you alter the first phoneme, you create rhymes:

Bat		*Word*		*Nick*		*Coat*	
sat	[sæt]	bird	[bɝd]	kick	[kɪk]	note	[noʊt]
cat	[kæt]	heard	[hɝd]	pick	[pɪk]	wrote	[roʊt]
hat	[hæt]	third	[θɝd]	tick	[tɪk]	vote	[voʊt]
mat	[mæt]	furred	[fɝd]	wick	[wɪk]	moat	[moʊt]

Now instead of rhyming by changing the first phoneme, make "sound-alikes" by changing either the second or third phoneme:

Bat		Word		Nick		Coat	
bit	[bɪt]	wed	[wɛd]	knack	[næk]	cut	[kʌt]
beat	[bit]	wad	[wɑd]	knock	[nɑk]	caught	[kɔt]
but	[bʌt]	weed	[wid]	neck	[nɛk]	kit	[kɪt]
bait	[beɪt]	wooed	[wud]	nook	[nʊk]	kite	[kaɪt]

Bat		Word		Nick		Coat	
bag	[bæg]	work	[wɝk]	nip	[nɪp]	comb	[koʊm]
ban	[bæn]	worm	[wɝm]	niche	[nɪtʃ]	cope	[koʊp]
bath	[bæθ]	worse	[wɝs]	near	[nɪr]	core	[koʊr]
back	[bæk]	worth	[wɝθ]	nil	[nɪl]	code	[koʊd]

The game consists of going around a circle several times with each person changing one phoneme, then telling the next person which position in the word—initial, medial, final—he or she should then change. For example,

Speaker	Says	Tells Next Person to Change
1:	sit	medial
2:	sat	final
3:	sap	initial
4:	nap	final
5:	gnat	medial
6:	knit	initial
7:	bit	medial, and so on . . .

Should any speaker inadvertently slip and repeat a word that has already been used, that person is eliminated.

"NO, WHAT YOU MEAN IS . . ." GAME

The group needs to become proficient at "Change Your Phoneme" before trying this next game, for it is a much more sophisticated version in which puns on word meanings are added. The first speaker deliberately uses a "sounds-alike" word while creating a sentence in which the word has a specific meaning. Here are two examples:

Example 1

Speaker 1: "Is that the <u>leash</u> you can do?"
Speaker 2: "No, what you mean is <u>least</u>."

Example 2

Speaker 1: "I could <u>share</u> less!"
Speaker 2: "No, what you mean is <u>care</u>."

The third speaker must do what the first speaker has done by creating another pun, moving the sound of the word <u>least</u> or <u>care</u> to a "sounds-alike" meaning in a new sentence.

Example 1

Speaker 3: "No, a <u>least</u> is what I signed when I moved into my apartment."

4: "No, what you mean is <u>lease</u>."

5: "No, <u>lease</u> is the opposite of tight."

6: "No, what you mean is <u>loose</u>."

7: "No, a <u>loose</u> is a mate to a gander."

8: "No, you mean a <u>goose</u>."

Example 2

Speaker 3: "No, a <u>care</u> is the hard center part of the apple."

4: "No, what you mean is <u>core</u>."

5: "No, <u>core</u> is what you do to ham to preserve it."

6: "No, what you mean is <u>cure</u>."

7: "No, <u>cure</u> is what you might call an adorable baby."

8: "No, you mean <u>cute</u>."

And so on, as long as you are able to play. The game can be played with just two or three players, alternating turns. As class members gain proficiency, try the game in a large group. Put a time limit of thirty seconds on how long any one member may have to think before responding, or else lose a turn.

When the group has become really good at "Change Your Phoneme" or "No, What You Mean Is . . ." branch into consonant clusters (*br, gl, st,* etc.) or into multi-syllabled words.

LABEL YOUR LOVER

In *Don Quixote,* Cervantes wrote:

> All true lovers ought to have the whole alphabet . . . Amiable, Bountiful, Constant, Daring, Enamoured, Faithful, Gallant, Honorable, Illustrious, Kind, Loyal, Mild, Noble, Obliging, Prudent, Quiet, Rich, and the Ss, as they say (slightly, sprightly, secret, and sincere); lastly true, valiant, and wise; the X suits him not, because it is a harsh letter; the Y, he is young; the Z, zealous of your honour.

Try to create your own list, following the orthographic alphabet as Cervantes did. Then try it using the International Phonetic Alphabet, as we have. Can you list both positive and negative characteristics?

OUR LIST		YOUR LIST	
Positive	*Negative*	*Positive*	*Negative*
eager	evil	_____	_____
interesting	insolent	_____	_____
elegant	ectomorphic	_____	_____
ambitious	adversarial	_____	_____
optimistic	omnivorous	_____	_____
awesome	audacious	_____	_____
(g)ood	(w)olf	_____	_____
oomph	oozing	_____	_____
earnest	irksome	_____	_____
(p)erceptive	(p)erfidious	_____	_____
understanding	ugly	_____	_____

OUR LIST		YOUR LIST	
Positive	*Negative*	*Positive*	*Negative*
amusing	abusive		
ablebodied	apelike		
idealistic	idle		
oilman	oinksome		
outstanding	outlandish		
open	oafish		
polite	pugnacious		
beloved	bum		
tidy	traitor		
delightful	dumb		
kind	conceited		
giving	gloomy		
fantastic	fickle		
vivacious	vain		
thin	thoughtless		
(fa)thomable	(hea)then		
sexy	stupid		
zesty	zoomorphic		
sharp	shameful		
(lei)surely	(trea)sureless		
healthy	hotheaded		
charming	cheap		
jaunty	judgmental		
magnificent	malevolent		
nice	nasty		
(si)ngle	(tha)nkless		
wonderful	wishy-washy		
whimsical	whimpering		
lively	liar		
relaxed	ruthless		
youthful	yahoo		

GRANDMOTHER'S TRUNK

In a similar vein to "Label Your Lover" is the old game, "I Packed My Grandmother's Trunk." The major difference is that here you must not only add a new word with the next letter of the alphabet, but you must also remember and repeat what others have said before you. A game might begin as follows:

Speaker 1:   I packed my grandmother's trunk with an <u>afghan</u>.

Speaker 2:   I packed my grandmother's trunk with an <u>afghan</u> and <u>binoculars</u>.

Speaker 3:   I packed my grandmother's trunk with an <u>afghan</u>, <u>binoculars</u> and a <u>cabbage</u>.

Speaker 4:   I packed my grandmother's trunk with an <u>afghan</u>, <u>binoculars</u>, a <u>cabbage</u>, and a <u>doily</u>.

Speaker 5:   I packed my grandmother's trunk with an <u>afghan</u>, <u>binoculars</u>, a <u>cabbage</u>, a <u>doily</u>, and an <u>elephant</u>.

The group should continue through the alphabet, with occasional group assistance provided for those who can't remember the whole list.

Variations

1. Starting with Z, go backward through the alphabet instead of forward.

2. Try it with the IPA instead of the orthographic alphabet, but do one game with consonants, then one with vowels and diphthongs. Otherwise the list gets too long.

3. For the ultimate challenge, try each list in *one* breath.

THE DICTIONARY GAME

English is a wonderfully fascinating, complex language. Our dictionaries contain hundreds of words that most of us have never heard before and certainly never use. A game built on these little-known words, called "Dictionary" by some people, "Fictionary" by others, enables you to try your hand at guessing word meanings after hearing a word pronounced. You take cues from the sounds in the word, hints such as common roots, prefixes, or suffixes, and your ability to make intelligent guesses. The game is played as described below.

One person is the Word Giver. The Word Giver takes the dictionary and browses until a word is found that probably no one will know. After checking the pronunciation in the dictionary, the Word Giver reads it aloud a couple of times. All the players then silently create their own imaginary definition for the word, each player writing on a slip of paper. The Word Giver writes the correct definition on a slip of paper, then collects all the slips.

With the actual definition inserted at some random spot in the stack of slips of paper, the Word Giver then reads through all the definitions, one at a time, giving players a chance to hear each carefully. The players then silently vote on the one they believe to be the correct definition. After the players have made their choices, the Word Giver identifies the correct definition. One point is scored for guessing the correct definition. One point is scored for a player each time a group member guesses that player's definition as correct when it is not. Players rotate being the Word Giver.

Here are a few of the interesting words we've discovered while playing "The Dictionary Game":

1.	ambagious	[æm ˈbeɪ dʒəs]	roundabout, circuitous.
2.	charabanc	[ˈʃæ rə bæŋ]	open-sided sightseeing bus.
3.	erythroid	[ɪ ˈrɪθ rɔɪd]	reddish; like red blood cells.
4.	enchiridion	[ɛn kaɪ ˈrɪd ɪ ən]	handbook, manual.
5.	ichneumon	[ɪk ˈnju mən]	carnivorous animal of Egypt; mongoose.
6.	icosahedron	[aɪ koʊ sə ˈhi drən]	solid figure having 20 faces.
7.	kakemono	[kɑk ɪ ˈmoʊ no]	Japanese scroll.
8.	lickerish	[ˈlɪk ə rɪʃ]	greedy, lustful.
9.	nictitating	[ˈnɪk təteɪ tɪŋ]	winking.
10.	ophidian	[o ˈfɪd ɪ ən]	snake.
11.	rodomontade	[rɑd ə mən ˈteɪd]	vainglorious, boasting or bragging.
12.	saxifrage	[ˈsæk sə freɪdʒ]	herb named for ability to break rocks.
13.	screed	[skrid]	long discourse or essay.
14.	tragacanth	[ˈtrædʒ ə kænθ]	substance used to impart firmness to pills.
15.	Ursprache	[ʊr ˈʃprɑk ə]	hypothetically reconstructed parent language.

WORDS FROM OTHER LANGUAGES

The following terms usually retain their original, foreign language pronunciation. They are sometimes mispronounced by American speakers of English. Check your dictionary for the preferred pronunciation and for the meaning if you do not know the word.

a cappella	coup de grace	haute couture
adagio	coup d'état	ingenue
ad hoc	cuisine	junta
aficionado	cul-de-sac	laissez-faire
andante	debonair	machismo
a priori	de facto	malaise
apropos	dénouement	mélange
arpeggio	détente	nouveau riche
avant-garde	deus ex machina	non sequitur
bon appétit	effete	pièce de résistance
bon vivant	élan	raison d'être
cause célèbre	enfant terrible	repartée
c'est la vie	esprit de corps	savoir faire
cher chez la femme	fait accompli	tête-a-tête
concierge	gourmet	tour de force

WORDS COMMONLY MISPRONOUNCED

Throughout this book you have been working on pronouncing words—identifying the various phonemes, forming them correctly, assimilating them smoothly, and producing them with a clear and interesting voice. As a final effort, study the following list of words we hear most frequently mispronounced. The mispronunciations may come from omitting, adding, or transposing sounds, from misplacing accents, or simply from not knowing the preferred pronunciation. We have used the IPA to indicate the usual mispronunciation and the preferred pronunciation. Some dictionaries show second and third options for pronunciation of some of these words; we suggest you use the one listed first. Remember the discussion from Chapter 2: pronunciation is a matter not so much of right and wrong or correct and incorrect as of suggested or preferred standards. We have left a few blank spaces for you to add words that you have trouble with or hear mispronounced.

		COMMON MISPRONUNCIATION	PREFERRED PRONUNCIATION
1.	abdomen	[æb 'dou mən]	['æb də mən]
2.	absolve	[æb 'zɑlv]	[æb 'sɑlv]
3.	absorb	[əb 'zɔrb]	[əb 'sɔrb]
4.	absurd	[əb 'zɚd]	[əb 'sɚd]
5.	accompaniment	[ə 'kʌmp ni mənt]	[ə 'kʌm pən ɪ mənt]
6.	accompanist	[ə 'kʌmpə ni ɪst]	[ə 'kʌm pə nɪst]
7.	accurate	['æk ə rɪt]	['æk jə rɪt]
8.	admirable	[æd 'maɪr əbl]	['æd mərəbl]
9.	adult	['æ dʌlt]	[ə 'dʌlt]
10.	alma mater	['ælmɚ mɑtə]	['ælmə mɑtɚ]
11.	almond	['æl mənd]	['ɑ mənd]

		COMMON MISPRONUNCIATION	PREFERRED PRONUNCIATION
12.	always	['ɔ wez]	['ɔl wez]
13.	amicable	[ə 'mɪk əbl]	['æm ɪ kəbl]
14.	analogous	[ə 'næl ə dʒəs]	[ə 'næl ə gəs]
15.	anesthetic	[ænəs 'tɛ tɪk]	[ænəs 'θɛ tɪk]
16.	antidote	['æn ɪk dot]	['æn tɪ dot]
17.	antithesis	[æn tɪ 'θi sɪs]	[æn 'tɪ θə sɪs]
18.	applicable	[æ 'plɪk əbl]	['æplɪkəbl]
19.	apricot	['æ prɪ kɑt]	[ei prɪ kɑt]
20.	archipelago	[ɑr tʃɪ pə 'lɛ goʊ]	[ɑr kə 'pɛlə goʊ]
21.	arctic	[ɑr tɪk]	['ɑrk tɪk]
22.	aria	['ɛr ɪ ɑ]	['ɑr ɪ ə]
23.	athlete	['æθ ə lit]	['æθ lit]
24.	au revoir	[orɪ 'vɔr]	[orə 'vwɑɚ]
25.	auxiliary	[ɔg 'zɪl ɪɛ rɪ]	[ɔg 'zil jə rɪ]
_____		[ ]	[ ]
_____		[ ]	[ ]
_____		[ ]	[ ]
26.	aviator	['ævɪ etɚ]	['eɪ vɪ etɚ]
27.	baptize	[bæb 'taɪz]	[bæp 'taɪz]
28.	behemoth	['bi hə məθ]	[bɪ 'hi məθ] [bi ə məθ]
29.	beige	[beɪdʒ]	[beɪʒ]
30.	beneficiary	[bɛ nə 'fi ʃi ɛrɪ]	[bɛ nə 'fɪ ʃərɪ]
31.	berserk	[bɝ 'zɝk]	[bɝ 'sɝk]
32.	bilingual	[baɪ 'lɪŋ gju wəl]	[baɪ 'lɪŋ gwəl]
33.	blackguard	[blæk gɑrd]	[blæ gɚd]
34.	blatant	[blæt nt]	[bleɪtnt]
35.	boatswain	[boʊt sweɪn]	[boʊsn]
36.	bouquet	[bu 'kɛt]	[bo 'keɪ] [bu 'keɪ]
37.	bravado	['brɑ və doʊ]	[brə 'vɑ doʊ]
38.	buoy	['bu wɪ]	[bɔɪ] or ['bu ɪ]
39.	bury	['bɝ rɪ]	['bɛ rɪ]
40.	cache	[kætʃ]	[kæʃ]
41.	camouflage	['kæmə flɑdʒ]	['kæ mə flɑʒ]
42.	candidate	['kæn ə det]	[k'æn də det]
43.	cashmere	['kæʒ mɪr]	['kæʃ mɪr]
44.	center	['sɪn ɚ]	['sɛn tɚ]
45.	cerebral	[sɛ 'ri brəl]	['sɛ rə brəl]
46.	chaise lounge	[tʃɛz 'lɑndʒ]	['ʃeɪz lɔŋ]
47.	charade	[ʃə 'rɑd]	[ʃə 'reɪd]
48.	chasm	['tʃæ zəm]	['kæ zəm]
49.	chimney	['tʃɪm lɪ]	['tʃɪm nɪ]
50.	coiffure	[kɔ fɚ]	[kwa 'fjʊr]

	COMMON MISPRONUNCIATION	PREFERRED PRONUNCIATION
_____	[ ]	[ ]
_____	[ ]	[ ]
_____	[ ]	[ ]
51. comparable	[kɑm 'pɛr əbl]	['kɑm pə rəbl]
52. corsage	[kɔr 'sɑdʒ]	[kɔr 'sɑʒ]
53. cuisine	[kə 'zin]	[kwɪ 'zin]
54. curriculum	[kə 'rɪk ə ləm]	[kə 'rɪk jə ləm]
55. despicable	[dɛs 'pɪk əbl]	['dɛspɪkɪbl]
56. diphtheria	[dɪp 'θɪrɪə]	[dɪf 'θɪrɪə]
57. diphthong	['dip θɔŋ]	['dif θɔŋ]
58. dirigible	[də 'rɪdʒ əbl]	['dɪrədʒəbl]
59. disparate	[dɪs 'pɛr ɪt]	['dɪs pərɪt]
60. divorce	['daɪ vors]	[də 'voʊrs]
61. drama	['dræ mə]	['drɑmə]
62. ecstatic	['ɛs tæ tɪk]	[ɪk 'stæ tɪk]
63. environment	[ɪn 'vaɪr mnt]	[ɪn 'vaɪ rən mnt]
64. escape	[ɛk 'skeɪp]	[ə 'skeɪp]
65. et cetera	[ɛk 'sɛt ərə]	[ɛt 'sɛt ərə]
66. etiquette	['ɛt ɪ kwɛt]	['ɛt ɪ kɛt]
67. exquisite	[ɛk 'skwɪzɪt]	['ɛk sk wɪz ɪt]
68. extraordinary	[ɛk strə 'ɔrdənɛrɪ]	[ɛk 'strɔd ənɛrɪ]
69. familiar	[fə 'mɪ jɚ]	[fə 'mɪl jɚ]
70. finale	[faɪ 'nælɪ]	[fɪ 'nɑlɪ]
71. formidable	[fɔr 'mɪd əbl]	['fɔr mɪd əbl]
72. genuine	[dʒɛn jʊ 'aɪn]	['dʒɛn jʊɪn]
73. gondola	[gɑn 'doʊ lə]	['gɑn də lə]
74. guarantee	[gɑrɛn 'ti]	[gærən 'ti]
75. height	[haɪθ]	[haɪt]
_____	[ ]	[ ]
_____	[ ]	[ ]
_____	[ ]	[ ]
76. hilarious	['haɪ lær ɪəs]	[hə 'lɛrɪəs]
77. human	['ju mən]	['hju mən]
78. hygienic	[haɪ 'dʒinɪk]	[haɪdʒɪ 'ɛnɪk]
79. idea	[aɪ dɪɚ]	[aɪ dɪə]
80. incomparable	[ɪn kɑm 'pɛr əbl]	[ɪn 'kɑm pər əbl]
81. interesting	['ɪnɚ ɛstɪŋ]	[ɪn tərɛstɪŋ]
82. iron	[ɑrn]	[aɪ ɚ n]
83. irreparable	[ɪ rɪ 'pɛr əbl]	[ɪ 'rɛp ər əbl]
84. Italian	[aɪ 'tæljən]	[ɪ 'tæljən]
85. kindergarten	['kɪn ə gɑrdn]	['kɪn dɚ gɑrtn]
86. laboratory	['læ bə torɪ]	['læ brə torɪ]
87. lamentable	[læ 'mɛnt əbl]	['læm ən təbl]
88. larynx	['lɑr nɪŋks]	['læ rɪŋks]

		COMMON MISPRONUNCIATION	PREFERRED PRONUNCIATION
89.	library	['laɪ bɛri]	['laɪ brɛri]
90.	maraschino	[mɛ rə 'ʃi noʊ]	[mæ rə 'ski noʊ]
91.	massage	[mə 'sadʒ]	[mə 'saʒ]
92.	mauve	[mɔv]	[moʊv]
93.	medieval	[mɪ 'di vl]	[mɪdɪ 'ivl]
94.	mischievous	[mɪs 'tʃi vɪəs]	['mɪs tʃɪ vəs]
95.	omnipotent	[am nɪ 'po tənt]	[am 'nɪ pə tənt]
96.	orgy	['ɔr gɪ]	['ɔr dʒɪ]
97.	particular	[pɚ 'tɪk ə lɚ]	[pɚ 'tɪk jələ˞]
98.	partition	[pɛ 'tɪ ʃən]	[pɚ 'tɪ ʃən]
99.	peculiarly	[pi kjul ɚ lɪ]	[pi 'kjul jə˞lɪ]
100.	pharynx	['fɛr nɪŋks]	['fæ rɪŋks]
_____		[ ]	[ ]
_____		[ ]	[ ]
_____		[ ]	[ ]
101.	plethora	[plɛ 'θorə]	['plɛ θərə]
102.	poem	[pom]	['po ɪm]
103.	poinsettia	[pɔn 'sɛ tə]	[pɔɪn 'sɛ tɪə]
104.	prerogative	[pɚ 'rag ə tɪv]	[prɪ 'rag ə tɪv]
105.	pronunciation	[pɚ naʊn sɪ 'eɪ ʃən]	[prə nʌn sɪ 'er ʃən]
106.	radiator	['ræ dɪ e tɚ]	['reɪ dɪ e tɚ]
107.	recipe	[rɪ 'sit]	['rɛ sə pɨ]
108.	reptile	[rɛp 'taɪl]	['rɛp tl]
109.	reputable	[rɪ 'pju təbl]	['rɛ pjə təbl]
110.	salmon	['sæl mən]	['sæ mən]
111.	sandwich	['sæm ɪtʃ]	['sænd wltʃ]
112.	schism	['skiz əm]	['sɪz əm]
113.	scion	['skaɪ ən]	['saɪ ən]
114.	secretary	['sɛ kə tɛ rɪ]	['sɛ krə tɛrɪ]
115.	sentence	['sin əns]	['sɛn təns]
116.	similar	['sɪ mju lɚ]	['sɪ mə lɚ]
117.	statistics	[stə 'stɪ stɪks]	[stə 'tɪs tɪks]
118.	strength	[strɛnθ]	[strɛŋθ]
119.	suggest	[sə 'dʒɛst]	[səg 'dʒɛst]
120.	superfluous	[sʊ pɚ 'flu əs]	[sʊ 'pɚ flʊ əs]
121.	theater	[θɪ 'eɪ tɚ]	['θi ə tɚ]
122.	tremendous	[trɪ 'mɛn dʒəs]	[trɪ 'mɛn dəs]
123.	wash	[warʃ]	[waʃ]
124.	victuals	['vɪk tʃʊ əlz]	['vɪ tlz]
125.	zoology	[zu 'al ədʒl]	[zo 'al ə dʒɪ]
_____		[ ]	[ ]
_____		[ ]	[ ]
_____		[ ]	[ ]

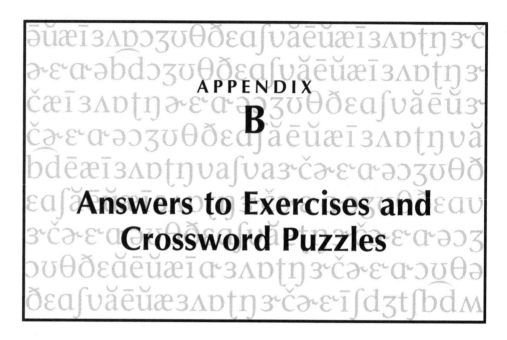

APPENDIX B

Answers to Exercises and Crossword Puzzles

ANSWER FOR CHAPTER 3

FYI, p. 18: The anagram of "one hug" is "enough"; the anagram of "a sentence of death" is "faces one at the end."

ANSWER FOR CHAPTER 9

Just for Fun, p. 131: There is no "e" in the paragraph.

ANSWERS FOR CHAPTER 10
Phonetics Practice (p. 156)

Orthographic Spelling		Phonetic Spelling	
1.	picked	1.	[pɪt]
2.	deep	2.	[bid]
3.	bagged	3.	[tæg]
4.	teak	4.	[gɛt]
5.	bid	5.	[kip]
6.	decked	6.	[dɛt]
7.	dig	7.	[pæk]
8.	apt	8.	[gæp]
9.	acted	9.	[kɛpt]
10.	egad!	10.	[ikt]
11.	bedded	11.	[gæbd]
12.	peak	12.	[ɛbd]
13.	bad	13.	[dɛd]
14.	eat	14.	[bɪ ˈgɛt]

Orthographic Spelling	*Phonetic Spelling*
15. capped	15. ['kæ tɪ]
16. deck	16. ['pɛ tɪ]
17. beady	17. [kid]
18. ditty	18. [pɪg]
19. tab	19. [tæb]
20. kicked	20. [ɛg]

CROSSWORD PUZZLE CHAPTER 10, p. 155

¹p	²æ	t		³d	⁴æ	b
⁵ɛ	d		⁶b	i	d	
⁷g	ɛ	⁸t		p		⁹k
	¹⁰d	ɪ	k		¹¹t	i
¹²b		k		¹³k	æ	p
¹⁴ɛ	g		¹⁵b	æ	g	
t		¹⁶d	i	d		

ANSWERS FOR CHAPTER 11

Phonetics Practice (p. 181–182)

PHONETICS PRACTICE 1   PHONETICS PRACTICE 2

		Orthographic Spelling	*Phonetic Spelling*
1. [suz]		1. foot	1. [gæf]
2. [θɔ]		2. give	2. [vɛst]
3. [ʃɑ]		3. thought	3. [buθ]
4. [hɔz]		4. these	4. [tið]
5. [hʊf]		5. sash	5. [hʊps]
6. [ʃɔ]		6. zoot suit	6. [gɑdz]
7. [suð]		7. shock	7. [pʊʃ]
8. [ɔf]		8. Zsa Zsa	8. [bɪhuv]
9. [hʊvz]		9. haughty	9. [fɔgɪ]
10. [suθ]		10. theft	10. [hɛvɪ]
11. [ɑz]		11. vapid	11. [θɪk]
12. [ɑv]		12. teeth	12. [gæsɪz]
13. [ʃuz]		13. this	13. [sið]
14. [hu]		14. fees	14. [zɪg zæg]
15. [zu]		15. soggy	15. [bʊʃɪz]
16. [huz]		16. shop	16. [bɪ hɛd]
17. [uz]		17. suited	17. [kukɪ]
18. [(bɪ) huv]		18. hopped	18. [fɔt]
19. [(ɾ) uʒ]		19. booked	19. [ɑpt]
20. [sɑf (mor)]		20. pots	20. [(de)ʒɑ vu]

CROSSWORD PUZZLE CHAPTER 11, p. 182

¹b	²u	³θ		⁴f	⁵ɑ	⁶p
ɑ	■	i	■	ɔ	■	ʊ
g	■	⁷f	⁸ɛ	t	⁹ɪ	ʃ
■	¹⁰h	■	g		t	■
¹¹v	æ	¹²t		¹³ð	ɪ	¹⁴s
¹⁵i	z	ɪ		æ		¹⁶u ¹⁷z
p	■	¹⁸f	ʊ	t		¹⁹ð i
²⁰s	ɪ	s	■		²¹ɑ	z

ANSWERS FOR CHAPTER 12

Phonetics Practice (p. 201–202)

PHONETICS PRACTICE 1		PHONETICS PRACTICE 2	
		Orthographics	*Phonetics*
1. [tʃʌm]		1. vaccine	1. [ə vɝt]
2. [tʃɝtʃ]		2. stitching	2. [tʃætɚ]
3. [dʒʌdʒ]		3. thank	3. [zɪ ðɚ]
4. [tʃɝn]		4. jerk	4. [æ ʒɚ]
5. [nʌm]		5. Cheshire	5. [hætʃ ət]
6. [əmʌŋ]		6. verge	6. [ɚ dʒənt]
7. [mʌtʃ]		7. mutter	7. [θʌn dɚ]
8. [nʌdʒ]		8. upper	8. [bʌm ɚ]
9. [nɝtʃɚ]		9. hanger	9. [hæŋ kɚ]
10. [mʌntʃ]		10. nervous	10. [tɝ nəp]
11. [mɝdʒ]		11. emergency	11. [ðʌs]
12. [ɝdʒ]		12. badinage	12. [pitʃ]
13. [dʒɝm]		13. chalk	13. [stɑdʒɪ]
14. [tʃɝnɚ]		14. gender	14. [fɝn]
15. [mɝdʒɚ]		15. thirty	15. [ðɛm]
16. [ɝmə]		16. seizure	16. [hʌfɪ]
17. [mɝnə]		17. again	17. [ʃɝk]
18. [tʃʌŋ]		18. hitch	18. [θɔŋ]
19. [tʃʌn]		19. singer	19. [nʌm bɚ]
20. [mɝmɚ]		20. journey	20. [dʒɛst ɪŋ]

CROSSWORD PUZZLE 12–1, p. 202

```
 1p  2ε  3t   ■   4t   i   5tʃ  ■
 7ɝ  8dʒ  I   z   ■   9k   ε  10n
  ■   ■  11n   u  12n   ■  13s   ɝ
14dʒ 15ʌ  t   ■  16ʌ  17s   ■   v
18ɝ  p   ■  19θ   i  20m
 k   ■  21æ  22I   z   I   t
  ■  23s   t   I   ŋ   ɝ   z
```

CROSSWORD PUZZLE 12–2, p. 202

```
 1m   2ɔ   3θ   ■   4ɔ   5t
 6æ   n    I    ■   7n   ʌ   8b
 9tʃ  I    n    ■  10k   ɝ
  ■   ŋ    ■  11æ   m
12dʒ  ■  13æ    n    ■  14h  15ɝ
16ε  17m   p    t  18I    ■   k
19t   u    t    ■  20n   ʌ   t
  ■   v    ■  21ɑ   d
22d   i    ■  23n    ■  24i   tʃ
  u   ■  25ɔ    ■   d
```

ANSWERS FOR CHAPTER 13

Phonetics Practice (p. 224–225)

PHONETICS PRACTICE 1	PHONETICS PRACTICE 2	
	Orthographics	Phonetics
1. [weɪ]	1. whirl	1. [liʒɚ]
2. [woʊ]	2. lawyer	2. [ʃeɪplɪ]
3. [loʊr]	3. rouge	3. [raɪmɪŋ]
4. [jeɪ]	4. treasure	4. [dʒɔɪnt]
5. [roʊl]	5. youthful	5. [raʊnd]
6. [waʊ]	6. creature	6. [oʊpənɪŋ]
7. [jeɪl]	7. enjoy	7. [kʊdnt]
8. [leɪ]	8. earthly	8. [tʃʌtnɪ]
9. [laɪl]	9. tabling	9. [rɪzɪst]
10. [lɔɪ(j)l]	10. withhold	10. [juʒjuəl]
11. [ʍaɪl]	11. although	11. [vaɪ ə lənt]
12. [ʍeɪl]	12. favorite	12. [hɔɪst]
13. [ɔɪl]	13. likely	13. [laʊdɚ]
14. [joʊr]	14. foible	14. [zoʊnd]
15. [reɪl]	15. mountain	15. [ʃɝkt]
16. [aʊl]	16. hopeless	16. [rɑʒɑ]
17. [waɪr]	17. voices	17. [wɔrmɪŋ]
18. [ʍaɪ]	18. yellow	18. [tʃeɪn]
19. [eɪl]	19. whiplash	19. [təgɛðɚ]
20. [rɔɪ(j)l]	20. unwitting	20. [kʌplz]

CROSSWORD PUZZLE 13–1, p. 225
All Sounds

¹θ	²r	³ɑ	⁴b	■	⁵f	⁶oʊ	■
⁷r	æ	t	ɪ	■	⁸ʃ	i	■
⁹ʌ	t	ɚ	l	¹⁰ɪ	■	¹¹s	i
s	■	¹²t	¹³r	aʊ	t	■	■
¹⁴t	¹⁵eɪ	¹⁶p	■	¹⁷æ	l	■	¹⁸aɪ
■	¹⁹m	ɔ	■	n	■	²⁰ɔɪ	l

CROSSWORD PUZZLE 13–2, p. 226
All Sounds

¹w	ɪ	n	²t	³ɚ	■	⁴t	oʊ
ɪ	■	⁵ɔ	r	■	⁶ə	■	■
n	■	⁷r	ɛ	⁸d	r	ɛ	⁹d
¹⁰d	u	■	¹¹d	r	aɪ	■	ɛ
f	■	■	i	■	■	¹²ɪ	f
ɔ	■	¹³m	æ	m	ɪ	■	■
l	■	ɪ	■	■	■	■	¹⁴k
■	¹⁵θ	ɔ	t	■	■	¹⁶ð	aʊ

CROSSWORD PUZZLE 13–3, p. 226
All Sounds

■	■	■	■	■	¹θ	ɝ	d	■	■
²b	■	³r	ɔ	■	r	■	■	■	■
l	■	u	■	⁴s	p	aɪ	z	■	■
ɑ	■	ɪ	■	aʊ	■	s	■	■	■
⁵b	⁶ə	n	æ	n	ə	■	⁷k	■	■
■	p	■	■	d	■	■	l	■	■
■	l	■	■	■	⁸k	r	ʌ	⁹s	¹⁰t
¹¹m	aɪ	z	ɚ	■	w	■	¹²b	l	u
i	■	■	■	■	oʊ	■	■	¹³eɪ	m
l	■	■	■	■	¹⁴ə	t	ɛ	s	t
■	■	■	■	■	ə	■	■	■	■

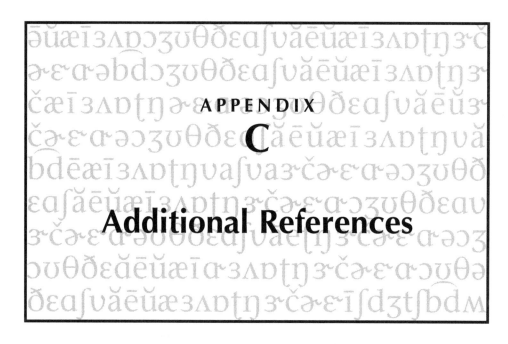

C

Additional References

ANDERSON, VIRGIL A. *Training the Speaking Voice,* 3rd ed. London: Oxford University Press, 1977.

BARKER, SARAH AND PETER HARRIGAN. *Introduction to Performance: Beginning the Creative Process of the Actor.* Dubuque, Iowa: Kendall-Hunt, 1994.

BOWLER, PETER. *The Superior Person's Book of Words.* Boston: Godine, 1985.

BOWLER, PETER. *The Superior Person's Second Book of Weird and Wondrous Words.* Boston: Godine, 1992.

COLAIANNI, LOUIS. *The Joy of Phonetics and Accents.* New York: Drama Books, 1994.

CRANNELL, KENNETH C. *Voice and Articulation.* 2nd ed. Belmont, CA: Wadsworth, 1991.

EISENSON, JON. *Voice and Diction: A Program for Improvement.* 6th ed. New York: Macmillan, 1991.

HAHNER, JEFFREY C., MARTIN A. SOKOLOFF, AND SANDRA L. SALISCH. *Speaking Clearly: Improving Your Voice and Diction.* 5th ed. New York: McGraw-Hill, 1997.

KENYON, JOHN S. *American Pronunciation.* 12th enl. rev. Ann Arbor, MI: Wahr, 1996.

KENYON, JOHN S. AND THOMAS A. KNOTT. *A Pronouncing Dictionary of American English.* Reprint ed. Springfield, MA: Merriam-Webster, 1995.

KING, ROBERT K. AND ELEANOR M. DIMICHAEL. *Voice and Diction Handbook.* Prospect Heights, IL: Waveland, 1991.

LESSAC, ABRAHAM AND BETTY. *The Use and Training of the Human Voice: A Bio-Dynamic Approach to Vocal Life.* 3rd ed. Mountain View, CA: Mayfield, 1996.

LINKLATER, KRISTIN. *Freeing the Natural Voice.* 2nd ed. New York: Drama Pubs., 1985.

MACKAY, IAN R. *Phonetics: The Science of Speech Production.* 2nd ed. Boston, MA: Allyn & Bacon, 1991.

MAYER, LYLE V. *Fundamentals of Voice and Diction.* 11th ed. Dubuque, Iowa: Brown, 1995.

MODISETT, NOAH F. AND JAMES G. LUTER, JR. *Speaking Clearly: The Basics of Voice and Articulation.* 3rd ed. Edina, MN: Burgess, 1988.

NEWMAN, FREDERICK R. *Mouthsounds.* New York: Workman, 1980.

RODENBURG, PATSY. *The Right to Speak: Working with the Voice*. New York: Routledge, Chapman & Hall, 1993.

SARNOFF, DOROTHY. *Never Be Nervous Again: Time Tested Techniques for Foolproof Control*. New York: Ivy, 1989.

TRASK, ROBERT L. *A Dictionary of Phonetics and Phonology*. New York: Routledge, 1995.

WELLS, LYNN K. *Articulate Voice: An Introduction to Voice and Diction*. Scottsdale, AZ: Gorsuch Scarisbrick, 1993.

Index